ETHNIC
WRITERS
IN AMERICA

ETHNIC
WRITERS
IN AMERICA

MYRON SIMON
University of California, Irvine

Harcourt Brace Jovanovich, Inc.

New York   Chicago   San Francisco   Atlanta   Dallas

400511859

Printed in the United States of America

ISBN 0–15–347070–4

CONTENTS

ETHNIC WRITERS IN AMERICA

☐ America has been known from its founding for the openness of its society and the energy of its people. These characteristics have constituted a kind of major premise upon which American culture, and therefore American literature also, has been built. The writers and readers of American literature have typically recognized, explicitly or implicitly, the centrality of these cultural features. They pervade the works of our great writers like a compelling theme upon which innumerable variations, each excellent in its way, have been played.

This theme of openness and energy has characterized America spiritually as well as physically. It was to America that men came to answer the invitation of a wild and virgin land—to succeed in their own ways and to think in their own ways. In Puritan accounts of wilderness life, in the autobiographical reflections of our Founding Fathers, in fictional and nonfictional explorations of the continent, in poetic invocations of nature, this theme persists. It has persisted through many shifts of literary fashion. It persists in contemporary writers as different as Robert Frost and John Steinbeck. Americans have been characteristically individualistic and independent, seeking the truth and thus drawn to mental as well as physical frontiers. On these frontiers, they have characteristically sought to translate ideas into actions, to build their own worlds.

The conditions of American society, from the beginning, have reinforced these tendencies. The physical factors of sharply varied landscape and climate have created an impatience with fixed boundaries and an eagerness to explore. The constant mixing of ethnic groups that had been traditionally separated and the open colliding of ancient and modern doctrines have shaken the American's beliefs in permanence, have encouraged a readiness and even a fondness for change. Americans—and especially American writers—have grown quickly tired of uniformity and have generated everywhere the healthy impulse to experiment.

The outcome has been a pluralistic society: plural in its values, plural in its habits and traditions, plural in its styles of life and manners of speech, and plural in its goals. Accompanying this pluralism, and partly because of it, there is the American's habit of self-examination and social criticism. Who am I? What am I? In what form do I originate and to what end am I destined? What is this America I call my home? Out of the confusing and exciting plurality of American life, these questions have arisen with special force and meaning. More than the citizen of any other nation the American has been obliged, sometimes forced, to reconsider his name, to find his true identity. The very fact that America is not purely anything, but rather a mixture of all, has disposed its people to reflect upon their personal experience, to come to grips with the mystery of self. All men have shared this concern, but the fluid and expansive conditions of American society have given this quest for identity a special urgency and practicability in the New World.

However, our writers responded slowly and indirectly to these new conditions. The creation of a body of distinctively American writing that would give resonant voice to the novel features of our culture lagged behind our assertion of political independence from England.

Well into the nineteenth century our writers remained colonial in their tendency to imitate English literary and social manners; they were content to gratify the taste of a genteel public for the "finer things." On the other hand—owing to ignorance, reformist zeal, or local pride—those of our writers whose work was more obviously "homemade" revealed a restricted angle of vision in their failure to see the America that lay beyond community and region. New England writers preoccupied with moral instruction, Southern novelists absorbed in conserving the chivalry and grace of older times, Western tellers of "tall tales" intent on unrestrained tributes to backwoods vigor and shrewdness—all were clearly provincial. In their choices of subject matter and modes of presentation, they revealed fully an immediate concern for their local audiences. They unhesitatingly declared their regional loyalties, and made it entirely plain by whom they wished to be understood and in what terms.

"America," as Robert Frost reminded us, "is hard to see." In order to discover America, our writers had to see themselves and their regions in broader perspective. They learned to use local materials with greater freedom, saw larger issues in what earlier had seemed to possess only local relevance, and became progressively disenchanted and uneasy with such stereotypes as the Puritan, the cavalier gentleman, and the "ring-tailed roarer."

When Nathaniel Hawthorne began to probe the psychological truths associated with the religious doctrine of man's sinfulness, his tales properly claimed an interest and an audience larger than Puritan New England. When Mark Twain recognized that in the openness of Southwestern frontier life the traditional conflict between innocence and experience might be realistically resolved without the defeat and capitulation of innocence, he passed from regional humor into national literature. When William Faulkner perceived the elements of human tragedy in the Southerner's unyielding attachment to myth, to the mind of the past, the boundaries of his fictional Mississippi were lost in time and space. There remains, of course, a sense in which Hawthorne, Twain, and Faulkner are inseparable from a particular earth and sky, which they understood in the almost intuitive way of native sons. But, at their artistic best, even the readiest acknowledgment of their status as American writers seems too limited to describe adequately their achievement.

Through the use of such terms as the "American Renaissance" and the "Flowering of American Literature," our attention and the world's has been drawn to the middle of the nineteenth century as the period marking the emergence of major American writers. From Emerson, Thoreau, and Whitman; Hawthorne, Melville, and James; Howells and Twain; Stephen Crane and E. A. Robinson; Dreiser, Sinclair Lewis, and O'Neill; Hemingway and Fitzgerald; to Flannery O'Connor and Robert Lowell, American writers have demonstrated how richly they could discern the national and the universal meanings momentarily embodied in regional landscapes. Thus, in their untiring and endlessly varied efforts to know the shapes of experience at first hand and to express them originally, they have given invaluable artistic expression to the enduring openness and energy of American life.

To the present day, American literature is in part still nourished by writers whose landscapes and language are drawn from New England or the South or the several regions of the West. But as America approached the twentieth century, its lengthening list of big cities signaled changing times. The widespread industrial and commercial booms following the Civil War had introduced modern American urban culture. Metropolitan settings and tempos and mixtures offered original material and fresh perspectives.

Amidst the novel minglings and confrontations of the big city, Americans grew far more conscious of some of the newer ethnic additions to their society. Large new immigrant communities like the Irish, the Jews, and the resettled urban Negroes forcibly reminded Americans of differences in race, nationality, religion, and class that are as much facts of American life as are the nation's regional differences. This awareness produced a heightened sense of both the promise and the failures of American life; and it stimulated bold reappraisals of America, together with a renewed spirit of experiment and reform.

The complicated awareness of America's ethnic pluralism has become one of the shaping principles of modern American literature. Toward the turn of the century, new sorts of American writers appeared whose perspectives were ethnic rather than regional. These ethnic writers began the task of illuminating the meanings of their own cultural traditions within the larger contexts of America and the world. Often, like the regional writers, they began by writing chiefly for their own people or by serving as the loyal interpreters of their people to the nation. In time, however, ethnic writers have appeared who are impatient with easy labels, comic dialect, and every kind of stereotyping. These writers have penetrated far beneath the surface of ethnic experience in search of its deepest meanings. They have discovered truths—not only about themselves, but truths about America and the world as well.

Like the regional literature which preceded it, ethnic writing has acquired its present status as a major component of modern American literature only after nearly a century of accommodation and experiment. The selections in this book have been arranged to illustrate the functional stages through which modern American ethnic literature has evolved and is still evolving.

PART 1

EARLY ETHNIC WRITERS

INTRODUCTION

☐ In one obvious sense, all American writers are essentially ethnic, the sons of immigrants, since—with the possible exception of the American Indian—there is no basic American stock. In this sense all Americans were at one time or another strangers to the American shores. But if we understand the word *ethnic* to mean immigrant groups speaking a language and possessing a culture other than English or belonging to a race other than the Caucasian, then it is evident that the distinction between the American and the immigrant has been a very real one, reaching virtually from the settlement of America to the present day.

In the colonial and early national periods, however, there was little sense that ethnic identity was a problem. The open spaces allowed those immigrants who wished to cling to their own language and customs to do so without seriously disturbing the established American communities. Similarly, the existence of open farmland allowed certain ethnic groups—like the Germans and Scandinavians—to become part of the new society easily. And black Americans—living in bondage, widely dispersed throughout the agrarian South, and without a unifying leadership—did not seem likely to disturb the existing social and economic arrangements, despite the many slave revolts preceding the Civil War. Thus, the ethnic groups of these early periods did not then appear to threaten the "traditional" values of American life.

But in the last decades of the nineteenth century, swollen tides of immigration flowed into our older big cities, like New York and Boston, and our new big cities, like Chicago and Los Angeles. This movement produced a direct confrontation between the native-born American and the immigrant. Also, in the years following the Civil War, a growing number of Negroes, uprooted from the countryside, moved to unfamiliar urban settings in another kind of immigration. In large numbers, Negroes found themselves in an environment in which hostility and deprivation assumed new forms and a different face.

Living side by side with these new ethnic groups in increasingly congested cities, the "American" often felt that his heritage and his way of life were being threatened. At the same time, the immigrant—whether European or Negro—was made more aware of his strangeness and even of his unwelcomeness. Groups favoring native-born Americans were quick to declare their hostility to the larger of these ethnic groups—the Irish, the blacks, and the Jews—and clamored wildly for the preservation of "Americanism." There were shrill demands that these "intruders" be thrown out of the country or, at least, that their growth and opportunity be limited.

The feeling of strangeness and unwelcomeness in America led the earliest writers of these ethnic groups to write primarily for their own people. And chiefly they wrote words of comfort. Later, when they started to write for the American public at large, they cast themselves in the role of good-will ambassadors. Wanting to be accepted, they naturally stressed those features of their ethnic life that seemed most attractive and ingratiating to those who deplored their presence. The early ethnic writers, accordingly, put their best foot forward, a strategy which frequently required that they idealize their group portraits. Their literary art unmistakably served social ends in stressing those qualities of their groups that might prove most charming and endearing to those who sullenly and belligerently asked, "Why don't you go back where you came from?"

1856–1915

BOOKER T. WASHINGTON

ESSAY

☐ *Booker T. Washington was born a slave in 1856. Twenty-five years later, in 1881, he founded Tuskegee Institute in Alabama as a college for training teachers. Washington became extraordinarily successful as an educator, and by the mid-1880's he was considered a national spokesman for the black American's educational needs. Since his educational views strongly emphasized such practical necessities as agricultural and industrial skills, Washington's appeals for assistance were generally regarded as appropriately modest and eminently reasonable. Since his social views urged the achievement of good will between the races by stressing the black American's capacity for self-improvement and acceptance of his separateness in white America, these arguments too were most acceptable to the general public—liberal and reactionary alike—who applauded this display of "common sense."*

Accordingly, Booker T. Washington's autobiography, Up from Slavery *(published in 1901), became and remained a best seller, for it presented a self-portrait of the Negro that was thoroughly ingratiating. Militant black intellectuals, then and now, have opposed Washington's position as spokesman for American blacks, on the grounds that he ignored the plain rights of black citizens and sought to cultivate educational programs and social attitudes which could only serve to prolong their bondage.*

☐ After the coming of freedom there were two points upon which practically all the people on our place were agreed, and I find that this was generally true throughout the South: that they must change their names, and that they must leave the old plantation for at least a few days or weeks in order that they might really feel sure that they were free.

In some way a feeling got among the colored people that it was far from proper for them to bear the surname of their former owners, and a great many of them took other surnames. This was one of the first signs of freedom. When they were slaves, a colored person was simply called "John" or "Susan." There was seldom occasion for more than the use of the one name. If "John" or "Susan" belonged to a white man by the name of "Hatcher," sometimes he was called "John Hatcher," or as often "Hatcher's John." But there was a feeling that "John Hatcher" or "Hatcher's John" was not the proper title by which to denote a freeman; and so in many cases "John Hatcher" was changed to "John S. Lincoln" or "John S. Sherman," the initial "S" standing for no name, it being simply a part of what the colored man proudly called his "entitles."

As I have stated, most of the colored people left the old plantation for a short while at least, so as to be sure, it seemed, that they could leave and try their freedom on to see how it felt. After they had remained away for a time, many of the older slaves, especially, returned to their old homes and made some kind of contract with their former owners by which they remained on the estate.

My mother's husband, who was the stepfather of my brother John and myself, did not belong to the same owners as did my mother. In fact, he seldom came to our plantation. I remember seeing him there perhaps once a year, that being about Christmas time. In some way, during the war, by running away and following the Federal soldiers, it seems, he found his way into the new state of West Virginia. As soon as freedom was declared, he sent for my mother to come to the Kanawha Valley, in West Virginia. At that time a journey from Virginia over the mountains to West Virginia was rather a tedious and in some cases a painful undertaking. What little clothing and few household goods we had were placed in a cart, but the children walked the greater portion of the distance, which was several hundred miles.

I do not think any of us ever had been very far from the plantation, and the taking of a long journey into another state was quite an event. The parting from our former owners and the members of our own race on the plantation was a serious occasion. From the time of our parting till their death we kept up a correspondence with the older members of the family, and in later years we have kept in touch with those who were the younger members. We were several weeks making the trip, and most of the time we slept in the open air and did our cooking over a log fire out of doors. One night I recall that we camped near an abandoned log cabin, and my mother decided to build a fire in that for cooking, and afterward to make a "pallet" on the floor for our sleeping. Just as the fire had gotten well started, a large black snake fully a yard and a half long dropped down the chimney and ran out on the floor. Of course we at once abandoned that cabin. Finally we reached our destination—a little town called Malden, which is about five miles from Charleston, the present capital of the state.

At that time salt-mining was the great industry in that part of West Virginia, and the little town of Malden was right in the midst of the salt-furnaces. My stepfather had already secured a job at a salt-furnace, and he had also secured a little cabin for us to live in. Our new house was no better than the one we had left on the old plantation in Virginia. In fact, in one respect it was worse. Notwithstanding the poor condition of our plantation cabin, we were at all times sure of pure air. Our new home was in the midst of a cluster of cabins crowded closely together, and as there were no sanitary regulations, the filth about the cabins was often intolerable. Some of our neighbors were colored people, and some were the poorest and most ignorant and degraded white people. It was a motley mixture. Drinking, gambling, quarrels, fights, and shockingly immoral practices were frequent. All who lived in the little town were in one way or another connected with the salt business. Though I was a mere child, my stepfather put me and my brother at work in one of the furnaces. Often I began work as early as four o'clock in the morning.

The first thing I ever learned in the way of book knowledge was while working in this salt-furnace. Each salt-packer had his barrels marked with a certain number. The number allotted to my stepfather was "18." At the close of the day's work the boss of the packers would come around and put "18" on each of our barrels, and I soon learned to recognize that figure wherever I saw it, and after a while got to the point where I could make that figure, though I knew nothing about any other figures or letters.

From the time that I can remember having any thoughts about anything, I recall that I had an intense longing to learn to read. I determined, when quite a small child, that, if I accomplished nothing else in life, I would in some way get enough education to enable me to read common books and newspapers. Soon after we got settled in some manner in our new cabin in West Virginia, I induced my mother to get hold of a book for me. How or where she got it I do not know, but in some way she procured an old copy of Webster's "blue-back" spelling-book, which contained the alphabet, followed by such meaningless words as "ab," "ba," "ca," "da." I began at once to devour this book, and I think that it was the first one I ever had in my hands. I had learned from somebody that the way to begin to read was to learn the alphabet, so I tried in all the ways I could think of to learn it—all of course without a teacher, for I could find no one to teach me. At that time there was not a single member of my race anywhere near us who could read, and I was too timid to approach any of the white people. In some way, within a few weeks, I mastered the greater portion of the alphabet. In all my efforts to learn to read my mother shared fully my ambition, and sympathized with me and aided me in every way that she could. Though she was totally ignorant, so far as mere book knowledge was concerned, she had high ambitions for her children, and a large fund of good, hard common sense which seemed to enable her to meet and master every situation. If I have done anything in life worth attention, I feel sure that I inherited the disposition from my mother.

In the midst of my struggles and longing for an education, a young colored boy who had learned to read in the state of Ohio came to Malden. As soon as the colored people found out that he could read, a newspaper was secured, and at the close of nearly every day's work this young man would be surrounded by a group of men and women who were anxious to hear him read the news contained in the papers. How I used to envy this man! He seemed to me to be the one young man in all the world who ought to be satisfied with his attainments.

About this time the question of having some kind of a school opened for the colored children in the village began to be discussed by members of the race. As it would be the first school for Negro children that had ever been opened in that part of Virginia, it was, of course, to be a great event, and the discussion excited the widest interest. The most perplexing question was where to find a teacher. The young man from Ohio who had learned to read the papers was considered, but his age was against him. In the midst of the discussion about a teacher, another young colored man from Ohio, who had been a soldier, in some way found his way into town. It was soon learned that he possessed considerable education, and he was engaged by the colored people to teach their first school. As yet no free schools had been started for colored people in that section, hence each family agreed to pay a certain amount per month, with the understanding that the teacher was to "board 'round"—that is, spend a day with each family. This was not bad for the teacher, for each family tried to provide the very best on the day the teacher was to be its guest. I recall that I looked forward with an anxious appetite to the "teacher's day" at our little cabin.

This experience of a whole race beginning to go to school for the first time presents one of the most interesting studies that has ever occurred in connection with the development of any race. Few people who were not right in the midst of the scenes can form any exact idea of the intense desire which the people of my race showed for an education. As I have stated, it was a whole race trying to go to school. Few were too young, and none too old, to make the attempt to learn. As fast as any kind of teachers could be secured, not only were day-schools filled, but night-schools as well. The great ambition of the older people was to try to learn to read the Bible before they died. With this end in view, men and women who were fifty or seventy-five years old would often be found in the night-school. Sunday-schools were formed soon after freedom, but the principal book studied in the Sunday-school was the spelling-book. Day-school, night-school, Sunday-school were always crowded, and often many had to be turned away for want of room.

The opening of the school in the Kanawha Valley, however, brought to me one of the keenest disappointments that I ever experienced. I had been working in a salt-furnace for several months, and my stepfather had discovered that I had a financial value, and so, when the school opened, he decided that he could not spare me from my work. This decision seemed to cloud my every ambition. The disappointment was made all the more severe by reason of the fact that my place of work was where I could see the happy children passing to and from school, mornings and afternoons. Despite this disappointment, however, I determined that I would learn something, anyway. I applied myself with greater earnestness than ever to the mastering of what was in the "blue-back" speller.

My mother sympathized with me in my disappointment, and sought to comfort me in all the ways she could, and to help me find a way to learn. After a while I succeeded in making arrangements with the teacher to give me some lessons at night, after the day's work was done. These night lessons were so welcome that I think I learned more at night than the other children did during the day. My own experiences in the night-school gave me faith in the night-school idea, with which, in after years, I had to do both at Hampton and Tuskegee.[1] But my boyish heart was still set upon going to the day-school, and I let no opportunity slip to push my case. Finally I won, and was permitted to go to the school in the day for a few months, with the understanding that I was to rise early in the morning and work in the furnace till nine o'clock, and return immediately after school closed in the afternoon for at least two more hours of work.

The schoolhouse was some distance from the furnace, and as I had to work till nine o'clock, and the school opened at nine, I found myself in a difficulty. School would always be begun before I reached it, and sometimes my class had recited. To get around this difficulty I yielded to a temptation for which most people, I suppose, will condemn me; but since it is a fact, I might as well state it. I have great faith in the power and influence of facts. It is seldom that anything is permanently gained by holding back a fact. There was a large clock in a little office in the furnace. This clock, of course, all the hundred or more workmen depended upon to regulate their hours of beginning and ending the day's work. I got the idea that the way for me to reach school on time was to move the clock hands from half-past eight up to the nine o'clock mark. This I found myself doing morning after morning, till the furnace "boss" discovered that something was wrong, and locked the clock in a case. I did not mean to inconvenience anybody. I simply meant to reach that schoolhouse in time.

When, however, I found myself at the school for the first time, I also found myself confronted with two other difficulties. In the first place, I found that all of the other children wore hats or caps on their heads, and I had neither hat nor cap. In fact, I do not remember that up to the time of going to school I had ever worn any kind of covering upon my head, nor do I recall that either I or anybody else had even thought anything about the need of

[1] *Hampton and Tuskegee:* Hampton Institute in Virginia was the Negro school from which Washington graduated in 1875. At Tuskegee, beginning with forty students "in a dilapidated shanty," Washington built a campus that by the end of his life had more than 100 buildings, over 1,500 students, and almost 200 faculty members; and it offered thirty-eight trade and professional programs.

covering for my head. But, of course, when I saw how all the other boys were dressed, I began to feel quite uncomfortable. As usual, I put the case before my mother, and she explained to me that she had no money with which to buy a "store hat," which was a rather new institution at that time among the members of my race and was considered quite the thing for young and old to own, but that she would find a way to help me out of the difficulty. She accordingly got two pieces of "homespun" (jeans) and sewed them together, and I was soon the proud possessor of my first cap.

The lesson that my mother taught me in this has always remained with me, and I have tried as best I could to teach it to others. I have always felt proud, whenever I think of the incident, that my mother had strength of character enough not to be led into the temptation of seeming to be that which she was not—of trying to impress my schoolmates and others with the fact that she was able to buy me a "store hat" when she was not. I have always felt proud that she refused to go into debt for that which she did not have the money to pay for. Since that time I have owned many kinds of caps and hats, but never one of which I have felt so proud as of the cap made of the two pieces of cloth sewed together by my mother. I have noted the fact, but without satisfaction, I need not add, that several of the boys who began their careers with "store hats" and who were my schoolmates and used to join in the sport that was made of me because I had only a "homespun" cap, have ended their careers in the penitentiary, while others are not able now to buy any kind of hat.

My second difficulty was with regard to my name, or rather *a* name. From the time when I could remember anything, I had been called simply "Booker." Before going to school it had never occurred to me that it was needful or appropriate to have an additional name. When I heard the school-roll called, I noticed that all of the children had at least two names, and some of them indulged in what seemed to me the extravagance of having three. I was in deep perplexity, because I knew that the teacher would demand of me at least two names, and I had only one. By the time the occasion came for the enrolling of my name, an idea occurred to me which I thought would make me equal to the situation; and so, when the teacher asked me what my full name was, I calmly told him "Booker Washington," as if I had been called by that name all my life; and by that name I have since been known. Later in my life I found that my mother had given me the name of "Booker Taliaferro" soon after I was born, but in some way that part of my name seemed to disappear, and for a long while was forgotten, but as soon as I found out about it I revived it, and made my full name "Booker Taliaferro Washington." I think there are not many men in our country who have had the privilege of naming themselves in the way that I have.

More than once I have tried to picture myself in the position of a boy or man with an honored and distinguished ancestry which I could trace back through a period of hundreds of years, and who had not only inherited a name, but fortune and a proud family homestead; and yet I have sometimes had the feeling that if I had inherited these, and had been a member of a more popular race, I should have been inclined to yield to the temptation of depending upon my ancestry and my color to do that for me which I should do for myself. Years ago I resolved that because I had no ancestry I would leave a record of which my children would be proud, and which might encourage them to still higher effort.

The world should not pass judgment upon the Negro, and especially the Negro youth, too quickly or too harshly. The Negro boy has obstacles, discouragements, and temptations to battle with that are little known to those not situated as he is. When a white boy undertakes a task, it is taken for granted that he will succeed. On the other hand, people are usually surprised if the Negro boy does not fail. In a word, the Negro youth starts out with the presumption against him.

The influence of ancestry, however, is important in helping forward any individual or race, if too much reliance is not placed upon it. Those who constantly direct attention to the Negro youth's moral weaknesses, and compare his advancement with that of white youths, do not consider the influence of the memories which cling about the old family homesteads. I have no idea, as I have stated elsewhere, who my grandmother was. I have, or have had, uncles and aunts and cousins, but I have no knowledge as to where most of them are. My case will illustrate that of hundreds of thousands of black people in every part of our country. The very fact that the white boy is conscious that, if he fails in life, he will disgrace the whole family record, extending back through many generations, is of tremendous value in helping him to resist temptations. The fact that the individual has behind and surrounding him proud family history and connection serves as a stimulus to help him to overcome obstacles when striving for success.

The time that I was permitted to attend school during the day was short, and my attendance was irregular. It was not long before I had to stop attending day-school altogether, and devote all of my time again to work. I resorted to the night-school again. In fact, the greater part of the education I secured in my boyhood was gathered through the night-school after my day's work was done. I had difficulty often in securing a satisfactory teacher. Sometimes, after I had secured some one to teach me at night, I would find, much to my disappointment, that the teacher knew but little more than I did. Often I would have to walk several miles at night in order to recite my night-school lessons. There was never a time in my youth, no matter how dark and discouraging the days might be, when one resolve did not continually remain with me, and that was a determination to secure an education at any cost.

Soon after we moved to West Virginia, my mother adopted into our family, notwithstanding our poverty, an orphan boy, to whom afterward we gave the name of James B. Washington. He has ever since remained a member of the family.

After I had worked in the salt-furnace for some time, work was secured for me in a coal-mine which was operated mainly for the purpose of securing fuel for the salt-furnace. Work in the coal-mine I always dreaded. One reason for this was that anyone who worked in a coal-mine was always unclean, at least while at work, and it was a very hard job to get one's skin clean after the day's work was over. Then it was fully a mile from the opening of the coal-mine to the face of the coal, and all, of course, was in the blackest darkness. I do not believe that one ever experiences anywhere else such darkness as he does in a coal-mine. The mine was divided into a large number of different "rooms" or departments, and, as I never was able to learn the location of all these "rooms," I many times found myself lost in the mine. To add to the horror of being lost, sometimes my light would go out, and then, if I did not happen to have a match, I would wander about in the darkness until by chance I found some one to give me a light. The work was not only hard, but it was dangerous. There was always the danger of being blown to pieces by a premature explosion of powder, or of being crushed by falling slate. Accidents from one or the other of these causes were frequently occurring, and this kept me in constant fear. Many children of the tenderest years were compelled then, as is now true I fear, in most coal-mining districts, to spend a large part of their lives in these coal-mines, with little opportunity to get an education; and, what is worse, I have often noted that, as a rule, young boys who begin life in a coal-mine are often physically and mentally dwarfed. They soon lose ambition to do anything else than to continue as a coal-miner.

In those days, and later as a young man, I used to try to picture in my imagination the feelings and ambitions of a white boy with absolutely no limit placed upon his aspirations and activities. I used to envy the white boy who had no obstacles placed in the way of his becoming a Congressman, Governor, Bishop, or President by reason of the accident of his birth or race. I used to picture the way that I would act under such circumstances; how I would begin at the bottom and keep rising until I reached the highest round of success.

In later years, I confess that I do not envy the white boy as I once did. I have learned that success is to be measured not so much by the position that one has reached in life as by the obstacles which he has overcome while trying to succeed. Looked at from this standpoint, I almost reach the conclusion that often the Negro boy's birth and connection with an unpopular race is an advantage, so far as real life is concerned. With few exceptions, the Negro youth must work harder and must perform his task even better than a white youth in order to secure recognition. But out of the hard and unusual struggle through which he is compelled to pass, he gets a strength, a confidence, that one misses whose pathway is comparatively smooth by reason of birth and race.

From any point of view, I had rather be what I am, a member of the Negro race, than be able to claim membership with the most favored of any other race. I have always been made sad when I have heard members of any race claiming rights and privileges, or certain badges of distinction, on the ground simply that they were members of this or that race, regardless of their own individual worth or attainments. I have been made to feel sad for such persons because I am conscious of the fact that mere connection with what is known as a superior race will not permanently carry an individual forward unless he has individual worth, and mere connection with what is regarded as an inferior race will not finally hold an individual back if he possesses intrinsic, individual merit. Every persecuted individual and race should get much consolation out of the great human law, which is universal and eternal, that merit, no matter under what skin found, is, in the long run, recognized and rewarded. This I have said here, not to call attention to myself as an individual, but to the race to which I am proud to belong.

for discussion

1. Why does Washington describe in such detail the making of his "homespun" cap? What lesson did Washington learn from this episode? Can you think of a current analogy to the "homespun" cap episode?
2. The rare experience of choosing a surname was one shared by many former Negro slaves. What does Washington think of this experience? What do you think is the difference between choosing your own name and having a name that someone gives you?

3. In your opinion, why does Washington include the detail that his mother adopted an orphan?

4. How would you describe the author's attitude toward the en-

vironment in which he was
raised?
5. How does Washington's de-

corous prose style influence the
response of a white reader?

born 1915

ALFRED KAZIN

☐ *Alfred Kazin was born in 1915 in Brownsville, a section
of Brooklyn then inhabited by poor Jewish immigrants.
He has noted that from his "first conscious moments"
he was absorbed "in the fire and color of immigrant life."
Educated in New York's public schools, Kazin earned his
bachelor's degree in 1935 at The City College of New
York and his master's degree at Columbia University
three years later. In 1942, after several years of teaching
in the evening and reading at the New York Public
Library during the day, he published* On Native Grounds,
*his widely admired history of modern American prose
literature. He has contributed to leading journals and
magazines many essays on American writers and their
social backgrounds. A selection of these essays,*
Contemporaries, *appeared in 1962. Kazin has taught at a
number of universities, and is presently Distinguished
Professor of English at the State University of New York's
Stony Brook campus.*

*As a literary historian and critic, Kazin has been
preoccupied with the relation between American
literature and its cultural setting. But his two
autobiographical volumes,* A Walker in the City *(1951)
and* Starting Out in the Thirties *(1965), reveal that he has
remained profoundly aware of his Jewishness, of how it
has served to define his feeling for America. Although
Kazin is no sentimentalist, his compelling sense of the
value of his past has moved him to provide warm and
appealing pictures of his home life. His memory revives
the Jew's consciousness of vulnerability and couples it*

*with a patient determination to endure, a talent for
survival. Kazin directs the reader's attention insistently to
the affectionate solidarity and self-sacrifice in Jewish
family life. He extends these qualities into a response to
all human suffering, and points thereby to the basis of the
Jew's association with reform movements and of his
dedication to hard work and learning. Most importantly,
Kazin endows the Jewish world that formed him with
traits that dispel older and uglier stereotypes of the Jew,
traits that make membership in Jewish culture seem
attractive and advantageous.*

the kitchen

☐ The last time I saw our kitchen this clearly was one
afternoon in London at the end of the war, when I waited
out the rain in the entrance to a music store. A radio was
playing into the street, and standing there I heard a broadcast of the first Sabbath service from Belsen Concentration
Camp. When the liberated Jewish prisoners recited the
Hear O Israel, the Lord Our God, the Lord is One, I felt
myself carried back to the Friday evenings at home, when
with the Sabbath at sundown a healing quietness would
come over Brownsville.[1]

It was the darkness and emptiness of the streets I liked
most about Friday evening, as if in preparation for that
day of rest and worship which the Jews greet "as a bride"
—that day when the very touch of money is prohibited,
all work, all travel, all household duties, even to the turning on and off of a light—Jewry had found its way past its

"The Kitchen" from *A Walker in the City*, copyright 1951 by Alfred
Kazin. Reprinted by permission of the publisher, Harcourt Brace Jovanovich, Inc.

[1] *Brownsville:* like Williamsburg, one of the sections of Brooklyn to
which large numbers of Jewish immigrants moved, after 1910, from the
Lower East Side of New York.

tormented heart to some ancient still center of itself. I waited for the streets to go dark on Friday evening as other children waited for the Christmas lights. Even Friday morning after the tests were over glowed in anticipation. When I returned home after three, the warm odor of a coffee cake baking in the oven and the sight of my mother on her hands and knees scrubbing the linoleum on the dining room floor filled me with such tenderness that I could feel my senses reaching out to embrace every single object in our household. One Friday, after a morning in school spent on the voyages of Henry Hudson, I returned with the phrase *Among the discoverers of the New World* singing in my mind as the theme of my own new-found freedom on the Sabbath.

My great moment came at six, when my father returned from work, his overalls smelling faintly of turpentine and shellac, white drops of silver paint still gleaming on his chin. Hanging his overcoat in the long dark hall that led into our kitchen, he would leave in one pocket a loosely folded copy of the New York *World;* and then everything that beckoned to me from that other hemisphere of my brain beyond the East River would start up from the smell of fresh newsprint and the sight of the globe on the front page. It was a paper that carried special associations for me with Brooklyn Bridge. They published the *World* under the green dome on Park Row overlooking the bridge; the fresh salt air of New York harbor lingered for me in the smell of paint and damp newsprint in the hall. I felt that my father brought the outside straight into our house with each day's copy of the *World.* The bridge somehow stood for freedom; the *World* for that rangy kindness and fraternalism and ease we found in Heywood Broun. My father would read aloud from "It Seems To Me"[2] with a delighted smile on his face. "A very clear and courageous man!" he would say. "Look how he stands up for our Sacco and Vanzetti! A real social conscience, that man! Practically a Socialist!" Then, taking off his

[2] *"It Seems To Me"*: a famous column which Broun (1888–1939) created in the New York *Tribune,* and brought with him to the *World* in 1921. He left the *World* in 1928 because of a disagreement with the publisher over Broun's indignant defense of Sacco and Vanzetti.

overalls, he would wash up at the kitchen sink, peeling and gnawing the paint off his nails with Gold Dust Washing Powder as I poured it into his hands, smacking his lips and grunting with pleasure as he washed himself clean of the job at last, and making me feel that I was really helping him, that I, too, was contributing to the greatness of the evening and the coming day.

By sundown the streets were empty, the curtains had been drawn, the world put to rights. Even the kitchen walls had been scrubbed and now gleamed in the Sabbath candles. On the long white tablecloth were the "company" dishes, filled for some with *gefillte* fish on lettuce leaves, ringed by red horseradish, sour and half-sour pickles, tomato salad with a light vinegar dressing; for others, with chopped liver in a bed of lettuce leaves and white radishes; the long white *khalleh*, the Sabbath loaf; chicken soup with noodles *and* dumplings; chicken, meat loaf, prunes, and sweet potatoes that had been baked all day into an open pie; compote of prunes and quince, apricots and orange rind; applesauce; a great brown nutcake filled with almonds, the traditional *lekakh*; [3] all surrounded by glasses of port wine, seltzer bottles with their nozzles staring down at us waiting to be pressed; a samovar of Russian tea, *svetouchnee* [4] from the little red box, always served in tall glasses, with lemon slices floating on top. My father and mother sipped it in Russian fashion, through lumps of sugar held between the teeth.

Afterwards we went into the "dining room" and, since we were not particularly orthodox, allowed ourselves little pleasures outside the Sabbath rule—an occasional game of Casino at the dining-room table where we never dined; and listening to the victrola. The evening was particularly good for me whenever the unmarried cousin who boarded with us had her two closest friends in after supper.

They were all dressmakers, like my mother; had worked with my mother in the same East Side sweatshops; were all passionately loyal members of the International

---

[3] *lekakh* (lek'ək): a honey cake.
[4] *svetouchnee* (sve·tuch'ne): originally a Russian brand name for bulk black tea; was used by Eastern European Jewish immigrants to mean virtually any black tea in bulk form.

Ladies Garment Workers Union; and were all unmarried. We were their only family. Despite my mother's frenzied matchmaking, she had never succeeded in pinning a husband down for any of them. As she said, they were all too *particular*—what a calamity for a Jewish woman to remain unmarried! But my cousin and her friends accepted their fate calmly, and prided themselves on their culture and their strong *progressive* interests. They felt they belonged not to the "kitchen world," like my mother, but to the enlightened tradition of the old Russian intelligentsia. Whenever my mother sighed over them, they would smile out of their greater knowledge of the world, and looking at me with a pointed appeal for recognition, would speak of novels they had read in Yiddish and Russian, of *Winesburg, Ohio,*[5] of some article in the *Nation.*[6]

Our cousin and her two friends were of my parents' generation, but I could never believe it—they seemed to enjoy life with such outspokenness. They were the first grown-up people I had ever met who used the word *love* without embarrassment. "*Libbe! Libbe!*"[7] my mother would explode whenever one of them protested that she could not, after all, marry a man she did not love. "What is this love you make such a stew about? You do not like the way he holds his cigarette? Marry him first and it will all come out right in the end!" It astonished me to realize there was a world in which even unmarried women no longer young were simply individual human beings with lives of their own. *Our* parents, whatever affection might offhandedly be expressed between them, always had the look of being committed to something deeper than *mere* love. Their marriages were neither happy nor unhappy; they were arrangements. However they had met —whether in Russia or in the steerage or, like my parents, in an East Side boarding house—whatever they still thought of each other, *love* was not a word they used easily. Marriage was an institution people entered into—

---

[5] *Winesburg, Ohio:* a collection of stories by Sherwood Anderson, published in 1919, and commonly regarded during the following decade as a shocking and controversial example of the new American realism.

[6] the *Nation:* a fervently liberal political weekly.

[7] *Libbe* (lib'ə): Yiddish for "love."

for all I could ever tell—only from immigrant loneliness, a need to be with one's own kind that mechanically resulted in the *family*. The *family* was a whole greater than all the individuals who made it up, yet made sense only in their untiring solidarity. I was perfectly sure that in my parents' minds *libbe* was something exotic and not wholly legitimate, reserved for "educated" people like their children, who were the sole end of their existence. My father and mother worked in a rage to put us above their level; they had married to make *us* possible. We were the only conceivable end to all their striving; we were their America.

So far as I knew, love was not an element admissible in my parents' experience. Any open talk of it between themselves would have seemed ridiculous. It would have suggested a wicked self-indulgence, a preposterous attention to one's own feelings, possible only to those who were free enough to choose. They did not consider themselves free. They were awed by us, as they were awed by their own imagined unworthiness, and looked on themselves only as instruments toward the ideal "American" future that would be lived by their children. As poor immigrants who had remained in Brownsville, painfully conscious of the *alrightniks* [8] on Eastern Parkway—oh, those successes of whom I was always hearing so much, and whom we admired despite all our socialism!—everything in their lives combined to make them look down on love as something *they* had no time for. Of course there was a deep resentment in this, and when on those Friday evenings our cousin or her two friends openly mentioned the unheard-of collapse of someone's marriage—

"Sórelle and Berke? [9] I don't believe it."

"But it's true."

"You must be joking!"

"No, it's true!"

"You're joking! You're joking!"

"No, it's true!"

[8] *alrightniks:* newly rich Jewish immigrants who had moved to more fashionable neighborhoods in New York.

[9] *Sórelle and Berke:* familiar, affectionate forms in Yiddish of the names whose nearest English equivalents are Sarah and Barry.

—I noticed that my parents' talk had an unnaturally hard edge to it, as if those who gave themselves up to love must inevitably come to grief. Love, they could have said, was not *serious*. Life was a battle to "make sure"; it had no place, as we had no time, for whims.

Love, in fact, was something for the movies, which my parents enjoyed, but a little ashamedly. They were the land of the impossible. On those few occasions when my mother closed her sewing machine in the evening and allowed herself a visit to the Supreme, or the Palace, or the Premier, she would return, her eyes gleaming with wonder and some distrust at the strangeness of it all, to report on erotic fanatics who were, thank God, like no one we knew. What heedlessness! What daring! What riches! To my mother riches alone were the gateway to romance, for only those who had money enough could afford the freedom, and the crazy boldness, to give themselves up to love.

Yet there they were in our own dining room, our cousin and her two friends—women, grown-up women—talking openly of the look on Garbo's face when John Gilbert took her in his arms, serenely disposing of each new *khayimyankel*,[10] poor wretch, my mother had picked for them, and arguing my father down on small points of Socialist doctrine. As they sat around the cut-glass bowl on the table—cracking walnuts, expertly peeling the skin off an apple in long even strips, cozily sipping at a glass of tea—they crossed their legs in comfort and gave off a deliciously musky fragrance of face powder that instantly framed them for me in all their dark coloring, brilliantly white teeth, and the rosy Russian blouses that swelled and rippled in terraces of embroidery over their opulent breasts.

They had a great flavor for me, those three women: they were the positive center of that togetherness that always meant so much to me in our dining room on Friday evenings. It was a quality that seemed to start in the prickly thickness of the cut-glass bowl laden with nuts and fruits; in the light from the long black-shaded lamp

[10] *khayimyankel* (khim·yonk′l): a Yiddish term indicating disapproval of a male by its connotation of insignificance and inadequacy, roughly translatable as "any Tom, Dick, or Harry."

hanging over the table as it shimmered against the thick surfaces of the bowl and softened that room where the lace curtains were drawn against the dark and empty streets—and then found its unexpectedly tender voice in the Yiddish folksongs and Socialist hymns they taught me—"*Let's Now Forgive Each Other*"; "*Tsuzamen*,[11] *Tsuzamen, All Together, Brothers!*" Those Friday evenings, I suddenly found myself enveloped in some old, primary Socialist idea that men could go beyond every barrier of race and nation and language, even of class! into some potential loving union of the whole human race. I was suddenly glad to be a Jew, as these women were Jews —simply and naturally glad of those Jewish dressmakers who spoke with enthusiastic familiarity of Sholem Aleichem and Peretz,[12] Gorky and Tolstoy, who glowed at every reminiscence of Nijinsky, of Nazimova[13] in *The Cherry Orchard*, of Pavlova in "The Swan."

Often, those Friday evenings, they spoke of *der heym*, "Home," and then it was hard for me. *Heym* was a terrible word. I saw millions of Jews lying dead under the Polish eagle with knives in their throats. I was afraid with my mother's fears, thought I should weep when she wept, lived again through every pogrom whose terrors she chanted. I associated with that old European life only pain, mud, and hopelessness, but I was of it still, through her. Whenever she would call through the roll of her many brothers and sisters and their children, remembering at each name that this one was dead, that one dead, another starving and sure soon to die—who knew *how* they were living these days in that miserable Poland?—I felt there was some supernatural Polish eagle across the sea whose face I should never see, but which sent out dark electrical rays to hold me fast.

In many ways *der heym* was entirely dim and abstract, nothing to do with me at all, alien as the skullcap and

---

[11] *Tsuzamen* (tsoo·zä′mən): Yiddish for "together."

[12] *Sholem Aleichem and Peretz*: the two leading figures in the flowering of Yiddish literature that occurred in Eastern Europe toward the end of the nineteenth century.

[13] *Nazimova*: a distinguished actress who achieved one of her greatest successes in *The Cherry Orchard* by the Russian dramatist Anton Chekhov.

beard and frock coat of my mother's father, whom I never saw, but whose calm orthodox dignity stared up at me from an old cracked photograph at the bottom of the bureau drawer. Yet I lived each of my mother's fears from Dugschitz [14] to Hamburg to London to Hester Street [15] to Brownsville through and through with such fidelity that there were times when I wished I had made that journey too, wished I could have seen Czarist Russia, since I had in any event to suffer it all over again. I often felt odd twinges of jealousy because my parents could talk about that more intense, somehow less *experimental* life than ours with so many private smiles between themselves. It was bewildering, it made me long constantly to get at some past nearer my own New York life, my having to live with all those running wounds of a world I had never seen.

Then, under cover of the talk those Friday evenings, I would take up *The Boy's Life of Theodore Roosevelt* again, and moodily call out to those strangers on the summer veranda in Oyster Bay until my father spoke *his* tale of arriving in America. That was hard, too, painful in another way—yet it always made him curiously lighthearted and left me swimming in space. For he had gone off painting box cars on the Union Pacific, had been as far west as Omaha, had actually seen Sidney Hillman toiling in Hart, Schaffner and Marx's Chicago factory, had heard his beloved Debs [16] making fools of Bryan and Taft in the 1908 campaign, had been offered a homestead in Colorado! *Omaha* was the most beautiful word I had ever heard,

[14] *Dugschitz:* a very small village in Russia.

[15] *Hester Street:* a street on the Lower East Side, especially noted for the noise and crowding produced by the pushcart vendors and immigrant shoppers who congregated there.

[16] Hillman . . . Debs: Sidney Hillman (1887–1946), American labor leader and pioneer of cooperation between workers and employers. In 1915 he became president of the Amalgamated Clothing Workers of America. Eugene Victor Debs (1855–1926) was a founder of the American Railway Union, the Industrial Workers of the World, and the Socialist Party of America. Five times the Socialist candidate for the Presidency of the U.S., Debs opposed Woodrow Wilson, William H. Taft and Theodore Roosevelt in the 1912 election and polled nearly a million votes.

homestead almost as beautiful; but I could never forgive him for not having accepted that homestead.

"What would I have done there? I'm no farmer."

"You should have taken it! Why do we always live here!"

"It would have been too lonely. Nobody I knew."

"What a chance!"

"Don't be childish. Nobody I knew."

"Why? Why?"

"Alfred, what do you want of us poor Jews?"

So it was: we had always to be together: believers and non-believers, we were a people; I was of that people. Unthinkable to go one's own way, to doubt or to escape the fact that I was a Jew. I had heard of Jews who pretended they were not, but could not understand them. We had all of us lived together so long that we would not have known how to separate even if we had wanted to. The most terrible word was *aleyn,* alone. I always had the same picture of a man desolately walking down a dark street, newspapers and cigarette butts contemptuously flying in his face as he tasted in the dusty grit the full measure of his strangeness. *Aleyn! Aleyn!* My father had been alone here in America as a boy. *His* father, whose name I bore, had died here at twenty-five of pneumonia caught on a garment workers' picket line, and his body flung in with thousands of other Jews who had perished those first years on the East Side. My father had never been able to find his father's grave. *Aleyn! Aleyn!* Did immigrant Jews, then, marry only out of loneliness? Was even Socialism just a happier way of keeping us together?

I trusted it to do that. Socialism would be one long Friday evening around the samovar and the cut-glass bowl laden with nuts and fruits, all of us singing *Tsuzamen, tsuzamen, ale tsuzamen!* Then the heroes of the Russian novel—*our* kind of people—would walk the world, and I —still wearing a circle-necked Russian blouse "*à la Tolstoy*"—would live forever with those I loved in that beautiful Russian country of the mind. Listening to our cousin and her two friends I, who had never seen it, who associated with it nothing but the names of great writers and my father's saying as we went through the Brooklyn Botanic Garden—"Nice! but you should have seen the Czar's summer palace at Tsarskoye-Selo!"—suddenly saw Russia as the grand antithesis to all bourgeois ideals, the spiritual home of all truly free people. I was perfectly sure that there was no literature in the world like the Russian; that the only warm hearts in the world were Russian, like our cousin and her two friends; that other people were always dully materialist, but that the Russian soul, like Nijinsky's dream of pure flight, would always leap outward, past all barriers, to a lyric world in which my ideal socialism and the fiery moodiness of Tchaikovsky's *Pathétique* would be entirely at home with each other. *Tsuzamen, alle tsuzamen!* How many millions would be with us! China was in our house those Friday evenings, Africa, the Indian masses. And it was those three unmarried dressmakers from the rank and file who fully wrapped me in that spell, with the worldly clang of their agate beads and the musky fragrance of their face powder and their embroidered Russian blouses, with the great names of Russian writers ringing against the cut-glass bowl under the black lamp. Never did the bowl look so laden, never did apples and tea smell so good, never did the samovar pour out with such steaming bounty, as on those Friday evenings when I tasted in the tea and the talk the evangelical heart of our cousin and her two friends, and realized that it was we—we!—who would someday put the world on its noblest course.

"*Kinder, kinder,*" [17] my mother would say. "Enough *discusye*.[18] Maybe now a little music? Alfred, play *Scheherazade!*"

You could melt their hearts with it; the effect of the violin on almost everyone I knew was uncanny. I could watch them softening, easing, already on the brink of tears —yet with their hands at rest in their laps, they stared straight ahead at the wall, breathing hard, an unforeseen smile of rapture on their mouths. Any slow movement, if only it were played lingeringly and sagely enough, seemed to come to them as a reminiscence of a reminiscence. It

[17] *Kinder* (kin'dər): Yiddish for "children."
[18] *discusye* (dis·cus'yə): Yiddish for "talk" or "debate."

seemed to have something to do with our being Jews. The depths of Jewish memory the violin could throw open apparently had no limit—for every slow movement was based on something "Russian," every plaintive melody even in Beethoven or Mozart was "Jewish." I could skip from composer to composer, from theme to theme, without any fear, ever, of being detected, for all slow movements fell into a single chant of *der heym* and of the great *Kol Nidre* [19] sung in the first evening hours of the Day of Atonement, in whose long rending cry—of contrition? of grief? of hopeless love for the Creator?—I relived all of the Jews' bitter intimacy with death.

Then I cranked up the old brown Victor, took our favorite records out of the red velvet pleated compartments, and we listened to John McCormack singing *Ave Maria*, Amelita Galli-Curci singing *Caro Nome* ("How ugly she is!" my parents would say wonderingly. "Have you seen her picture? Incredible! But how she sings!"), and Alma Gluck singing *Comin' Thro' the Rye*. The high point was Caruso singing from *La Juive*.[20] He inspired in my father and mother such helpless, intimidated adoration that I came to think of what was always humbly referred to as his *golden voice* as the invocation of a god. The pleasure he gave us was beyond all music. When Mischa Elman [21] played some well-known melody we sighed familiarly at each other—his tone was so *warm;* he bubbled slowly in my ears like the sound of chicken fat crackling in the pan. But Caruso, "that *Italyéner,*" seemed to me the echo of some outrageously pagan voice at the roof of the world. While I pushed at the hand-crank and the wheezy sounds of the orchestra in the background came to me as the whispered turnings, sighs and alarms of the crowd around the circus pit, there on high, and rising higher and higher with each note, that voice, that *golden voice,* leaped its way from one trapeze to another. We sat hunched in our won-

[19] *Kol Nidre* (kôl nid′rə): song sung by the cantor in the synagogue on Yom Kippur, the most solemn Jewish holy day.
[20] *La Juive* (lä zhwēv′): *The Jewess,* a French opera by Jacques Halévy in which Caruso performed to great acclaim the role of Eléazar, a Jewish goldsmith.
[21] *Mischa Elman:* a celebrated violinist.

der, our adoration, our fear. Would he make it? Could any human being find that last impossible rung?

Rachel! Quand du Seigneur la grâce tutélaire. . . .[22]

Then, suddenly bounding back to earth again, there he was before us again, secretly smiling, the tones welling out of him with such brazen strength, such irresistible energy, that he left us gasping. I could see him standing inside the victrola box—a centaur just out of the woods, not quite human, with that enigmatic, almost contemptuous smile on his face. "What a voice!" my father would say over and over, deeply shaken. "What a voice! It's not human! Never was there a voice like it! Only the other day I was reading that when they opened him up after he died they found his vocal chords were ab-solutely unique!" Then, his face white with pleasure, with amazement, with wonder: "Oh that *Italyéner!* Oh that *Italyéner!* What a power he has, that *Italyéner!*"

In Brownsville tenements the kitchen is always the largest room and the center of the household. As a child I felt that we lived in a kitchen to which four other rooms were annexed. My mother, a "home" dressmaker, had her workshop in the kitchen. She told me once that she had begun dressmaking in Poland at thirteen; as far back as I can remember, she was always making dresses for the local women. She had an innate sense of design, a quick eye for all the subtleties in the latest fashions, even when she despised them, and great boldness. For three or four dollars she would study the fashion magazines with a customer, go with the customer to the remnants store on Belmont Avenue to pick out the material, argue the owner down—all remnants stores, for some reason, were supposed to be shady, as if the owners dealt in stolen goods—and then for days would patiently fit and baste and sew and fit again. Our apartment was always full of women in their housedresses sitting around the kitchen table waiting for a fitting. My little bedroom next to the kitchen was the fitting room. The sewing machine, an old nut-brown Singer with golden

---

[22] "*Rachel! . . . tutélaire. . . .*": the opening of the famous, highly emotional aria sung by Caruso in Act IV of *La Juive.*

scrolls painted along the black arm and engraved along the two tiers of little drawers massed with needles and thread on each side of the treadle, stood next to the window and the great coal-black stove which up to my last year in college was our main source of heat. By December the two outer bedrooms were closed off, and used to chill bottles of milk and cream, cold borscht [23] and jellied calves' feet.

The kitchen held our lives together. My mother worked in it all day long, we ate in it almost all meals except the Passover *seder*,[24] I did my homework and first writing at the kitchen table, and in winter I often had a bed made up for me on three kitchen chairs near the stove. On the wall just over the table hung a long horizontal mirror that sloped to a ship's prow at each end and was lined in cherry wood. It took up the whole wall, and drew every object in the kitchen to itself. The walls were a fiercely stippled whitewash, so often rewhitened by my father in slack seasons that the paint looked as if it had been squeezed and cracked into the walls. A large electric bulb hung down the center of the kitchen at the end of a chain that had been hooked into the ceiling; the old gas ring and key still jutted out of the wall like antlers. In the corner next to the toilet was the sink at which we washed, and the square tub in which my mother did our clothes. Above it, tacked to the shelf on which were pleasantly ranged square, blue-bordered white sugar and spice jars, hung calendars from the Public National Bank on Pitkin Avenue and the Minsker Progressive Branch of the Workman's Circle; receipts for the payment of insurance premiums, and household bills on a spindle; two little boxes engraved with Hebrew letters. One of these was for the poor, the other to buy back the Land of Israel. Each spring a bearded little man would suddenly appear in our kitchen, salute us with a hurried Hebrew blessing, empty the boxes (sometimes with a sidelong look of disdain if they were not full), hurriedly bless us again for remembering our less fortunate Jewish brothers

[23] *borscht* (bôrsht): a kind of beet soup popular in Eastern Europe.
[24] *seder* (sâ′dər): the meal incorporating the traditional foods and rituals associated with the observance of Passover, which commemorates the exodus of the Jews from Egyptian bondage.

and sisters, and so take his departure until the next spring, after vainly trying to persuade my mother to take still another box. We did occasionally remember to drop coins in the boxes, but this was usually only on the dreaded morning of "mid-terms" and final examinations, because my mother thought it would bring me luck. She was extremely superstitious, but embarrassed about it, and always laughed at herself whenever, on the morning of an examination, she counseled me to leave the house on my right foot. "I know it's silly," her smile seemed to say, "but what harm can it do? It may calm God down."

The kitchen gave a special character to our lives; my mother's character. All my memories of that kitchen are dominated by the nearness of my mother sitting all day long at her sewing machine, by the clacking of the treadle against the linoleum floor, by the patient twist of her right shoulder as she automatically pushed at the wheel with one hand or lifted the foot to free the needle where it had got stuck in a thick piece of material. The kitchen was her life. Year by year, as I began to take in her fantastic capacity for labor and her anxious zeal, I realized it was ourselves she kept stitched together. I can never remember a time when she was not working. She worked because the law of her life was work, work and anxiety; she worked because she would have found life meaningless without work. She read almost no English; she could read the Yiddish paper, but never felt she had time to. We were always talking of a time when I would teach her how to read, but somehow there was never time. When I awoke in the morning she was already at her machine, or in the great morning crowd of housewives at the grocery getting fresh rolls for breakfast. When I returned from school she was at her machine, or conferring over *McCall's* with some neighborhood woman who had come in pointing hopefully to an illustration—"Mrs. Kazin! Mrs. Kazin! Make me a dress like it shows here in the picture!" When my father came home from work she had somehow mysteriously interrupted herself to make supper for us, and the dishes cleared and washed, was back at her machine. When I went to bed at night, often she was still there, pounding away at the treadle, hunched over the wheel, her hands steering a piece of gauze under the needle with a finesse that always contrasted sharply with her swollen hands and broken nails. Her left hand had been pierced through when as a girl she had worked in the infamous Triangle Shirtwaist Factory [25] on the East Side. A needle had gone straight through the palm, severing a large vein. They had sewn it up for her so clumsily that a tuft of flesh always lay folded over the palm.

The kitchen was the great machine that set our lives running; it whirred down a little only on Saturdays and holy days. From my mother's kitchen I gained my first picture of life as a white, overheated, starkly lit workshop redolent with Jewish cooking, crowded with women in housedresses, strewn with fashion magazines, patterns, dress material, spools of thread—and at whose center, so lashed to her machine that bolts of energy seemed to dance out of her hands and feet as she worked, my mother stamped the treadle hard against the floor, hard, hard, and silently, grimly at war, beat out the first rhythm of the world for me.

Every sound from the street roared and trembled at our windows—a mother feeding her child on the doorstep, the screech of the trolley cars on Rockaway Avenue, the eternal smash of a handball against the wall of our house, the clatter of *"der Italyéner"*'s cart packed with watermelons, the sing-song of the old-clothes men walking Chester Street, the cries *"Árbes! Árbes! Kinder! Kinder! Heyse gute árbes!"* [26] All day long people streamed into our apartment as a matter of course—"customers," upstairs neighbors, downstairs neighbors, women who would stop in for a half-hour's talk, salesmen, relatives, insurance agents.

[25] *Triangle Shirtwaist Factory:* "infamous" because of its wretched working conditions and because 146 of its 850 employees—mostly girls—were killed there in a fire in 1911. The disaster deeply affected the Jewish immigrant community of the Lower East Side, since the Triangle workers—like so many employed in New York's garment factories—were largely of this community.

[26] *"Árbes! ... gute árbes":* the cry of vendors, "Chickpeas, chickpeas, kids, good hot chickpeas." The chickpeas were roasted and salted for flavor.

Usually they came in without ringing the bell—everyone knew my mother was always at home. I would hear the front door opening, the wind whistling through our front hall, and then some familiar face would appear in our kitchen with the same bland, matter-of-fact inquiring look: no need to stand on ceremony: my mother and her kitchen were available to everyone all day long.

At night the kitchen contracted around the blaze of light on the cloth, the patterns, the ironing board where the iron had burned a black border around the tear in the muslin cover; the finished dresses looked so frilly as they jostled on their wire hangers after all the work my mother had put into them. And then I would get that strangely ominous smell of tension from the dress fabrics and the burn in the cover of the ironing board—as if each piece of cloth and paper crushed with light under the naked bulb might suddenly go up in flames. Whenever I pass some small tailoring shop still lit up at night and see the owner hunched over his steam press; whenever in some poorer neighborhood of the city I see through a window some small crowded kitchen naked under the harsh light glittering in the ceiling, I still smell that fiery breath, that warning of imminent fire. I was always holding my breath. What I must have felt most about ourselves, I see now, was that we ourselves were like kindling—that all the hard-pressed pieces of ourselves and all the hard-used objects in that kitchen were like so many slivers of wood that might go up in flames if we came too near the white-blazing filaments in that naked bulb. Our tension itself was fire, we ourselves were forever burning—to live, to get down the foreboding in our souls, to make good.

Twice a year, on the anniversaries of her parents' deaths, my mother placed on top of the ice-box an ordinary kitchen glass packed with wax, the *yortsayt*,[27] and lit the candle in it. Sitting at the kitchen table over my homework, I would look across the threshold to that mourning-glass, and sense that for my mother the distance from our kitchen to *der heym*, from life to death, was only

[27] *yortsayt* (yôr′tsĭt): the date on which a relative's death is remembered in the manner described by Kazin.

a flame's length away. Poor as we were, it was not poverty that drove my mother so hard; it was loneliness—some endless bitter brooding over all those left behind, dead or dying or soon to die; a loneliness locked up in her kitchen that dwelt every day on the hazardousness of life and the nearness of death, but still kept struggling in the lock, trying to get us through by endless labor.

With us, life started up again only on the last shore. There seemed to be no middle ground between despair and the fury of our ambition. Whenever my mother spoke of her hopes for us, it was with such unbelievingness that the likes of us would ever come to anything, such abashed hope and readiness for pain, that I finally came to see in the flame burning on top of the ice-box death itself burning away the bones of poor Jews, burning out in us everything but courage, the blind resolution to live. In the light of that mourning-candle, there were ranged around me how many dead and dying—how many eras of pain, of exile, of dispersion, of cringing before the powers of this world!

It was always at dusk that my mother's loneliness came home most to me. Painfully alert to every shift in the light at her window, she would suddenly confess her fatigue by removing her pince-nez, and then wearily pushing aside the great mound of fabrics on her machine, would stare at the street as if to warm herself in the last of the sun. "How sad it is!" I once heard her say. "It grips me! It grips me!" Twilight was the bottommost part of the day, the chillest and loneliest time for her. Always so near to her moods, I knew she was fighting some deep inner dread, struggling against the returning tide of darkness along the streets that invariably assailed her heart with the same foreboding—Where? Where now? Where is the day taking us now?

Yet one good look at the street would revive her. I see her now, perched against the windowsill, with her face against the glass, her eyes almost asleep in enjoyment, just as she starts up with the guilty cry—"What foolishness is this in me!"—and goes to the stove to prepare supper for us: a moment, only a moment, watching the evening crowd of women gathering at the grocery for fresh bread and milk. But between my mother's pent-up face at the window and the winter sun dying in the fabrics—"Alfred, see how beautiful!"—she has drawn for me one single line of sentience.

The unmarried cousin who boarded with us had English books in her room—the only English books in our house I did not bring into it myself. Half an hour before supper, I liked nothing better than to stray into her room, and sitting on the India print spread of her bed next to the yellow wicker bookstand, look through her books and smell the musky face powder that filled her room. There was no closet: her embroidered Russian blouses and red velvet suits hung behind a curtain, and the lint seemed to float off the velvet and swim in multicolored motes through the air. On the wall over her bed hung a picture of two half-nude lovers fleeing from a storm, and an oval-framed picture of Psyche perched on a rock. On the wicker bookstand, in a star-shaped frame of thick glass, was a photograph of our cousin's brother, missing since the Battle of Tannenberg, in the uniform of a Czarist Army private.

In that wicker bookstand, below the blue set of Sholem Aleichem in Yiddish and the scattered volumes of Russian novels, were the books I would never have to drag from the Stone Avenue Library myself—THE WORLD'S GREATEST SELECTED SHORT STORIES; a biography of Alfred E. Smith entitled *Up From the City Streets;* a Grosset and Dunlap edition of *The Sheik;* [28] and in English, a volume of stories by Alexander Kuprin.[29] Day after day at five-thirty, half an hour before supper, I would sit myself carefully on the India print, and fondle those books with such rapture that they were actually *there,* for me to look through whenever I liked, that on some days I could not bear to open them at all, but sat as close to the sun in the windows as I could, breathing the lint in, and the sun still hot on the India spread.

On the roof just across the street, the older boys now

[28] *The Sheik:* a best-selling exotic romance of the desert by Edith M. Hull, published in 1921; its popularity was extended by the silent movie version starring Rudolph Valentino.

[29] *Alexander Kuprin:* a Russian short story writer and novelist (1870–1938) whose works displayed a vigorous, earthy realism and a striking zest for life.

home from work would spring their pigeons from the traps. You could see the feathers glistening faintly in the last light, beating thinly against their sides—they, too, sucking air as the birds leaped up from their wire cages. Then, widening and widening their flight each time they came over our roof again, they went round a sycamore and the spire of the church without stopping. The sun fell straight on the India spread—how the thin prickly material burned in my nostrils—and glowed along the bony gnarled bumps in the legs of the yellow wicker bookstand. Happiness was warmth. Beyond Chester Street, beyond even Rockaway, I could see to where the Italians lived on broken streets that rose up to a hill topped by a church. The church seemed to be thickly surrounded by trees. In his star-shaped glass on the bookstand, that Russian soldier missing since the Battle of Tannenberg looked steadily at me from under his round forage cap. His chest bulged against two rows of gold buttons up and down his black blouse. Where? Where now? Had they put him, too, into a great pit? Suddenly it did not matter. Happiness was the sun on the India spread, the hot languid sands lapping at the tent of the Sheik—*"Monseigneur! My desert prince!"*—the summer smell of the scum on the East River just off Oliver Street where Alfred E. Smith worked in the Fulton Fish Market. In the Kuprin stories an old man and a boy went wandering up a road in the Crimea. There was dust on the road, dust on the leaves—*hoo! hoo! my son! how it is hot!* But they were happy. It was summer in the Crimea, and just to walk along with them made me happy. When they got hungry they stopped at a spring, took black bread, salt, and tomatoes out of their knapsacks, and ate. The ripe open tomatoes gushed red from their mouths, the black bread and salt were good, very good, and when they leaned over to drink at the spring, the water was so icy cold it made my teeth ache. I read that story over and over, sometimes skipping pages to get to the part about the bread, the salt, the tomatoes, the icy water. *I could taste that bread, that salt, those tomatoes, that icy spring.*

Now the light begins to die. Twilight is also the mind's grazing time. Twilight is the bottom of that arc down which we had fallen the whole long day, but where I now sit at our cousin's window in some strange silence of attention, watching the pigeons go round and round to the leafy smell of soupgreens from the stove. In the cool of that first evening hour, as I sit at the table waiting for supper and my father and the New York *World*, everything is so rich to overflowing, I hardly know where to begin.

for discussion

1. What conflicting loyalties are revealed in this selection by the linking of Hudson's discovery of the New World and Kazin's boyhood freedom on the Sabbath?

2. How did the "kitchen world" of Kazin's mother differ from the "progressive" world of the unmarried cousin? Why do you think the author saw the unmarried cousin and her friends as the "positive center" of the dining room discussions?

3. Kazin states: "With us, life started up again only on the last shore. There seemed to be no middle ground between despair and the fury of our ambition." What does this statement reveal about the conflicting emotions of Jewish immigrants in America?

4. Did the tensions between the European traditions of the Jewish community and the characteristics of life in America oppose each other? Or were they complementary?

1871–1938

JAMES WELDON JOHNSON

☐ *In his lifetime, James Weldon Johnson played many roles. He was a lawyer in Florida, a musical comedy lyricist in New York, a consul in Venezuela, a newspaper editor in New York, an early leader of the National Association for the Advancement of Colored People (NAACP), a professor of creative literature at Fisk University, and a poet and novelist. From these many roles, Johnson became equally renowned for his social and his literary contributions. As the author of a novel,* The Autobiography of an Ex-Colored Man *(1912), which sensitively probed the realities of Negro life in America, and as a leader of the NAACP, he spoke with eloquence and force of the problems confronting the black American. As a poet and a student of black cultural history, he inspired the New Negro art movement of the 1920's with its new pride in the value of the Afro-American past. Thus, Johnson is often associated with the beginnings of Negro social and literary protest.*

However, his popularity with his contemporaries came largely from his poems, which often conformed to the public image of the Negro as a happy, rural, hymn-singing innocent whose patience was virtually endless. That these poems were frequently written in dialect added to their public appeal by rendering their good-humored stereotypes of Negro life more "authentic." On the other hand, Johnson also attempted to make his poetry more artistically attractive by demonstrating that he could write in a highly formal manner. Whether writing in dialect or in "literary" English, Johnson represented the Afro-American as a devoutly religious man with a "natural" tendency to expresss this religious spirit rhythmically. Consequently, Johnson's poetry commanded much the same sympathetic response that white audiences had already accorded the widely admired spirituals. The first collection of Johnson's poetry, Fifty Years and Other Poems, *was published in*

1917. It was followed in 1927 by God's Trombones—
*Johnson's poetic re-creations of the black folk sermon—
and in 1930 by* Saint Peter Relates an Incident of the
Resurrection Day. *Johnson edited* The Book of American
Negro Poetry *in 1922 and two books of spirituals in the
mid-1920's.*

o black and unknown bards

O black and unknown bards of long ago,
How came your lips to touch the sacred fire?
How, in your darkness, did you come to know
The power and beauty of the minstrel's lyre?
Who first from midst his bonds lifted his eyes?
Who first from out the still watch, lone and long,
Feeling the ancient faith of prophets rise
Within his dark-kept soul, burst into song?

Heart of what slave poured out such melody
As "Steal away to Jesus"? On its strains
His spirit must have nightly floated free,
Though still about his hands he felt his chains.
Who heard great "Jordan roll"? Whose starward eye
Saw chariot "swing low"? And who was he
That breathed that comforting, melodic sigh,
"Nobody knows de trouble I see"?

What merely living clod, what captive thing,
Could up toward God through all its darkness grope,
And find within its deadened heart to sing
These songs of sorrow, love and faith, and hope?

How did it catch that subtle undertone,
That note in music heard not with the ears?
How sound the elusive reed so seldom blown,
Which stirs the soul or melts the heart to tears.

Not that great German master in his dream
Of harmonies that thundered amongst the stars
At the creation, ever heard a theme
Nobler than "Go down, Moses." Mark its bars
How like a mighty trumpet-call they stir
The blood. Such are the notes that men have sung
Going to valorous deeds; such tones there were
That helped make history when Time was young.

There is a wide, wide wonder in it all,
That from degraded rest and servile toil
The fiery spirit of the seer should call
These simple children of the sun and soil.
O black slave singers, gone, forgot, unfamed,
You—you alone, of all the long, long line
Of those who've sung untaught, unknown, unnamed,
Have stretched out upward, seeking the divine.

You sang not deeds of heroes or of kings;
No chant of bloody war, no exulting paean
Of arms-won triumphs; but your humble strings
You touched in chord with music empyrean.
You sang far better than you knew; the songs
That for your listeners' hungry hearts sufficed
Still live,—but more than this to you belongs:
You sang a race from wood and stone to Christ.

for discussion

1. Look up the word *bard* in a dictionary. What is the effect of the poet's addressing the unknown creators of the spiritual as "bards"?
2. What comparison does Johnson suggest by the reference to Negro bondage and "the ancient faith of prophets" in the Bible?
3. In what way does Johnson declare the black folk poets superior to the bards and minstrels of antiquity?

1902–1967

LANGSTON HUGHES

☐ *Born and raised in the Midwest, Langston Hughes
graduated from a Cleveland high school in 1920, spent the
following year in Mexico, and arrived in New York in
the fall of 1921 to attend Columbia University. After a
year he left school, moved into Harlem, and formed the
close bond with its everyday scenes and styles of
expression that was ever after characteristic of his
writing. Beginning with "The Negro Speaks of Rivers"
in 1921, Hughes's poems were published in such
important black journals as* The Crisis *and* Opportunity
*during the early 1920's. But poverty forced him to
undertake the usual run of menial jobs; and from the
spring of 1923 to the fall of 1924, he traveled as a seaman
to Africa and Europe, worked as a dishwasher and waiter
in the jazz clubs of Paris, and finally—still penniless—
worked his way back to Harlem on a freighter. At the end
of 1924, Hughes joined his mother and younger brother
in Washington, D.C., where he worked as a bus boy
at the Wardman Park Hotel. One day in December 1925,
he excitedly glimpsed the poet Vachel Lindsay, who had
come to the hotel to give a public reading. In his
autobiography,* The Big Sea *(1940), Hughes described the
circumstances that led to three of his poems being
recited by Lindsay at the reading that night:*

> *That afternoon I wrote out three of my poems,
> "Jazzonia," "Negro Dancers," and "The Weary
> Blues," on some pieces of paper and put them in the
> pocket of my white bus boy's coat. In the evening
> when Mr. Lindsay came down to dinner, quickly I
> laid them beside his plate and went away, afraid to
> say anything to so famous a poet, except to tell him I
> liked his poems and that these were poems of mine.
> I looked back once and saw Mr. Lindsay reading the*

poems, as I picked up a tray of dirty dishes from a
side table.°

On the next day, newspapers throughout America
announced Lindsay's "discovery" of a new Negro poet.
The following years were encouraging ones for Hughes,
who had now been identified as a major poetic voice of
the Harlem Renaissance: earlier that year he had won a
poetry contest; and in 1926 he won a second poetry prize
and published his first book, The Weary Blues. In 1926
he also enrolled at Lincoln University in Pennsylvania,
from which he graduated in 1929.

If James Weldon Johnson's poetry and researches into
black culture did much to establish among the new
poets of the Harlem Renaissance a sense of the dignity
and power of their folk traditions, Langston Hughes was
one of the most notable heirs to this influence. Hughes
reached proudly back into the past for themes and
attitudes that dispelled the myth of Negro inferiority by
showing an ancient and wealthy cultural legacy, a quietly
heroic determination to endure, and a buoyant mood of
hope. The blacks who people Hughes's early poems
"stand tall" and express a stirring awareness of their
heritage.

° From The Big Sea by Langston Hughes. Reprinted by permission of
the publisher, Hill and Wang Incorporated.

the negro speaks of rivers

I've known rivers:
I've known rivers ancient as the world and older than the
      flow of human blood in human veins.

My soul has grown deep like the rivers.

I bathed in the Euphrates when dawns were young.
I built my hut near the Congo and it lulled me to sleep.
I looked upon the Nile and raised the pyramids above it.
I heard the singing of the Mississippi when Abe Lincoln
     went down to New Orleans, and I've seen its muddy
     bosom turn all golden in the sunset.

I've known rivers:
Ancient, dusky rivers.

My soul has grown deep like the rivers.

still here

I've been scarred and battered.
My hopes the wind done scattered.
Snow has friz me, sun has baked me.
     Looks like between 'em
     They done tried to make me
Stop laughin', stop lovin', stop livin'—
     But I don't care!
     I'm still here!

Well, son, I'll tell you:
Life for me ain't been no crystal stair.
It's had tacks in it,
And splinters,
And boards torn up,
And places with no carpet on the floor—
Bare.
But all the time
I'se been a-climbin' on,
And reachin' landin's,
And turnin' corners,
And sometimes goin' in the dark
Where there ain't been no light.
So boy, don't you turn back.
Don't you set down on the steps
'Cause you finds it's kinder hard.
Don't you fall now—
For I'se still goin', honey,
I'se still climbin',
And life for me ain't been no crystal stair.

for discussion

1. Compare the last line in "The Negro Speaks of Rivers" with the last line in "Still Here." How are the speakers' attitudes different in the two poems? How are they the same? How does the poet's language reveal these attitudes?

2. In what way is the speaker in "Mother to Son" like the speaker in "Still Here"? In what way is she like the speaker in "The Negro Speaks of Rivers"?

3. How does the informal, "spoken" language in "Still Here" and "Mother to Son" effect a different image of the black than does Johnson's formal language in "O Black and Unknown Bards."

STERLING BROWN

☐ Sterling Brown was educated at Williams College and at Harvard. In 1932 he published Southern Road, his only book of poems thus far. Since then he has occasionally published poems in magazines, but increasingly he has turned his attention to the study of Negro writing in America. A faculty member at Howard University since 1929, Brown wrote both The Negro in American Fiction and Negro Poetry and Drama in 1937; and he was an editor of one of the best anthologies of American Negro literature—The Negro Caravan, published in 1941. Thus, Sterling Brown has gained wide recognition for his poetry and for his commanding knowledge of American Negro writing.

His poetry illustrates both of the contrasting forms practiced by black poets intent upon brightening the image of the Afro-American. First, there is the dialect poetry, expressing the modest, benevolent, quietly optimistic tone encouraged by "realistic" reformers like Booker T. Washington. Alternatively, there is the heavily "educated" poetic performance, remote in its style and substance from Negro life. These two forms of ethnic poetry are opposed only in appearance. Whether by stressing familiar Afro-American virtues or by ignoring them in order to function more generally in the Anglo-American literary tradition, Brown—like James Weldon Johnson—wished to accelerate the processes of social and artistic assimilation. In this common desire, he testified to his faith in the American Dream, to his belief in the promise of American life.

He snuggles his fingers
In the blacker loam
The lean months are done with,
The fat to come.

His eyes are set
On a brushwood-fire
But his heart is soaring
Higher and higher.

Though he stands ragged
An old scarecrow,
This is the way
His swift thoughts go,

"Butter beans fo' Clara
Sugar corn fo' Grace
An' fo' de little feller
Runnin' space.

"Radishes and lettuce
Eggplants and beets
Turnips fo' de winter
An' candied sweets.

"Homespun tobacco
Apples in de bin
Fo' smokin' an' fo' cider
When de folks draps in."

He thinks with the winter
His troubles are gone;
Ten acres unplanted
To raise dreams on.

"After Winter" from *Southern Road* by Sterling A. Brown, published by Harcourt Brace Jovanovich, Inc., 1932. Reprinted by permission of the author.

The lean months are done with,
The fat to come.
His hopes, winter wanderers,
Hasten home.

"Butterbeans fo' Clara
Sugar corn fo' Grace
An' fo' de little feller
Runnin' space. . . ."

virginia portrait

Winter is settling on the place; the sedge
Is dry and lifeless and the woods stand bare.
The late autumnal flowers, nipped by frost,
Break from the sear stalks in the trim, neat garden,
And fall unheeded on the bleak, brown earth.

The winter of her year has come to her,
This wizened woman, spare of frame, but great
Of heart, erect, and undefeated yet.

Grief has been hers, before this wintry time.
Death has paid calls, unmannered, uninvited;
Low mounds have swollen in the fenced off corner,
Over brown children, marked by white-washed stones.
She has seen hopes that promised a fine harvest
Burnt by the drought; or bitten by the hoarfrost;
Or washed up and drowned out by unlooked for rains.
And as a warning blast of her own winter,
Death, the harsh overseer, shouted to her man,
Who answering slowly went over the hill.

"Virginia Portrait" from *Southern Road* by Sterling A. Brown, published by Harcourt Brace Jovanovich, Inc., 1932. Reprinted by permission of the author.

She, puffing on a jagged slow-burning pipe,
By the low hearthfire, knows her winter now.
But she has strength and steadfast hardihood.
Deep-rooted is she, even as the oaks,
Hardy as perennials about her door.
The circle of the seasons brings no fear,
"Folks all gits used to what dey sees so often";
And she has helps that throng her glowing fire
Mixed with the smoke hugging her grizzled head:

Warm friends, the love of her full-blooded spouse,
Quiet companionship as age crept on him,
Laughter of babies, and their shrewd, sane raising;
These simple joys, not poor to her at all;
The sight of smokeclouds pouring from the flue;
Her stalwart son deep busied with "book larnin',"
After the weary fields; the kettle's purr
In duet with the sleek and pampered mouser;
Twanging of dominickers; [1] lowing of Betsey;
Old folksongs chanted underneath the stars. . . .

Even when winter settles on her heart,
She keeps a wonted, quiet nonchalance,
A courtly dignity of speech and carriage,
Unlooked for in these distant rural ways.

She has found faith sufficient for her grief,
The song of earth for bearing heavy years,
She with slow speech, and spurts of heartfelt laughter,
Illiterate, and somehow very wise.

She has been happy, and her heart is grateful.
Now she looks out, and forecasts unperturbed
Her following slowly over the lonesome hill,
Her *"layin' down her burdens, bye and bye."*

[1] *dominickers:* chickens.

for discussion

1. How would you describe the two voices in "After Winter"? Do they have the same point of view?

2. Describe the language of "Virginia Portrait." How does it contrast with the actual circumstances of the woman?

3. In "Virginia Portrait," what effect does the author achieve from the contrast between the real world and his poetic language?

1860–1951

ABRAHAM CAHAN

☐ Born to poor but literate Jewish parents in an Eastern European village, Abraham Cahan came to America in 1882 when the great tide of Jewish immigration was just beginning. His only resource was his fiercely independent desire to educate himself. On the boat to America, he struggled alone to master English grammar. And after his arrival in New York, the twenty-two-year-old Cahan eagerly attended an East Side elementary school—where he sat with twelve- and thirteen-year-old pupils—in order to improve his command of English. Within a year he was teaching English to newly arrived Jewish immigrants. Thereafter, as a writer, newspaper editor, and reformer, Cahan was deeply involved in helping America's Jewish immigrants to learn the ways of their new country and to better their lives.

As the author of some of the earliest fiction written in English about Jewish immigrants, Abraham Cahan tried to illuminate America's understanding of these Yiddish-speaking strangers. Indeed, it was Cahan who first acquainted the American reading public with the hopes and fears of the new dwellers on New York's East Side. In Yekl: A Tale of the New York Ghetto (published in 1896), The Imported Bridegroom and Other Stories of the New York Ghetto (1898), and The Rise of David Levinsky (1917), he dramatized the difficult life of the "greenhorn": its loneliness, its uprootedness, its wretched poverty and susceptibility to exploitation.

Cahan was admirably suited to serve as the Jewish community's first literary ambassador to America: his life bridged both worlds, and he wrote successfully in both Yiddish and English. On the one hand, he greatly influenced the Jewish immigrants through his reports in the Yiddish press and his editorship of the Jewish Daily Forward, the most widely read Yiddish newspaper in America. On the other hand, his writings in American newspapers and magazines earned the praise of Lincoln

Steffens, William Dean Howells, and other critics who favored greater realism in American literature. A pioneer of American realism, Cahan dedicated himself to providing honest narrative accounts of what he had closely observed. And for the most part, he resisted the urge to sentimentalize his immigrant characters. Anxious to gain the sympathy of the American reading public for the Jewish immigrant's dilemmas, Cahan painstakingly documented his stories in order to gain that sympathy by showing things as they really were.

a sweat-shop romance

☐ Leizer Lipman was one of those contract tailors who are classed by their hands [1] under the head of "cockroaches," which—translating the term into lay English—means that he ran a very small shop, giving employment to a single team of one sewing-machine operator, one baster, one finisher, and one presser.

The shop was one of a suite of three rooms on the third floor of a rickety old tenement house on Essex Street, and did the additional duty of the family's kitchen and dining-room. It faced a dingy little courtyard, and was connected by a windowless bedroom with the parlor, which commanded the very heart of the Jewish markets. Bundles of cloth, cut to be made into coats, littered the floor, lay in chaotic piles by one of the walls, cumbered Mrs. Lipman's kitchen table and one or two chairs, and formed, in a corner, an improvised bed upon which a dirty two-year-old boy, Leizer's heir apparent, was enjoying his siesta.

Dangling against the door or scattered among the bundles, there were cooking utensils, dirty linen, Lipman's velvet skull-cap, hats, shoes, shears, cotton-spools, and whatnot. A red-hot kitchen stove and a blazing grate full of

---

[1] *hands:* workers.

glowing flat-irons combined to keep up the overpowering temperature of the room, and helped to justify its nickname of sweat-shop in the literal sense of the epithet.

Work was rather scarce, but the designer of the Broadway clothing firm, of whose army of contractors Lipman was a member, was a second cousin to the latter's wife, and he saw to it that his relative's husband was kept busy. And so operations in Leizer's shop were in full swing. Heyman, the operator, with his bared brawny arms, pushed away at an unfinished coat, over which his head, presenting to view a wealth of curly brown hair, hung like an eagle bent on his prey. He swayed in unison to the rhythmic whirr of his machine, whose music, supported by the energetic thumps of Meyer's press-iron, formed an orchestral accompaniment to the sonorous and plaintive strains of a vocal duet performed by Beile, the finisher girl, and David, the baster.

Leizer was gone to the Broadway firm's offices, while Zlate, his wife, was out on a prolonged haggling expedition among the tradeswomen of Hester Street. This circumstance gave the hands a respite from the restrictions usually placed on their liberties by the presence of the "boss" and the "Missis," and they freely beguiled the tedium and fatigue of their work, now by singing, now by a bantering match at the expense of their employer and his wife, or of each other.

"Well, I suppose you might as well quit," said Meyer, a chubby, red-haired, freckled fellow of forty, emphasizing his remark by an angry stroke of his iron. "You have been over that song now fifty times without taking breath. You make me tired."

"Don't you like it? Stuff up your ears, then," Beile retorted, without lifting her head from the coat in her lap.

"Why, I do like it, first-rate and a half," Meyer returned, "but when you keep your mouth shut I like it better still, see?"

The silvery tinkle of Beile's voice, as she was singing, thrilled Heyman with delicious melancholy, gave him fresh relish for his work, and infused additional activity into his limbs; and as her singing was interrupted by the presser's gibe, he involuntarily stopped his machine with that annoying feeling which is experienced by dancers when brought to an unexpected standstill by an abrupt pause of the music.

"And you?"—he addressed himself to Meyer, facing about on his chair with an irritated countenance. "It's all right enough when you speak, but it is much better when you hold your tongue. Don't mind him, Beile. Sing away!" he then said to the girl, his dazzlingly fair face relaxing and his little eyes shutting into a sweet smile of self-confident gallantry.

"You had better stick to your work, Heyman. Why, you might have made half a cent the while," Meyer fired back, with an ironical look, which had reference to the operator's reputation of being a niggardly fellow, who overworked himself, denied himself every pleasure, and grew fat by feasting his eyes on his savings-bank book.

A sharp altercation ensued, which drifted to the subject of Heyman's servile conduct toward his employer.

"It was you, wasn't it," Meyer said, "who started that collection for a birthday present for the boss? Of course, we couldn't help chipping in. Why is David independent?"

"Did I compel you?" Heyman rejoined. "And am I to blame that it was to me that the boss threw out the hint about that present? It is so slack everywhere, and you ought to thank God for the steady job you have here," he concluded, pouncing down upon the coat on his machine.

David, who had also cut short his singing, kept silently plying his needle upon pieces of stuff which lay stretched on his master's dining-table. Presently he paused to adjust his disheveled jet-black hair, with his fingers for a comb, and to wipe the perspiration from his swarthy, beardless, and typically Israelitic face with his shirt-sleeve.

While this was in progress, his languid hazel eyes were fixed on the finisher girl. She instinctively became conscious of his gaze, and raised her head from the needle. Her fresh buxom face, flushed with the heat of the room and with exertion, shone full upon the young baster. Their eyes met. David colored, and, to conceal his embarrassment, he asked: "Well, is he going to raise your wages?"

Beile nodded affirmatively, and again plunged her head into her work.

"He is? So you will now get five dollars a week. I am afraid you will be putting on airs now, won't you?"

"Do you begrudge me? Then I am willing to swap wages with you. I'll let you have my five dollars, and I'll take your twelve dollars every week."

Lipman's was a task shop, and, according to the signification which the term has in the political economy of the sweating world, his operator, baster, and finisher, while nominally engaged at so much a week, were in reality paid by the piece, the economical week being determined by a stipulated quantity of made-up coats rather than by a fixed number of the earth's revolutions around its axis; for the sweat-shop day will not coincide with the solar day unless a given amount of work be accomplished in its course. As to the presser, he is invariably a piece-worker, pure and simple.

For a more lucid account of the task system in the tailoring branch, I beg to refer the reader to David, although his exposition happens to be presented rather in the form of a satire on the subject. Indeed, David, while rather inclined to taciturnity, was an inveterate jester, and what few remarks he indulged in during his work would often cause boisterous merriment among his shopmates, although he delivered them with a nonchalant manner and with the same look of good-humored irony, mingled in strange harmony with a general expression of gruffness, which his face usually wore.

"My twelve dollars every week?" David echoed. "Oh, I see; you mean a week of twelve days!" And his needle resumed its duck-like sport in the cloth.

"How do you make it out?" Meyer demanded, in order to elicit a joke from the witty young man by his side.

"Of course, *you* don't know how to make that out. But ask Heyman or Beile. The three of us do."

"Tell him, then, and he will know too," Beile urged, laughing in advance at the expected fun.

A request coming from the finisher was—yet unknown to herself—resistless with David, and in the present instance it loosened his tongue.

"Well, I get twelve dollars a week, and Heyman fourteen. Now a working week has six days, but—hem—that 'but' gets stuck in my throat—but a day is neither a Sunday nor a Monday nor anything unless we make twelve coats. The calendars are a lot of liars."

"What do you mean?"

"They say a day has twenty-four hours. That's a bluff. A day has twelve coats."

Beile's rapturous chuckle whetted his appetite for persiflage, and he went on:—

"They read the Tuesday Psalm in the synagogue this morning, but I should have read the Monday one."

"Why?"

"You see, Meyer's wife will soon come up with his dinner, and here I have still two coats to make of the twelve that I got yesterday. So it's still Monday with me. My Tuesday won't begin before about two o'clock this afternoon."

"How much will you make this week?" Meyer questioned.

"I don't expect to finish more than four days' work by the end of the week, and will only get eight dollars on Friday—that is, provided the missis has not spent our wages by that time. So when it's Friday I'll call it Wednesday, see?"

"When I am married," he added, after a pause, "and the old woman asks me for Sabbath expenses, I'll tell her it is only Wednesday—it isn't yet Friday—and I have no money to give her."

David relapsed into silence, but mutely continued his burlesque, hopping from subject to subject.

David thought himself a very queer fellow. He often wondered at the pranks which his own imagination was in the habit of playing, and at the grotesque combinations it frequently evolved. As he now stood, leaning over his work, he was striving to make out how it was that Meyer reminded him of the figure "7."

"What nonsense!" he inwardly exclaimed, branding himself for a crank. "And what does Heyman look like?" his mind queried, as though for spite. He contemplated the operator askance, and ran over all the digits of the Arabic system, and even the whole Hebrew alphabet, in quest of a counterpart to the young man, but failed to find anything suitable. "His face would much better become a girl," he at last decided, and mentally proceeded to envelop Heyman's head in Beile's shawl. But the proceeding somehow stung him, and he went on to meditate upon the operator's chunky nose. "No, that nose is too ugly for a girl. It wants a little planing. It's an unfinished job, as it were. But for that nose Heyman would really be the nice fellow they say he is. His snow-white skin—his elegant heavy mustache— yes, if he did not have that nose he would be all right," he maliciously joked in his heart. "And I, too, would be all right if Heyman were noseless," he added, transferring his thoughts to Beile, and wondering why she looked so sweet. "Why, *her* nose is not much of a beauty, either. Entirely too straight, and too—too foolish. Her eyes look old and as if constantly on the point of bursting into tears. Ah, but then her lips—that kindly smile of theirs, coming out of one corner of her mouth!" And a strong impulse seized him to throw himself on those lips and to kiss them, which he did mentally, and which shot an electric current through his whole frame. And at this Beile's old-looking eyes both charmed and pierced him to the heart, and her nose, far from looking foolish, seemed to contemplate him contemptuously, triumphantly, and knowingly, as if it had read his thoughts.

While this was going on in David's brain and heart, Beile was taken up with Heyman and with their mutual relations. His attentions to her were an open secret. He did not go out of his way to conceal them. On the contrary, he regularly escorted her home after work, and took her out to balls and picnics—a thing involving great sacrifices to a fellow who trembled over every cent he spent, and who was sure to make up for these losses to his pocketbook by foregoing his meals. While alone with her in the hallway of her mother's residence, his voice would become so tender, so tremulous, and on several occasions he even addressed her by the endearing form of Beilinke. And yet all this had been going on now for over three months, and he had not as much as alluded to marriage, nor even bought her the most trifling present.

Her mother made life a burden to her, and urged the point-blank declaration of the alternative between a formal engagement and an arrest for breach of promise. Beile would have died rather than make herself the heroine of such a sensation; and, besides, the idea of Heyman handcuffed to a police detective was too terrible to entertain even for a moment.

She loved him. She liked his blooming face, his gentleman-like mustache, the quaint jerk of his head, as he walked; she was fond of his company; she was sure she was in love with him: her confidante, her fellow country girl and playmate, who had recently married Meyer, the presser, had told her so.

But somehow she felt disappointed. She had imagined love to be a much sweeter thing. She had thought that a girl in love admired *everything* in the object of her affections, and was blind to all his faults. She had heard that love was something like a perpetual blissful fluttering of the heart.

"I feel as if something was melting here," a girl friend who was about to be married once confided to her, pointing to her heart. "You see, it aches and yet it is so sweet at the same time." And here she never feels anything melting, nor can she help disliking some things about Heyman. His smile sometimes appears to her fulsome. Ah, if he did not shut his eyes as he does when smiling! That he is so slow to spend money is rather one of the things she likes in him. If he ever marries her she will be sure to get every cent of his wages. But then when they are together at a ball he never goes up to the bar to treat her to a glass of soda, as the other fellows do to their girls, and all he offers her is an apple or a pear, which he generally stops to buy on the street on their way to the dancing-hall. Is she in love at all? Maybe she is mistaken? But no! he is after all so dear to her. She must have herself to blame. It is not in vain that her mother calls her a whimpering, nagging thing, who gives no peace to herself nor to anybody around her. But why does he not come out with his declaration? Is it because he is too stingy to wish to support a wife? Has he been making a fool of her? What does he take her for, then?

In fairness to Heyman, it must be stated that on the point of his intentions, at least, her judgment of him was without foundation, and her misgivings gratuitous. Pecuniary considerations had nothing to do with his slowness in proposing to her. And if she could have watched him and penetrated his mind at the moments when he examined his bankbook—which he did quite often—she would have ascertained that little images of herself kept hovering before his eyes between the figures of its credit columns, and that the sum total conjured up to him a picture of prospective felicity with her for a central figure.

Poor thing; she did not know that when he lingeringly fondled her hand, on taking his leave in the hallway, the proposal lay on the tip of his tongue, and that, lacking the strength to relieve himself of its burden, he every time left her, consoling himself that the moment was inopportune and that "tomorrow he would surely settle it." She did not know that only two days ago the idea had occurred to him to have recourse to the aid of a messenger in the form of a lady's watch, and that while she now sat worrying lest she was being made a fool of, the golden emissary lay in Heyman's vest-pocket, throbbing in company with his heart with impatient expectation of the evening hour, which had been fixed for the delivery of its message.

"I shall let mother speak to him," Beile resolved, in her musings over her needle. She went on to picture the scene, but at this point her meditations were suddenly broken by something clutching and pulling at her hair. It was her employer's boy. He had just got up from his after-dinner nap, and, for want of any other occupation, he passed his dirty little hand into her raven locks.

"He is practicing to be a boss," observed David, whose attention was attracted to the spectacle by the finisher's shriek.

Beile's voice brought Heyman to his feet, and disentangling the little fellow's fingers from the girl's hair, he fell to "plastering his nasty cheeks for him," as he put it. At this juncture the door opened to admit the little culprit's father. Heyman skulked away to his seat, and, burying his head in his work, he proceeded to drown, in the whir-r, whir-r of his machine, the screams of the boy, who would have struck a much higher key had his mamma happened on the spot.

Lipman took off his coat, substituted his greasy velvet

skull-cap for his derby, and lighting a cigar with an air of good-natured business-like importance, he advanced to Meyer's corner and fell to examining a coat.

"And what does *he* look like?" David asked himself, scrutinizing his task-master. "Like a broom with its stick downward," he concluded to his own satisfaction. "And his snuff-box?"—meaning Lipman's huge nose—"A perfect fiddle—And his mouth? Deaf-mutes usually have such mouths. And his beard? He has entirely too much of it, and it's too pretty for his face. It must have got there by mistake."

Presently the door again flew open, and Mrs. Lipman, heavily loaded with parcels and panting for breath, came waddling in with an elderly couple in tow.

"Greenhorns," Meyer remarked. "Must be fellow townspeople of hers—lately arrived."

"She looks like a tea-kettle, and she is puffing like one, too," David thought, after an indifferent gaze at the newcomers, looking askance at his stout, dowdyish little "Missis." "No," he then corrected himself, "she rather resembles a broom with its stick out. That's it! And wouldn't it be a treat to tie a stick to her head and to sweep the floor with the horrid thing! And her mouth? Why, it makes me think she does nothing but sneeze."

"Here is Leizer! Leizer, look at the guests I have brought you!" Zlate exclaimed, as she threw down her bundles. "Be seated, Reb [2] Avrom; be seated, Basse. This is our factory," she went on, with a smile of mixed welcome and triumph, after the demonstrative greetings were over. "It is rather too small, isn't it? But we are going to move into larger and better quarters."

Meyer was not mistaken. Zlate's visitors had recently arrived from her birthplace, a poor town in western Russia, where they had occupied a much higher social position than their present hostess, and Mrs. Lipman, coming upon them on Hester Street, lost no time in inviting them to her house, in order to overwhelm them with her American achievements.

[2] *Reb:* a respectful form of personal address, roughly equivalent to "Mister."

"Come, I want to show you my parlor," Mrs. Lipman said, beckoning to her country people, and before they were given an opportunity to avail themselves of the chairs which she had offered them, they were towed into the front room.

When the procession returned, Leizer, in obedience to an order from his wife, took Reb Avrom in charge and proceeded to initiate him into the secrets of the "American style of tailoring."

"Oh, my!" Zlate suddenly ejaculated, with a smile. "I came near forgetting to treat. Beilke!" she then addressed herself to the finisher girl in a tone of imperious nonchalance, "here is a nickel. Fetch two bottles of soda from the grocery."

"Don't go, Beile!" David whispered across his table, perceiving the girl's reluctance.

It was not unusual for Beile to go on an errand for the wife of her employer, though she always did it unwillingly, and merely for fear of losing her place; but then Zlate generally exacted these services as a favor. In the present instance, however, Beile felt mortally offended by her commanding tone, and the idea of being paraded before the strangers as a domestic cut her to the quick, as a stream of color rushing into her face indicated. Nevertheless the prospect of having to look for a job again persuaded her to avoid trouble with Zlate, and she was about to reach out her hand for the coin, when David's exhortation piqued her sense of self-esteem, and she went on with her sewing. Heyman, who, being interrupted in his work by the visitor's inspection, was a witness of the scene, at this point turned his face from it, and cringing by his machine, he made a pretense of busying himself with the shuttle. His heart shrank with the awkwardness of his situation, and he nervously grated his teeth and shut his eyes, awaiting still more painful developments. His veins tingled with pity for his sweetheart and with deadly hatred for David. What could he do? he apologized to himself. Isn't it foolish to risk losing a steady job at this slack season on account of such a trifle as fetching up a bottle of soda? What business has David to interfere?

"You are not deaf, are you? I say go and bring some soda, quick!" Mrs. Lipman screamed, fearing lest she was going too far.

"Don't budge, Beile!" the baster prompted, with fire in his eyes.

Beile did not.

"I say go!" Zlate thundered, reddening like a beet, to use a phrase in vogue with herself.

"Never mind, Zlate," Basse interposed, to relieve the embarrassing situation. "We just had tea."

"Never mind. It is not worth the trouble," Avrom chimed in.

But this only served to lash Zlate into a greater fury, and unmindful of consequences, she strode up to the cause of her predicament, and tearing the coat out of her hands, she squeaked out:

"Either fetch the soda, or leave my shop at once!"

Heyman was about to say, to do something, he knew not exactly what, but his tongue seemed seized with palsy, the blood turned chill in his veins, and he could neither speak nor stir.

Leizer, who was of a quiet, peaceful disposition, and very much under the thumb of his wife, stood nervously smiling and toying with his beard.

David grew ashen pale, and trembling with rage, he said aloud and in deliberate accents:

"Don't mind her, Beile, and never worry. Come along. I'll find you a better job. This racket won't work, Missis. Your friends see through it, anyhow, don't you?" he addressed himself to the newcomers. "She wanted to brag to you. That's what she troubled you for. She showed off her parlor carpet to you, didn't she? But did she tell you that it had been bought on the installment plan, and that the custom-peddler threatened to take it away unless she paid more regularly?"

"Leizer! are you—are you drunk?" Mrs. Lipman gasped, her face distorted with rage and desperation.

"Get out of here!" Leizer said, in a tone which would have been better suited to a cordial invitation.

The command was unnecessary, however, for by this time David was buttoning up his overcoat, and had his hat on. Involuntarily following his example, Beile also dressed to go. And as she stood in her new beaver cloak and freshly trimmed large old hat by the side of her discomfited commander, Basse reflected that it was the finisher girl who looked like a lady, with Zlate for her servant, rather than the reverse.

"See that you have our wages ready for Friday, and all the arrears, too!" was David's parting shot as the two left the room with a defiant slam of the door.

"That's like America!" Zlate remarked, with an attempt at a scornful smile. "The meanest beggar girl will put on airs."

"Why *should* one be ordered about like that? She is no servant, is she?" Heyman murmured, addressing the corner of the room, and fell to at his machine to smother his misery.

When his day's work was over, Heyman's heart failed him to face Beile, and although he was panting to see her, he did not call at her house. On the following morning he awoke with a headache, and this he used as a pretext to himself for going to bed right after supper.

On the next evening he did betake himself to the Division Street tenement house, where his sweetheart lived with her mother on the top floor, but on coming in front of the building his courage melted away. Added to his cowardly part in the memorable scene of two days before, there now was his apparent indifference to the finisher, as manifested by his two evenings' absence at such a critical time. He armed himself with a fib to explain his conduct. But all in vain; he could not nerve himself up to the terrible meeting. And so day after day passed, each day increasing the barrier to the coveted visit.

At last, one evening, about a fortnight after the date of Mrs. Lipman's fiasco, Heyman, forgetting to lose courage, as it were, briskly mounted the four flights of stairs of the Division Street tenement. As he was about to rap for admission he was greeted by a sharp noise within of something, like a china plate or a bowl, being dashed to pieces against the very door which he was going to open. The noise was followed by merry voices: "Good luck! Good luck!" and there was no mistaking its meaning. There was evidently an engagement party inside. The Rabbi had just read the writ of betrothment, and it was the mutual pledges of the contracting parties which were emphasized by the "breaking of the plate." [3]

Presently Heyman heard exclamations which dissipated his every doubt as to the identity of the chief actors in the ceremony which had just been completed within.

"Good luck to you, David! Good luck to you, Beile! May you live to a happy old age together!" "Feige, why don't you take some cake? Don't be so bashful!" "Here is luck!" came through the door, piercing a muffled hum inside.

Heyman was dumbfounded, and with his head swimming, he made a hasty retreat.

Ever since the tragi-comical incident at Lipman's shop, Heyman was not present to Beile's thoughts except in the pitiful, cowering attitude in which he had sat through that awful scene by his machine. She was sure she hated him now. And yet her heart was, during the first few days, constantly throbbing with the expectation of his visit; and as she settled in her mind that even if he came she would have nothing to do with him, her deeper consciousness seemed to say, with a smile of conviction: "Oh no, you know you would not refuse him. You wouldn't risk to remain an old maid, would you?" The idea of his jilting her harrowed her day and night. Did he avail himself of her leaving Lipman's shop to back out of the proposal which was naturally expected of him, but which he never perhaps contemplated? Did he make game of her?

When a week had elapsed without Heyman's putting in an appearance, she determined to let her mother see a lawyer about breach-of-promise proceedings. But an image, whose outlines had kept defining themselves in her heart for several days past, overruled this decision. It was the image of a pluckier fellow than Heyman—of one with whom there was more protection in store for a wife, who

[3] "breaking . . . plate": a custom symbolizing the permanence of the wedding contract by suggesting that a breach of the contract is no more possible than the restoration of the plate to its unbroken condition.

inspired her with more respect and confidence, and, what is more, who seemed on the point of proposing to her.

It was the image of David. The young baster pursued his courtship with a quiet persistency and a suppressed fervor which was not long in winning the girl's heart. He found work for her and for himself in the same shop; saw her home every evening; regularly came after supper to take her out for a walk, in the course of which he would treat her to candy and invite her to a coffee saloon—a thing which Heyman had never done—kept her chuckling over his jokes; and at the end of ten days, while sitting by her side in Central Park one night, he said, in reply to her remark that it was so dark that she knew not where she was:

"I'll tell you where you are—guess."

"Where?"

"Here, in my heart, and keeping me awake nights, too. Say, Beile, what have I ever done to you to have my rest disturbed by you in that manner?"

Her heart was beating like a sledge-hammer. She tried to laugh, as she returned:

"I don't know—You can never stop making fun, can you?"

"Fun? Do you want me to cry? I will gladly, if I only know that you will agree to have an engagement party," he rejoined, deeply blushing under cover of the darkness.

"When?" she questioned, the word crossing her lips before she knew it.

"On my part, tomorrow."

for discussion

1. A "romance" may be either a love affair or a type of literature that is about extravagant adventures far removed from common life—a type of literature criticized by "realistic" storytellers like Cahan. How is Cahan's use of the word *romance* in the title ironic?

2. How does Zlate use *meanest* in the statement "The meanest beggar girl will put on airs" (page 67)? Is this usage appropriate to the speech of an immigrant? What does this suggest about Cahan's desire both to serve as a spokesman for the Jewish community and to be rec-

ognized as an American writer?

3. Through which details of character and action does Cahan manage to introduce a pleasant and attractive quality into his portrayal of Jewish immigrant life?

born 1908
LEO ROSTEN

☐ *Raised and educated in Chicago, Leo Rosten earned a Ph.D. at the University of Chicago, where his main interest was in the social sciences. He has been a teacher briefly at Yale, Columbia, and the University of California. But he is best known to the general public as a prolific journalist whose articles on many topics have regularly appeared in popular magazines. In 1968 he published* The Joys of Yiddish, *a charmingly anecdotal dictionary of Yiddish culture that has become a best seller. It was, however, under the penname of Leonard Q. Ross that Rosten began contributing his Hyman Kaplan stories to* The New Yorker *magazine in the mid-1930's. The first collection of these stories,* The Education of H*y*m*a*n K*a*p*l*a*n, *was published in 1937; its successor,* The Return of H*y*m*a*n K*a*p*l*a*n, *appeared in 1959. Like other literary ambassadors of good will, Leo Rosten has made heavy use of dialect to convey the special flavor of an ethnic group, in his case the Jewish immigrant community. Rosten's use of dialect also suggests the objectivity of his group portrait, even while it adds to the attractiveness of his amusing characters.*

Hyman Kaplan is, in fact, undeniably brash and rather harsh with his night school rivals. Yet he remains an extraordinarily appealing figure. He is appealing—at times irresistible—because he has an agile imagination and a dramatic sense that turn near disasters into stunning triumphs. More than a survivor, Hyman Kaplan is a winner. He possesses the unshakable self-confidence

*and endless vitality that the American public has long
associated with success. Significantly, the night school
teacher, Mr. Parkhill—the "native" American through
whose eyes Hyman Kaplan is presented to us—is
obviously impressed by Kaplan and thoroughly approves
of him. Kaplan's spirit is so unquenchable, his resolve
so unyielding, his good humor so boundless that we are
drawn to him and somehow become his allies.*

mr. k*a*p*l*a*n and the magi

☐ When Mr. Parkhill saw that Miss Mitnick, Mr. Bloom,
and Mr. Hyman Kaplan were absent, and that a strange excitement pervaded the beginners' grade, he realized that
it was indeed the last night before the holidays and that
Christmas was only a few days off. Each Christmas the
classes in the American Night Preparatory School for
Adults gave presents to their respective teachers. Mr.
Parkhill, a veteran of many sentimental Yuletides, had
come to know the procedure. That night, before the class
session had begun, there must have been a hurried collection; a Gift Committee of three had been chosen; at
this moment the Committee was probably in Mickey
Goldstein's Arcade, bargaining feverishly, arguing about
the appropriateness of a pair of pajamas or the color of a
dozen linen handkerchiefs, debating whether Mr. Parkhill
would prefer a pair of fleece-lined slippers to a set of
mother-of-pearl cuff links.

"We shall concentrate on—er—spelling drill tonight,"
Mr. Parkhill announced.

The students smiled wisely, glanced at the three empty
seats, exchanged knowing nods, and prepared for spelling

"Mr. Kaplan and the Magi" from *The Education of Hyman Kaplan* by
Leonard Q. Ross, copyright 1937 by Harcourt Brace Jovanovich, Inc.;
renewed 1965 by Leo Rosten. Reprinted by permission of the publisher.

drill. Miss Rochelle Goldberg giggled, then looked ashamed as Mrs. Rodriguez shot her a glare of reproval.

Mr. Parkhill always chose a spelling drill for the night before the Christmas vacation: it kept all the students busy simultaneously; it dampened the excitement of the occasion; above all, it kept him from the necessity of resorting to elaborate pedagogical efforts in order to hide his own embarrassment.

Mr. Parkhill called off the first words. Pens and pencils scratched, smiles died away, eyes grew serious, preoccupied, as the beginners' grade assaulted the spelling of "Banana . . . Romance . . . Groaning." Mr. Parkhill sighed. The class seemed incomplete without its star student, Miss Mitnick, and barren without its most remarkable one, Mr. Hyman Kaplan. Mr. Kaplan's most recent linguistic triumph had been a fervent speech extolling the D'Oyly Carte Company's performance of an operetta by two English gentlemen referred to as "Goldberg and Solomon."

"Charming . . . Horses . . . Float," Mr. Parkhill called off.

Mr. Parkhill's mind was not really on "Charming . . . Horses . . . Float." He could not help thinking of the momentous event which would take place that night. After the recess the students would come in with flushed faces and shining eyes. The Committee would be with them, and one member of the Committee, carrying an elaborately bound Christmas package, would be surrounded by several of the largest students in the class, who would try to hide the parcel from Mr. Parkhill's eyes. The class would come to order with uncommon rapidity. Then, just as Mr. Parkhill resumed the lesson, one member of the Committee would rise, apologize nervously for interrupting, place the package on Mr. Parkhill's desk, utter a few half-swallowed words, and rush back to his or her seat. Mr. Parkhill would say a few halting phrases of gratitude and surprise, everyone would smile and fidget uneasily, and the lesson would drag on, somehow, to the final and distant bell.

"*Accept . . . Except . . . Cucumber.*"

And as the students filed out after the final bell, they would cry "Merry Christmas, Happy New Year!" in joyous voices. The Committee would crowd around Mr. Parkhill with tremendous smiles to say that if the present wasn't *just right* in size or color (if it was something to wear) or in design (if it was something to use), Mr. Parkhill could exchange it. He didn't *have* to abide by the Committee's choice. He could exchange the present for *any*thing. They would have arranged all that carefully with Mr. Mickey Goldstein himself.

That was the ritual, fixed and unchanging, of the last night of school before Christmas.

"Nervous . . .Goose . . . Violets."

The hand on the clock crawled around to eight. Mr. Parkhill could not keep his eyes off the three seats, so eloquent in their vacancy, which Miss Mitnick, Mr. Bloom, and Mr. Kaplan ordinarily graced with their presences. He could almost see these three in the last throes of decision in Mickey Goldstein's Arcade, harassed by the competitive attractions of gloves, neckties, an electric clock, a cane, spats, a "lifetime" fountain pen. Mr. Parkhill grew cold as he thought of a fountain pen. Three times already he had been presented with "lifetime" fountain pens, twice with "lifetime" pencils to match. Mr. Parkhill had exchanged these gifts: he had a fountain pen. Once he had chosen a woollen vest instead; once a pair of mittens and a watch chain. Mr. Parkhill hoped it wouldn't be a fountain pen. Or a smoking jacket. He had never been able to understand how the Committee in '32 had decided upon a smoking jacket. Mr. Parkhill did not smoke. He had exchanged it for fur-lined gloves.

Just as Mr. Parkhill called off "Sardine . . . *Exquisite* . . . Palace" the recess bell rang. The heads of the students bobbed up as if propelled by a single spring. There was a rush to the door, Mr. Sam Pinsky well in the lead. Then, from the corridor, their voices rose. Mr. Parkhill began to print "Banana" on the blackboard, so that the students could correct their own papers after recess. He tried not to listen, but the voices in the corridor were like the chatter of a flock of sparrows.

"Hollo, Mitnick!"

"Bloom, Bloom, vat is it?"

"So vat did you gat, Keplen? Tell!"

Mr. Parkhill could hear Miss Mitnick's shy "We

bought—" interrupted by Mr. Kaplan's stern cry, "Mitnick! Don' say! Plizz, faller-students! Come *don* mit de voices! Titcher vill awreddy hearink, you hollerink so lod! Still! Order! Plizz!" There was no question about it: Mr. Kaplan was born to command.

"Did you bought a Tsheaffer's Fontain Pan Sat, guarantee for de whole life, like *I* said?" one voice came through the door. A Sheaffer Fountain Pen Set, Guaranteed. That was Mrs. Moskowitz. Poor Mrs. Moskowitz, she showed so little imagination, even in her homework. "Moskovitz! Mein Gott!" the stentorian whisper of Mr. Kaplan soared through the air. "Vy you don' open op de door Titcher should *positivel* hear? Ha! Let's goink to odder and fromm de hall!"

The voices of the beginners' grade died away as they moved to the "odder and" of the corridor, like the chorus of *Aïda* vanishing into Egyptian wings.

Mr. Parkhill printed "Charming" and "Horses" on the board. For a moment he thought he heard Mrs. Moskowitz's voice repeating stubbornly, "Did—you—bought—a—Tsheaffer—Fontain—Pan—Sat—*Guarantee?*"

Mr. Parkhill began to say to himself, "Thank you, all of you. It's *just* what I wanted," again and again. One Christmas he hadn't said "It's just what I wanted" and poor Mrs. Oppenheimer, chairman of the Committee that year, had been hounded by the students' recriminations for a month.

It seemed an eternity before the recess bell rang again. The class came in *en masse,* and hastened to the seats from which they would view the impending spectacle. The air hummed with silence.

Mr. Parkhill was printing "Cucumber." He did not turn his face from the board as he said, "Er—please begin correcting your own spelling. I have printed most of the words on the board."

There was a low and heated whispering. "Stend op, Mitnick!" he heard Mr. Kaplan hiss. "You should stend op *too!*"

"The *whole* Committee," Mr. Bloom whispered. "Stand op!"

Apparently Miss Mitnick, a gazelle choked with embarrassment, did not have the fortitude to "stend op" with her colleagues.

"A fine raprezantitif *you'll* gonna make!" Mr. Kaplan hissed scornfully. "Isn't for *mine* sek I'm eskink, Mitnick. Plizz *stend op!*"

There was a confused, half-muted murmur, and the anguished voice of Miss Mitnick saying, "I *can't*." Mr. Parkhill printed "Violets" on the board. Then there was a tense silence. And then the voice of Mr. Kaplan rose, firmly, clearly, with a decision and dignity which left no doubt as to its purpose.

"Podden me, Mr. Pockheel!"

It had come.

"Er—yes?" Mr. Parkhill turned to face the class.

Messrs. Bloom and Kaplan were standing side by side in front of Miss Mitnick's chair, holding between them a large, long package, wrapped in cellophane and tied with huge red ribbons. A pair of small hands touched the bottom of the box, listlessly. The owner of the hands, seated in the front row, was hidden by the box.

"De hends is Mitnick," Mr. Kaplan said apologetically.

Mr. Parkhill gazed at the tableau. It was touching.

"Er—yes?" he said again feebly, as if he had forgotten his lines and was repeating his cue.

"Hau Kay!" Mr. Kaplan whispered to his confreres. The hands disappeared behind the package. Mr. Kaplan and Mr. Bloom strode to the platform with the box. Mr. Kaplan was beaming, his smile rapturous, exalted. They placed the package on Mr. Parkhill's desk, Mr. Bloom dropped back a few paces, and Mr. Kaplan said, "Mr. Pockheel! Is mine beeg honor, becawss I'm Chairman fromm de Buyink an' Deliverink to You a Prazent Committee, to givink to you dis fine peckitch."

Mr. Parkhill was about to stammer, "Oh, thank you," when Mr. Kaplan added hastily, "Also I'll sayink a few voids."

Mr. Kaplan took an envelope out of his pocket. He whispered loudly, "Mitnick, *you still got time to comm op mit de Committee*," but Miss Mitnick only blushed furiously and lowered her eyes. Mr. Kaplan sighed, straightened the envelope, smiled proudly at Mr. Parkhill, and read.

"Dear Titcher—dat's de beginnink. Ve stendink on de adge fromm a beeg holiday." He cleared his throat. "Ufcawss is all kinds holidays in U.S.A. Holidays for politic, for religious, an' *plain* holidays. In Fabrary, ve got Judge Vashington's boitday, a *fine* holiday. Also Abram Lincohen's. In May ve got Memorable Day, for dad soldiers. In July comms, netcheral, Fort July. Also ve have Labor Day, Denksgivink, for de Peelgrims, an' for de feenish fromm de Voild Var, *Armistress* Day."

Mr. Parkhill played with a piece of chalk nervously.

"But arond dis time year ve have a *difference* kind holiday, a spacial, movvellous time. Dat's called—Chrissmas."

Mr. Parkhill put the chalk down.

"All hover de voild," Mr. Kaplan mused, "is pipple celebraking dis vunderful time. Becawss for som pipple is Chrissmas like for *odder* pipple is Passover. Or Chanukah, batter. De most fine, de most beauriful, de most *secret* holiday fromm de whole bunch!"

(" 'Sacred,' Mr. Kaplan, 'sacred,' " Mr. Parkhill thought, ever the pedagogue.)

"Ven ve valkink don de stritt an' is snow on de floor an' all kinds tarrible cold!" Mr. Kaplan's hand leaped up dramatically, like a flame. "Ven ve see in de vindows trees mit rad an' grin laktric lights boinink! Ven is de time for tellink de fancy-tales abot Sandy Claws commink fromm Naut Pole on rain-enimals, an' climbink don de jiminies mit *stockings* for all de leetle kits! Ven ve hearink abot de beauriful toughts of de Tree Vise Guys who vere follerink a star fromm de dasert! Ven pipple sayink, 'Oh, Mary Chrissmas! Oh, Heppy Noo Yiss! Oh, bast regotts!' Den ve *all* got a varm fillink in de heart for all humanity vhich should be brodders!"

Mr. Feigenbaum nodded philosophically at this profound thought; Mr. Kaplan, pleased, nodded back.

"*You* got de fillink, Mr. Pockheel. *I* got de fillink, dat's no qvastion abot! Bloom, Pinsky, Caravello, Schneiderman, even Mitnick"—Mr. Kaplan was punishing Miss Mitnick tenfold for her perfidy—"got de fillink! An' vat is it?" There was a momentous pause. "De Chrissmas Spirits!"

(" 'Spir*it*,' Mr. Kaplan, 'spir*it*,' " the voice of Mr. Parkhill's conscience said.)

"Now I'll givink de prazent," Mr. Kaplan announced subtly. Mr. Bloom shifted his weight. "Becawss you a foist-cless titcher, Mr. Pockheel, an' learn abot gremmer an' spallink an' de hoddest pots pernonciation—ve know is a planty hod jop mit soch students—so ve fill you should havink a sample fromm our—fromm our—" Mr. Kaplan turned the envelope over hastily—"aha! Fromm our santimental!"

Mr. Parkhill stared at the long package and the huge red ribbons.

"Fromm de cless, to our lovely Mr. Pockheel!"

Mr. Parkhill started. "Er—?" he asked involuntarily.

"Fromm de cless, to our lovely Mr. Pockheel!" Mr. Kaplan repeated with pride.

(" '*Beloved*,' Mr. Kaplan, '*beloved*.' ")

A hush had fallen over the room. Mr. Kaplan, his eyes bright with joy, waited for Mr. Parkhill to take up the ritual. Mr. Parkhill tried to say, "Thank you, Mr. Kaplan," but the phrase seemed meaningless, so big, so ungainly, that it could not get through his throat. Without a word Mr. Parkhill began to open the package. He slid the big red ribbons off. He broke the tissue paper inside. For some reason his vision was blurred and it took him a moment to identify the present. It was a smoking jacket. It was black and gold, and a dragon with a green tongue was embroidered on the breast pocket.

"Horyantal style," Mr. Kaplan whispered delicately.

Mr. Parkhill nodded. The air trembled with the tension. Miss Mitnick looked as if she were ready to cry. Mr. Bloom peered intently over Mr. Kaplan's shoulder. Mrs. Moskowitz sat entranced, sighing with behemothian gasps. She looked as if she were at her daughter's wedding.

"Thank you," Mr. Parkhill stammered at last. "Thank you, all of you."

Mr. Bloom said, "Hold it op everyone should see."

Mr. Kaplan turned on Mr. Bloom with an icy look. "*I'm* de chairman!" he hissed.

"I—er—I can't tell you how much I appreciate your kindness," Mr. Parkhill said without lifting his eyes.

Mr. Kaplan smiled. "So now you'll plizz hold op de prazent. Plizz."

Mr. Parkhill took the smoking jacket out of the box and held it up for all to see. There were gasps—"Oh!"s and "Ah!"s and Mr. Kaplan's own ecstatic "My! Is beauriful!" The green tongue on the dragon seemed alive.

"Maybe ve made a mistake," Mr. Kaplan said hastily. "Maybe you don' smoke—dat's how *Mitnick* tought." The scorn dripped. "But I said, "Ufcawss is Titcher smokink! Not in de cless, netcheral. At home! At least a *pipe!*'"

"No, no, you didn't make a mistake. It's—it's *just* what I wanted!"

The great smile on Mr. Kaplan's face became dazzling. "Hooray! Vear in de bast fromm helt!" he cried impetuously. "Mary Chrissmas! Heppy Noo Yiss! You should have a *hondert* more!"

This was the signal for a chorus of acclaim. "Mary Chrissmas!" "Wear in best of health!" "Happy New Year!" Miss Schneiderman burst into applause, followed by Mr. Scymzak and Mr. Weinstein. Miss Caravello, carried away by all the excitement, uttered some felicitations in rapid Italian. Mrs. Moskowitz sighed once more and said, "Soch a *sveet* ceremonia." Miss Mitnick smiled feebly, blushing, and twisted her handkerchief.

The ceremony was over. Mr. Parkhill began to put the smoking jacket back into the box with fumbling hands. Mr. Bloom marched back to his seat. But Mr. Kaplan stepped a little closer to the desk. The smile had congealed on Mr. Kaplan's face. It was poignant and profoundly earnest.

"Er—thank you, Mr. Kaplan," Mr. Parkhill said gently.

Mr. Kaplan shuffled his feet, looking at the floor. For the first time since Mr. Parkhill had known him, Mr. Kaplan seemed to be embarrassed. Then, just as he turned to rush back to his seat, Mr. Kaplan whispered, so softly that no ears but Mr. Parkhill's heard it, "Maybe de spitch I rad vas too *formmal*. But avery void I said—it came fromm *below mine heart!*"

Mr. Parkhill felt that, for all his weird, unorthodox

English, Mr. Kaplan had spoken with the tongues of the Magi.

for discussion

1. Mr. Parkhill expected the usual "half-swallowed" words from a Committee member, but instead Hyman Kaplan spoke "with the tongues of the Magi." What effect did Kaplan's speech have on Parkhill? How does this affect the reader's reaction to Kaplan?

2. In what ways are Hyman Kaplan, Miss Mitnick, and Mr. Bloom like the Magi? How does this comparison make the immigrant Hyman Kaplan attractive to non-Jewish readers?

1858–1932

CHARLES WADDELL CHESNUTT

☐ *Charles Waddell Chesnutt became, shortly before 1900, one of the first black Americans writing about the lives of black people to win popular literary recognition. His books sold very well, and Chesnutt the artist was enthusiastically championed by William Dean Howells and other influential American intellectuals.*

Chesnutt was born in Cleveland, the son of free Negroes. At the end of the Civil War his parents moved the family to Fayetteville, North Carolina, where he was educated in a Negro school. While still in his teens Chesnutt became a teacher in the Negro schools of North Carolina; and in 1880, when he was twenty-two, he became principal of the State Normal School for Negroes at Fayetteville. Chesnutt was largely self-taught, and read widely in classical and modern languages. More important to his later life was the stenography he taught himself. This skill made it possible for him to leave the security of Fayetteville with the confidence that he could provide a living up North for his wife and children. In 1883 he moved to Cleveland, where he was to live for the rest of his long life. In 1887 he was admitted to the practice of law in Ohio. During his many years in Cleveland, he worked chiefly as a court stenographic reporter and attorney. But he was so powerfully motivated to write stories that any scattered moments he could spare he gave to literature.

At twenty-one, when Chesnutt first considered a literary career, he concluded that the purpose of his writing would be to try to remove the color line. "This work," he once noted, "is of a two-fold character. The Negro's part is to prepare himself for recognition and equality, and it is the province of literature to open the way for him to get it—to accustom the public mind to the idea; to lead people out, imperceptibly, unconsciously, step by step, to the desired state of feeling. If I can do anything to further this work, and can see any likelihood of obtaining success in it, I would gladly devote my life to it."°

Chesnutt's literary career was truly launched in 1887 when his stories began to appear in the Atlantic Monthly. But it was the publication of "The Wife of His Youth" in 1898 that provoked the first excited public response and made his reputation. Shortly after the publication of this story, Chesnutt wrote triumphantly to his editor at the Atlantic, "I get compliments right and left from the best people of Cleveland on the ethics, the English, and the interest of 'The Wife of His Youth.'"

Two volumes of Chesnutt's short stories were published in 1899: his plantation tales in dialect were published in The Conjure Woman, and his stories dealing with the race problem were collected in The Wife of His Youth and Other Stories of the Color Line. Chesnutt later published three novels: The House Behind the Cedars in 1900, The Marrow of Tradition in 1901, and The Colonel's Dream in 1905.

° From *Charles Waddell Chesnutt: Pioneer of the Color Line* by Helen M. Chesnutt. Reprinted by permission of the publisher, The University of North Carolina Press.

the wife of his youth

I

☐ Mr. Ryder was going to give a ball. There were several reasons why this was an opportune time for such an event.

Mr. Ryder might aptly be called the dean of the Blue Veins. The original Blue Veins were a little society of colored persons organized in a certain Northern city shortly after the war. Its purpose was to establish and maintain correct social standards among a people whose social condition presented almost unlimited room for improvement. By accident, combined perhaps with some natural affinity, the society consisted of individuals who were, generally speaking, more white than black. Some envious outsider made the suggestion that no one was eligible for membership who was not white enough to show blue veins. The suggestion was readily adopted by those who were not of the favored few, and since that time the society, though possessing a longer and more pretentious name, had been known far and wide as the "Blue Vein Society," and its members as the "Blue Veins."

The Blue Veins did not allow that any such requirement existed for admission to their circle, but, on the contrary, declared that character and culture were the only things considered; and that if most of their members were light-colored, it was because such persons, as a rule, had had better opportunities to qualify themselves for membership. Opinions differed, too, as to the usefulness of the society. There were those who had been known to assail it violently as a glaring example of the very prejudice from which the colored race had suffered most; and later, when such critics had succeeded in getting on the inside, they had been heard to maintain with zeal and earnestness that the society was a lifeboat, an anchor, a bulwark and a shield—a pillar of cloud by day and of fire by night, to guide their people through the social wilderness. Another alleged prerequisite for Blue Vein membership was that of free birth; and while there was really no such requirement, it is doubtless true that very few of the members would have been unable to meet it if there had been. If there were one or two of the older members who had come up from the South and from slavery, their history presented enough romantic circumstances to rob their servile origin of its grosser aspects.

While there were no such tests of eligibility, it is true that the Blue Veins had their notions on these subjects, and that not all of them were equally liberal in regard to the things they collectively disclaimed. Mr. Ryder was one of the most conservative. Though he had not been among the founders of the society, but had come in some years later, his genius for social leadership was such that he had speedily become its recognized adviser and head, the custodian of its standards, and the preserver of its traditions. He shaped its social policy, was active in providing for its entertainment, and when the interest fell off, as it sometimes did, he fanned the embers until they burst again into a cheerful flame.

There were still other reasons for his popularity. While he was not as white as some of the Blue Veins, his appearance was such as to confer distinction upon them. His features were of a refined type, his hair was almost straight; he was always neatly dressed; his manners were irreproachable, and his morals above suspicion. He had come to Groveland a young man, and, obtaining employment in the office of a railroad company as messenger, had in time worked himself up to the position of stationery clerk, having charge of the distribution of the office supplies for the whole company. Although the lack of early training had hindered the orderly development of a naturally fine mind, it had not prevented him from doing a great deal of reading or from forming decidedly literary tastes. Poetry was his passion. He could repeat whole pages of the great English poets; and if his pronunciation was sometimes faulty, his eye, his voice, his gestures, would respond to the changing sentiment with a precision that revealed a poetic soul and disarmed criticism. He was economical, and had saved money; he owned and occupied a very comfortable house on a respectable street. His residence was handsomely furnished, containing among other things a good library, especially rich in poetry, a piano, and some choice engravings. He generally shared his house with some young couple, who looked after his wants and were company for him; for Mr. Ryder was a single man. In the early days of his connection with the Blue Veins he had been regarded as quite a catch, and young ladies and their mothers had maneuvered with much ingenuity to capture him. Not, however, until Mrs. Molly Dixon visited Groveland had any woman ever made him wish to change his condition to that of a married man.

Mrs. Dixon had come to Groveland from Washington in the spring, and before the summer was over she had won Mr. Ryder's heart. She possessed many attractive qualities. She was much younger than he; in fact, he was old enough to have been her father, though no one knew exactly how old he was. She was whiter than he, and better educated. She had moved in the best colored society of the country, at Washington, and had taught in the schools of that city. Such a superior person had been eagerly welcomed to the Blue Vein Society, and had taken a leading part in its activities. Mr. Ryder had at first been attracted by her charms of person, for she was very good-looking and not over twenty-five; then by her refined manners and the vivacity of her wit. Her husband had been a government clerk, and at his death had left a considerable life insurance. She was visiting friends in Groveland, and, finding the town and the people to her liking, had prolonged her stay indefinitely. She had not seemed displeased at Mr. Ryder's attentions, but on the contrary had given him every proper encouragement; indeed, a younger and less cautious man would long since have spoken. But he had made up his mind, and had only to determine the time when he would ask her to be his wife. He decided to give a ball in her honor, and at some time during the evening of the ball to offer her his heart and hand. He had no special fears about the outcome, but, with a little touch of romance, he wanted the surroundings to be in harmony with his own feelings when he should have received the answer he expected.

Mr. Ryder resolved that this ball should mark an epoch in the social history of Groveland. He knew, of course—

no one could know better—the entertainments that had taken place in past years, and what must be done to surpass them. His ball must be worthy of the lady in whose honor it was to be given, and must, by the quality of its guests, set an example for the future. He had observed of late a growing liberality, almost a laxity, in social matters, even among members of his own set, and had several times been forced to meet in a social way persons whose complexions and callings in life were hardly up to the standard which he considered proper for the society to maintain. He had a theory of his own.

"I have no race prejudice," he would say, "but we people of mixed blood are ground between the upper and the nether millstone. Our fate lies between absorption by the white race and extinction in the black. The one doesn't want us yet, but may take us in time. The other would welcome us, but it would be for us a backward step. 'With malice toward none, with charity for all,' we must do the best we can for ourselves and those who are to follow us. Self-preservation is the first law of nature."

His ball would serve by its exclusiveness to counteract leveling tendencies, and his marriage with Mrs. Dixon would help to further the upward process of absorption he had been wishing and waiting for.

II

The ball was to take place on Friday night. The house had been put in order, the carpets covered with canvas, the halls and stairs decorated with palms and potted plants; and in the afternoon Mr. Ryder sat on his front porch, which the shade of a vine running up over a wire netting made a cool and pleasant lounging place. He expected to respond to the toast "The Ladies" at the supper, and from a volume of Tennyson—his favorite poet—was fortifying himself with apt quotations. The volume was open at "A Dream of Fair Women." His eyes fell on these lines, and he read them aloud to judge better of their effect:

At length I saw a lady within call,
  Stiller than chisell'd marble, standing there;
A daughter of the gods, divinely tall,
  And most divinely fair.

He marked the verse, and, turning the page, read the stanza beginning,

O sweet pale Margaret,
  O rare pale Margaret.

He weighed the passage a moment, and decided that it would not do. Mrs. Dixon was the palest lady he expected at the ball, and she was of a rather ruddy complexion, and of lively disposition and buxom build. So he ran over the leaves until his eye rested on the description of Queen Guinevere:

She seem'd a part of joyous Spring:
A gown of grass-green silk she wore,
Buckled with golden clasps before;
A light-green tuft of plumes she bore
Closed in a golden ring.

.   .   .   .   .   .

She look'd so lovely, as she sway'd
The rein with dainty finger-tips,
A man had given all other bliss,
And all his worldly worth for this,
To waste his whole heart in one kiss
Upon her perfect lips.

As Mr. Ryder murmured these words audibly, with an appreciative thrill, he heard the latch of his gate click, and a light footfall sounding on the steps. He turned his head, and saw a woman standing before his door.

She was a little woman, not five feet tall, and proportioned to her height. Although she stood erect, and looked around her with very bright and restless eyes, she seemed quite old; for her face was crossed and recrossed with a hundred wrinkles, and around the edges of her bonnet could be seen protruding here and there a tuft of short gray wool. She wore a blue calico gown of ancient cut, a little red shawl fastened around her shoulders with an old-fashioned brass brooch, and a large bonnet profusely ornamented with faded red and yellow artificial flowers. And she was very black—so black that her toothless gums, revealed when she opened her mouth to speak, were not red, but blue. She looked like a bit of the old plantation life, summoned up from the past by the wave of a magician's wand, as the poet's fancy had called into being the gracious shapes of which Mr. Ryder had just been reading.

He rose from his chair and came over to where she stood.

"Good-afternoon, madam," he said.

"Good-evenin', suh," she answered, ducking suddenly with a quaint curtsy. Her voice was shrill and piping, but softened somewhat by age. "Is dis yere whar Mistuh Ryduh lib, suh?" she asked, looking around her doubtfully, and glancing into the open windows, through which some of the preparations for the evening were visible.

"Yes," he replied, with an air of kindly patronage, unconsciously flattered by her manner, "I am Mr. Ryder. Did you want to see me?"

"Yas, suh, ef I ain't 'sturbin' of you too much."

"Not at all. Have a seat over here behind the vine, where it is cool. What can I do for you?"

" 'Scuse me, suh," she continued, when she had sat down on the edge of a chair, " 'scuse me, suh, I's lookin' for my husban'. I heerd you wuz a big man an' had libbed heah a long time, an' I 'lowed you wouldn't min' ef I'd come roun' an' ax you ef you'd ever heerd of a merlatter man by de name er Sam Taylor 'quirin' roun' in de chu'ches ermongs' de people fer his wife 'Liza Jane?"

Mr. Ryder seemed to think for a moment.

"There used to be many such cases right after the war," he said, "but it has been so long that I have forgotten them. There are very few now. But tell me your story, and it may refresh my memory."

She sat back farther in her chair so as to be more comfortable, and folded her withered hands in her lap.

"My name's 'Liza," she began, " 'Liza Jane. W'en I wuz young I us'ter b'long ter Marse Bob Smif, down in ole

Missoura. I wuz bawn down dere. W'en I wuz a gal I wuz married ter a man named Jim. But Jim died, an' after dat I married a merlatter man named Sam Taylor. Sam wuz free-bawn, but his mammy and daddy died, an' de w'ite folks 'prenticed him ter my marster fer ter work fer 'im 'tel he wuz growed up. Sam worked in de fiel', an' I wuz de cook. One day Ma'y Ann, ole miss's maid, came rushin' out ter de kitchen, an' says she, ' 'Liza Jane, ole marse gwine sell yo' Sam down de ribber.'

" 'Go way f'm yere,' says I; 'my husban's free!'

" 'Don' make no diff'ence. I heerd ole marse tell ole miss he wuz gwine take yo' Sam 'way wid 'im ter-morrow, fer he needed money, an' he knowed whar he could git a t'ousan' dollars fer Sam an' no questions axed.'

"W'en Sam come home f'm de fiel' dat night, I tole him 'bout ole marse gwine steal 'im, an' Sam run erway. His time wuz mos' up, an' he swo' dat w'en he wuz twenty-one he would come back an' he'p me run erway, er else save up de money ter buy my freedom. An' I know he'd 'a' done it, fer he thought a heap er me, Sam did. But w'en he come back he didn' fin' me, fer I wuzn' dere. Ole marse had heerd dat I warned Sam, so he had me whip' an' sol' down de ribber.

"Den de wah broke out, an' w'en it wuz ober de cullud folks wuz scattered. I went back ter de ole home; but Sam wuzn' dere, an' I couldn' l'arn nuffin' 'bout-'im. But I knowed he'd be'n dere to look fer me an' hadn' foun' me, an' had gone erway ter hunt fer me.

"I's be'n lookin' fer 'im eber sence," she added simply, as though twenty-five years were but a couple of weeks, "an' I knows he's be'n lookin' fer me. Fer he sot a heap er sto' by me, Sam did, an' I know he's be'n huntin' fer me all dese years—'less'n he's be'n sick er sump'n, so he couldn' work, er out'n his head, so he couldn' 'member his promise. I went back down de ribber, fer I 'lowed he'd gone down dere lookin' fer me. I's be'n ter Noo Orleens, an' Atlanty, an' Charleston, an' Richmon'; an' w'en I'd be'n all ober de Souf I come ter de Norf. Fer I knows I'll fin' 'im some er dese days," she added softly, "er he'll fin' me, an' den we'll bofe be as happy in freedom as we wuz in de ole days befo' de wah." A smile stole over her withered countenance as she paused a moment, and her bright eyes softened into a far-away look.

This was the substance of the old woman's story. She had wandered a little here and there. Mr. Ryder was looking at her curiously when she finished.

"How have you lived all these years?" he asked.

"Cookin', suh. I's a good cook. Does you know anybody w'at needs a good cook, suh? I's stoppin' wid a cullud fam'ly roun' de corner yonder 'tel I kin git a place."

"Do you really expect to find your husband? He may be dead long ago."

She shook her head emphatically. "Oh no, he ain' dead. De signs an' de tokens tells me. I dremp three nights runnin' on'y dis las' week dat I foun' him."

"He may have married another woman. Your slave marriage would not have prevented him, for you never lived with him after the war, and without that your marriage doesn't count."

"Wouldn' make no diff'ence wid Sam. He wouldn' marry no yuther 'ooman 'tel he foun' out 'bout me. I knows it," she added. "Sump'n's be'n tellin' me all dese years dat I's gwine fin' Sam 'fo' I dies."

"Perhaps he's outgrown you, and climbed up in the world where he wouldn't care to have you find him."

"No, indeed, suh," she replied, "Sam ain' dat kin' er man. He wuz good ter me, Sam wuz, but he wuzn' much good ter nobody e'se, fer he wuz one er de triflin'es' han's on de plantation. I 'spec's ter haf ter suppo't 'im w'en I fin' 'im, fer he nebber would work 'less'n he had ter. But den he wuz free, an' he didn' git no pay fer his work, an' I don' blame 'im much. Mebbe he's done better sence he run erway, but I ain' 'spectin' much."

"You may have passed him on the street a hundred times during the twenty-five years, and not have known him; time works great changes."

She smiled incredulously. "I'd know 'im 'mongs' a hund'ed men. Fer dey wuzn' no yuther merlatter man like my man Sam, an' I couldn' be mistook. I's toted his picture roun' wid me twenty-five years."

"May I see it?" asked Mr. Ryder. "It might help me to remember whether I have seen the original."

As she drew a small parcel from her bosom, he saw that it was fastened to a string that went around her neck. Removing several wrappers, she brought to light an old-fashioned daguerreotype in a black case. He looked long and intently at the portrait. It was faded with time, but the features were still distinct, and it was easy to see what manner of man it had represented.

He closed the case, and with a slow movement handed it back to her.

"I don't know of any man in town who goes by that name," he said, "nor have I heard of any one making such inquiries. But if you will leave me your address, I will give the matter some attention, and if I find out anything I will let you know."

She gave him the number of a house in the neighborhood, and went away, after thanking him warmly.

He wrote the address on the fly-leaf of the volume of Tennyson, and, when she had gone, rose to his feet and stood looking after her curiously. As she walked down the street with mincing step, he saw several persons whom she passed turn and look back at her with a smile of kindly amusement. When she had turned the corner, he went upstairs to his bedroom, and stood for a long time before the mirror of his dressing-case, gazing thoughtfully at the reflection of his own face.

III

At eight o'clock the ballroom was a blaze of light and the guests had begun to assemble; for there was a literary program and some routine business of the society to be gone through with before the dancing. A black servant in evening dress waited at the door and directed the guests to the dressing-rooms.

The occasion was long memorable among the colored people of the city; not alone for the dress and display, but for the high average of intelligence and culture that distinguished the gathering as a whole. There were a number of school-teachers, several young doctors, three or four lawyers, some professional singers, an editor, a lieutenant in the United States Army spending his furlough in the city, and others in various polite callings; these were colored, though most of them would not have attracted even a casual glance because of any marked difference from white people. Most of the ladies were in evening costume, and dress coats and dancing pumps were the rule among the men. A band of string music, stationed in an alcove behind a row of palms, played popular airs while the guests were gathering.

The dancing began at half past nine. At eleven o'clock supper was served. Mr. Ryder had left the ballroom some little time before the intermission, but reappeared at the supper-table. The spread was worthy of the occasion, and the guests did full justice to it. When the coffee had been served, the toast-master, Mr. Solomon Sadler, rapped for order. He made a brief introductory speech, complimenting host and guests, and then presented in their order the toasts of the evening. They were responded to with a very fair display of after-dinner wit.

"The last toast," said the toast-master, when he reached the end of the list, "is one which must appeal to us all. There is no one of us of the sterner sex who is not at some time dependent upon woman—in infancy for protection, in manhood for companionship, in old age for care and comforting. Our good host has been trying to live alone, but the fair faces I see around me tonight prove that he too is largely dependent upon the gentler sex for most that makes life worth living—the society and love of friends— and rumor is at fault if he does not soon yield entire subjection to one of them. Mr. Ryder will now respond to the toast—The Ladies."

There was a pensive look in Mr. Ryder's eyes as he took the floor and adjusted his eye-glasses. He began by speaking of woman as the gift of Heaven to man, and after some general observations on the relations of the sexes he said: "But perhaps the quality which most distinguishes woman is her fidelity and devotion to those she loves. History is full of examples, but has recorded none more striking than one which only today came under my notice."

He then related, simply but effectively, the story told by his visitor of the afternoon. He gave it in the same soft dialect, which came readily to his lips, while the company listened attentively and sympathetically. For the story had awakened a responsive thrill in many hearts. There were some present who had seen, and others who had heard their fathers and grandfathers tell, the wrongs and sufferings of this past generation, and all of them still felt, in their darker moments, the shadow hanging over them. Mr. Ryder went on:

"Such devotion and confidence are rare even among women. There are many who would have searched a year, some who would have waited five years, a few who might have hoped ten years; but for twenty-five years this woman has retained her affection for and her faith in a man she has not seen or heard of in all that time.

"She came to me today in the hope that I might be able to help her find this long-lost husband. And when she was gone I gave my fancy rein, and imagined a case I will put to you.

"Suppose that this husband, soon after his escape, had learned that his wife had been sold away, and that such inquiries as he could make brought no information of her whereabouts. Suppose that he was young, and she much older than he; that he was light, and she was black; that their marriage was a slave marriage, and legally binding only if they chose to make it so after the war. Suppose, too, that he made his way to the North, as some of us have done, and there, where he had larger opportunities, had improved them, and had in the course of all these years grown to be as different from the ignorant boy who ran away from fear of slavery as the day is from the night. Suppose, even, that he had qualified himself, by industry, by thrift, and by study, to win the friendship and be considered worthy of the society of such people as these I see around me tonight, gracing my board and filling my heart with gladness; for I am old enough to remember the day when such a gathering would not have been possible in this land. Suppose, too, that, as the years went by, this man's memory of the past grew more and more indistinct, until at last it was rarely, except in his dreams, that any image of this bygone period rose before his mind. And then suppose that accident should bring to his knowledge the fact that the wife of his youth, the wife he had left behind him—not one who had walked by his side and kept pace with him in his upward struggle, but one upon whom advancing years and a laborious life had set their mark—was alive and seeking him, but that he was absolutely safe from recognition or discovery, unless he chose to reveal himself. My friends, what would the man do? I will presume that he was one who loved honor, and tried to deal justly with all men. I will even carry the case further, and suppose that perhaps he had set his heart upon another, whom he had hoped to call his own. What would he do, or rather what ought he to do, in such a crisis of a lifetime?

"It seemed to me that he might hesitate, and I imagined that I was an old friend, a near friend, and that he had come to me for advice; and I argued the case with him. I tried to discuss it impartially. After we had looked upon the matter from every point of view, I said to him, in words that we all know:

> This above all: to thine own self be true,
> And it must follow, as the night the day,
> Thou canst not then be false to any man.

Then, finally, I put the question to him, 'Shall you acknowledge her?'

"And now, ladies and gentlemen, friends and companions, I ask you, what should he have done?"

There was something in Mr. Ryder's voice that stirred the hearts of those who sat around him. It suggested more than mere sympathy with an imaginary situation; it seemed rather in the nature of a personal appeal. It was observed, too, that his look rested more especially upon Mrs. Dixon, with a mingled expression of renunciation and inquiry.

She had listened, with parted lips and streaming eyes. She was the first to speak: "He should have acknowledged her."

"Yes," they all echoed, "he should have acknowledged her."

"My friends and companions," responded Mr. Ryder,

"I thank you, one and all. It is the answer I expected, for I knew your hearts."

He turned and walked toward the closed door of an adjoining room, while every eye followed him in wondering curiosity. He came back in a moment, leading by the hand his visitor of the afternoon, who stood startled and trembling at the sudden plunge into this scene of brilliant gaiety. She was neatly dressed in gray, and wore the white cap of an elderly woman.

"Ladies and gentlemen," he said, "this is the woman, and I am the man, whose story I have told you. Permit me to introduce to you the wife of my youth."

for discussion

1. "The Wife of His Youth" was published in 1898, just thirty-three years after the Civil War. In your opinion, why would the predominantly white, middle-class audience in 1898 have found Mr. Ryder an appealing figure? Is Mr. Ryder in any way like such moderate leaders as Booker T. Washington?

2. What might have been the readers' reaction to Chesnutt's mildly satiric description of the "Blue Vein Society"? How does this gentle satire contribute to the objectivity of the story?

3. What is the nature of the choice presented to Mr. Ryder by the old lady's appearance on the day of the ball? What are the implications of Mr. Ryder's decision to identify himself to the old woman?

born 1906

THEODORE POSTON

☐ *A generation younger than Charles Waddell Chesnutt, Theodore Poston was born in Kentucky, received his undergraduate education in Tennessee, and then did graduate work in editorial and short story writing in New York. In 1937, after holding a variety of minor journalistic jobs, Ted Poston became a feature writer and reporter* on the New York Post. *He was one of the first black men to hold such a position on a major daily newspaper. Poston also served as a publicist for several federal agencies and commissions in Washington during the Roosevelt and Truman administrations. His articles and stories have been published in many periodicals and anthologies.*

Ted Poston's stories inhabit the disputed ground between fiction and history, between real and imagined autobiography. They grow out of his exploration of incidents remembered from childhood. Thus, like Chesnutt's, his stories possess a marked authenticity; they are honest and accurate portraits of life in a segregated society. And, again like Chesnutt's, his stories feature people whose dignity, sense of justice, and resourcefulness are badges of ethnic worth. Both Chesnutt and Poston have a remarkable capacity to savor the genuinely comic moments and the particular absurdities that occur—or might occur—in a racially segregated society. Through the author's perspective of comic realism, the characters in these stories earn our affection and respect, their circumstances and "cause" subtly enlist our sympathy.

In "Rat Joiner Routs the Klan," Poston presents a surprisingly low-keyed account of an event which has been the occasion of much national controversy since 1915—the showing of D. W. Griffith's silent film The Birth of a Nation. *Griffith based the film upon* The Clansman, *a novel written in 1905 by Thomas Dixon. The novel gave a highly conservative Southerner's view of the race problem during the Civil War and the Reconstruction. Dixon's novel sensationally dramatized the stereotyped opinion that "in his place" the Negro was a manageable child, but that out of it he became savage and uncontrollable. The film, like the novel, showed black Union soldiers behaving bestially; alternatively, it showed the Ku Klux Klan behaving heroically. Hence, by arousing racial fears and hatred, the film seemed to support the effort to return Negroes to social and legal bondage. Many citizens—both black and white—have opposed the showing of the film on the grounds that it increases*

*racial antagonism. In fact, Chesnutt led the fight to
prevent the film from being shown in Ohio. More
constructively, however, the stories of both Chesnutt
and Poston challenge the stereotyped view of black
Americans—which received its most powerful cinematic
expression in* The Birth of a Nation—*by introducing
characters who either are more attractively stereotyped or
are too individualized to lend support to any stereotype.*

rat joiner routs the klan

☐ There had never been a Ku Klux Klan in Hopkinsville,
Kentucky. So it was sort of surprising how our leading
colored citizens got all worked up when they heard that
The Birth of a Nation was coming to the Rex Theater down
on Ninth Street.

It was we young ones who brought them the news—
although it didn't mean anything to us. And it was we
young ones who got them out of it when the situation
finally reached a stalemate.

The whole thing started one Saturday morning when
Bronco Billy Anderson was being featured at the Rex in
The Revenge of the Ranger. And, of course, not a one of
us could afford to miss that.

Naturally, the Booker T. Washington Colored Grammar School was not open on Saturdays, but that meant
only one extra hour's sleep. For all of us had to be at the
Rex at 9 A.M. to be sure that we could get front row seats
in the peanut gallery which was reserved for all of our
colored citizens.

It was absolutely essential that we be there when the
doors first opened or else the bigger boys would get there
first and take the choice seats.

We always thought the big boys were unfair, but there

"Rat Joiner Routs the Klan" by Ted Poston from *Soon, One Morning*,
edited by Herbert Hill. Reprinted by permission of the author.

was nothing we could do about it. No self-respecting young colored citizen would dream of squealing to the white folks about it. And furthermore, if we did, we knew the big boys would bop us for doing it.

But this was our problem: The Rex Theater charged only five cents admission for all of our colored citizens under ten years of age. But since Miss Lucy, the white ticket lady who took our nickels, was nearsighted, and saw us only through a peephole as we stood in line in the alley, there was a rumor around the colored community that none of us grew any older after we were nine years old until we suddenly reached twenty-one or more. For all you had to do was bend your knees, look up innocently, and slip your nickel through the slot, and she'd pass you right up the gallery stairs.

There was a story—which I never believed—that Jelly Roll Benson never paid more than a nickel to get into the Rex until he was thirty-five years old.

"That's why he walks with a stoop in his shoulders and a bend in his knees to this day," Rat Joiner always insisted. "He got that way from fooling Miss Lucy. He'd still be doing it now, but he forgot to shave one morning. And she suspected for the first time that he was over ten."

But all this happened before that historic Saturday when we all rushed to see Bronco Billy Anderson in *The Revenge of the Ranger*. All of us were crazy about Bronco Billy, but there was also another reason for going to see him. For in every picture, Bronco Billy's main side-kick was a cowboy named Buffalo Pete. And, believe it or not, Buffalo Pete was as highly visible and 100 per cent colored as any citizen up on Billy Goat Hill.

He was the only colored cowboy or colored anything we ever saw in the movies in those days, and we wouldn't think of missing him. Our enthusiasm was not even dimmed by the cynicism of Rat Joiner, who observed one day: "They don't never let him kill none of them white mens, no matter how evil they is. Oh yeah, they let him knock off a Indian every now and then. But only Bronco Billy kills them white bad mens."

There was an unconfirmed rumor around town that another movie actor, named Noble Johnson, had Negro blood. But we didn't pay that no mind. We figured that the high-yallers [1] in our colored community had dreamed up that story for prestige purposes. And anyway, Noble Johnson played in those silly love stories they showed at the Rex on weekday nights. And who would pay five cents to see one of them?

But *The Revenge of the Ranger* that Saturday was a real knock-down picture, and we saw it eight times before they put us out at 5 P.M. in order to let the grownups in for the evening, at fifteen cents a head.

We got downstairs and out of the alley at just about the same time that the little white boys were being put out also, and we noticed that they were all carrying handbills in their fists. Nobody had passed out any handbills upstairs, but we had no difficulty getting some when we found out that Tack Haired Baker had been paid twenty-five cents to stand by the front door in the lobby and pass them out.

We were a little disappointed when we read them, because it didn't mean anything to us then. Bronco Billy and Buffalo Pete weren't even mentioned anywhere on the handbills. They read:

Special   *Special*   *Special*
THE SOUTH RISES AGAIN
Come see D. W. Griffith's:
"THE BIRTH OF A NATION"
(Based on "The Clansman")
Every night——Tuesday Through Friday.
Admission 25 cents.

Most of us threw the handbills away before we got home, and I don't remember how I happened to hold on to mine.

But I still had it in my hand when I climbed up our front steps and tried to make my way through the usual Saturday crowd of elders and sporting men who were holding their weekly session with Papa. Papa was Professor E. Poston, dean of men at Kentucky State Industrial College for Negroes in Frankfort and the official arbiter

[1] *high yallers:* exceedingly light-skinned Negroes.

of all bets and disputes which piled up during his two-weekly absences from home.

My sister Lillian, who is only three years older than I, was showing off by sitting next to Papa while he explained that a Negro jockey named Isaac Murphy was the first man to ride three winners in the Kentucky Derby, in 1884, 1890, and 1891. So as I stepped around Smoky Smith, our leading colored gambling man, who had raised the question, I handed Lillian the handbill. This *Birth of a Nation* thing sounded like one of those silly love-story movies she was always going to, so I thought I was doing her a favor.

But I was absolutely unprepared for the commotion that was raised when Mr. Freddie Williams, the first deacon of our Virginia Street Baptist Church, happened to glance at the handbill and let out a screech.

"Don't that say *The Birth of a Nation?*" he yelled as he snatched it out of Lillian's hands. "And coming to the Rex Theater here?"

He thrust the crumpled handbill in Papa's face and said: "Professor Poston, you've got to do something about this right away."

I still had no idea what had caused the commotion, but Mr. J. B. Petty, our local insurance man–historian, very soon put me right.

It seemed that this novel, *The Clansman,* and the moving picture *The Birth of a Nation* were something about a bunch of peckerwoods [2] who dressed up in sheets and went around whipping the heads of unsuspecting colored citizens and yelling about white supremacy. And there was one place in both things about some Negro—"played by a white man," Mr. J. B. Petty explained—who chased some poor white woman off the top of a rock quarry, with her yelling "Death before dishonor."

Mr. Freddie Williams was putting it right up to Papa.

"You know what it will mean to show this sort of thing

[2] *peckerwoods:* The literal meaning of "peckerwood" in the Southern and Western states is "woodpecker"; however, owing to the red head of this bird, the word has been figuratively applied to the poor white in the South, the "redneck."

to these hillbillies and peckerwoods around here, Professor Poston," he kept saying. "And I'm sure that the quality white folks will agree with you if you put it up to them right. I'm surprised that Mr. Max Kaplan even thought of letting this happen."

Now even I knew that Mr. Max Kaplan, who owned the Rex, was not exactly quality white folks in the eyes of Hopkinsville, Kentucky, even if he was a very popular white citizen in the colored community.

And neither was Judge Hezekiah Witherspoon, our veteran Republican leader, quality either. But he ran Hopkinsville, Kentucky, and it was to him that the group decided that Papa should make his first appeal.

Papa went right down to see him that Saturday night, but the meeting wasn't altogether successful. As I heard Papa explaining it to Mama when he finally got home, Judge Witherspoon started talking about private enterprise and what were the Negroes excited about anyhow? But Papa had one more weapon up his sleeve, he explained to Mama.

"So I finally said to him," Papa recalled, " 'I don't know if you read the book, Judge Witherspoon, but the whole thing is about the terrible things the scalawags and carpetbaggers did to the people of the South during Reconstruction. And although I didn't want to mention the subject, Judge, you must remember that all of those scalawags and carpetbaggers were Republicans, so I wonder if you want people reminded of that?' "

Papa chuckled as he recalled Judge Witherspoon's reaction.

" 'Eph, you damn Democrat,' he yelled at me," Papa said. " 'You keep your politics out of this.' But I could see that he was shaken, and I just let him rave for a few minutes.

"But finally he said: 'I'm not gonna get mixed up in this thing. But you go and see Max Kaplan and tell him how the colored people feel about this thing. And tell him I'll back him up if he feels he's got to do something about it.' "

Papa was very set up about the meeting. "I'm going out

to see Mr. Max Kaplan tomorrow morning. After all, Sunday is not his Sabbath and he won't be averse to talking a little business."

I still didn't quite understand what the shouting was all about. But I had no doubt that Mr. Max Kaplan would side with our colored citizens if Papa asked him to. For Mr. Max Kaplan was quite an unusual citizen even in Hopkinsville, Kentucky. He had come there years before I was born and had got into hot water the minute he built the Rex Theater, because he had planned only ground-floor seats for white and colored citizens alike.

Of course, the white folks, including the quality ones, had beaten him down on that, and he had been forced to spend extra money to fix the peanut gallery up for us.

Reaching Pete Washington, a classmate of mine in the Booker T. Washington Colored Grammar School, once said he was glad Mr. Max Kaplan lost that fight. Reaching Pete didn't have a nickel one Saturday when The Clutching Hand serial was playing the Rex, so he kept on up the alley and slipped through the fire-escape door on the ground floor where the white folks sat.

It was dark, of course, and nobody noticed that Reaching Pete had slipped in. But everybody knew it a few minutes later. For when Pete looked up, he was right under the screen and the pictures were twenty feet tall. And just at that moment, the Clutching Hand, a very mean crook who had a claw in place of his right hand, was reaching out for his next victim, and Pete thought he was reaching for him.

Pete closed his eyes and screamed so loud that they had to turn on the lights in the whole theater to find out what was going on. The cops wanted to lock Reaching Pete up, but Mr. Max Kaplan wouldn't let them. He even let Reaching Pete go upstairs free of charge.

But that wasn't the only thing that endeared Mr. Max Kaplan to our colored community. There was the matter of Tapper Johnson, our motion-picture projectionist. When the white folks balked Mr. Max Kaplan and made him build a whole peanut gallery (after starting a whispering campaign that he was trying to bring his New York City ideas to Hopkinsville), he made up his mind to get even. So he decided to make his most highly paid employee one of our colored citizens. That was when he hired Tapper and trained him to be the only moving-picture-machine operator in all of Hopkinsville. And he paid Tapper thirty-five dollars each and every week.

And Tapper paid Mr. Max Kaplan back real nice too. He became the best moving-picture operator for his size and age in all of Kentucky, and there were rumors that he could have gotten five dollars more a week in Clarksville, Tennessee, if Mr. Kaplan had ever given him a vacation or a day off to go see about it.

But Tapper didn't want a day off. He had only two loves in his life—his motion-picture machine and little Cecelia Penrod, with whom he had been in love long before he quit the fourth grade in the Booker T. Washington Colored Grammar School.

His love affair with the Rex Theater moving-picture machine went along smoothly. But not his love affair with little Cecelia. For Cecelia was one of the nieces of Mrs. Nixola Green, our high-yaller social leader. And she felt that Tapper was too dark to become a member of her family.

In fact, my sister Lillian was always saying that Mrs. Nixola was trying to marry Cecelia off to Pat Slaker (who naturally was yaller), but that Pat and Cecelia weren't paying each other any mind. Cecelia was in love with Tapper, Lillian said, although there wasn't much she could do about it. She never got to go to the Rex Theater alone. Mrs. Nixola always insisted on accompanying her.

Papa probably had all this in mind that Sunday morning when he hopefully set out for Mr. Max Kaplan's home. But Papa was in for a disappointment. Mr. Kaplan wasn't in town. He'd left three weeks ago for California and he wasn't expected home until Wednesday.

Now *The Birth of a Nation* was due to start running Tuesday night. Time was running out as the elders of Freeman Methodist Chapel and the Virginia Street Baptist Church met that afternoon to receive Papa's report.

"Professor Poston," Mr. Freddie Williams finally said after the discussion had gone on for hours, "I know how you feel about poor white trash. But with Mr. Max Kaplan out of town, there's nothing we can do but appeal to S. J. Bolton."

It took some talking on the part of the elders, but Papa was finally persuaded to lay the matter before Mr. S. J. Bolton, Mr. Kaplan's manager of the Rex, and the results were disastrous, as he reported it to Mama later.

"This clay-eating cracker,"[3] Papa said later, in as near an approach to profanity as he ever permitted himself, "had the nerve to call me Eph. He said to me: 'Eph, what are you Nigras upset about? Why, my grandfather was one of the founders of the Klan. No Nigra who knows his place has anything to worry about in this glorious story of the re-rise of the South.'

"And then he added," Papa said, " 'Why, Eph, you must know what my initials, S. J., stand for. Stonewall Jackson Bolton, of course.' "

Papa's indignation at the outcome of his conference was far exceeded by the reaction of the elders who met on our lawn that Sunday afternoon to hear his report.

But none of us young ones felt personally involved until Mr. Freddie Williams summed up the feelings of our elders.

"All right," he said, "if that is the way the white folks feel about it, let them. But I move that if *The Birth of a Nation* opens at the Rex Tuesday evening, then 'The Death of the Rex' should set in that very night. Because if we don't patronize that peanut gallery Mr. Max Kaplan has for us, then they ain't gonna make enough money each week to pay even Tapper's salary. And that means not only us staying away, but our kids as well—Bronco Billy and Buffalo Pete notwithstanding."

Now this created a very desperate situation indeed, as I explained to my classmates at the Booker T. Washington Colored Grammar School the next morning.

But what could we do about it? We were all pretty downcast until Rat Joiner said: "I think I got an idea." And then he explained.

And as soon as school was out that day, we all went

---

[3] *cracker:* another derisive term for a poor white in the Southern states.

to work to raise the fifteen cents Rat said was necessary for the success of his plan. Coca-Cola bottles, scrap wire, everything, went into the pot until we had the fifteen cents.

There was no picket line at the Rex the next night, but some of our most responsible colored citizens were loitering around the alley from the minute the evening tickets went on sale. And most of them were very upset when Rat Joiner, the pride of Billy Goat Hill, showed up as the only colored customer that night who plunked down fifteen cents and requested a peanut-gallery ticket from Miss Lucy.

In fact, there was talk about mentioning the fact to Reverend Timberlake, and having him read Roosevelt Alonzo Taylor Joiner out of the congregation of the Dirt's Avenue Methodist Church.

But that was before they found out the nature of Rat's mission.

For Rat entered the Rex just thirty minutes before the main feature was to go on, just when Tapper was preparing to rewind the film for Hopkinsville's first showing of *The Birth of a Nation.*

Rat knocked on the door of the projection room, then came right to the matter at hand.

"Tapper," he said, "Mrs. Nixola Green has finally persuaded Cecelia to run off and marry Pat Slaker. They're up at Mrs. Nixola's house on First Street and they're going to head for Clarksville any minute. I know it ain't none of my business, but you always been fair to us and—"

Tapper waited to hear no more. He dashed out of the projection room and headed first for Mrs. Nixola's house on First Street.

Of course, Cecelia wasn't there; the whole family was over in Earlington, Kentucky, attending a family reunion.

But Tapper didn't know this. He rushed down to Irving's Livery Stable and rented the fastest horse and rig for an emergency dash to Clarksville, Tennessee, where he hoped to head off the nuptials.

Well, the downstairs section of the Rex Theater was crowded (with only Rat in the peanut gallery) before Mr. S. J. Bolton learned that Hopkinsville's only movie projectionist was no longer in the Rex Theater. He tried to stall the showing for a half hour, but when Tapper didn't show up then, Mr. S. J. Bolton tried to run the machine himself.

Rat, who had decided to stay inside since he had paid an unheard-of fifteen cents to be there anyway, explained to us later what happened.

"Tapper had started rewinding the film backward to get to the front," he said, "but Mr. S. J. Bolton didn't know that. So he picked up the first film roll he saw and started running it on that picture thing.

"Well, it turned out that it was the middle of the picture and backwards besides. So, instead of that colored gentleman (played by some white man) chasing that white lady off the top of the quarry, it started with the white lady at the bottom of the quarry. And she was leaping to the top of the quarry so that the colored gentleman (who was really a white man) could grab her.

"The white folks didn't see much of the picture, because Mr. S. J. Bolton yanked that part off so fast that he tore up the whole thing. I waited around another half hour and nothing else came on, so all of us went home."

So Hopkinsville, Kentucky, never got to see *The Birth of a Nation*. Mr. Max Kaplan came back the next day and substituted another film for *The Birth of a Nation*. There were always two schools of thought in the colored community after that—and even Papa couldn't settle the dispute.

One school held that Mr. Max Kaplan would never have let *The Birth of a Nation* be booked for the Rex if he had known anything about it and if he hadn't been in Los Angeles. And the other school contended that Mr. S. J. Bolton had so messed up the original print in trying to run it without Tapper that it couldn't have been shown anyway.

In any case, Mr. Max Kaplan took steps to see that a certain situation never obtained again. He had little Cecelia Penrod smuggled out of her house while Mrs. Nixola wasn't watching. And he took her and Tapper down to Judge Hezekiah Witherspoon, who married both of them on the spot. Mrs. Nixola Green collapsed at the news and went over to Clarksville, Tennessee, to recuperate at the home of some of her high-yaller relatives.

When she came back she boasted that she had passed for white and had seen *The Birth of a Nation* at the Princess Theater there.

"And it was a very good picture," she said, "I don't know what all the fuss over here was about."

for discussion

1. How would you characterize the tone of the narrator? What is his attitude toward the events he describes? Does his attitude make the characters more or less believable?

2. Why is it significant that the young black boys find a solution after the adult leaders of the black and white communities fail?

3. How does the narrator's attitude toward both the white and black communities of Hopkinsville help to shape the reader's response to this portrait of a segregated society?

1867–1936

FINLEY PETER DUNNE

☐ *Finley Peter Dunne was born in Chicago and raised on its West Side, in the Irish section surrounding Archer Avenue—the "Archey Road" where he situated the saloon of his literary creation Mr. Dooley, barkeeper and philosopher. A reporter and editor on major newspapers in Chicago and New York, Dunne possessed an active social conscience which compelled him to speak out against corruption and hypocrisy in both domestic and international affairs. In the fashion of earlier satiric commentators on the human scene, he invented in 1893 a disarmingly humble and engaging character through whom he could speak—more or less safely—the unvarnished truth. Martin Dooley is a shrewd,* tough-minded observer of the social scene who holds forth in his saloon mainly for the benefit of a rather dense patron named Hennessy. Although his sharp insights are generally lost upon Hennessy, they gained him the attentive ear and the admiration of the country. Dunne wrote most of his "Mr. Dooley" sketches between 1893 and 1905; and since they were originally published in newspapers, their audience was vast. When the sketches were collected into Mr. Dooley in Peace and in War (1898) and Mr. Dooley in the Hearts of His Countrymen (1899), both books became national best sellers.

It is important to note that at this time the Irish were frequently singled out for ridicule and contempt. In the stereotyped public view of the Irish—to which writers as distinguished as Henry David Thoreau had contributed—they were regarded as low and brutish shanty-dwellers, fit only for brawling and working on the railroad or as menials. Through Mr. Dooley, Dunne stressed the practical wisdom of the Irish, their vivid and witty speech, adventurous spirit, and great personal warmth. It is not, indeed, too much to say that Mr. Dooley played a major part in the assimilation of the Irish into American culture.

on the popularity of firemen

☐ "I knowed a man be th' name iv Clancy wanst, Jawn. He was fr'm th' County May-o, but a good man f'r all that; an', whin he'd growed to be a big, sthrappin' fellow, he wint on to th' fire departmint. They'se an Irishman 'r two on th' fire departmint an' in th' army, too, Jawn, though ye'd think be hearin' some talk they was all runnin' prim'-ries an' thryin' to be cinthral comitymen. So ye wud. Ye niver hear iv thim on'y whin they die; an' thin, murther, what funerals they have!

"On the Popularity of Firemen" from *Mr. Dooley in Peace and War* by Finley Peter Dunne, published by Small, Maynard and Co., 1899.

"Well, this Clancy wint on th' fire departmint, an' they give him a place in thruck twinty-three. All th' r-road was proud iv him, an' faith he was proud iv himsilf. He r-rode free on th' sthreet ca-ars, an' was th' champeen hand-ball player f'r miles around. Ye shud see him goin' down th' sthreet, with his blue shirt an' his blue coat with th' buttons on it, an' his cap on his ear. But ne'er a cap or coat'd he wear whin they was a fire. He might be shiv'rin' be th' stove in th' ingine house with a buffalo robe over his head; but, whin th' gong sthruck, 'twas off with coat an' cap an' buffalo robe, an' out come me brave Clancy, bare-headed an' bare hand, dhrivin' with wan line an' spillin' th' hose cart on wan wheel at ivry jump iv th' horse. Did anny wan iver see a fireman with his coat on or a polisman with his off? Why, wanst, whin Clancy was standin' up f'r Grogan's eighth, his son come runnin' in to tell him they was a fire in Vogel's packin' house. He dhropped th' kid at Father Kelly's feet, an' whipped off his long coat an' wint tearin' f'r th' dure, kickin' over th' poorbox an' buttin' ol' Mis' O'Neill that'd come in to say th' stations.[1] 'Twas lucky 'twas wan iv th' Grogans. They're a fine family f'r falls. Jawn Grogan was wurrukin' on th' top iv Metzri an' O'Connell's brewery wanst, with a man be th' name iv Dorsey. He slipped an' fell wan hundherd feet. Whin they come to see if he was dead, he got up, an' says he: 'Lave me at him.' 'At who?' says they. 'He's deliryous,' they says. 'At Dorsey,' says Grogan. 'He thripped me.' So it didn't hurt Grogan's eighth to fall four 'r five feet.

"Well, Clancy wint to fires an' fires. Whin th' big organ facthry burnt, he carrid th' hose up to th' fourth story an' was squirtin' whin th' walls fell. They dug him out with pick an' shovel, an' he come up fr'm th' brick an' boards an' saluted th' chief. 'Clancy,' says th' chief, 'ye betther go over an' get a dhrink.' He did so, Jawn. I heerd it. An' Clancy was that proud!

"Whin th' Hogan flats on Halsted Sthreet took fire, they got all th' people out but wan; an' she was a woman asleep on th' fourth flure. 'Who'll go up?' says Bill Musham. 'Sure, sir,' says Clancy, 'I'll go'; an' up he wint. His captain was

[1] *stations:* the stations of the cross, a form of meditation in the Catholic Church.

a man be th' name iv O'Connell, fr'm th' County Kerry; an' he had his fut on th' ladder whin Clancy started. Well, th' good man wint into th' smoke, with his wife faintin' down below. 'He'll be kilt,' says his brother. 'Ye don't know him,' says Bill Musham. An' sure enough, whin ivry wan'd give him up, out comes me brave Clancy, as black as a Turk, with th' girl in his arms. Th' others wint up like monkeys, but he shtud wavin' thim off, an' come down th' ladder face forward. 'Where'd ye larn that?' says Bill Musham. 'I seen a man do it at th' Lyceem [2] whin I was a kid,' says Clancy. 'Was it all right?' 'I'll have ye up before th' ol' man,' says Bill Musham. 'I'll teach ye to come down a laddher as if ye was in a quadhrille, ye horse-stealin', hamsthringin' May-o man,' he says. But he didn't. Clancy wint over to see his wife. 'Oh Mike,' says she, ' 'twas fine,' she says. 'But why d'ye take th' risk?' she says. 'Did ye see th' captain?' he says with a scowl. 'He wanted to go. Did ye think I'd follow a Kerry man with all th' ward lukkin' on?' he says.

"Well, so he wint dhrivin' th' hose-cart on wan wheel, an' jumpin' whin he heerd a man so much as hit a glass to make it ring. All th' people looked up to him, an' th' kids followed him down th' sthreet; an' 'twas th' gr-reatest priv'lige f'r anny wan f'r to play dominos with him near th' joker. But about a year ago he come in to see me, an' says he, 'Well, I'm goin' to quit.' 'Why,' says I, 'ye'er a young man yet,' I says. 'Faith,' he says, 'look at me hair,' he says—'young heart, ol' head. I've been at it these twenty year, an' th' good woman's wantin' to see more iv me thin blowin' into a saucer iv coffee,' he says. 'I'm goin' to quit,' he says, 'on'y I want to see wan more good fire,' he says. 'A rale good ol' hot wan,' he says, 'with th' win' blowin' f'r it an' a good dhraft in th' ilivator-shaft, an' about two stories, with pitcher-frames an' gasoline an' excelsior, an' to hear th' chief yellin': "Play 'way, sivinteen. What th' hell an' damnation are ye standin' aroun' with that pipe

<hr />

[2] Lyceem: Irish dialect for "Lyceum"; originally the name for an association providing public lectures and for the building in which the program was given. The term later was applied to many forms of public entertainment and was used as the name of countless vaudeville and movie houses.

f'r? Is this a fire 'r a dam livin' pitcher? I'll break ivry man iv eighteen, four, six, an' chem'cal five to-morrah mornin' befure breakfast." Oh,' he says, bringin' his fist down, 'wan more, an' I'll quit.'

"An' he did, Jawn. Th' day th' Carpenter Brothers' box factory burnt. 'Twas wan iv thim big, fine-lookin' buildings that pious men built out iv celluloid an' plasther iv Paris. An' Clancy was wan iv th' men undher whin th' wall fell. I seen thim bringin' him home; an' th' little woman met him at th' dure, rumplin' her apron in her hands."

the big fine

☐ "That was a splendid fine they soaked Jawn D. with," said Mr. Dooley.[1]

"What did they give him?" asked Mr. Hennessy.

"Twinty-nine millyon dollars," said Mr. Dooley.

"Oh, great!" said Mr. Hennessy. "That's a grand fine. It's a gorjous fine. I can't hardly believe it."

"It's thrue, though," said Mr. Dooley. "Twinty-nine millyon dollars. Divvle th' cent less. I can't exactly make out what th' charge was that they arrested him on, but th' gin'ral idee is that Jawn D. was goin' around loaded up to th' guards with Standard Ile, exceedin' th' speed limit in acquirin' money, an' singin' 'A charge to keep I have' till th' neighbors cud stand it no longer. The judge says: 'Ye're an old offender an' I'll have to make an example iv ye. Twinty-nine millyon dollars or fifty-eight millyon days. Call th' next case, Misther Clerk.

"Did he pay th' fine? He did not. Iv coorse he cud if he wanted to. He wuddent have to pawn annything to get th'

"The Big Fine" from *Mr. Dooley Says* by Finley Peter Dunne, copyright 1910 Charles Scribner's Sons; renewal copyright 1938 by Margaret Dunne. Reprinted by permission of the publisher.

[1] In 1907, U.S. Judge Kenesaw Mountain Landis ruled that John D. Rockefeller's Standard Oil Company would have to pay a fine of more than 29 million dollars for unfair business practices. The judgment was later set aside by a higher court, and Standard Oil was never obliged to pay this immense fine.

money, ye can bet on that. All he'd have to do would be to put his hand down in his pocket, skin twenty-nine millyon dollar bills off iv his roll an' hurl thim at th' clerk. But he refused to pay as a matter iv principle. 'Twas not that he needed th' money. He don't care f'r money in th' passionate way that you an' me do, Hinnissy. Th' likes iv us are as crazy about a dollar as a man is about his child whin he has on'y wan. Th' chances are we'll spoil it. But Jawn D., havin' a large an' growin' fam'ly iv dollars, takes on'y a kind iv gin'ral inthrest in thim. He's issued a statement sayin' that he's a custojeen iv money appinted be himsilf. He looks afther his own money an' th' money iv other people. He takes it an' puts it where it won't hurt thim an' they won't spoil it. He's a kind iv a society f'r th' previntion of croolty to money. If he finds a man misusing his money, he takes it away fr'm him an' adopts it. Ivry Saturdah night he lets th' man see it f'r a few hours. An' he says he's surprised to find that whin, with th' purest intintions in th' wurruld, he is found thryin' to coax our little money to his home where it'll find conjanial surroundings an' have other money to play with, th' people thry to lynch him an' th' polis arrest him f'r abduction.

"So as a matther iv principle he appealed th' case. An appeal, Hinnissy, is where ye ask wan coort to show its contempt f'r another coort. 'Tis sthrange that all th' pathrites [2] that have wanted to hang Willum Jennings Bryan an' mesilf f'r not showin' proper respect f'r th' joodicyary, are now showin' their respect f'r th' joodicyary be appealin' fr'm their decisions. Ye'd think Jawn D. wud bow his head reverentially in th' awful presence iv Kenesaw Mt. Landis an' sob out: 'Thank ye'er honor. This here noble fine fills me with joy. But d'ye think ye give me enough? If agreeable I'd like to make it an even thirty millyons.' But he doesn't. He's like mesilf. Him an' me bows to th' decisions iv th' coorts on'y if they bow first.

"I have gr-reat respect f'r th' joodicyary, as fine a lot iv cross an' indignant men as ye'll find annywhere. I have th' same respect f'r thim as they have f'r each other. But I niver bow to a decision iv a judge onless, first, it's pleasant

---

[2] *pathrites:* Irish dialect for "patriots."

to me, an', second, other judges bow to it. Ye can't be too careful about what decisions ye bow to. A decision that seems agreeable may turn out like an acquaintance ye scrape up at a picnic. Ye may be ashamed iv it to-morrah. Manny's th' time I've bowed to a decree iv a coort on'y to see it go up gayly to th' supreem coort, knock at th' dure an' be kicked down stairs be an angry old gintleman in a black silk petticoat. A decree iv th' coort has got to be pretty vinrable befure I do more thin greet it with a pleasant smile.

"Me idee was whin I read about Jawn D.'s fine that he'd settle at wanst, payin' twenty-eight millyon dollars in millyon dollar bills an' th' other millyon in chicken-feed like ten thousand dollar bills just to annoy th' clerk. But I ought to've known betther. Manny's th' time I've bent me proud neck to a decision iv a coort that lasted no longer thin it took th' lawyer f'r th' definse to call up another judge on th' tillyphone. A judge listens to a case f'r days an' hears, while he's figurin' a possible goluf score on his blotting pad, th' argymints iv two or three lawyers that no wan wud dare to offer a judgeship to. Gin'rally speakin', judges are lawyers. They get to be judges because they have what Hogan calls th' joodicyal timp'ramint, which is why annybody gets a job. Th' other kind iv people won't take a job. They'd rather take a chance. Th' judge listens to a case f'r days an' decides it th' way he intinded to. D'ye find th' larned counsel that's just been beat climbin' up on th' bench an' throwin' his arms around th' judge? Ye bet ye don't. He gathers his law books into his arms, gives th' magistrate a look that means 'There's an eliction next year,' an' runs down th' hall to another judge. Th' other judge hears his kick an' says he: 'I don't know annything about this here case except what ye've whispered to me, but I know me larned collague an' I wuddent thrust him to referee a roller-skatin' contest. Don't pay th' fine till ye hear fr'm me.' Th' on'y wan that bows to th' decision is th' fellow that won, an' pretty soon he sees he's made a mistake, f'r wan day th' other coort comes out an' declares that th' decision of th' lower coort is another argymint in favor iv abolishing night law schools.

"That's th' way Jawn D. felt about it an' he didn't

settle. I wondher will they put him away if he don't pay ivinchooly? 'Twill be a long sentence. A frind iv mine wanst got full iv kerosene an' attempted to juggle a polisman. They thried him whin he come out iv th' emergency hospital an' fined him a hundhred dollars. He didn't happen to have that amount with him at th' moment or at anny moment since th' day he was born. But the judge was very lenient with him. He said he needn't pay it if he cudden't. Th' coort wud give him a letther of inthroduction to th' bridewell [3] an' he cud stay there f'r two hundhred days. At that rate it'll be a long time befure Jawn D. an' me meet again on the goluf-links. Hogan has it figured out that if Jawn D. refuses to go back on his Puritan principles an' separate himsilf fr'm his money he'll be wan hundhred an' fifty-eight thousand years in cold storage. A man ought to be pretty good at th' lock step in a hundhred an' fifty-eight thousand years.

"Well, sir, glory be but times has changed whin they land me gr-reat an' good frind with a fine that's about akel to three millyon dhrunk an' disorderly cases. 'Twud've been cheaper if he'd took to dhrink arly in life. I've made a vow, Hinnissy, niver to be very rich. I'd like to be a little rich, but not rich enough f'r anny wan to notice that me pockets bulged. Time was whin I dhreamed iv havin' money an' lots iv it. 'Tis thrue I begun me dhreams at th' wrong end, spent th' money befure I got it. I was always clear about th' way to spend it but oncertain about th' way to get it. If th' Lord had intinded me to be a rich man, He'd've turned me dhreams around an' made me clear about makin' th' money but very awkward an' shy about gettin' rid iv it. There are two halves to ivry dollar. Wan is knowin' how to make it an' th' other is not knowin' how to spend it comfortably. Whin I hear iv a man with gr-reat business capacity, I know he's got an akel amount iv spending incapacity. No matter how much he knew about business, he wuddent be rich if he wasn't totally ignorant iv a science that we have developed as far as our means will allow. But now, I tell ye, I don't dhream iv bein' rich. I'm afraid

---

[3] *bridewell:* from Bridewell, London house of correction established in the 16th century; the name has become a term for any jail or prison.

iv it. In th' good old days th' polis coorts were crowded with th' poor. They weren't charged with poverty, iv coorse, but with the results iv poverty, d'ye mind. Now, be Hivens, th' rich have invaded even th' coorts an' the bridewell. Manny a face wearin' side whiskers an' gold-rimmed specs peers fr'm th' windows iv th' black Maria.[4] 'What's this man charged with?' says th' coort. 'He was found in possession iv tin millyon dollars,' says th' polisman. An' th' judge puts on th' black cap."

"Well," said Mr. Hennessy, " 'tis time they got what was comin' to thim."

"I'll not say ye're wrong," said Mr. Dooley. "I see th' way me frind Jawn D. feels about it. He thinks he's doin' a great sarvice to th' worruld collectin' all th' money in sight. It might remain in incompetint hands if he didn't get it. 'Twud be a shame to lave it where it'd be misthreated. But th' on'y throuble with Jawn is that he don't see how th' other fellow feels about it. As a father iv about thirty dollars I want to bring thim up mesilf in me own foolish way. I may not do what's right be thim. I may be too in-dulgent with thim. Their home life may not be happy. Per-haps 'tis clear that if they wint to th' Rockyfellar institution f'r th' care iv money they'd be in bether surroundings, but whin Jawn thries to carry thim off I raise a cry iv 'Polis,' a mob iv people that niver had a dollar iv their own an' niver will have wan, pounce on th' misguided man, th' polis pinch him, an' th' governmint condemns th' institution an' lets out th' inmates an' a good manny iv thim go to th' bad."

"D'ye think he'll iver sarve out his fine?" asked Mr. Hennessy.

"I don't know," said Mr. Dooley. "But if he does, whin he comes out at the end iv a hundhred an' fifty-eight thou-sand years, he'll find a great manny changes in men's hats an' th' means iv transportation but not much in annything else. He may find flyin' machines, though it'll be arly f'r thim, but he'll see a good manny people still walkin' to their wurruk."

---

[4] *black Maria:* a police patrol wagon or van used to transport prisoners.

for discussion

1. What specific criticism of the Irish does Dunne attempt to counter in "On the Popularity of Firemen"? In what way does the characterization of Clancy further this intention?

2. In what ways is Mr. Dooley like Leo Rosten's character Hyman Kaplan? In what ways are these literary ambassadors of good will different?

born 1908

WILLIAM SAROYAN

▢ *William Saroyan, who was raised in San Francisco, was the first Armenian-American writer to become famous. He burst dramatically onto the American literary scene in 1934 with the publication of his first book of short stories,* The Daring Young Man on the Flying Trapeze. *Speaking of this event, Nona Balakian, a literary critic of Armenian descent, remarked that "American readers heard the word* Armenian *used for the first time not in a pitiful context but in a gay and triumphant one. Perhaps nothing that the Armenians had achieved in this country until that time had left so favorable an impression on Americans."*

In 1939 Saroyan also became known as a dramatist with the opening of My Heart's in the Highlands, *and in 1940 he was awarded the Pulitzer Prize in drama for* The Time of Your Life. *He has published numerous collections of stories and plays, several novels, and an autobiography. His stories display enormous affection for humanity in its many forms and varied surroundings. They reveal an unmistakable joy, an expansive faith in the fundamental worth of people. Whether children or adults, his Armenian characters are typically good-humored and irrepressibly buoyant. But they also possess a certain folk wisdom—an inbred shrewdness and practicality—together with unyielding determination and endurance. The old-world attributes of Saroyan's characters blend easily with those of the American self-image, and make the Armenian immigrant seem somehow less foreign.*

the insurance salesman, the peasant, the rug merchant, and the potted plant

☐ Arshag Gorobakian was a small man who earned his living as a salesman for the New York Life Insurance Company. He worked exclusively among his own people, the Armenians. In twenty years, he often told a new client, I have sold three hundred policies, and so far two hundred of my clients have died. He did not utter this remark with sorrow and it was not intended to be a commentary on the sadness of life. On the contrary, Gorobakian's smile indicated that what he meant by two hundred of them dying was simply that these were men who had cheated death of its awful victory, and at the same time made a monkey out of the New York Life Insurance Company. All shrewd men, he often told a new client. Men like yourself, in all things practical and brilliant. They said to themselves, Yes, we shall die, there is no way out of that, let us face the facts.

Here the insurance salesman would bring the printed charts and statistics out of his inside coat pocket and say, Here are the facts. You are forty-seven years of age, and by the grace of God in good health. According to the facts you will be dead in five years.

He would smile gently, sharing with the new client the thrill of dying in five years and earning thereby an enormous sum of money. In five years, he would say, you will

"The Insurance Salesman, the Peasant, the Rug Merchant, and the Potted Plant" from *Peace, It's Wonderful* by William Saroyan. Reprinted by permission of the author.

have paid my company three hundred and eighty-seven dollars, and on dying you will have earned twenty thousand dollars, or a net profit of nineteen thousand six hundred and thirteen dollars.

That, he would say, is a fair profit on any investment.

Once, however, he talked to a peasant in Kingsburg who didn't believe he would be dead in five years.

Come back in seventeen or eighteen years, the peasant said.

But you are sixty-seven years old now, the insurance salesman said.

I know, the peasant said. But I shall not be swindled in an affair like this. I shall be alive twenty years from now. I have planted three hundred new olive trees and I know I shall not be dead until they are full grown. Not to mention the mulberry trees, and the pomegranate trees, and the walnut and almond trees.

No, the peasant said, the time is not ripe for a bargain of this sort. I know I shall be alive twenty years from now. I can feel it in my bones. Shall I say something?

Yes, the insurance salesman said.

I shall live *thirty* years longer, not twenty. You will admit I should be cheated in a deal of this sort.

The insurance salesman was small, courteous, quiet-spoken, and never aggressive.

I can see, he said, that you are a man of giant strength—

Giant strength? the peasant roared. Shall I say something?

The insurance salesman nodded.

What you say is the truth, he said. I am a man of giant strength. What death? Why should I die? For what reason, countryman? I am in no hurry. Money? Yes. It is good. But I am not going to die.

The insurance salesman smoked his cigar calmly, although inwardly he was in a state of great agitation, like a routed cavalry officer trying desperately to round up his men and organize another offensive.

Death to you? he said to the peasant. God forbid. In all my life I have never wished another man's death. Life is what we enjoy. The taste of the watermelon in the summer is the thing we cherish.

May I say something? the peasant interrupted.

Again the insurance salesman nodded.

What you say is true, he said. The thing we cherish is the taste of the watermelon in the summertime. And bread and cheese and grapes in the cool of evening, under the trees. Please go on.

I do not wish any man's departure from this warm scene of life, the insurance salesman said. We must face the facts, however.

He shook the documents in his hand.

Our world is a crazy world, he said. You are a strong man. You enjoy the taste of the watermelon. You are walking in the city. An automobile strikes you and where are you? You are dead.

The peasant frowned.

Ah, yes, he said. The automobile.

In the event that you are killed accidentally, which God forbid, the insurance salesman said, you will be rewarded doubly.

The confounded automobiles, the peasant said. I shall be very careful in the streets.

We are all careful, the insurance salesman said, but what good does it do us? More people are killed every year in automobile accidents than in one year of a great war.

May I say something? the peasant said.

Say it, the insurance salesman said.

I have half a mind to be protected, the peasant said. I have half a mind to take out an insurance policy.

That is a wise plan, the insurance salesman said.

The peasant purchased a policy and began making payments. Two years later he called the insurance salesman to his house and reprimanded him severely, although politely. He complained that although he had spent several hundred dollars, he had not so much as come anywhere near being killed, which he considered very odd.

I do not want the policy any longer, he said.

The insurance salesman told the ironic story of another man who gave up his policy after two years, and three weeks later was gored to death by an angry bull. But the peasant was not impressed with the story.

May I say something? he said. There is no bull in the

world strong enough to gore me. I would break his neck. No thank you, I do not want to be insured. I have made up my mind not to die, even for a profit. I have had a hundred chances of walking in front of an automobile, but always I have stepped back cautiously and allowed it to go by.

That was fourteen years ago, and the peasant, a man named Hakimian, is still alive.

The insurance salesman, however, preferred people more enlightened than peasants. He himself was a graduate of college. His preference was for men with whom he could talk for hours about other things, and then little by little move in with the insurance speech. He would often drive two hundred miles to San Francisco to talk with a dentist who had graduated from college.

Once he decided to drive his Buick across the country to Boston. It was a journey of ten days. Along the way there would be much to see, and in Boston he would visit his sister and her husband and their eleven children. He drove to Boston, visited his sister and her family, and met a rug merchant who was a college graduate. Three times in ten days he called at this man's home and carried on pleasant conversations. The man's name was Haroutunian and he was extremely fond of conversation. The insurance salesman found him brilliant on all subjects. But when the subject of life insurance was introduced, he discovered that his friend was, bluntly, in no mood for it. At least, not for the present.

The time came for the insurance salesman to return to California. Before departing he was paid a visit by the rug merchant, Haroutunian, who was carrying a small potted plant.

My friend, the rug merchant said, I have a brother in Bakersfield which is near where you live. I have not seen him in twenty years. Will you do me a favor?

Of course, the insurance salesman said.

Carry this plant to my brother with my greetings, the rug merchant said.

Gladly, the insurance salesman said. What plant is this?

I do not know, the rug merchant said, but the leaf has a wonderful odor. Smell it.

The insurance salesman smelled the plant and was disappointed in the smell of the leaf.

It is truly a heavenly smell, he said.

The rug merchant gave the insurance salesman the name and address of his brother, and then said:

One more thing. The agricultural department in each state demands that a plant being transported be examined for plant insects. There are none on this plant, but the law is the law. You will have to stop a minute at the agricultural department of each state. A formality.

Oh, the insurance salesman said.

His word had been given, however, so he put the plant into his car and made his departure from Boston.

He was a very law-abiding man and the plant caused him quite a little trouble. Very often even after he had found the agricultural department of each state, the inspector was out of town and wouldn't be back for several days.

The result of the whole thing was that the insurance salesman got home in twenty-one days instead of ten. He drove a hundred miles to Bakersfield and found the rug merchant's brother.

The plant was safe and was now growing small red blossoms that gave off an odor which to the insurance salesman was extremely unpleasant.

Three thousand six hundred and seventy-eight miles I have carried this wonderful plant, the insurance salesman said, from the home of your brother in Boston to your home in Bakersfield. Your brother sends greetings.

The rug merchant's brother liked the plant even less than the insurance salesman did.

I do not want the plant, he said.

The insurance salesman was a man who was hardly ever amazed by anything. He accepted the brother's indifference and took the plant home with him.

He planted it in the finest soil in his backyard, bought fertilizer for it, watered it, and took very good care of it.

It is not the plant, he told a neighbor. It nauseates me. But some day I shall perhaps be going back to Boston to visit my sister and when I see the rug merchant again I know he shall ask about the plant and I shall be pleased to tell him that it is flourishing. I feel that I have as good a chance as any man to sell him an insurance policy some day.

for discussion

1. What does the author suggest by observing that the insurance salesman "preferred people more enlightened than peasants"?

2. What is shown about the insurance salesman when he agrees to take the potted plant to California, even though he will be greatly inconvenienced?

3. Although he realistically acknowledges the human weaknesses of his characters, Saroyan has in fact produced a generally favorable portrait. How does he accomplish this?

PART 2

VOICES
OF ALIENATION
AND PROTEST

INTRODUCTION

☐ The patient mood of America's ethnic writers changed as they experienced two quite different kinds of frustration. Once eager to serve as "ambassadors" from their ethnic communities to the larger American community, they sometimes found themselves adrift between two worlds—no longer at home in the one, not really welcome in the other. Once confident that their communities were on the way to realizing the promise of American life, they were shaken and angered by the stubborn opposition that persisted, openly and covertly. Thus, they increasingly felt a sense of their separateness, felt betrayed by the social values they had embraced. Consequently, they were more disposed than the earlier ethnic writers to speak defensively and combatively.

Alienation is a feeling of insecurity arising from one's awareness that once-firm ties to others, to geographical places, to traditions and beliefs have been cut. It is the frightening sensation of being detached from a once-secure anchorage, of finding oneself a stranger or an outsider in what appeared to be friendly surroundings. Accordingly, one may feel alienated both from himself and from his society; and one's response to the sense of alienation may be expressed both through the exploration of this puzzling condition and through protest against the harsh social circumstances that produce such acute human distress.

One may, of course, be alienated from himself by the ordinary burdens of human experience. All men feel some manner of discontent with the limitations and uncertainties that compose life; and the fluidity of our society has created for virtually all Americans a problem of identity that has left many of them with a keen sense of personal alienation. But truly extraordinary physical and psychological burdens and inescapable questions of identity have made alienation from oneself almost the distinguishing mark of the individuals who constitute America's ethnic minorities. At the turn of the century,

W. E. B. Du Bois provided this account of a black American's personal reality:

> It is a peculiar sensation, this double-consciousness, this sense of always looking at one's self through the eyes of others, of measuring one's soul by the tape of a world that looks on in amused contempt and pity. One ever feels his two-ness—an American, a Negro—two souls, two thoughts, two unreconciled strivings; two warring ideals in one dark body, whose dogged strength alone keeps it from being torn asunder.

More than six decades later, the social scientist Horace Cayton offered this description of his experience as a black man:

> I discovered at a very early age, perhaps three or four, that I was a Negro. And I became aware that I would always be one and that Negroes would always be underprivileged and stigmatized, a group of people set apart. I also knew that I was an American, and, in school as well as in the home, I learned that America had a dream of freedom. These two identities, both of which I had internalized, seemed to be in constant conflict. When I became aware of the conflict, I was confused.°

This fundamental uncertainty is apparent in the poetry of Paul Laurence Dunbar and Countee Cullen, both of whom wrote alternately in dialect and in elevated literary language without fully "belonging" to either tradition. For those ethnic writers who felt most sharply the anxieties of self-alienation, writing became the means of either escaping or better understanding their confusion.

On the other hand, in other ethnic writers the feeling of alienation served primarily to heighten their sense of social injustice. Their personal distress made them more conscious of the suffering of their fellows and of the

° From selection by Horace Cayton from *Anger, and Beyond: The Negro Writer in the United States,* edited by Herbert Hill. Reprinted by permission of Harper & Row, Publishers, Inc.

social and economic restrictions which produced such misery. They expressed their alienation from a society which condoned such restrictions by crying out against it, by demanding change. They lashed out angrily, even savagely, at the inequities of a society that had promised so much and given so little. These writers viewed literature as a weapon designed to shock the complacent and to generate indignation. Speaking of the aims of the black American writer in 1935, Langston Hughes said, "Something has got to change in America—and change soon. We must help that change to come."

1893–1967

MICHAEL GOLD

ESSAY

☐ *Irwin Granich, best known by his penname, Michael Gold, was born on the East Side of New York to poor Jewish immigrants. He grew up among the almost unrelieved miseries and frustrations of tenement life. Before he was thirteen, he had been compelled by his family's poverty to leave school and become a laborer. These harsh experiences of social injustice led Gold first to despair and then to a missionary determination to change the world. In his early twenties he became a socialist. Heavily influenced by the poet Walt Whitman and by the movement for economic reform, he was one of the earliest American writers to call for a new kind of literature, a "proletarian" literature, by workers and about the realities of working-class life. Michael Gold identified himself fully with the American masses, and with all the world's "bottom dogs." Consequently, he insisted that art should originate in the artist's close association with the people.*

Gold wrote for and edited several of the most vigorous left-wing periodicals in America during the three decades following the first World War. His uncompromising dedication to the struggle for a better world led him to turn his literary talents entirely to political journalism. Thus, although his most famous book was the autobiographical novel Jews Without Money, *published in 1930, Gold addressed his readers really neither as a Jew nor as a novelist. He was driven to speak, rather, by a general compassion for the exploited —whatever their nationality or religion—and by a seething anger against the exploiters of humanity.*

the soul of a landlord

I

☐ On the East Side people buy their groceries a pinch at a time; three cents' worth of sugar, five cents' worth of butter, everything in penny fractions. The good Jewish black bread that smells of harvest-time is sliced into a dozen parts and sold for pennies. But that winter even pennies were scarce.

There was a panic on Wall Street. Multitudes were without work; there were strikes, suicides, and food riots. The prostitutes roamed our street like wolves; never was there so much competition among them.

Life froze. The sun vanished from the deathly gray sky. The streets reeked with snow and slush. There were hundreds of evictions. I walked down a street between dripping tenement walls. The rotten slush ate through my shoes. The wind beat on my face. I saw a stack of furniture before a tenement: tables, chairs, a washtub packed with crockery and bed-clothes, a broom, a dresser, a lamp.

The snow covered them. The snow fell, too, on a little Jew and his wife and three children. They huddled in a mournful group by their possessions. They had placed a saucer on one of the tables. An old woman with a market bag mumbled a prayer in passing. She dropped a penny in the saucer. Other people did the same. Each time the evicted family lowered its eyes in shame. They were not beggars, but "respectable" people. But if enough pennies fell in the saucer, they might have rent for a new home. This was the one hope left them.

Winter. Building a snow fort one morning, we boys dug out a litter of frozen kittens and their mother. The little ones were still blind. They had been born into it, but had never seen our world.

Other dogs and cats were frozen. Men and women, too, were found dead in hallways and on docks. Mary Sugar

"The Soul of a Landlord" from *Jews Without Money* by Michael Gold. Reprinted by permission of Evelyn Singer Agency.

Bum met her end in an alley. She was found half-naked, clutching a whisky bottle in her blue claw. This was her last "love" affair.

Horses slipped on the icy pavement, and quivered there for hours with broken legs, until a policeman arrived to shoot them.

The boys built a snow man. His eyes were two coals; his nose a potato. He wore a derby hat and smoked a corn-cob pipe. His arms were flung wide; in one of them he held a broom, in the other a newspaper. This Golem [1] with his amazed eyes and idiotic grin amused us all for an afternoon.

The next morning we found him strangely altered. His eyes and nose had been torn out; his grin smashed, like a war victim's. Who had played this joke? The winter wind.

II

Mrs. Rosenbaum owned a grocery store on our street. She was a widow with four children, and lived in two rooms back of the store. She slaved from dawn until midnight; a big, clumsy woman with a chapped face and masses of untidy hair; always grumbling, groaning, gossiping about her ailments. Sometimes she was nervous and screamed at her children, and beat them. But she was a kind-hearted woman, and that winter suffered a great deal. Everyone was very poor, and she was too good not to give them groceries on credit.

"I'm crazy to do it!" she grumbled in her icy store. "I'm a fool! But when a child comes for a loaf of bread, and I have the bread, and I know her family is starving, how can I refuse her? Yet I have my own children to think of! I am being ruined! The store is being emptied! I can't meet my bills!"

She was kind. Kindness is a form of suicide in a world based on the law of competition.

One day we watched the rewards of kindness. The sheriff's men arrived to seize Mrs. Rosenbaum's grocery.

[1] *Golem* (gō′ləm): a kind of Frankenstein monster described in Jewish legends.

They tore down the shelves and fixtures, they carted off tubs of butter, drums of kerosene, sacks of rice, flour, and potatoes.

Mrs. Rosenbaum stood by, watching her own funeral. Her fat, kind face was swollen with crying as with toothache. Her eyes blinked in bewilderment. Her children clung to her skirts and cried. Snow fell from the sky, a crowd muttered its sympathy, a policeman twirled his club.

What happened to her after that, I don't know. Maybe the Organized Charities helped her; or maybe she died. O golden dyspeptic God of America, you were in a bad mood that winter. We were poor, and you punished us harshly for this worst of sins.

III

My father lay in bed. His shattered feet ached in each bone. His painter's sickness came back on him; he suffered with lung and kidney pains.

He was always depressed. His only distraction was to read the Yiddish newspapers, and to make gloomy conversation at night over the suicides, the hungry families, the robberies, murders, and catastrophes that newspapers record.

"It will come to an end!" said my father. "People are turning into wolves! They will soon eat each other! They will tear down the cities, and destroy the world in flames and blood!"

"Drink your tea," said my mother cheerfully, "God is still in the world. You will get better and work and laugh again. Let us not lose courage."

My father was fretful and nervous with an invalid's fears.

"But what if we are evicted, Katie?"

"We won't be evicted, not while I have my two hands and can work," said my mother.

"But I don't want you to work!" my father cried. "It breaks up our home!"

"It doesn't!" said my mother. "I have time and strength for everything."

IV

At first my mother had feared going out to work in a cafeteria among Christians. But after a few days she settled easily into the life of the polyglot kitchen, and learned to fight, scold, and mother the Poles, Germans, Italians, Irish, and Negroes who worked there. They liked her, and soon called her "Momma," which made her vain.

"You should hear how a big black dishwasher named Joe, how he comes to me today, and says, 'Momma, I'm going to quit. Everyone is against me here because I am black,' he says. 'The whole world is against us black people.'

"So I said to him, 'Joe, I am not against you. Don't be foolish, don't go out to be a bum again. The trouble with you here is you are lazy. If you would work harder the others would like you, too.' So he said, 'Momma, all right, I'll stay.' So that's how it is in the restaurant. They call me Momma, even the black ones."

It was a large, high-priced cafeteria for businessmen on lower Broadway. My mother was a chef's helper, and peeled and scoured tons of vegetables for cooking. Her wages were seven dollars a week.

She woke at five, cooked our breakfast at home, then had to walk a mile to her job. She came home at five-thirty, and made supper, cleaned the house, was busy on her feet until bedtime. It hurt my father's masculine pride to see his wife working for wages. But my mother liked it all; she was proud of earning money, and she liked her fights in the restaurant.

My dear, tireless, little dark-faced mother! Why did she always have to fight? Why did she have to give my father a new variety of headache with accounts of her battles for "justice" in the cafeteria? The manager there was a fat, blond Swede with a *Kaiserliche* [2] mustache, and the manners of a Mussolini. All the workers feared this bull-necked tyrant, except my mother. She told him "what was what." When the meat was rotten, when the drains were

---

[2] *Kaiserliche* (kī′zər·lĭḵ): Yiddish for a full mustache, twisted and pointed at the ends, like the one worn by the Kaiser, or Emperor, of Germany at the end of the nineteenth century.

clogged and smelly, or the dishwashers overworked, she told him so. She scolded him as if he were her child, and he listened meekly. The other workers fell into the habit of telling their complaints to my mother, and she would relay them to the Swedish manager.

"It's because he needs me," said my mother proudly. "That's why he lets me scold him. I am one of his best workers; he can depend on me in the rush. And he knows I am not like the other kitchen help; they work a day or two, then quit, but I stay on. So he's afraid to fire me, and I tell him what is what."

It was one of those super-cafeterias, with flowers on the tables, a string orchestra during the lunch hour, and other trimmings. But my mother had no respect for it. She would never eat the lunch served there to the employees, but took along two cheese sandwiches from home.

"Your food is *Dreck*,[3] it is fit only for pigs," she told the manager bluntly. And once she begged me to promise never to eat hamburger steak in a restaurant when I grew up.

"Swear it to me, Mikey!" she said. "Never, never eat hamburger!"

"I swear it, momma."

"Poison!" she went on passionately. "They don't care if they poison the people, so long as there's money in it. I've seen with my own eyes. If I could write English, I'd write a letter to all the newspapers."

"Mind your own business!" my father growled. "Such things are for Americans. It is their country and their hamburger steak."

for discussion

1. What is the social significance of the narrator's remark that the eyes and nose of the snowman "had been torn out"?
2. In what way is the statement "Kindness is a form of suicide in a world based on the law of competition" critical of the American way of life?

3. How does the last section reveal the separation immigrants felt between themselves and native-born Americans?

[3] *Dreck* (drek): Yiddish for "garbage."

1918–1956

ISAAC ROSENFELD

☐ *Isaac Rosenfeld was born in Chicago in 1918. In 1941,
after completing his education at the University of
Chicago, he moved to New York. There he briefly took
graduate courses in philosophy and worked as an editor
for several of the liberal political periodicals. By the
mid-1940's, Rosenfeld had been recognized as one of the
most promising young essayists and short story writers
in New York.*

*From 1941 to 1952 Isaac Rosenfeld lived in New York.
But in one sense he never made New York, or Chicago,
his home; he seems always to have felt he was an
outsider, at home nowhere. Rosenfeld was acutely
sensitive to being a Jew and an American. But he was no
less aware that he was something more—a human. In his
life, he acted out all of these roles with an extraordinary
honesty and selflessness. His writing constantly reflects
his attempt to define his identity and to integrate his life.
Unfortunately, whether as Jew or American or human
being, Rosenfeld seems to have felt himself an alienated
man who survived only by his wits and his psychological
toughness. But as a writer he took brilliant advantage
of the insight into the personal and social anxieties of our
time that came from his own alienated vision. Out of
Rosenfeld's need to define his identity and to chart his
world came the autobiographical novel* Passage from
Home *(published in 1946), the essays in* An Age of
Enormity *(1962), and the stories in* Alpha and Omega
(1966).

the situation of the jewish writer

☐ All discussions pertaining to the Jews must begin with some very gloomy observations. The Jews are, everywhere, a minority group, and it is a particular misfortune these days [1] to be a minority group in the United States. A conscious member of such a group is necessarily overconscious: he is distracted by race and religion, distressed by differences which in a healthy society would be considered healthful. The very simple state of being a Jew—and it should occupy no more of a man's attention than any ordinary fact of his history—has created traumas, fears of violence, defenses against aggression. These are about the worst conditions under which an artist could seek to carry on his work. An artist should first of all have the security of a dignified neutrality. He should be able to consider himself a *mensch mit alle menschen gleich*—that is, an equal, a man among men, a representative even if extraordinary individual. But a Jewish writer unconsciously feels that he may at any time be called to account not for his art, nor even for his life, but for his Jewishness. Only a brave man can be a brave artist, let alone a good one, in a hostile world. It is therefore clear to me that whatever contribution Jewish writers may make to American literature will depend on matters beyond their control as writers.

But the position of Jewish writers—artists and intellectuals in general—is not entirely an unfortunate one. For the most part, the young Jewish writers of today are the children of immigrants, and as such—not completely integrated in society and yet not wholly foreign to it—they enjoy a critical advantage over the life that surrounds them. They are bound to observe much that is hidden to the more accustomed native eye.

The insight available to most Jewish writers is a natural

[1] This essay was first published in 1944.

result of their position in American life and culture. Jews are marginal men. As marginal men, living in cities and coming from the middle classes, they are open to more influences than perhaps any other group. I vaguely recall a Yiddish proverb to the effect that bad luck always knows where to find a Jew; and as a barometer of political calamity the Jews in this country are second only to the Negroes. But even gentler influences, short of fatality, know where to find Jews—in the middle, in the overlapping area where events converge. And the middle position has its cultural correlate, that of being centrally exposed to all movements in art and in thought. This position of cultural exposure gives the Jewish writer the advantage of access. (There is much more to be said about this point—more than I have the space or the knowledge to disclose. But, generally speaking, the position of Jewish writers illustrates one of the strangest phenomena of modern life. Since modern life is so complex that no man can possess it in its entirety, the outsider often finds himself the perfect insider.)

Close as they are to the main developments in America, some Jewish writers may retain more than a little of European culture. Either through their position in the Jewish community, their childhood, or the influence of their immigrant parents, they may possess a sense of reference to an earlier community. I don't know how widespread this old-world feeling is among Jewish writers. But if it is at all common, I should say it is a valuable thing. Jews in America have relatively little contact with country life, with small-town folk and farmers. But through cultural retention, through a subliminal orientation to more primitive surroundings, they may still find in themselves access to rural life, understanding of its character and traditions.

But it is one thing to consider the Jewish writer's social equipment, and quite another to regard his actual position in society. As a member of an internationally insecure group, he has grown personally acquainted with some of the fundamental themes of insecurity that run through modern literature. He is a specialist in alienation (the one international banking system the Jews actually control). Alienation puts him in touch with his own past traditions, the history of the Diaspora;[2] with the present predicament of almost all intellectuals and, for all one knows, with the future conditions of civilized humanity. Today nearly all sensibility —thought, creation, perception—is in exile, alienated from the society in which it barely managed to stay alive.

But alienation from society, like the paradox of the outsider, may function as a condition of entrance into society. Surely it is not a condition for the Jew's re-entrance into the world that has rejected him. But persecution may lead him, as it has in the past, to a further effort to envisage the good society. No man suffers injustice without learning, vaguely but surely, what justice is. The desire for justice, once it passes beyond revenge, becomes the deepest motive for social change. Out of their recent sufferings one may expect Jewish writers to make certain inevitable moral discoveries. These discoveries, enough to indict the world, may also be crucial to its salvation.

I do not want to make too much of alienation. It is the only possible condition, the theme we have to work with, but it is undesirable, for it falls short of the full human range. Besides, in every society, in every group, there are what Saul Bellow has called "colonies of the spirit." Artists create their colonies. Some day these may become empires.

for discussion

1. What does Rosenfeld mean when he says that, owing to the complexity of modern American life, "the outsider often finds himself the perfect insider"?

2. Explain why the author thinks it desirable that urban Jewish writers should possess some understanding of rural life.

3. What, according to Rosenfeld, is the advantage of the artist's existing in an alienated condition? What is the disadvantage?

[2] *Diaspora:* the scattering of the Jews throughout Asia and Europe that began with the destruction of their nation by the Assyrians and Babylonians during the eighth, seventh, and sixth centuries B.C.

born 1914

RALPH ELLISON

☐ *Born and reared in Oklahoma City, Ralph Ellison left Oklahoma in 1933 to study music at Tuskegee Institute in Alabama. He had played the trumpet since he was eight years old, and when he entered college it seemed certain that he was bound for a career in music. But while in college Ellison began to read widely in American literature, and by the time he moved to New York in 1936 his interests had broadened to include sculpture and literature.*

The first publication of Ralph Ellison's writing came in 1937, when he wrote a book review for a little magazine edited by Richard Wright in New York. But Ellison was not generally recognized as a writer until the early 1950's. In 1953 he became widely known by winning the National Book Award for his novel Invisible Man, *which was published in 1952. Since that occasion, Ralph Ellison has been firmly established as one of the most talented contemporary American writers. His conception of the black American as an "invisible man" has been admired for its insight into human relations in America and into human behavior generally. But this breadth of vision was not always so clearly the mark of Ellison's art. Very early in his career, during the late 1930's and early 1940's, Ellison expressed more directly his sense of frustration with his society and his anger against its injustices. Although even these early writings are very different from the raw, documentary realism of the "protest" writers of that period, they reveal an Ellison more troubled by the fact and the consequences of being black than was the author of* Invisible Man.

☐ The boy looked at me through the cracked door and stood staring with his large eyes until his mother came and invited me in. It was an average Harlem apartment, cool now with the shift in the fall weather. The room was clean and furnished with the old-fashioned furniture found so often up our way, two old upholstered chairs and a divan upon a faded blue and red rug. It was painfully clean, and the furniture crowded the narrow room.

"Sit right there, sir," the woman said. "It's where Wilbur use to sit before he went to camp, it's pretty comfortable."

I watched her ease herself tiredly upon the divan, the light from the large red lamp reflected upon her face from the top of a mirrored side table.

She must have been fifty, her hair slightly graying. The portrait of a young soldier smiled back from the top of a radio cabinet beside her.

She pointed. "That's my boy Wilbur right there," she said proudly. "He's a sergeant."

"Wilbur's got a medal for shooting so good," the boy said.

"You just be quiet and go eat your supper," she said. "All you can think about is guns and shooting." She spoke with the harsh tenderness so often used by Negro mothers.

The boy went, reluctantly opening the door. The odor of peas and rice and pork chops drifted through.

"Who was it, Tommy?" shrilled a voice on the other side.

"You two be quiet in there and eat your supper now," Mrs. Jackson called. "Them two just keeps my hands full. They just get into something *all* the time. I was coming up the street the other day and like to got the fright of my life.

"The Way It Is" by Ralph Ellison, copyright 1942 by Weekly Masses Co., Inc., from *Shadow and Act* by Ralph Ellison. Reprinted by permission of the publisher, Random House, Inc.

There was Tommy hanging on the back of a streetcar! But didn't I tan his bottom! I bet he won't even *look* at a streetcar for a long, long time. It ain't really that he's a *bad* child, it's just that he tries to do what he sees the other boys do. I wanted to send both him and his sister away to camp for the summer, but things was so tight this year that I couldn't do it. Raising kids in Harlem nowadays is more than a notion."

As is true so often in Negro American life, Mrs. Jackson, the mother, is the head of her family. Her husband had died several years ago; the smaller children were babies. She had kept going by doing domestic work and had kept the family together with the help of the older boy.

There is a quiet courage about Mrs. Jackson. And yet now and then the clenching and unclenching of her work-hardened fingers betray an anxiety that does not register in her face. I offer to wait until after she has eaten, but she says no, that she is too tired right now and she would rather talk than eat.

"You finding the writing business any better since the war?" she asked.

"I'm afraid not," I said.

"Is that so? Well, I don't know nothing about the writing business. I just know that don't many colored go in for it. But I guess like everything else, some folks is doing good while others ain't. The other day I was over on 126th Street and saw them dispossessing a lawyer! Yes, sir, it was like back in the thirties. Things piled all over the sidewalk, the Negroes a-hanging out of the windows, and the poor man rushing around trying to get his stuff off the streets before it got dark, and everything."

I remembered the incident myself, having passed through the street that afternoon. Files, chest of drawers, bedsteads, tables and barrels had been piled along the sidewalk; with pink, blue, and white mattresses and bundles of table linen and bedclothing piled on top. And the crowd had been as she described: some indignant, some curious, and all talking in subdued tones so as not to offend the evicted family. Law books had been piled upon the sidewalk near where a black and white kitten—and these are no writer's details

—played games with itself in the coils of an upright bed-spring. I told her I had seen the incident.

"Lord," she said. "And did you see all those law books he had? Looks like to me that anybody with all those books of law oughtn't to never get dispossessed.

"I was dispossessed, myself, back in thirty-seven, when we were all out of work. And they threatened me once since Wilbur's been in the Army. But I stood up for my rights and when the government sent the check we pulled through. Anybody's liable to get dispossessed though." She said it defensively.

"Just how do you find it otherwise?" I asked.

"Things is mighty tight, son. . . . You'll have to excuse me for calling you 'son,' because I suspect you must be just about Wilbur's age."

She sat back abruptly. "How come you not in the Army?" she asked.

"I've a wife and dependents," I said.

"I see," she pondered. "Wilbur would have got married too, but he was helping me with the kids."

"That's the way it goes," I said.

"Things is tight," she said again. "With food so high and everything I sometimes don't know what's going to happen. Then, too, with Wilbur in the Army we naturally misses the money he use to bring in."

She regarded me shrewdly. "So you want to know about how we're doing? Don't you live in Harlem?"

"Oh, yes, but I want to know what *you* think about it."

"So's you can write it up?"

"Some of it, sure. But I won't use your name."

"Oh I don't care 'bout that. I *want* them to know how I feel."

She became silent. Then, "You didn't tell me where you live, you know," she said cagily. I had to laugh and she laughed too.

"I live up near Amsterdam Avenue," I said.

"You telling me the truth?"

"Honest."

"And is your place a nice one?"

"Just average. You know how they go," I said.

"I bet you live up there on Sugar Hill." [1]

"Not me," I said.

"And you're sure you're not one of these investigators?"

"Of course not."

"I bet you are too." She smiled.

I shook my head and she laughed.

"They always starting something new," she said. "You can't keep up with them."

But now she seemed reassured and settled down to talk, her hands clasped loosely in her lap against the checkered design of her dress.

"Well, we're carrying on somehow. I'm still working and I manage to keep the young uns in school, and I pays the rent too. I guess maybe it would be a little better if the government would send the checks on time. . . ."

She paused and pointed across the room to the picture of a young woman. "And it would be even better if Mary, that's my next oldest after Wilbur—if she could get some of that defense training so she could get a job what pays decent money. But don't look like she's going to get anything. She was out to the Western Electric plant in Kearney, New Jersey, the other day and they give her some kind of test, but that was the end of that."

"Did she pass the test?" I asked.

"Sure she passed. But they just put her name down on a card and told her they would keep her in mind. They always do that. They ask her a lot of questions, then they want to know if she ever had any experience in running machines, and when she says she ain't, they just take down her name. Now where is a colored girl going to get any experience in running all these kinds of machines they never even seen before?"

When I could not answer she threw up her hands.

"Well, there you have it, they got you any which way you turn. A few gets jobs, but most don't."

"Things are much better outside of New York," I said.

[1] *Sugar Hill:* a section of Harlem in which wealthy Negroes lived at the time this essay was written. Amsterdam Avenue is a long street passing through impoverished, comfortable, and affluent neighborhoods, including Sugar Hill.

"So I hear," she said. "Guess if I was younger I'd take the kids and move to Jersey or up to Connecticut, where I hear there's some jobs for colored. Or even down South. Only I keep hearing about the trouble they're having down there. And I don't want the kids to grow up down there nohow. Had enough of that when I was a kid. . . . ."

"Have any of your friends gotten work through the F.E.P.C.?" [2]

She thought for a moment.

"No, son. It seems to me that that committee is doing something everywhere but here in New York. Maybe that's why it's so bad for us—and you know it's bad 'cause you're colored yourself."

As I heard the clatter of dishes coming from the kitchen, her face suddenly assumed an outraged expression.

"Now you take my sister's boy, William. God bless his poor soul. William went to the trade schools and learned all about machines. He got so he could take any kind of machine apart and fix it and put it together again. He was machine-crazy! But he was a smart boy and a good boy. He got good marks in school too. But when he went to get a job in one of those factories where they make war machines of some kind, they wouldn't take him 'cause he was colored—*and they told him so!*"

She paused for breath, a red flush dyeing her skin. The tinted portrait of a brown mother holding a brown, shiny-haired baby posed madonna-like from a calendar above her head.

"Well, when they wouldn't take him some of the folks over to the church told him to take his case to the F.E.P.C., and he did. But they had so many cases and it took so long that William got discouraged and joined up in the Merchant Marine. That poor boy was just so disgusted that he said that he would have enlisted in the Army, only that his mamma's got two little ones like I have. So he went out on that boat 'cause it paid good money and a good bonus. It was real good money and he helped his mamma a heap. But

[2] *F.E.P.C.*: the federal Fair Employment Practices Commission, created by presidential order in 1941 in response to threats of massive protest by Negroes against discriminatory employment practices, especially in defense industries.

it didn't last long before one of those submarines sunk the boat."

Her eyes strayed to the window, where a line of potted plants crowded the sill: a profusion of green things, slowly becoming silhouettes in the fading light. Snake plants, English ivy, and others, a potato plant in a glass jar, its vines twining around a cross of wood and its thousand thread-fine roots pushing hungrily against the wall of glass. A single red bloom pushed above the rest, and in one corner a corn plant threatened to touch the ceiling from the floor with its blade-like leaves.

The light was fading and her voice had slipped into the intense detachment of recent grief. "It was just about four months yesterday," she said. "He was such a fine boy. Everybody liked William."

She shook her head silently, her fingers gripping her folded arms as she swallowed tensely.

"It hurts to think about it," she said, getting up and snapping on another light, revealing a child's airplane model beneath the table. "Well, the folks from his union is being very nice to my sister, the whites as well as the colored. And you know," she added, leaning toward me, "it really makes you feel a little better when they come round—the white ones, I mean—and really tries to help. Like some of these ole relief investigators who come in wanting to run your life for you, but really like they interested in you. Something like colored folks in a way. We used to get after William for being with white folks so much, but these sure have shown themselves to be real friends."

She stared at me as though it was a fact which she deeply feared to accept.

"Some of them is going to try and see that my sister gets some sort of defense work. But what I'm trying to tell you is that it's a sin and a shame that a fine boy like William had to go fooling round on them ships when ever since he was a little ole boy he'd been crazy about machines."

"But don't you think that the Merchant Marine is helping to win the war?" I said. "It takes brave men to go out there, and they've done a lot."

"Sure they have," she said. "Sure they have. But I'm not talking about that. Anybody could do what they had him doing on that boat. Anybody can wait tables who's got sense enough to keep his fingernails clean! Waiting tables, when he could *make* things on a machine!

"You see that radio there? Well, William made that radio. It ain't no store set, no, sir, even though it looks like one. William made it for the kids. Made everything but the cabinet, and you can hear way down to Cuba and Mexico with it. And to think of that boy! Oh, it makes me so mad I don't know what to do! He ought to be here right now helping his mamma and lil brother and sister. But what can you do? You educated, son, you one of our educated Negroes that's been to college and everything. Now you tell me, *what can we do?*" She paused. "I'm a colored woman, and colored women can take it. I can hit the chillies [3] to the subway every morning and stand in the white folks' kitchen all day long, but so much is happening in the world that I don't know which way to turn. First it's my sister's boy and then they sends my own boy down to Fort Bragg. I tells you I'm even afraid to open Wilbur's letters, some of the things he tells is so awful. I'm even afraid to open letters that the *government* sends sometimes about his insurance or something like that, 'cause I'm afraid it might be a message that Wilbur's been beaten up or killed by some of those white folks down there. Then I gets so mad I don't know what to do. I use to pray, but praying don't do no good. And too, like the union folks was telling us when we was so broken up about William, we got to fight the big Hitler over yonder even with all the little Hitlers over here. I wish they'd hurry up and send Wilbur on out of the country 'cause then maybe my mind would know some ease. Lord!" she sighed. "If it wasn't so serious I'd break down and laugh at my ownself."

She smiled now and the tension eased from her face and she leaned back against the divan and laughed. Then she became serious again.

"But, son, you really can't laugh about it. Not honestly laugh like you can about some things. It reminds me of that

[3] *chillies:* cold, unfriendly streets.

crazy man what's always running up and down the streets up here. You know, the one who's always hollering at the cars and making out like he's throwing bombs?"

"Of course, I've seen him often," I said.

"Sure you have. Well, I use to laugh at that poor man when he'd start acting the fool—you know how it is, you feel sorry for him but you can't help but laugh. They say he got that way in the last war. Well, I can understand him better now. Course I ain't had no bombs bursting in my ears like he had. But yet and still, with things pulling me thisaway and thataway, I sometimes feel that I'm going to go screaming up and down the streets just like that poor fellow does."

"He's shell-shocked," I said. "Sometimes I've seen him talking and acting just as normal as anyone."

"Is that so?" she said. "I always thought it was funny he never got hit by a car. I've seen them almost hit him, but he goes right back. One day I heard a man say, Lord, if that crazy fellow really had some bombs he'd get rid of every car in Harlem!"

We laughed and I prepared to go.

"Sorry you found me so gloomy today, son. But you know, things have a way of just piling up these days and I just had to talk about them. Anyway, you asked for me to tell you what I thought."

She walked with me to the door. Street lamps glowed on the avenue, lighting the early dark. The after-school cries of children drifted dimly in from the sidewalk.

She shivered close beside me.

"It's getting chilly already," she said. "I'm wondering what's going to happen this winter about the oil and coal situation. These ole holes we have to live in can get mighty cold. Now can't they though?"

I agreed.

"A friend of mine that moved up on Amsterdam Avenue about a month ago wanted to know why I don't move out of Harlem. So I told her it wouldn't do no good to move 'cause anywhere they let us go gets to be Harlem right on. I done moved round too much not to know that. Oh yes!"

She shook her head knowingly.

"Harlem's like that old song says:

> *It's so high you can't get over it*
> *So low, you can't get under it,*
> *And so wide, you can't get round it. . . .*

"That's the way it really is," she said. "Well, good-bye, son."

And as I went down the dimmed-out street the verse completed itself in my mind, *You must come through by the living gate. . . .*

So there you have Mrs. Jackson. And that's the way "it really is" for her and many like her who are searching for that gate of freedom. In the very texture of their lives there is confusion, war-made confusion. And the problem is to get around, over, under, and through this confusion. They do not ask for a lighter share of necessary war sacrifices than other Americans have to bear. But they do ask for equal reasons to believe that their sacrifices are worthwhile, and they *do* want to be rid of the heavy resentment and bitterness which has been theirs for long before the war.

Forced in normal times to live at standards much lower than those the war has brought to the United States generally, they find it emotionally difficult to give their attention to the war. The struggle for existence constitutes a war in itself. The Mrs. Jacksons of Harlem offer one of the best arguments for the stabilization of prices and the freezing of rents. For twenty-five percent of those still on relief come from our five percent of New York's population. Mrs. Jackson finds it increasingly difficult to feed her children. She must pay six cents more on the dollar for food than do the mothers of similar-income sections of the city. And with the prospect of a heatless winter, Harlem, with its poor housing and high tuberculosis death rate, will know an increase of hardship.

It is an old story. Touch any phase of urban living in our democracy and its worst aspects are to be found in Harlem. Our housing is the poorest, and our rents the highest. Our people are the sickest, and Harlem Hospital the most overcrowded and understaffed. Our unemployment is the greatest, and our cost of food the most exorbitant. Our crime the most understandable and easily corrected, but the policemen sent among us the most brutal. Our desire to rid the world of fascism the most burning, and the obstacles placed in our way the most frustrating. Our need to see the war as a struggle between democracy and fascism the most intense, and our temptation to interpret it as a "color" war the most compelling. Our need to believe in the age of the "common man" the most hope-inspiring, and our reasons to doubt that it will include us the most disheartening (this is no Whitmanesque catalogue of democratic exultations, while more than anything else we wish that it could be). And that's the way it is.

Many of Mrs. Jackson's neighbors are joining in the fight to freeze rents and for the broadening of the F.E.P.C., for Negroes and all other Americans. Their very lives demand that they back the President's stabilization program. That they must be victorious is one of the necessities upon which our democratic freedom rests. The Mrs. Jacksons cannot make the sacrifices necessary to participate in a total war if the conditions under which they live, the very ground on which they must fight, continues its offensive against them. Nor is this something to be solved by propaganda. Morale grows out of realities, not out of words alone. Only concrete action will be effective—lest irritation and confusion turn into exasperation, and exasperation change to disgust and finally into anti-war sentiment (and there is such a danger). Mrs. Jackson's reality must be democratized so that she may clarify her thinking and her emotions. And that's the way it really is.

for discussion

1. In presenting his report on the way things "really" are, Ellison relies heavily upon the direct testimony of Mrs. Jackson. What does his narrative gain from this manner of presentation?

2. In what way do the constant references to the second World War intensify the social criticism expressed by Mrs. Jackson and by the narrator?

3. What does Mrs. Jackson's evident suspicion of the narrator suggest to you?

4. Does the narrator speak entirely as a black man? How would you define the narrator's cultural identity?

1872–1906

PAUL LAURENCE DUNBAR

☐ *Paul Laurence Dunbar was born in Dayton, Ohio, and attended its public schools. After graduating from high school, he stayed in Dayton, working as an elevator operator and occasionally publishing his poems in local newspapers. In 1893, at his own expense, he published a booklet of his poems,* Oak and Ivy. *Encouraged by friends, Dunbar published a second book of poems,* Majors and Minors, *in 1895. A copy of this book came to the attention of William Dean Howells, the leader of the new movement toward greater realism in American writing. Howells's strongly approving review of* Majors and Minors *dramatically raised Dunbar in 1896 out of total obscurity into the bright light of national acclaim. Dunbar's most famous book,* Lyrics of Lowly Life, *was published later the same year, with an introduction by Howells that proclaimed Dunbar the first black American to achieve genuine literary distinction.*

To Dunbar's sorrow and frustration, what Howells and the public most relished was the supposed authenticity of the sentimental and uncomplaining plantation lyrics Dunbar wrote in such dialect poems as "A Banjo Song":

> Oh, dere's lots o' keer an' trouble
>   In dis world to swaller down;
> An' ol' Sorrer's purty lively
>   In her way o' gittin' roun'.
> Yet dere's times when I furgit 'em—
>   Aches an' pains an' troubles all—
> An' it's when I tek at ebenin'
>   My ol' banjo f'om de wall.

Dunbar felt alienated from his success as a black good-will ambassador to the white literary world, and he felt artistically unfulfilled as a balladeer of black rural life. He longed to write solely as a poet of the English language, as a voice of universally human values, as a lover of beauty for whom the consideration of race was irrelevant. Thus, many of the poems in Lyrics of Lowly Life were written in an elegantly formal language which in no way reveals that their author is black. The poem written after the death of the black abolitionist Frederick Douglass is such a poem:

> A hush is over all the teeming lists,
>   And there is pause, a breath-space in the strife;
> A spirit brave has passed beyond the mists
>   And vapors that obscure the sun of life.

But the advocates of literary realism, on the one hand, and the white reading public with its stereotyped view of Negroes, on the other, reserved their enthusiasm for Dunbar's dialect lyrics of plantation life. Surely it was out of his own despair that Dunbar wrote "The Poet," which follows.

Nevertheless, in a few of his poems, the agonizing ambiguity of his experience as a black American took full possession of his pen, so that he spoke neither as a plantation hand nor as a latter-day English Romantic poet. In "We Wear the Mask," Dunbar achieved a remarkably effective fusion of art and anger.

the poet

> He sang of life, serenely sweet,
>   With, now and then, a deeper note.
>   From some high peak, nigh yet remote,
> He voiced the world's absorbing beat.
>
> He sang of love when earth was young,
>   And Love, itself, was in his lays.
>   But ah, the world, it turned to praise
> A jingle in a broken tongue.

we wear the mask

We wear the mask that grins and lies,
It hides our cheeks and shades our eyes—
This debt we pay to human guile;
With torn and bleeding hearts we smile,
And mouth with myriad subtleties.

Why should the world be over-wise,
In counting all our tears and sighs?
Nay, let them only see us, while
    We wear the mask.

We smile, but, O great Christ, our cries
To thee from tortured souls arise.
We sing, but oh the clay is vile
Beneath our feet, and long the mile;
But let the world dream otherwise,
    We wear the mask!

for discussion

1. In "The Poet," what is "some high peak, nigh yet remote"? What is the "broken tongue"?

2. What is the most obvious interpretation of the statement "We wear the mask"? What are some of the meanings of the word *mask* that make it an especially good metaphor for the social situation of black Americans?

3. Does the speaker regard his "mask" as self-imposed or socially imposed? Or both? Is his tone one of resignation or reproach?

4. Is there a veiled threat in the last line which is not present in the first statement that "We wear the mask"?

"We Wear the Mask" from *The Complete Poems of Paul Laurence Dunbar.* Reprinted by permission of the publisher, Dodd, Mead & Company, Inc.

1903–1946
COUNTEE CULLEN

☐ Except for a year of graduate study at Harvard and
frequent visits to Europe, Countee Cullen spent nearly all
of his life in New York City. He was raised in Harlem.
He graduated from the New York public schools and
from New York University. And during the last decade of
his life he was a public school teacher in Harlem.

As a high school student, Cullen excitedly discovered
the poems of Paul Laurence Dunbar; but he did not
share the popular enthusiasm for Dunbar's dialect poems
of plantation life. Instead he admired Dunbar's verses
in "literary" English. Intelligent and ambitious, Cullen
quickly established himself as one of the most cultivated
poets of the Harlem Renaissance. In college Cullen had
read widely in European and English literature. He
was drawn to the Romantic poets and especially to Keats
and Tennyson. Accordingly, many of Cullen's poems
are nonracial in perspective. In these poems he writes of
universal human experiences and reveals his consuming
desire to achieve recognition as a genuine poet of the
English language.

But a significant number of Cullen's poems—while
carefully avoiding dialect—testify to his unmistakable
personal distress over the frustrations of black
Americans and protest the indignities that are the
common experience of blacks. Thus, he was torn by
his divided loyalties: he felt alternately at home and a
stranger in America; he felt by turns a poet and a Negro.
Cullen was acutely conscious of his dilemma, as the
following self-characterization shows:

A number of times I have said I wanted to be a poet
and known as such and not as a Negro poet.
Somehow or other, however, I find my poetry of
itself treating of the Negro, of his joys and his

sorrows—mostly of the latter—and of the heights
and depths of emotion which I feel as a Negro.°

Countee Cullen's first book of poems was Color,
which was published in 1925 while he was still a college
student. It was followed by Copper Sun *and* The Black
Christ, *published in 1927 and 1929. Shortly before his*
death in 1946, Cullen made a selection of the poems by
which he wished finally to be represented. Titled
On These I Stand, *the book was published in 1947.*

°From selection by Countee Cullen from *Living Authors: A Book of Biographies,* edited by Dilly Tante. Reprinted by permission of the publisher, The H. W. Wilson Co.

to certain critics

Then call me traitor if you must,
Shout treason and default!
Say I betray a sacred trust
Aching beyond this vault.
I'll bear your censure as your praise,
For never shall the clan
Confine my singing to its ways
Beyond the ways of man.

No racial option narrows grief,
Pain is no patriot,
And sorrow plaits her dismal leaf
For all as lief as not.
With blind sheep groping every hill,
Searching an oriflamme,
How shall the shepherd heart then thrill
To only the darker lamb?

"To Certain Critics" from *On These I Stand* by Countee Cullen, copyright 1929 by Harper & Brothers; renewed 1957 by Ida M. Cullen. Reprinted by permission of the publisher, Harper & Row Publishers, Inc.

yet do i marvel

I doubt not God is good, well-meaning, kind,
And did He stoop to quibble could tell why
The little buried mole continues blind,
Why flesh that mirrors Him must some day die,
Make plain the reason tortured Tantalus
Is baited by the fickle fruit, declare
If merely brute caprice dooms Sisyphus
To struggle up a never-ending stair.
Inscrutable His ways are, and immune
To catechism by a mind too strewn
With petty cares to slightly understand
What awful brain compels His awful hand.
Yet do I marvel at this curious thing:
To make a poet black, and bid him sing!

incident

Once riding in old Baltimore,
    Heart-filled, head-filled with glee,
I saw a Baltimorean
    Keep looking straight at me.

Now I was eight and very small,
    And he was no whit bigger,
And so I smiled, but he poked out
    His tongue, and called me "Nigger."

I saw the whole of Baltimore
From May until December;
Of all the things that happened there
That's all that I remember.

for discussion

1. Who are the "blind sheep" in "To Certain Critics"? If the shepherd heart did thrill "To only the darker lamb," how might Cullen's poetry have been affected?
2. What is the chief meaning of "awful" in the twelfth line of "Yet Do I Marvel"? How are other meanings of *awful* relevant to the poem?

3. All of Cullen's poems reveal his close attention to the craft of poetry in their customary precision and symmetry. Does this concern with formal orderliness and correctness seem to you a virtue or a defect in his poetry? Does the insistent regularity of Cullen's verses seem less effective in one poem than in another?

1902–1967

LANGSTON HUGHES

☐ *Although Hughes first came to Harlem in 1921 as a young man from the Midwest, he quickly found himself at home there and soon became Harlem's best-known literary spokesman. By 1925 he had become closely associated with the Harlem Renaissance. This vigorous new movement of young black artists and intellectuals encouraged black Americans to feel greater pride in the black community—on the one hand, by demonstrating the richness of black culture; on the other, by showing white Americans that black artists could produce work which met traditional standards of artistic merit. Hughes was especially interested in revealing the distinctive features of Negro life, its characteristic attitudes and its essential emotions. He aimed to make his poetry as expressive of the Negro's angle of vision as spirituals and jazz are. Thus, Hughes disagreed with those Harlem*

Renaissance poets who wished to show their artistry by "rising above" racial themes to the lofty plane of universal experience. He called such writers "the Nordicized Negro intelligentsia."

Hughes identified with the uneducated, working-class blacks who "live on Seventh Street in Washington or State Street in Chicago and . . . do not particularly care whether they are like white folks or anybody else." "These common people," said Hughes, "are not afraid of spirituals, as for a long time their more intellectual brethren were, and jazz is their child." In order to distinguish his brand of Harlem Renaissance poetry from that of poets such as Countee Cullen, he said in 1926, "Most of my own poems are racial in theme and treatment, derived from the life I know."

Since his earliest sympathies were with working-class blacks, it is not surprising that Hughes turned increasingly to social protest writing as the twenties gave way to the years of the great Depression. Following The Weary Blues in 1926, Hughes published many books of poems, culminating in the publication of his Selected Poems in 1959. His last books of poems were Ask Your Mama (1961) and The Panther and the Lash (1967).

as i grew older

It was a long time ago.
I have almost forgotten my dream.
But it was there then,
In front of me,
Bright like a sun—
My dream.

"As I Grew Older" by Langston Hughes, copyright 1926 by Alfred A. Knopf, Inc.; renewed 1954 by Langston Hughes, from *Selected Poems* by Langston Hughes. Reprinted by permission of the publisher, Alfred A. Knopf, Inc.

And then the wall rose,
Rose slowly,
Slowly,
Between me and my dream.
Rose slowly, slowly,
Dimming,
Hiding,
The light of my dream.
Rose until it touched the sky—
The wall.

Shadow.
I am black.

I lie down in the shadow.
No longer the light of my dream before me,
Above me.
Only the thick wall.
Only the shadow.

My hands!
My dark hands!
Break through the wall!
Find my dream!
Help me to shatter this darkness,
To smash this night,

To break this shadow
Into a thousand lights of sun,
Into a thousand whirling dreams
Of sun!

What happens to a dream deferred?

Does it dry up
like a raisin in the sun?
Or fester like a sore—
And then run?
Does it stink like rotten meat?
Or crust and sugar over—
like a syrupy sweet?

Maybe it just sags
like a heavy load.

Or does it explode?

for discussion

1. "As I Grew Older" and "Harlem" together speak of a dream once bright, now "deferred" and "almost forgotten." What is this dream?

2. Contrast the tone of the speaker in "As I Grew Older" with that of the speaker in "Harlem."

1908–1960

RICHARD WRIGHT

☐ *Anger is the ruling emotion in the art of Richard Wright. His autobiography,* Black Boy *(1945), reveals that he was early driven to feel and to express rage: the rage growing out of fear and hunger and frustration. Born and raised in the Deep South, Wright grew up in a world far removed from the Harlem Renaissance; he was reared in places where discrimination against black people was severe. Thus, not racial pride but the more primal concern for survival preoccupied him: "Watching the white people eat would make my empty stomach churn and I would grow vaguely angry. Why could I not eat when I was hungry?"*

Also, he came to fear "white" justice. He learned that black people were often treated brutally, that they were often beaten and killed by whites. In Black Boy, *he says the news that whites had killed the brother of one of his friends—for an alleged violation of the color line— left him with the belief that the "penalty of death awaited me if I made a false move." Lynching was a grim fact of life in the South during Wright's boyhood, and it produced in him terror and anger.*

between the world and me

And one morning while in the woods I stumbled suddenly
    upon the thing,
Stumbled upon it in a grassy clearing guarded by scaly oaks
    and elms.

"Between the World and Me" by Richard Wright from *Partisan Review*, Volume II, Number 8, July–August 1935, copyright 1935 by Richard Wright. Reprinted by permission of Paul R. Reynolds, Inc.

And the sooty details of the scene rose, thrusting themselves between the world and me. . . .

There was a design of white bones slumbering forgottenly upon a cushion of ashes.
There was a charred stump of a sapling pointing a blunt finger accusingly at the sky.
There were torn tree limbs, tiny veins of burnt leaves, and a scorched coil of greasy hemp;
A vacant shoe, an empty tie, a ripped shirt, a lonely hat, and a pair of trousers stiff with black blood.
And upon the trampled grass were buttons, dead matches, butt-ends of cigars and cigarettes, peanut shells, a drained gin-flask, and a whore's lipstick;
Scattered traces of tar, restless arrays of feathers, and the lingering smell of gasoline.
And through the morning air the sun poured yellow surprise into the eye sockets of a stony skull. . . .
And while I stood my mind was frozen with a cold pity for the life that was gone.
The ground gripped my feet and my heart was circled by icy walls of fear—
The sun died in the sky; a night wind muttered in the grass and fumbled the leaves in the trees; the woods poured forth the hungry yelping of hounds; the darkness screamed with thirsty voices; and the witnesses rose and lived:
The dry bones stirred, rattled, lifted, melting themselves into my bones.
The gray ashes formed flesh firm and black, entering into my flesh.
The gin-flask passed from mouth to mouth; cigars and cigarettes glowed, the whore smeared the lipstick red upon her lips,
And a thousand faces swirled around me, clamoring that my life be burned. . . .

And then they had me, stripped me, battering my teeth into my throat till I swallowed my own blood.
My voice was drowned in the roar of their voices, and my black wet body slipped and rolled in their hands as they bound me to the sapling.

And my skin clung to the bubbling hot tar, falling from me
   in limp patches.
And the down and quills of the white feathers sank into
   my raw flesh, and I moaned in my agony.
Then my blood was cooled mercifully, cooled by a baptism
   of gasoline.
And in a blaze of red I leaped to the sky as pain rose like
   water, boiling my limbs.
Panting, begging I clutched childlike, clutched to the hot
   sides of death.
Now I am dry bones and my face a stony skull staring in
   yellow surprise at the sun. . . .

for discussion

1. In what way does the repetition of words and details contribute to the poem's effect?
2. The poem obviously presents an account of a lynching, but that description is only part of the poem. As the title suggests, the speaker is centrally implicated in the poem's meaning. What change or development in the speaker's attitude toward life may be observed in his description of the lynching?

1900–1966

MELVIN B. TOLSON

☐ *Born in Missouri, Melvin Tolson was educated at Fisk, Lincoln, and Columbia universities. As a student, he displayed exceptional ability in classical studies, theater, and debate. And during a long career as a college teacher, he carried forward both his scholarly and his dramatic interests. At Langston University, he was both professor of creative literature and director of the Dust Bowl Theater.*

But Tolson was no less dedicated to the struggle of the black man in America. Long before it became fashionable for Negro intellectuals to do so, Tolson was

a "facer of mobs" and a defender of African culture.
He was a powerful and exciting speaker, at his best in
face-to-face confrontations. Tolson was a man of vast
range and energy—an encyclopedic student of Western
civilization, on the one hand; the four-term mayor of
Langston, Oklahoma, on the other. Asked to describe his
cross-grained and adventurous life, Tolson replied that
he was a part of all he had met

> as shoeshine boy, stevedore, soldier, janitor,
> packinghouse worker, cook on a railroad, waiter in
> beach-front hotels, boxer, actor, football coach,
> director of drama, lecturer for the NAACP, organizer
> of sharecroppers' unions, teacher, father of Ph.D.'s,
> poet laureate of a foreign country, painter,
> newspaper columnist, four-time mayor of a town,
> facer of mobs.°

Asked to describe the sources of his poetry, Tolson said
that he liked "to go about places, hobnob with people,
gather rich epithets and proverbs in churches and
taverns, in cotton fields and dance halls, in streets and
toilets." Tolson's life was a fertile union of his intellectual
and emotional appetites. He savored both ideas and
action, was equally responsive to great writers and
common humanity. What gave Tolson's unusually varied
life its unifying perspective was his full acceptance of his
identity as a black man and his primary loyalty to
Afro-American culture. Thus, he could say, "I, as a black
poet, have absorbed the Great Ideas of the Great White
World, and interpreted them in the melting-pot idiom
of my people. My roots are in Africa, Europe, and
America."

   Tolson's first book of poems, Rendezvous with
America, was published in 1944. Much of
Tolson's poetry of the thirties and early forties revealed
his anguished, outraged reaction to the plain
contradiction between the practice of racial segregation
and the avowed principles of American democracy. His
first book expressed defiance of that ugly contradiction,

°From selection by Melvin Tolson from Anger, and Beyond: The Negro
Writer in the United States, edited by Herbert Hill. Reprinted by permission of Harper & Row, Publishers, Inc.

but it also expressed a faith in the potential of American society for true fellowship.

dark symphony

I

Allegro Moderato [1]

Black Crispus Attucks [2] taught
           Us how to die
Before white Patrick Henry's bugle breath
Uttered the vertical
           Transmitting cry:
"Yea, give me liberty or give me death."

And from that day to this
           Men black and strong
For Justice and Democracy have stood,
Steeled in the faith that Right
           Will conquer Wrong
And Time will usher in one brotherhood.

No Banquo's ghost [3] can rise
           Against us now
And say we crushed men with a tyrant's boot
Or pressed the crown of thorns
           On Labor's brow,
Or ravaged lands and carted off the loot.

[1] *Allegro Moderato:* moderately fast tempo.

[2] *Crispus Attucks:* A black sailor who, together with four white colonists, was killed by British soldiers in the famous "Boston Massacre" of 1770. Their deaths aroused the determination of American colonists to insist upon their rights and, ultimately, to demand their freedom.

[3] *Banquo's ghost:* the ghost of the general whose murder was arranged by Shakespeare's Macbeth (*Macbeth*, Act III).

II

Lento Grave [4]

The centuries-old pathos in our voices
Saddens the great white world,
And the wizardry of our dusky rhythms
Conjures up shadow-shapes of ante-bellum years:

Black slaves singing *One More River to Cross*
In the torture tombs of slave-ships,
Black slaves singing *Steal Away to Jesus*
In jungle swamps,
Black slaves singing *The Crucifixion*
In slave-pens at midnight,
Black slaves singing *Swing Low, Sweet Chariot*
In cabins of death,
Black slaves singing *Go Down, Moses*
In the canebrakes of the Southern Pharaohs.

III

Andante Sostenuto [5]

They tell us to forget
The Golgotha [6] we tread . . .
We who are scourged with hate,
A price upon our head.
They who have shackled us
Require of us a song,
They who have wasted us
Bid us condone the wrong.

They tell us to forget
Democracy is spurned.
They tell us to forget
The Bill of Rights is burned.
Three hundred years we slaved,

[4] *Lento Grave:* slow and solemn.
[5] *Andante Sostenuto:* very moderate pace, between Allegro and Lento.
[6] *Golgotha:* Calvary; any place of torture.

We slave and suffer yet:
Though flesh and bone rebel,
They tell us to forget!

Oh, how can we forget
Our human rights denied?
Oh, how can we forget
Our manhood crucified?
When Justice is profaned
And plea with curse is met,
When Freedom's gates are barred,
Oh, how can we forget?

IV

Tempo Primo [7]

The New Negro strides upon the continent
In seven-league boots . . .
The New Negro
Who sprang from the vigor-stout loins
Of Nat Turner,[8] gallows-martyr for Freedom,
Of Joseph Cinquez,[9] Black Moses of the Amistad Mutiny,
Of Frederick Douglass,[10] oracle of the catholic Man,
Of Sojourner Truth,[11] eye and ear of Lincoln's legions,

[7] *Tempo Primo:* resume original speed (Allegro Moderato).

[8] *Nat Turner:* a Virginia slave who led a small but violent revolt against plantation slaveholders in 1831.

[9] *Joseph Cinquez:* the leader in a rebellion of fifty-three African slaves against their two Spanish masters in 1839. While being transported on the schooner *Amistad* from Havana to another Cuban seaport, the slaves seized the ship in a desperate effort to return to Africa. However, they were deceived by their captives into sailing north and west and were taken into custody off New York by an American warship. They were brought to trial; and, after much public and legal debate, the U.S. Supreme Court in 1841 ordered them set free.

[10] *Frederick Douglass:* a fugitive slave who became—largely through his ability as an orator—the foremost Negro abolitionist before the Civil War and one of the most effective black leaders of the postemancipation struggle to achieve genuine social equality for the black man in America.

[11] *Sojourner Truth:* a woman who was born a slave in upstate New York but became free in 1827 and traveled across America, speaking out powerfully against slavery. During the Civil War, she served as a lookout and spy for "Lincoln's legions."

Of Harriet Tubman, Saint Bernard [12] of the Underground
Railroad.

The New Negro
Breaks the icons of his detractors,
Wipes out the conspiracy of silence,
Speaks to *his* America:
"My history-molding ancestors
Planted the first crops of wheat on these shores,
Built ships to conquer the seven seas,
Erected the Cotton Empire,
Flung railroads across a hemisphere,
Disemboweled the earth's iron and coal,
Tunneled the mountains and bridged rivers,
Harvested the grain and hewed forests,
Sentineled the Thirteen Colonies,
Unfurled Old Glory at the North Pole,
Fought a hundred battles for the Republic."

The New Negro:
His giant hands fling murals upon high chambers,
His drama teaches a world to laugh and weep,
His music leads continents captive,
His voice thunders the Brotherhood of Labor,
His science creates seven wonders,
His Republic of Letters challenges the Negro-baiters.

The New Negro,
Hard-muscled, Fascist-hating, Democracy-ensouled,
Strides in seven-league boots
Along the Highway of Today
Toward the Promised Land of Tomorrow!

[12] *Harriet Tubman, Saint Bernard:* Harriet Tubman was an escaped
slave who made nineteen trips back into slave country and led more
than 300 slaves north to freedom on the Underground Railroad. Saint
Bernard is the patron saint of mountain climbers.

V

Larghetto [13]

None in the Land can say
To us black men Today:
You send the tractors on their bloody path,
And create Okies for *The Grapes of Wrath*.[14]
You breed the slum that breeds a *Native Son* [15]
To damn the good earth Pilgrim Fathers won.

None in the Land can say
To us black men Today:
You dupe the poor with rags-to-riches tales,
And leave the workers empty dinner pails.
You stuff the ballot box, and honest men
Are muzzled by your demagogic din.

None in the Land can say
To us black men Today:
You smash stock markets with your coined blitzkriegs,
And make a hundred million guinea pigs.
You counterfeit our Christianity,
And bring contempt upon Democracy.

None in the Land can say
To us black men Today:
You prowl when citizens are fast asleep,
And hatch Fifth Column [16] plots to blast the deep
Foundations of the State and leave the Land
A vast Sahara with a Fascist brand.

---

[13] *Larghetto:* slightly slower than Lento.
[14] *The Grapes of Wrath:* John Steinbeck's documentary novel (1939) portraying the misery of the "poor white" tenant farmers who migrated from the Oklahoma dustbowl to California during the 1930's.
[15] *Native Son:* Bigger Thomas, the trapped "hero" of Richard Wright's novel *Native Son.*
[16] *Fifth Column:* enemy sympathizers; traitors.

None in the Land can say
To us black men Today:
You send flame-gutting tanks, like swarms of flies,
And plump a hell from dynamiting skies.
You fill machine-gunned towns with rotting dead—
A No Man's Land where children cry for bread.

VI

Tempo di Marcia [17]

Out of abysses of Illiteracy,
Through labyrinths of Lies,
Across waste lands of Disease . . .
We advance!

Out of dead-ends of Poverty,
Through wildernesses of Superstition,
Across barricades of Jim Crowism . . .
We advance!

With the Peoples of the World . . .
We advance!

[17] *Tempo di Marcia:* march tempo.

the man inside

(*To the memory of V. F. Calverton*) °

They told me—the voices of hates in the land—
They told me that White is White and Black is Black;
That the children of Africa are scarred with a brand
Ineradicable as the spots on the leopard's back.

"The Man Inside" from *Rendezvous with America* by Melvin B. Tolson, copyright 1944 by Dodd, Mead & Company, Inc. Reprinted by permission of the publisher.

° *V. F. Calverton* (1900–1940): sociologist, writer, and editor whose novel *The Man Inside* (1936) presented the general thesis that, although most individuals fear the loss of their personal and ethnic identities, the true freedom of "the man inside" arises from the recognition by individuals of their fundamental sameness.

They told me that gulfs unbridgeable lie
In the no-man's seascapes of unlike hues,
As wide as the vertical of earth and sky,
As ancient as the grief in the seagull's mews.

They told me that Black is an isle with a ban
Beyond the pilgrims' Continent of Man.

I yearned for the mainland where my brothers live.
The cancerous isolation behind, I swarm
Into the deeps, a naked fugitive,
Defying tribal fetishes that maim and damn.

And when the typhoon of jeers smote me and hope
Died like a burnt-out world and on the shore
The hates beat savage breasts, you threw the rope
And drew me into the catholic Evermore.

We stood on common ground, in transfiguring light,
Where the man inside is neither Black nor White.

for discussion

1. In a symphony, a composer blends the richly varied voices of many musical instruments into different themes, moods, and movements which have an underlying unity. How does Tolson use the "symphonic" form in "Dark Symphony"? How do the tempo marks of the six movements help us understand Tolson's point of view?
2. What is "the pilgrims' Continent of Man" in the poem "The Man Inside"? Who are the "brothers" who live on the "mainland"?

3. Tolson uses the word *catholic* in both "Dark Symphony" and "The Man Inside." In what specific sense does Tolson indicate that both the black Frederick Douglass and the white V. F. Calverton were "catholic"?

born 1915

MARGARET WALKER

☐ *Margaret Walker was born in Birmingham, Alabama.
She received her college education in the Midwest and
for many years has taught English at colleges in West
Virginia and Mississippi. Although she has not published
a large amount of poetry and fiction, what has been
published is of conspicuously high quality. Her poetry has
been frequently included in anthologies; and her first
book of poems,* For My People, *was included in 1942 in
the distinguished Yale University Series of Younger Poets.
Her second book of poems,* Prophets for a New Day,
appeared in 1970. Her novel Jubilee *won the Houghton
Mifflin Award in 1966.*

*Some of the poems Margaret Walker wrote during
the late 1930's are urgent appeals for understanding of
the black man's plight in America. Other poems, more
militant, seem designed to mobilize a greater sense of
black solidarity and an unflinching resolve for
immediate change.*

we have been believers

We have been believers believing in the black gods of an
      old land, believing in the secrets of the seeress and
      the magic of the charmers and the power of the
      devil's evil ones.
And in the white gods of a new land we have been believers
      believing in the mercy of our masters and the

beauty of our brothers, believing in the conjure [1] of
the humble and the faithful and the pure.

Neither the slavers' whip nor the lynchers' rope nor the
bayonet could kill our black belief. In our hunger
we beheld the welcome table and in our nakedness
the glory of a long white robe. We have been
believers in the new Jerusalem.

We have been believers feeding greedy grinning gods, like
a Moloch [2] demanding our sons and our daughters,
our strength and our wills and our spirits of pain.
We have been believers, silent and stolid and
stubborn and strong.

We have been believers yielding substance for the world.
With our hands have we fed a people and out of our
strength have they wrung the necessities of a
nation. Our song has filled the twilight and our
hope has heralded the dawn.

Now we stand ready for the touch of one fiery iron, for the
cleansing breath of many molten truths, that the
eyes of the blind may see and the ears of the deaf
may hear and the tongues of the people be filled
with living fire.

Where are our gods that they leave us asleep? Surely the
priests and the preachers and the powers will hear.
Surely now that our hands are empty and our hearts
too full to pray they will understand. Surely the
sires of the people will send us a sign.

We have been believers believing in our burdens and our
demigods too long. Now the needy no longer weep
and pray; the long-suffering arise, and our fists
bleed against the bars with a strange insistency.

[1] *conjure:* magic or witchcraft, here with particular reference to the
ancient African beliefs described in the first stanza.
[2] *Moloch:* a tyrannical power that is calmed by sacrifice of human
life.

for discussion

1. What contrast is drawn between the beliefs defined in the first two stanzas? The word *conjure* would seem to belong more obviously in the first stanza than in the second. What point about these two kinds of belief is implied through the introduction of the word *conjure* into the second stanza? In what sense, then, does the speaker appear to regard these contrasted beliefs as fundamentally the same?

2. Is the "black belief" described in the third stanza different from the beliefs described in the first two stanzas? What are the characteristics of this "black belief"?

3. What is the structural relationship of the fourth stanza to the group of three stanzas preceding it?

4. The first five stanzas indicate several of the ways in which black people have been believers. In the final stanzas, what conclusions are drawn from this complicated definition? What judgments are made?

1902–1967

LANGSTON HUGHES

☐ *Although Langston Hughes was himself securely anchored in the Afro-American community, he had an excellent opportunity during the 1920's to observe those black artists who oscillated between the white and black worlds. Young Harlem Renaissance writers like Countee Cullen and Jean Toomer enjoyed the praise of the white literary world and tried to become biracial or even nonracial authors. They assumed the difficult burden of trying to live and to write as cultural amphibians; and they became seriously alienated men, without secure roots in either black or white society.*

Unlike them, Hughes identified fully with the lives of fellow black people. Like many other blacks, he became increasingly alienated from white America, from a society that had fallen short of meeting its democratic and its human obligations. Many of his stories breathe black protest; they voice the frustrations of working-class Harlemites who know "the way it is" and tell it straight, simply and honestly.

The most famous of Hughes's fictional Harlemites is named Simple; his full name is Jess B. Semple (just be simple). This slogan was a guiding principle of both the art and the politics of Langston Hughes. Hughes's first collection of stories, The Ways of White Folks, *was published in 1934; and another collection,* Laughing to Keep from Crying, *in 1952. There have been several volumes of the "Simple" stories, beginning with* Simple Speaks His Mind *in 1950.*

who's passing for who?

☐ One of the great difficulties about being a member of a minority race is that so many kindhearted, well-meaning bores gather around to help. Usually, to tell the truth, they have nothing to help with, except their company—which is often appallingly dull.

Some members of the Negro race seem very well able to put up with it, though, in these uplifting years. Such was Caleb Johnson, colored social worker, who was always dragging around with him some nondescript white person or two, inviting them to dinner, showing them Harlem, ending up at the Savoy—much to the displeasure of whatever friends of his might be out that evening for fun, not sociology.

Friends are friends and, unfortunately, overearnest uplifters are uplifters—no matter what color they may be. If it were the white race that was ground down instead of Negroes, Caleb Johnson would be one of the first to offer Nordics the sympathy of his utterly inane society, under the impression that somehow he would be doing them a great deal of good.

You see, Caleb, and his white friends, too, were all bores. Or so we who lived in Harlem's literary bohemia during the "Negro Renaissance" thought. We literary ones considered ourselves too broad-minded to be bothered with questions of color. We liked people of any race who smoked incessantly, drank liberally, wore complexion and morality as loose garments, and made fun of anyone who didn't do likewise. We snubbed and high-hatted any Negro or white luckless enough not to understand Gertrude Stein, Ulysses, Man Ray, the theremin, Jean Toomer, or George Antheil.[1] By the end of the 1920's Caleb was just catching

[1] *Gertrude Stein ... George Antheil:* referring to the experimental art of the 1920's. Gertrude Stein (1874–1946) left America for Paris in

up to Dos Passos. He thought H. G. Wells good.[2]

We met Caleb one night in Small's.[3] He had three assorted white folks in tow. We would have passed him by with but a nod had he not hailed us enthusiastically, risen, and introduced us with great acclaim to his friends, who turned out to be schoolteachers from Iowa, a woman and two men. They appeared amazed and delighted to meet all at once two Negro writers and a black painter in the flesh. They invited us to have a drink with them. Money being scarce with us, we deigned to sit down at their table.

The white lady said, "I've never met a Negro writer before."

The two men added, "Neither have we."

"Why, we know any number of *white* writers," we three dark bohemians declared with bored nonchalance.

"But Negro writers are much more rare," said the lady.

"There are plenty in Harlem," we said.

"But not in Iowa," said one of the men, shaking his mop of red hair.

"There are no good *white* writers in Iowa either, are there?" we asked superciliously.

"Oh, yes, Ruth Suckow came from there."

Whereupon we proceeded to light in upon Ruth Suckow

1903. She presided over many of the young experimental artists from America who, in flight from commercialism and provincialism, settled in Paris during the years following the first World War. *Ulysses* is the innovative novel by James Joyce, published in Paris in 1922 and banned in America until 1934. Man Ray (born 1890) helped to introduce abstract painting and experimental photography into this country. The theremin is an electronic musical instrument invented in 1924. Jean Toomer (1894–1967), a black American author, published in 1923 the poetic novel *Cane*, a highly original fantasia on the relations between the races in America. George Antheil (1900–1959), an American composer, wrote ultramodern music. His *Ballet méchanique* (1925), scored for automobile horns and machines, outraged conventional audiences.

[2] *Dos Passos, H. G. Wells:* The English social critic H. G. Wells (1866–1946) and the American writer John Dos Passos (1896–1970) both wrote novels that realistically document social problems. But Dos Passos employed new narrative techniques—such as the Newsreel and the Camera Eye—which gave his realism a more modern quality.

[3] *Small's:* Like the Savoy, Small's Paradise is a well-known Harlem cabaret.

as old hat and to annihilate her in favor of Kay Boyle.[4] The way we flung names around seemed to impress both Caleb and his white guests. This, of course, delighted us, though we were too young and too proud to admit it.

The drinks came and everything was going well, all of us drinking, and we three showing off in a high-brow manner, when suddenly at the table just behind us a man got up and knocked down a woman. He was a brownskin man. The woman was blonde. As she rose he knocked her down again. Then the red-haired man from Iowa got up and knocked the colored man down.

He said, "Keep your hands off that white woman."

The man got up and said, "She's not a white woman. She's my wife."

One of the waiters added, "She's not white, sir, she's colored."

Whereupon the man from Iowa looked puzzled, dropped his fists, and said, "I'm sorry."

The colored man said, "What are you doing up here in Harlem anyway, interfering with my family affairs?"

The white man said, "I thought she was a white woman."

The woman who had been on the floor rose and said, "Well, I'm not a white woman, I'm colored, and you leave my husband alone."

Then they both lit in on the gentleman from Iowa. It took all of us and several waiters, too, to separate them. When it was over the manager requested us to kindly pay our bill and get out. He said we were disturbing the peace. So we all left. We went to a fish restaurant down the street. Caleb was terribly apologetic to his white friends. We artists were both mad and amused.

"Why did you say you were sorry," said the colored painter to the visitor from Iowa, "after you'd hit that man —and then found out it wasn't a white woman you were

[4] *Ruth Suckow, Kay Boyle:* Ruth Suckow (1892–1960) was a Midwestern novelist who wrote in a realistic style about the farms and small towns in that part of the country. Kay Boyle (born 1903) comes from the Midwest but went to Paris in 1922 and has spent much of her life since then in Europe. The setting of her stories is frequently European, and her style was shaped in the experimental school.

defending, but merely a light colored woman who looked white?"

"Well," answered the red-haired Iowan, "I didn't mean to be butting in if they were all the same race."

"Don't you think a woman needs defending from a brute, no matter what race she may be?" asked the painter.

"Yes, but I think it's up to you to defend your own women."

"Oh, so you'd divide up a brawl according to races, no matter who was right?"

"Well, I wouldn't say that."

"You mean you wouldn't defend a colored woman whose husband was knocking her down?" asked the poet.

Before the visitor had time to answer, the painter said, "No! You just got mad because you thought a black man was hitting a *white* woman."

"But she *looked* like a white woman," countered the man.

"Maybe she was just passing for colored," I said.

"Like some Negroes pass for white," Caleb interposed.

"Anyhow, I don't like it," said the colored painter, "the way you stopped defending her when you found out she wasn't white."

"No, we don't like it," we all agreed except Caleb.

Caleb said in extenuation, "But Mr. Stubblefield is new to Harlem."

The red-haired white man said, "Yes, it's my first time here."

"Maybe Mr. Stubblefield ought to stay out of Harlem," we observed.

"I agree," Mr. Stubblefield said. "Good night."

He got up then and there and left the café. He stalked as he walked. His red head disappeared into the night.

"Oh, that's too bad," said the white couple who remained. "Stubby's temper just got the best of him. But explain to us, are many colored folks really as fair as that woman?"

"Sure, lots of them have more white blood than colored, and pass for white."

"Do they?" said the lady and gentleman from Iowa.

"You never read Nella Larsen?" [5] we asked.

"She writes novels," Caleb explained. "She's part white herself."

"Read her," we advised. "Also read the *Autobiography of an Ex-colored Man.*" [6] Not that we had read it ourselves —because we paid but little attention to the older colored writers—but we knew it was about passing for white.

We all ordered fish and settled down comfortably to shocking our white friends with tales about how many Negroes there were passing for white all over America. We were determined to *épater le bourgeois* [7] real good via this white couple we had cornered, when the woman leaned over the table in the midst of our dissertations and said, "Listen, gentlemen, you needn't spread the word, but me and my husband aren't white either. We've just been *passing* for white for the last fifteen years."

"What?"

"We're colored, too, just like you," said the husband. "But it's better passing for white because we make more money."

Well, that took the wind out of us. It took the wind out of Caleb, too. He thought all the time he was showing some fine white folks Harlem—and they were as colored as he was!

Caleb almost never cursed. But this time he said, "I'll be damned!"

Then everybody laughed. And laughed! We almost had hysterics. All at once we dropped our professionally self-conscious "Negro" manners, became natural, ate fish, and talked and kidded freely like colored folks do when there are no white folks around. We really had fun then, joking about that red-haired guy who mistook a fair colored woman for white. After the fish we went to two or three

[5] *Nella Larsen:* One of the best novelists of the Harlem Renaissance, Nella Larsen was born in the Virgin Islands of a Danish mother and a Negro father. Her novel *Passing* (1929) explores the problems of a black woman of mixed parentage who crosses the color line.

[6] *Autobiography of an Ex-colored Man:* James Weldon Johnson's novel about a man of partly Negro parentage who, after some shifting of racial identity, is finally driven by shame and fear to pass as white.

[7] *épater le bourgeois* (ā·pa′tā lə boor·shwa′): French for "shock conventional people."

more night spots and drank until five o'clock in the morning.

Finally we put the light-colored people in a taxi heading downtown. They turned to shout a last good-by. The cab was just about to move off, when the woman called to the driver to stop.

She leaned out the window and said with a grin, "Listen, boys! I hate to confuse you again. But, to tell the truth, my husband and I aren't really colored at all. We're white. We just thought we'd kid you by passing for colored a little while—just as you said Negroes sometimes pass for white."

She laughed as they sped off toward Central Park, waving, "Good-by!"

We didn't say a thing. We just stood there on the corner in Harlem dumbfounded—not knowing now *which* way we'd been fooled. Were they really white—passing for colored? Or colored—passing for white?

Whatever race they were, they had had too much fun at our expense—even if they did pay for the drinks.

duty is not snooty

☐ "I remember one time you told me that you thought that if white people who *say* they love Negroes really *do* love them, then they ought to live like Negroes live. Didn't you say that?"

"I did," said Simple, "especially when they go down South."

"That means then that our white friends should ride in Jim Crow cars, too?"

"It does," said Simple.

"Why?" I asked.

"To prove that they love me," said Simple, "otherwise, I do not believe them. White folks that love me and care about my race ought to sleep in colored hotels when they travel—which are mostly not built for sleeping. They also ought to eat in colored restaurants—which in small towns is generally greasy spoons. They should also wait an hour for a colored taxi in them places where white cabs won't haul Negroes. Also let my white friends what plan to stay in the South awhile, send their children to the colored not-yet-integrated school, which is most generally across the railroad track in a hovel. And when they get on the buses to come home, let them ride in the back of the buses. If the back seats for colored is crowded, then let them stand up, even if some of the white seats is empty—which colored dare not set in for fear of getting shot through the windows. When nice white folks got through with all that Jim Crow, from eating to sleeping to schools to Jim Crow cars, then we would see how they feel for real."

"If you are expecting our good white friends to go through all of that, then you are expecting them to be superhuman," I said.

"I ride in Jim Crow cars and I am not superhuman."

"You ride in them because you have to," I said.

"I believe in share and share alike," declared Simple. "Them white folks that really loves me should share them Jim Crow cars with me, and not be setting back up in the hindpart of the train all air-cooled and everything whilst I rides up by the engine in an old half-baggage car. Also, I want my white friends to experience a Jim Crow toilet. There is nothing like a COLORED toilet in a Southern train station! Half the time, no mirror, no paper towels, sometimes no sink even to wash your hands. They is separate, all right, but not equal. Let them try one, then them nice white folks, who are always asking me what more do I want since the Supreme Court decided I could vote, would understand what I want. I wants me a train-station toilet with everything in it everybody else has got."

"You know it is against local law for white people to use COLORED waiting rooms down South, or for colored people to use WHITE. Do you want decent white folks to get locked up just to prove they love you?"

"I'd get locked up for going in their waiting rooms, so why shouldn't they get locked up for going in mine? It ain't right for friends to be separated."

"What good would it do us for our white friends to get locked up?"

"It would teach them how dumb it is to have WHITE and COLORED signs all over Dixie."

"Liberal whites already agree that is stupid," I said.

"They would agree more if they experienced it," said Simple. "And if they got locked up a few times, them signs would come down! White folks do not put up with whatever they don't like. Just let a white man get turned down when he goes in a restaurant hungry. He will turn the joint out. If I get turned down, all they do is turn me out. White folks has got a theoretical knowledge of prejudice. I want them to have a real one. That is why I say when these nice white folks from up North goes down to Florida in the winter, let them go Jim Crow. When they get there let them stay at one of them colored hotels where they don't have no bell boys to wait on them hand and foot, also no valet service, and no nice room service for breakfast on a push wagon, and where the elevator is liable to be broke down, if they got one. Let them live colored for just *one* vacation. I bet they will not be so sweet-tempered then. They would not like it. They would be mad! It is not enough for white folks just to be nice and shake my hand and tell me I am equal. I know I am equal. What I want is to be *treated* equal. So maybe if the nice white folks really find out *what* it is like *not* to be treated equal—after they live Jim Crow themselves—I bet you, things will change! You know, white folks would not put up with Jim Crow—if they ever got Jim Crowed themselves. They don't really know what Jim Crow is. But it is their duty to find out, and duty cannot be snooty."

"Your flights of fancy are rather intriguing," I said, "but you know none of what you are saying is going to happen. Good people are not *that* good. To tell the truth, if I were white, no matter how much I loved Negroes, I doubt that I would submit myself to Jim Crow living conditions just to prove my love."

"Neither would I," said Simple.

"Then you would not be very good, either."
"No," said Simple, "but I would be white."

for discussion

1. In "Who's Passing for Who?" what does the narrator's description of his literary preferences tell us about him? What happened to the narrator's attitude toward the couple from Iowa when he learned that they were themselves "passing" for white? What does this tell us about the narrator?

2. What appears to be Hughes's attitude toward the narrator? Is it admiring, critical, or neutral? How does Hughes establish his implied attitude toward the narrator in this story?

3. What are the differences in speech and outlook between the narrator in "Who's Passing for Who?" and Simple in "Duty Is Not Snooty"?

4. At which segment of the white population is Simple's protest directed? What is his principal criticism of this group?

5. How does Hughes's use of dialogue add to the persuasiveness of the argument that Simple puts forward? What are the characteristics of this other speaker, who opens the discussion so provocatively?

1908–1960

RICHARD WRIGHT

☐ *Fear and anger compelled protest and escape: this was the recurrent pattern of Richard Wright's life, from his birth in Mississippi in 1908 to his death in France in 1960. His exodus in 1947 from America to Paris climaxed his lifelong effort to find an acceptable home, a place where it was neither dangerous nor humiliating to be black. Deserted at the age of six by his father in Memphis, driven two years later with his mother and aunt from a small town in Arkansas where his uncle was murdered by whites, forced at twelve by his mother's illness to resettle in Jackson, Mississippi, Wright endured a starved and fugitive childhood among impoverished, cowed blacks who were sharply segregated from their*

overbearing white neighbors. After graduating from
the ninth grade of the Negro school in Jackson—his only
formal education—Wright returned at seventeen to
Memphis, where he hoped to earn enough money to
escape from a society in which he felt trapped and
threatened. His intense desire for independence—fed by
such authors as H. L. Mencken, Theodore Dreiser, and
Sinclair Lewis—only added to his acute awareness of his
plight. He despised the way of life prescribed for "good"
Negroes, but was obliged to respect it in order to avoid
provoking suspicion and abuse. Fear for his life taught
him to mask both his anger and his ambitions.
Consequently, throughout Wright's boyhood he wished
to escape northward; in his teens, the wish grew almost
obsessive. In 1927, at nineteen, he left Memphis and
came by train to Chicago.

Wright found in Chicago only the menial jobs to
which he had been restricted earlier. He worked as a
porter and dishwasher, later as a postal clerk. Living on
Chicago's South Side through most of the Depression,
Wright experienced gnawing hunger again and observed
human misery in the Northern black belt fully
comparable to what he had seen as a boy. But he also
noticed that blacks displayed less fear and greater
solidarity in Chicago than in their former surroundings.
Despite unemployment and hunger, Wright in the early
1930's began to feel a sense of hope and purpose;
he began to believe in the possibility of meaningful
protest:

> I was slowly beginning to comprehend the meaning
> of my environment; a sense of direction was
> beginning to emerge from the conditions of my life.
> I began to feel something more powerful than I could
> express. My speech and manner changed. My
> cynicism slid from me. I grew open and questioning.
> I wanted to know.°

Out of this dawning confidence grew Wright's
self-education in sociology and psychology, his

°From *Richard Wright: A Biography* by Constance Webb. Reprinted by
permission of the publisher, G. P. Putnam's Sons.

involvement in radical politics, and his redoubled effort
to launch the career in literature for which he had been
preparing himself since his arrival in Chicago. In the
mid-1930's his poems, stories, and essays started to appear
in print, largely in left-wing periodicals.

In 1937 Wright moved from Chicago to New York,
where he lived for the next ten years. Here he gained his
greatest literary triumphs with the publication of Uncle
Tom's Children (1938), Native Son (1940), and Black Boy
(1945). Wright's stories imaged his life, for his main
characters are "black boys" on the run. Driven by fear
and suppressed anger, they give way to violent impulses
—expressed sometimes in fantasy or talk, sometimes in
sudden reflexlike actions of which they seem hardly
conscious. The unvarying consequence of their violence
is flight: typically, Wright's heroes are trapped creatures
frantically trying to get free.

As the author of the best seller Native Son, Wright
became the leader of those "protest" writers who
dedicated their literary talents to the battle against
racism. However, he was increasingly troubled in the
mid-1940's by the realization that neither his literary
successes nor the war Americans were fighting abroad
for human rights had really altered his situation as a
black man in white America. He still had to frequent
black barbershops, he was still denied service in white
restaurants, and he still could not rent or purchase
housing where he wished. Despairing and angry once
more, he fled the United States in 1947, and spent the
last fourteen years of his life moving restlessly about
Europe and Africa. From this self-imposed exile came
two more novels, The Outsider (1953) and The Long
Dream (1958). Wright's foreign residence and travels also
inspired two prophetic works of nonfiction, Black Power
(1954) and White Man, Listen! (1957). A new collection of
Wright's stories, Eight Men, was published the year
after his death.

A number of black American authors had achieved
recognition before Wright appeared on the American
literary scene. But he was the first black American writer
to reach a mass reading audience. And he shook that

audience by exposing the inner and outer lives of black people in America with a degree of realism and anger vastly beyond that of writers who had preceded him.

the man who was almost a man

☐ Dave struck out across the fields, looking homeward through paling light. Whut's the use talkin wid em niggers in the field? Anyhow, his mother was putting supper on the table. Them niggers can't understan nothing. One of these days he was going to get a gun and practice shooting, then they couldn't talk to him as though he were a little boy. He slowed, looking at the ground. Shucks, Ah ain scareda them even ef they are biggern me! Aw, Ah know whut Ahma do. Ahm going by ol Joe's sto n git that Sears Roebuck catlog n look at them guns. Mebbe Ma will lemme buy one when she gits mah pay from ol man Hawkins. Ahma beg her t gimme some money. Ahm ol ernough to hava gun. Ahm seventeen. Almost a man. He strode, feeling his long loose-jointed limbs. Shucks, a man oughta hava little gun aftah he done worked hard all day.

He came in sight of Joe's store. A yellow lantern glowed on the front porch. He mounted steps and went through the screen door, hearing it bang behind him. There was a strong smell of coal oil and mackerel fish. He felt very confident until he saw fat Joe walk in through the rear door, then his courage began to ooze.

"Howdy, Dave! Whutcha want?"

"How yuh, Mistah Joe? Aw, Ah don wanna buy nothing. Ah jus wanted t see ef yuhd lemme look at tha catlog erwhile."

"Sure! You wanna see it here?"

"Nawsuh. Ah wans t take it home wid me. Ah'll bring it back termorrow when Ah come in from the fiels."

"You plannin on buying something?"

"Yessuh."

"Your ma lettin you have your own money now?"

"Shucks. Mistah Joe, Ahm gittin t be a man like anybody else!"

Joe laughed and wiped his greasy white face with a red bandanna.

"Whut you plannin on buyin?"

Dave looked at the floor, scratched his head, scratched his thigh, and smiled. Then he looked up shyly.

"Ah'll tell yuh, Mistah Joe, ef yuh promise yuh won't tell."

"I promise."

"Waal, Ahma buy a gun."

"A gun? Whut you want with a gun?"

"Ah wanna keep it."

"You ain't nothing but a boy. You don't need a gun."

"Aw, lemme have the catlog, Mistah Joe. Ah'll bring it back."

Joe walked through the rear door. Dave was elated. He looked around at barrels of sugar and flour. He heard Joe coming back. He craned his neck to see if he were bringing the book. Yeah, he's got it. Gawddog, he's got it!

"Here, but be sure you bring it back. It's the only one I got."

"Sho, Mistah Joe."

"Say, if you wanna buy a gun, why don't you buy one from me? I gotta gun to sell."

"Will it shoot?"

"Sure it'll shoot."

"Whut kind is it?"

"Oh, it's kinda old . . . a left-hand Wheeler. A pistol. A big one."

"Is it got bullets in it?"

"It's loaded."

"Kin Ah see it?"

"Where's your money?"

"Whut yuh wan fer it?"

"I'll let you have it for two dollars."

"Just two dollahs? Shucks, Ah could buy tha when Ah git mah pay."

"I'll have it here when you want it."

"Awright, suh. Ah be in fer it."

He went through the door, hearing it slam again behind him. Ahma git some money from Ma n buy me a gun! Only two dollahs! He tucked the thick catalogue under his arm and hurried.

"Where yuh been, boy?" His mother held a steaming dish of black-eyed peas.

"Aw, Ma, Ah jus stopped down the road t talk wid the boys."

"Yuh know bettah t keep suppah waitin."

He sat down, resting the catalogue on the edge of the table.

"Yuh git up from there and git to the well n wash yosef! Ah ain feedin no hogs in mah house!"

She grabbed his shoulder and pushed him. He stumbled out of the room, then came back to get the catalogue.

"Whut this?"

"Aw, Ma, it's jusa catlog."

"Who yuh git it from?"

"From Joe, down at the sto."

"Waal, thas good. We kin use it in the outhouse."

"Naw, Ma." He grabbed for it. "Gimme ma catlog, Ma."

She held onto it and glared at him.

"Quit hollerin at me! Whut's wrong wid yuh? Yuh crazy?"

"But Ma, please. It ain mine! It's Joe's! He tol me t bring it back t im termorrow."

She gave up the book. He stumbled down the back steps, hugging the thick book under his arm. When he had splashed water on his face and hands, he groped back to the kitchen and fumbled in a corner for the towel. He bumped into a chair; it clattered to the floor. The catalogue sprawled at his feet. When he had dried his eyes he snatched up the book and held it again under his arm. His mother stood watching him.

"Now, ef yuh gonna act a fool over that ol book, Ah'll take it n burn it up."

"Naw, Ma, please."

"Waal, set down n be still!"

He sat down and drew the oil lamp close. He thumbed page after page, unaware of the food his mother set on the table. His father came in. Then his small brother.

"Whutcha got there, Dave?" his father asked.

"Jusa catlog," he answered, not looking up.

"Yeah, here they is!" His eyes glowed at blue-and-black revolvers. He glanced up, feeling sudden guilt. His father was watching him. He eased the book under the table and rested it on his knees. After the blessing was asked, he ate. He scooped up peas and swallowed fat meat without chewing. Buttermilk helped to wash it down. He did not want to mention money before his father. He would do much better by cornering his mother when she was alone. He looked at his father uneasily out of the edge of his eye.

"Boy, how come yuh don quit foolin wid tha book n eat yo suppah?"

"Yessuh."

"How you n ol man Hawkins gitten erlong?"

"Suh?"

"Can't yuh hear? Why don yuh lissen? Ah ast yu how wuz yuh n ol man Hawkins gittin erlong?"

"Oh, swell, Pa. Ah plows mo lan than anybody over there."

"Waal, yuh oughta keep yo mind on whut yuh doin."

"Yessuh."

He poured his plate full of molasses and sopped it up slowly with a chunk of cornbread. When his father and brother had left the kitchen, he still sat and looked again at the guns in the catalogue, longing to muster courage enough to present his case to his mother. Lawd, ef Ah only had tha pretty one! He could almost feel the slickness of the weapon with his fingers. If he had a gun like that he would polish it and keep it shining so it would never rust. N Ah'd keep it loaded, by Gawd!

"Ma?" His voice was hesitant.

"Hunh?"

"Ol man Hawkins give yuh mah money yit?"

"Yeah, but ain no usa yuh thinking bout throwin nona it erway. Ahm keepin tha money sos yuh kin have cloes t go to school this winter."

He rose and went to her side with the open catalogue in his palms. She was washing dishes, her head bent low over a pan. Shyly he raised the book. When he spoke, his voice was husky, faint.

"Ma, Gawd knows Ah wans one of these."

"One of whut?" she asked, not raising her eyes.

"One of these," he said again, not daring even to point. She glanced up at the page, then at him with wide eyes.

"Nigger, is yuh gone plumb crazy?"

"Aw, Ma—"

"Git outta here! Don yuh talk t me bout no gun! Yuh a fool!"

"Ma, Ah kin buy one fer two dollahs."

"Not ef Ah knows it, yuh ain!"

"But yuh promised me one—"

"Ah don care whut Ah promised! Yuh ain nothing but a boy yit!"

"Ma, ef yuh lemme buy one Ah'll *never* ast yuh fer nothing no mo."

"Ah tol yuh t git outta here! Yuh ain gonna toucha penny of tha money fer no gun! Thas how come Ah has Mistah Hawkins t pay yo wages t me, cause Ah knows yuh ain got no sense."

"But, Ma, we needa gun. Pa ain got no gun. We needa gun in the house. Yuh kin never tell whut might happen."

"Now don yuh try to maka fool outta me, boy! Ef we did hava gun, yuh wouldn't have it!"

He laid the catalogue down and slipped his arm around her waist.

"Aw, Ma, Ah done worked hard alla summer n ain ast yuh fer nothin, is Ah, now?"

"Thas whut yuh spose t do!"

"But Ma, Ah wans a gun. Yuh kin lemme have two dollahs outta mah money. Please, Ma. I kin give it to Pa . . . Please, Ma! Ah loves yuh, Ma."

When she spoke her voice came soft and low.

"Whut yuh wan wida gun, Dave? Yuh don need no gun.

Yuh'll git in trouble. N ef yo pa jus thought Ah let yuh have money t buy a gun he'd hava fit."

"Ah'll hide it, Ma. It ain but two dollahs."

"Lawd, chil, whut's wrong wid yuh?"

"Ain nothin wrong, Ma. Ahm almos a man now. Ah wans a gun."

"Who gonna sell yuh a gun?"

"Ol Joe at the sto."

"N it don cos but two dollahs?"

"Thas all, Ma. Jus two dollahs. Please, Ma."

She was stacking the plates away; her hands moved slowly, reflectively. Dave kept an anxious silence. Finally, she turned to him.

"Ah'll let yuh git tha gun ef yuh promise me one thing."

"Whut's tha, Ma?"

"Yuh bring it straight back t me, yuh hear? It be fer Pa."

"Yessum! Lemme go now, Ma."

She stooped, turned slightly to one side, raised the hem of her dress, rolled down the top of her stocking, and came up with a slender wad of bills.

"Here," she said. "Lawd knows yuh don need no gun. But yer pa does. Yuh bring it right back t me, yuh hear? Ahma put it up. Now ef yuh don, Ahma have yuh pa lick yuh so hard yuh won fergit it."

"Yessum."

He took the money, ran down the steps, and across the yard.

"Dave! Yuuuuuh Daaaaave!"

He heard, but he was not going to stop now. "Naw, Lawd!"

The first movement he made the following morning was to reach under his pillow for the gun. In the gray light of dawn he held it loosely, feeling a sense of power. Could kill a man with a gun like this. Kill anybody, black or white. And if he were holding his gun in his hand, nobody could run over him; they would have to respect him. It was a big gun, with a long barrel and a heavy handle. He raised and lowered it in his hand, marveling at its weight.

He had not come straight home with it as his mother had asked; instead he had stayed out in the fields, holding the weapon in his hand, aiming it now and then at some imaginary foe. But he had not fired it; he had been afraid that his father might hear. Also he was not sure he knew how to fire it.

To avoid surrendering the pistol he had not come into the house until he knew that they were all asleep. When his mother had tiptoed to his bedside late that night and demanded the gun, he had first played possum; then he had told her that the gun was hidden outdoors, that he would bring it to her in the morning. Now he lay turning it slowly in his hands. He broke it, took out the cartridges, felt them, and then put them back.

He slid out of bed, got a long strip of old flannel from a trunk, wrapped the gun in it, and tied it to his naked thigh while it was still loaded. He did not go in to break-fast. Even though it was not yet daylight, he started for Jim Hawkins' plantation. Just as the sun was rising he reached the barns where the mules and plows were kept.

"Hey! That you, Dave?"

He turned. Jim Hawkins stood eying him suspiciously.

"What're yuh doing here so early?"

"Ah didn't know Ah wuz gittin up so early, Mistah Hawkins. Ah wuz fixin t hitch up ol Jenny n take her t the fiels."

"Good. Since you're so early, how about plowing that stretch down by the woods?"

"Suits me, Mistah Hawkins."

"O.K. Go to it!"

He hitched Jenny to a plow and started across the fields. Hot dog! This was just what he wanted. If he could get down by the woods, he could shoot his gun and nobody would hear. He walked behind the plow, hearing the traces creaking, feeling the gun tied tight to his thigh.

When he reached the woods, he plowed two whole rows before he decided to take out the gun. Finally, he stopped, looked in all directions, then untied the gun and held it in his hand. He turned to the mule and smiled.

"Know whut this is, Jenny? Naw, yuh wouldn know! Yuhs jusa ol mule! Anyhow, this is a gun, n it kin shoot, by Gawd!"

He held the gun at arm's length. Whut t hell, Ahma shoot this thing! He looked at Jenny again.

"Lissen here, Jenny! When Ah pull this ol trigger, Ah don wan yuh t run n acka fool now!"

Jenny stood with head down, her short ears pricked straight. Dave walked off about twenty feet, held the gun far out from him at arm's length, and turned his head. Hell, he told himself, Ah ain afraid. The gun felt loose in his fingers; he waved it wildly for a moment. Then he shut his eyes and tightened his forefinger. Bloom! A report half deafened him and he thought his right hand was torn from his arm. He heard Jenny whinnying and galloping over the field, and he found himself on his knees, squeezing his fingers hard between his legs. His hand was numb; he jammed it into his mouth, trying to warm it, trying to stop the pain. The gun lay at his feet. He did not quite know what had happened. He stood up and stared at the gun as though it were a living thing. He gritted his teeth and kicked the gun. Yuh almos broke mah arm! He turned to look for Jenny; she was far over the fields, tossing her head and kicking wildly.

"Hol on there, ol mule!"

When he caught up with her she stood trembling, walling her big white eyes at him. The plow was far away; the traces had broken. Then Dave stopped short, looking, not believing. Jenny was bleeding. Her left side was red and wet with blood. He went closer. Lawd, have mercy! Wondah did Ah shoot this mule? He grabbed for Jenny's mane. She flinched, snorted, whirled, tossing her head.

"Hol on now! Hol on."

Then he saw the hole in Jenny's side, right between the ribs. It was round, wet, red. A crimson stream streaked down the front leg, flowing fast. Good Gawd! Ah wuzn't shootin at tha mule. He felt panic. He knew he had to stop that blood, or Jenny would bleed to death. He had never seen so much blood in all his life. He chased the mule for half a mile, trying to catch her. Finally she stopped, breathing hard, stumpy tail half arched. He caught her mane and led her back to where the plow and gun lay. Then he stooped and grabbed handfuls of damp black earth and tried to plug the bullet hole. Jenny shuddered, whinnied, and broke from him.

"Hol on! Hol on now!"

He tried to plug it again, but blood came anyhow. His fingers were hot and sticky. He rubbed dirt into his palms, trying to dry them. Then again he attempted to plug the bullet hole, but Jenny shied away, kicking her heels high. He stood helpless. He had to do something. He ran at Jenny; she dodged him. He watched a red stream of blood flow down Jenny's leg and form a bright pool at her feet.

"Jenny . . . Jenny," he called weakly.

His lips trembled. She's bleeding t death! He looked in the direction of home, wanting to go back, wanting to get help. But he saw the pistol lying in the damp black clay. He had a queer feeling that if he only did something, this would not be; Jenny would not be there bleeding to death.

When he went to her this time, she did not move. She stood with sleepy, dreamy eyes; and when he touched her she gave a low-pitched whinny and knelt to the ground, her front knees slopping in blood.

"Jenny . . . Jenny . . ." he whispered.

For a long time she held her neck erect; then her head sank, slowly. Her ribs swelled with a mighty heave and she went over.

Dave's stomach felt empty, very empty. He picked up the gun and held it gingerly between his thumb and forefinger. He buried it at the foot of a tree. He took a stick and tried to cover the pool of blood with dirt—but what was the use? There was Jenny lying with her mouth open and her eyes walled and glassy. He could not tell Jim Hawkins he had shot his mule. But he had to tell something. Yeah, Ah'll tell em Jenny started gittin wil n fell on the joint of the plow. . . . But that would hardly happen to a mule. He walked across the field slowly, head down.

It was sunset. Two of Jim Hawkins' men were over near the edge of the woods digging a hole in which to bury Jenny. Dave was surrounded by a knot of people, all of whom were looking down at the dead mule.

"I don't see how in the world it happened," said Jim Hawkins for the tenth time.

The crowd parted and Dave's mother, father, and small brother pushed into the center.

"Where Dave?" his mother called.

"There he is," said Jim Hawkins.

His mother grabbed him.

"Whut happened, Dave? Whut yuh done?"

"Nothin."

"C mon, boy, talk," his father said.

Dave took a deep breath and told the story he knew nobody believed.

"Waal," he drawled, "Ah brung ol Jenny down here sos Ah could do mah plowin. Ah plowed bout two rows, just like yuh see." He stopped and pointed at the long rows of upturned earth. "Then somethin musta been wrong wid ol Jenny. She wouldn ack right a-tall. She started snortin n kickin her heels. Ah tried t hol her, but she pulled erway, rearin n goin in. Then when the point of the plow was stickin up in the air, she swung erroun n twisted herself back on it. . . . She stuck herself n started t bleed. N fo Ah could do anything, she wuz dead."

"Did you ever hear of anything like that in all your life?" asked Jim Hawkins.

There were white and black standing in the crowd. They murmured. Dave's mother came close to him and looked hard into his face. "Tell the truth, Dave," she said.

"Looks like a bullet hole to me," said one man.

"Dave, whut yuh do wid the gun?" his mother asked.

The crowd surged in, looking at him. He jammed his hands into his pockets, shook his head slowly from left to right, and backed away. His eyes were wide and painful.

"Did he hava gun?" asked Jim Hawkins.

"By Gawd, Ah tol yuh tha wuz a gun wound," said a man, slapping his thigh.

His father caught his shoulders and shook him till his teeth rattled.

"Tell whut happened, yuh rascal! Tell whut. . . ."

Dave looked at Jenny's stiff legs and began to cry.

"Whut yuh do wid tha gun?" his mother asked.

"Whut wuz he doin wida gun?" his father asked.

"Come on and tell the truth," said Hawkins. "Ain't nobody going to hurt you. . . ."

His mother crowded close to him.

"Did yuh shoot tha mule, Dave?"

Dave cried, seeing blurred white and black faces.

"Ahh ddinn gggo tt sshooot hher . . . Ah sssswear ffo Gawd Ah ddin. . . . Ah wuz a-tryin t sssee ef the old gggun would sshoot—"

"Where yuh git the gun from?" his father asked.

"Ah got it from Joe, at the sto."

"Where yuh git the money?"

"Ma give it t me."

"He kept worryin me, Bob. Ah had t. Ah tol im t bring the gun right back t me. . . . It was fer yuh, the gun."

"But how yuh happen to shoot that mule?" asked Jim Hawkins.

"Ah wuzn shootin at the mule, Mistah Hawkins. The gun jumped when Ah pulled the trigger. . . . N fo Ah knowed anythin Jenny was there a-bleedin."

Somebody in the crowd laughed. Jim Hawkins walked close to Dave and looked into his face.

"Well, looks like you have bought you a mule, Dave."

"Ah swear fo Gawd, Ah didn go t kill the mule, Mistah Hawkins!"

"But you killed her!"

All the crowd was laughing now. They stood on tiptoe and poked heads over one another's shoulders.

"Well, boy, looks like yuh done bought a dead mule! Hahaha!"

"Ain tha ershame."

"Hohohohoho."

Dave stood, head down, twisting his feet in the dirt.

"Well, you needn't worry about it, Bob," said Jim Hawkins to Dave's father. "Just let the boy keep on working and pay me two dollars a month."

"Whut yuh wan fer yo mule, Mistah Hawkins?"

Jim Hawkins screwed up his eyes.

"Fifty dollars."

"Whut yuh do wid tha gun?" Dave's father demanded.

Dave said nothing.

"Yuh wan me t take a tree n beat yuh till yuh talk!"

"Nawsuh!"

"Whut yuh do wid it?"

"Ah throwed it erway."

"Where?"

"Ah . . . Ah throwed it in the creek."

"Waal, c mon home. N firs thing in the mawnin git to tha creek n fin tha gun."

"Yessuh."

"Whut yuh pay fer it?"

"Two dollahs."

"Take tha gun n git yo money back n carry it t Mistah Hawkins, yuh hear? N don fergit Ahma lam you black bottom good fer this! Now march yosef on home, suh!"

Dave turned and walked slowly. He heard people laughing. Dave glared, his eyes welling with tears. Hot anger bubbled in him. Then he swallowed and stumbled on.

That night Dave did not sleep. He was glad that he had gotten out of killing the mule so easily, but he was hurt. Something hot seemed to turn over inside him each time he remembered how they had laughed. He tossed on his bed, feeling his hard pillow. N Pa says he's gonna beat me. . . . He remembered other beatings, and his back quivered. Naw, naw, Ah sho don wan im t beat me tha way no mo. Dam em all! Nobody ever gave him anything. All he did was work. They treat me like a mule, n then they beat me. He gritted his teeth. N Ma had t tell on me.

Well, if he had to, he would take old man Hawkins that two dollars. But that meant selling the gun. And he wanted to keep that gun. Fifty dollars for a dead mule.

He turned over, thinking how he had fired the gun. He had an itch to fire it again. Ef other men kin shoota gun, by Gawd, Ah kin! He was still, listening. Mebbe they all sleepin now. The house was still. He heard the soft breathing of his brother. Yes, now! He would go down and get that gun and see if he could fire it! He eased out of bed and slipped into overalls.

The moon was bright. He ran almost all the way to the edge of the woods. He stumbled over the ground, looking for the spot where he had buried the gun. Yeah, here it is. Like a hungry dog scratching for a bone, he pawed it up.

He puffed his black cheeks and blew dirt from the trigger and barrel. He broke it and found four cartridges unshot. He looked around; the fields were filled with silence and moonlight. He clutched the gun stiff and hard in his fingers. But, as soon as he wanted to pull the trigger, he shut his eyes and turned his head. Naw, Ah can't shoot wid mah eyes closed n mah head turned. With effort he held his eyes open; then he squeezed. *Blooooom!* He was stiff, not breathing. The gun was still in his hands. Dammit, he'd done it. He fired again. *Blooooom!* He smiled. *Bloooom! Blooooom! Click, click.* There! It was empty. If anybody could shoot a gun, he could. He put the gun into his hip pocket and started across the fields.

When he reached the top of a ridge he stood straight and proud in the moonlight, looking at Jim Hawkins' big white house, feeling the gun sagging in his pocket. Lawd, ef Ah had just one mo bullet Ah'd taka shot at tha house. Ah'd like t scare ol man Hawkins jusa little. . . . Jusa enough t let im know Dave Saunders is a man.

To his left the road curved, running to the tracks of the Illinois Central. He jerked his head, listening. From far off came a faint *hoooof-hoooof; hoooof-hoooof; hoooof-hoooof.* . . . He stood rigid. Two dollahs a month. Les see now. . . . Tha means it'll take bout two years. Shucks! Ah'll be dam!

He started down the road, toward the tracks. Yeah, here she comes! He stood beside the track and held himself stiffly. Here she comes, erroun the ben. . . . C mon, yuh slow poke! C mon! He had his hand on his gun; something quivered in his stomach. Then the train thundered past, the gray and brown box cars rumbling and clinking. He gripped the gun tightly; then he jerked his hand out of his pocket. Ah betcha Bill wouldn't do it! Ah betcha. . . . The cars slid past, steel grinding upon steel. Ahm ridin yuh ternight, so hep me Gawd! He was hot all over. He hesitated just a moment; then he grabbed, pulled atop of a car, and lay flat. He felt his pocket; the gun was still there. Ahead the long rails were glinting in the moonlight, stretching away, away to somewhere, somewhere where he could be a man. . . .

1. As the story begins, Dave is described as feeling misunderstood. What is it that the boys to whom he has been speaking do not understand? Why does Dave feel that speaking to them is useless?

2. When "Mistah" Joe says, "You ain't nothing but a boy," he may be referring only partly to Dave's age. What other meaning could the statement have?

3. What observations by the narrator define the way in which Dave and Mistah Joe perceive each other?

4. How is Dave's desire to own a gun related to his desire to be respected as a man? Is this a desire that any boy might experience, or is Dave's desire to be a man specially conditioned by the nature of his environment?

5. Wright first published this story with the title "Almos' a Man," which he later changed to "The Man Who Was Almost a Man." Does this revision help to convey the point of Wright's implied protest?

born 1904

ALBERT HALPER

☐ *Albert Halper was born on Chicago's West Side, the son of poor Jewish immigrants from Lithuania who had come to America in the early 1890's. He attended the public schools of Chicago, and after graduating from high school drifted into what he called "dreary bread-and-butter labor." He was a clerk in a mail-order warehouse, a machine operator in a factory, a shipping clerk and plate stamper in an electrotype foundry, and a sorter on the night shift of the Chicago central post office.*

Determined to become a writer, Halper left Chicago at the age of twenty-five and journeyed to New York, where his first story had just been published in The Dial. *New York has remained his home since 1929, although Chicago has served as the background of most of his fiction. In 1934 he published a collection of stories titled* On the Shore: Young Writer Remembering Chicago. *But he is better known for such novels as*

Union Square (1933), The Foundry (1934), The Chute (1937), and The Little People (1942). Halper chronicled that segment of modern American society out of which he himself came, the urban working class. His stories and novels are detailed accounts of an environment he knew first-hand: the daily lives of proletarians who toiled wearily and often hopelessly in the factories, stores, and offices of America's big cities during the 1920's and 1930's.

Despite the doctrinaire times in which these books were written, Halper's fiction adhered to no party line and argued no economic thesis. Halper's point of view is broadly humanitarian:

> I am sorry for many things in life. I am sorry for the small folk who live thin twisted lives, who have to hold onto their job and look alive when the big chief passes by. I am sorry for the broken men who stand against buildings when the wind howls down the street and the snow whirls past the arc lamps. I am sorry for clerks working in big stockrooms, for all my old buddies down at the Post Office—the whites, the Negroes, and the Filipinos, who stand hour on hour tossing mail.°

The Jews who appear in Halper's stories and novels are largely indistinguishable from other American "bottom dogs." His Jewish characters are blended into the masses struggling to survive hard times. Halper observed that poverty oppressed the native-born American as well as the immigrant, and he perceived that what they suffered drew them into a kind of brotherhood.

Halper's social portraits are drawn in language that some readers have found "too raw and awkward, too unfinished and slangy." But Halper has offered this explanation of his style:

> I was born in a raw slangy city, in a raw slangy neighborhood. I lived near railroads, and on warm nights I could smell the strong odor from the

°From *On the Shore: Young Writer Remembering Chicago* by Albert Halper, copyright 1934 by Albert Halper; renewal copyright 1962 by Albert Halper. Reprinted by permission of the author.

*stockyards rolling in heavy waves all the way from
the South Side. Just try to write in the classic tradition
with that stink in your nostrils, sit down and spin
out smooth poetic sentences with the roar of railroads
in your ears.*°

Scab!

☐ I pulled out of the Big Garage on West Fifty-fourth
Street early in the morning, because I thought the pickets
wouldn't be on the job yet. But they were. At the door,
Mrs. Steur, the wife of the fleet manager, checked me out,
holding the big book in her hand. I spoke my number so
low she didn't hear me at first. She stuck her head into
the cab.

"1544," I said again.

"Listen," she told me, "don't let them scare you, fella,
the police are behind us, they can't do anything to you,"
and she gave me a big smile as I zoomed out of the garage.

Mrs. Steur is big and getting stout and knows how to
give the boys a big smile. Since this strike has been going
on she has done a lot of smiling, especially when we roll
out of the garage in the morning, but she isn't fooling any
of us. She wears a fur coat that must have cost her five
hundred dollars if it cost her a nickel, and every time
I look at it I think of my own wife and two kids and I get
mad around the mouth. Damn her anyway. Last week, just
before the strike started, she used to give us dirty looks
every time she checked us out in the morning, and her
dirty looks said: "You bums are lousy drivers, you don't
know how to hack, all you do is to warm your fannies in
our nice comfortable cabs while Jake and me worry over

the intake." But now she calls us sonny and fella and all that baloney.

I zoomed out of the Big Garage in third and saw the pickets strung all along the street with signs on their backs. But luck was with me. The green light was showing up the block so I hit the bus up to forty-five miles an hour and none of them jumped on my running-board to argue with me. I've been working for the Steurs for over two years now and every hack-man in the garage knows I'm a square-shooter, and they can't figure out why I'm driving with the strike going on. Only a few know about the hole I'm in and about the wife's operation— But what the hell, I'm not telling everybody about my troubles, everybody's got plenty of their own these days, so I don't say anything to anybody.

I whizzed up the block as fast as I could hit it up. There were two cops on motorcycles resting at the corner and though I was going way over the speed limit they didn't stop me but waved their hands and smiled. I smiled back, but it was not the same kind of smile they gave to me. My smile said, "To hell with you, beefsteaks!"

Two blocks down, three of the boys started running toward my cab, so I had to cut west on Fifty-second. This is a bad street with some deep holes in it, but I shook them off. Then I cut east again and headed toward Fifth Avenue, praying for a fare. It was already half-past seven in the morning and the city was waking up. As I sent the car along, I could see pieces of fog floating up the street. I like to drive early in the morning. There is something about cruising in an empty cab with the fog coming up the street which gets me. I don't know what it is. Sometimes I can almost smell it. A lot of times, if business has been good the day before, that is, if I make over three dollars, I will coast about in the East Sixties and Seventies for a good half hour just to get that feeling on a foggy morning. In the East Sixties and Seventies there is not even a dog in sight at 7 A.M. and most of the houses are boarded up because the rich people that own them spend their time mostly down in Florida or in Europe, so it's nice and still and quiet there early in the morning.

But I was out for business today, so I didn't stall

around. I picked up a fare on Eighth Avenue and carried him to Fifth and Fifty-ninth. The fare was one of those tall rich guys around fifty who like to bend forward and act chummy with the driver, just to show you he's a regular fella. I know those kind. They tip dimes and always expect you to say thank-you twice.

"Do you mind if I turn the radio off?" he asks me, leaning forward.

I felt like telling him he could throw it out the window for all I cared. When I hear that sad music early in the morning I keep on thinking about the wife and how the doctors bungled the job and it gets me nuts sometimes. Why did they have to put radios in cabs for anyway?

"How is the strike going?" the man asks me next.

"I guess it's going," I mumbled back.

He kind of laughed soft-like and said the men didn't have a chance. With my left arm I reached around and turned the radio on again, real loud, because I started feeling down at the mouth again. It was those exercises this time: "One-two, bend from the waist, three-four, take a deep breath." You know those kind of daily dozen business they have on the air in the morning.

I was glad when the fare stepped out. But he sure surprised me. I mean he gave me fifteen cents. I picked up another load and took her to Grand Central. She wore a classy shiny brown fur coat and looked to be the bucks. Just before she got out she says to me, "You men are having trouble with your employers, aren't you?" I said yes. Then she gave me a quarter tip. "Well, I hope you win out," she said, in a kind of nice tone. "I like to see you men put up a fight."

I sat in the cab burning up after she was gone. Did she say that to me on purpose, just to get my goat? Didn't she know I was a scab?

Then I heard someone hollering at me and when I looked back I saw a big guy in a cap running toward me. I wasn't taking any chances, so I started roaring up the block away from him. When I looked back again he was still hollering and waving at me, and then I saw him step into another cab. He wasn't out to slug me after all. He was a fare. I got my nerve back, turned around in the middle of the block, and played the line on Lexington Avenue. There were only three cabs in line. In half a minute all of us got fares.

Luck was with me all morning. I mean that every single fare I carried wasn't near Times Square or downtown. It was mostly East Side business with swell tips. By eleven o'clock I took in almost seven dollars. This is swell business even in a snowstorm.

But after noon the trouble started. I was passing Thirty-fourth Street and Seventh Avenue when another cab cruises up to me and the driver calls out, "They're burning and wrecking cabs downtown, don't go below Fourteenth Street."

So I turned one fare down. I told the man I'd take him as far as Eighteenth Street where he could get a subway, but he looked at me disgusted and called another cab. I wasn't taking any chances. What would happen to Ethel and the kids if I got put away in the hospital? Damn the whole business anyway! Why can't it be worked out some-how that we men could get paid a decent wage so that we wouldn't have to go out on strike and have the papers say nasty and untrue things about us? Why can't—dammit, I forgot. I'm a scab! I'm a—

"Hey, you!" yelled a blonde dame. "Can you take me to Twelfth Street?"

"Sure," I hollered back, sore at myself. "I'll take you anywheres."

"What a man!" she sings out and steps high, wide, and handsome into the cab and when she gets inside she lights a cigarette and starts humming a song. I had a feeling right away she was good for a two-bit tip. "Play, taxi, play!" she sings out and turned on the radio. It was one of those damn sad songs again which I can't stand right after noon and I started thinking of Ethel and the doctors, but I didn't tell the fare to turn it off. She was painted up like hell, but I saw right away she was a good sport.

At Sixteenth Street they stopped me. There must have been over fifty of them. There were three cops, but the cops couldn't do anything.

"Come on, lady, get out," the drivers hollered.

The fare told them to go to hell. I had to hand it to her.

"Come on, get out, or we'll knock you out!"

"You and who else?" she hollers at them.

"Turn that damn radio off!" they yelled at me.

I turned it off. Then two of them hopped on the running-board and I had to kill the engine. They bunched all around me. The cops tried to get to me, but the boys kept shoving them away. They shoved in a kind of good-natured way, but they meant business. It was a kind of shoving that told the cops that all they had to do was to just start to get fresh and the boys would have flattened them. Then one of the boys who jumped onto the running-board poked his head inside, and I saw it was Goldstein.

"It's Tom Davlin," he said, and he started talking to the others to let me alone.

"To hell with that!" the others told him. "Let's drag him out if he doesn't turn around and shoot back to the garage right away. Let's drag him out!"

But Goldstein kept on arguing. Goldie is one of the few fellows in the Big Garage who knows what a hole I'm in. I heard him whispering something and I felt cheap as hell sitting there, but they wouldn't listen to him. "Drag him out!" they said again. I sat there wringing wet. "Drag him out!" they hollered, and I thought they were going to give it to me for sure, and I wouldn't have put up a battle, because I knew just how they felt. But just then three patrol cars came up with their sirens screaming and the cops piled out. They started swinging their clubs and cleared a way for my cab. I shot the car into second and tore like hell down the street.

"What was that pal of yours whispering to the others?" the fare asked me when we were about a block away. "Have you fellas got a magic password?"

"I don't know nothing," I said.

"Oh, so that's the way you feel about it," she said, then turned on the radio again. "Play, taxi, play!" she sang out, and what a nice long beautiful throat that woman had! She was singing happy over something and couldn't keep it down. She must have gotten a good hunk of cash from her daddy or something, I figured to myself.

"Hey, you," she called to me from the back seat, "hey, you, do you know what?"

"What?" I says, not turning around.

"I'm going to have a baby," she sings out to me, "and I feel so damned happy."

Then I knew she was tight. Any girl like that who feels happy over a kid must be either tight or crazy. I figured she was nutty.

She gave me the address and I stopped in front of a doctor's place.

"Here, sweetheart," she says and gives me two one-dollar bills. "Keep the change, handsome," and then she goes up to the door and rings the doctor's bell. A girl dressed like a nurse opens it. Then the door closed again.

What a tip! A dollar and twenty cents! I took time out and went into a coffee pot on Bank Street for some grub. There were two or three guys at the counter looking funny at me, so my meal was spoiled. I got up and paid and walked out. Dammit, I'm a scab! I said to myself.

I shot the car into third and cruised east. When I hit Fourth Avenue I heard a lot of yelling and hollering. I got off at University Place and let the motor run. Then I hoofed it to Fourth.

There was a mob there, almost three hundred drivers. They were burning three taxicabs, while a big crowd of people were watching on the sidewalks. The cops couldn't do anything. They hit a few of the boys, but the boys socked them back. I saw them stepping on one policeman. They got him down and started tearing his overcoat to pieces. You ought to have seen their faces when they were doing that! The cop reached for his gun, but they stepped on his hand. They were yelling and screaming at him all the time. I got into the crowd and started helping them. A cop came for me, but I cracked him one. Then I got a sweet blow behind the ear and the next thing I knew I was laying on the street. Two of the boys helped me up and I sat on the curb for a while with my head in my hands. I was half-unconscious but I could smell burnt rubber, burnt paint, and the stink of gasoline. And all the while the crowd was yelling crazy.

I got up again, but by this time the cops on horseback came up. They started hitting the boys right and left. It was terrible. One fellow's ear was hanging by a piece of flesh and he kept holding his hand to his ear trying to put it back. The cops went for him and cracked him another one. There were a few women, and nice looking ones, standing on the curb who started screaming at the cops to let the poor boy alone. One of them even came over to the horses and started to argue.

Then the fire engines came. They tried to put out the flames. They lay hoses from Tenth and Eleventh Street, but by the time the water was turned on the cabs weren't worth a dime. Then the gang started toward Union Square.[1] I started with them, then suddenly remembered I had my bus parked up the street. I started thinking of Ethel and the kids again. Dammit anyway!

I walked back to the cab and shot it west. I picked up a fare and took her uptown to Forty-fourth Street. She tipped me twenty cents. My pockets were heavy with silver so I got out and went into a restaurant and had it changed to paper money. The cashier looked funny at me. I felt so lousy that I didn't count my money twice and maybe he gypped me out of a quarter or so, because I remember—

Then I heard yelling on Seventh Avenue. I ran out and started the bus in a hurry. I didn't stop until I got to the Sixties. I cruised up and down those side streets until I got my nerve back. It started raining a little. A fare hailed me, but I didn't stop because I didn't have a good grip on myself yet. But in another minute I got another, this time for Ninety-second Street.

When I dropped that fare the rain stopped for a while. I was good and hungry again, because I had only taken a few bites out of my sandwich in that coffee pot on Bank Street, so I went into a place on Ninety-third, but first I put my hat in the cab.

But when I came in, some truck drivers at the counter recognized that I was a hackman anyway. You can al-

---

[1] *Union Square:* at Fourteenth Street and Broadway in downtown New York. Famous since the 1880's as the public forum of radical orators, it was often the scene of mass protest meetings during the Depression.

ways tell one if you know them. We all have clothes shiny around the seat, and that shininess is a special cab driver's gloss. I can't just describe it, but the gloss gives us away. I can be walking down the street with the missus and if I see a fellow walking ahead of me with that gloss on his rear-end, I can turn to the wife and say, "Two to one that guy is a hacker." Ethel knows that I am not the betting kind, but she gets sore at me sometimes. "Can't you forget your lousy business even when you're not working?" she asks me. This gets me sore sometimes, but I know she hasn't been herself since the operation. So I just keep quiet.

Anyway, when I sat down and ordered a bowl of soup I saw the truck drivers giving me the once-over. Then one of them started talking louder. "I bet he's a scab," he said. I turned around with murder in my eye. "Damn you, what if I am?" I hollered at him and I was so worked up that I started spilling all about my wife and the kids and the deep hole I'm in. The cook came out from the kitchen and looked at me. By the time I was through I was almost screaming. The guy who had called me a scab didn't know what to say and sat there looking at the counter.

"All right, all right," he says kind of quiet and he wanted to let the matter drop.

"All right hell!" I screamed at him and got up and went out.

The cook hollered at me to pay the check, but I told him to come outside and I'd beat hell out of him, and he didn't make a move when I told him that.

I got into the bus and had to cruise around for a good fifteen minutes to cool off. I was so hopping mad I felt like speeding the car up to sixty miles an hour and driving square into a building.

But when a fare hailed me, I calmed down. I started to think of Ethel and the kids and I realized I couldn't act like a damn fool.

So I picked up the fare and cooled off. It started to rain again. When I dropped the fare, I got another right away. I kept uptown. Business was heavy and I was on the jump all the time.

I worked straight through until eight o'clock, then I bought a newspaper to see how the strike was coming on.

The headlines said the strike was still deadlocked. There was a lot of stuff written about what the fleet owners said about company unions, but we all know what those company unions are. The boys were still putting up a fight. I parked my bus in a side street and read the piece to the last line. When I read about the fights and the riots and the burning of the cabs I felt so thrilled I wanted to sing and scream with happiness. Then all of a sudden I remembered I wasn't in it, and the feeling flopped inside of me.

A half hour later, when I pulled into the Big Garage, Mrs. Steur let out a big sigh of relief. "Oh thank God," she said, "I thought they burned your cab."

Then she saw the dented fenders and the broken windows and her face fell. She started cursing the strikers to beat the band. I never heard her swear like that before. Then she told me to check in and go home and get a good night's rest and report for duty in the morning. When she saw the meter reading she complimented me, but she was still swearing at the drivers.

I got home an hour later, tired as a dog. The first thing when I closed the door, Ethel asked me how much I made. I put eleven dollars on the table. It was the most I had ever made in a single day's hacking. She looked at my face and didn't say anything. I started to tell her I was through until the strike was over, when I heard Sonny start to bawl in the bedroom. Then I kept my mouth shut.

When we sat down to eat Ethel got me to talk. I told her how I had seen the burning cabs, how they had stopped me, and how Goldie and the cops had saved me from getting slugged. I didn't tell her how I got out and socked a cop and then got flattened out. Women sometimes can't see things a man's way.

"You'd think they'd let a man work in peace," she said finally, and then I got sore as hell. I started to holler. I couldn't help myself. I told her how I had gone to the coffee pots and couldn't eat because I was looked at in a funny way, I told her how I felt about it, and I said something about the fog drifting up the street and the East Sixties and the Seventies where the houses were boarded up with the rich people spending the winter down in Florida or over in Europe, and the first thing I knew I was standing up and screaming at her across the table.

The kids started bawling in the bedroom. Ethel hollered at me, but I couldn't stop.

"Damn it to hell," I screamed, "I'm through! I'm not the only guy driving a hack with a wife and kids on his hands. I'm through, I tell you. How do you suppose I feel at the wheel of my cab making money with my buddies out on strike? I tell you I'm through. I'm not reporting in the morning, nor the day after. I don't care if we starve. I'm going tearing through the streets with the other drivers because that's where I belong. I'm going to help them burn and wreck every damn cab in sight!"

And then I told Ethel something I promised myself I would never tell to anybody.

I told her about how just before I started back to the garage I parked in a side street and took out my tire-wrench and bashed in the fenders of my cab and then broke every damned window with my own hands. I screamed that out to her. She asked me why I had done it, and I didn't know what to answer.

Then I hollered out, louder than ever: "A man's got to keep some of his self-respect, don't he? What do you take me for, a scab?"

for discussion

1. Why does Tom Davlin insist that, in returning the smiles of the two motorcycle policemen, "it was not the same kind of smile they gave to me"? Why does he turn his radio on again "real loud" after his passenger has turned it off?

2. Francis Bacon said, "He that hath wife and children hath given hostages to fortune; for they are impediments to great enterprises, either of virtue or mischief." Tom Davlin says, "Any girl like that who feels happy over a kid must be either tight or crazy." What is the relevance of Bacon's statement to Tom's dilemma?

3. What other details in the story reveal the nature of Tom's conflicting loyalties?

JAMES T. FARRELL

☐ James T. Farrell was born in Chicago in 1904. Though his parents were native-born, his grandparents had emigrated from Ireland. His father, a teamster, was hard pressed to support his large family, so from the time he was three Farrell was raised by his maternal grandmother. He grew up on the South Side, in a middle-class Irish neighborhood then in the process of becoming the city's Negro section. Farrell attended parochial schools and graduated from high school in 1923. As his books show, he was also educated in the streets of Chicago and at the Amalgamated Express Company, where he was employed while in high school and for about a year after his graduation. From 1925 to 1929 he attempted to work his way through the University of Chicago, where by 1927 he had elected to become a writer. While still a student at the University, he published his first short stories and began to write about Studs Lonigan. After a year in Paris in 1931, Farrell took up residence in New York City. There, almost overnight, he became famous in 1932 with the publication of Young Lonigan: A Boyhood in Chicago Streets. The appearance of The Young Manhood of Studs Lonigan in 1934 and Judgment Day in 1935 completed the Studs Lonigan trilogy.

Farrell's main subject has been the Chicago Irish, but in describing them he carefully omitted most of the traits usually associated with the Irish. Their fabled charm and wit and vivacity are not evident in Farrell's literary portraits. A committed student of environmental influence, Farrell was less interested in some imagined Irishness of his characters than in their actual adjustments to the harsh urban conditions in which they fought for comfort and respectability. In many novels and stories, he recorded the bleak lives, the defeats, and the flickering hopes of people whose Irishness is largely a matter of sociological detail, a part of "a world they never made." Through his portrayal of the tragic emptiness of Studs Lonigan's wasted life, Farrell presented his larger case against American economic and social institutions. Farrell's central point is unmistakable: Lonigan's natural promise was twisted and destroyed by an unfavorable environment.

It should be noted, however, that Farrell never subscribed to the formularized literary Marxism of the 1930's. He was opposed to didactic fiction, and argued against the production of stories which conformed mechanically to the "correct" view of the class struggle. His implied criticism of American society emerges not from party dogma but from experience accurately and perceptively reported.

It should also be noted that Farrell's environmentalism is not rigidly deterministic. He read William James and John Dewey, and concluded that through the education of his reason a man might both escape and improve an unfavorable environment. Even while he was writing the Studs Lonigan trilogy, Farrell believed that through the creative exercise of knowledge a man may reshape his relation to the physical circumstances surrounding him. This affirmative side of Farrell's social vision is revealed in his five Danny O'Neill novels: A World I Never Made (1936), No Star Is Lost (1938), Father and Son (1940), My Days of Anger (1943), and The Face of Time (1953).

Farrell has written many other novels, including Gas-House McGinty (1933) and Ellen Rogers (1941). He has published more than 200 short stories. And he has defined his theory of literature in A Note on Literary Criticism (1936), The League of Frightened Philistines (1945), Literature and Morality (1947), and Reflections at Fifty (1954).

the oratory contest

I

☐ Facing the bathroom mirror, Gerry O'Dell practiced for the contest, and he imagined the thunder of applause that would greet him at the conclusion of his oration. His mother called him, and he said that he was coming. He met his dad in the hallway, and Mr. O'Dell looked at his narrow-faced, small, sixteen-year-old son with a mingling of pride and humility.

"Well, Gerry, how do you feel? The old soupbone in your throat loosened up?" the father asked.

"Yes, Dad," Gerry nervously answered.

"Gerry, your mother and I are mighty proud of you, and we'll be giving you all the ... the moral support we can tonight. Don't get worried because you're speaking in public, or because of the size of the crowd. Ah, anyway, Gerry, oratory is certainly a great gift for a boy to have," the father said, putting his hairy hands into his blue trouser pockets and rocking backward on his heels. "Gerry, if a man has the makings of a great orator in him, he need have no fears of getting ahead in life."

"George, don't be making the boy nervous. Gerald, supper is ready," the mother called.

"Martha, I was only explaining to him," the father apologetically explained.

"Father, you mustn't be saying any more now," she said in a nagging tone.

The father followed his son into the dining room, and he seemed to have been hurt as the family sat down for supper.

"Well, Sis, how did school go today?" the father asked, cutting into his lamb chop and looking at his pigtailed daughter while Gerry talked with his brother, Michael,

"The Oratory Contest" from *The Short Stories of James T. Farrell*, copyright 1937, 1964 by James T. Farrell. Reprinted by permission of the publisher, Vanguard Press, Inc.

about Sister Sylvester, the eighth-grade teacher at Saint Catherine's grammar school.

"I was spelled down," Ellen said.

"What word did you miss, Sis?"

"Interest, Daddy."

"Maybe you'll do better the next time."

"But, gee, Daddy, I tried so hard. I could have cried right then and there like a baby," she said.

"That's just too bad! Too bad that you couldn't show off before Georgie Schaeffer," Michael said, making a wry face at his sister.

"Is that so!"

Mrs. O'Dell told her younger children to stop arguing and eat their supper. It was no time to be disturbing Gerald. The family ate, and the father cast continued glances of approval and pride at his oldest son.

"Gerry, where did you learn the things you're talking about tonight? You must certainly have studied a lot to learn them," the father said.

"I read the Constitution, and the editorials on it that have been printed recently in *The Chicago Questioner*. And then, of course, there was my civics course, and Father Robert gave me lots of suggestions, and he spent an awful lot of time helping me rehearse my speech. He helped me get it written and to get my delivery set in my mind," Gerry said.

"Gerry, when I heard you give your oration at the semi-finals, I was a mighty proud father, I was."

Gerry smiled self-consciously.

"After you finish high school, you'll have to go to college. I want you to get a fine education."

"But, Dad, how can I?" Gerry said, looking hopefully at his father.

"You ought to be able to get a job and study law in the evenings downtown at Saint Vincent's."

"That's what I'll have to do," Gerry said disconsolately.

"Of course, something might turn up," the father said.

"George, that is what you've been saying for twenty years," Mrs. O'Dell said sarcastically.

"Martha, you can't say that I ain't tried. I've provided

for you and the children as well as I could, and I always brought my pay home to you untouched. I don't see where you have any right to complain when a man has always done his best."

"George, I'm not complaining. It's just that after all these years I'm tired out. Look how long we're married, and we don't even own our own home."

"We will yet. I mean it! I swear we will! A fellow at the barns was telling me yesterday that he can get a ticket on the English Sweepstakes. Now suppose I should win that! One hundred thousand dollars! Say, we'd be rolling in wealth. You know, Martha, you never can tell what will happen in life. Now last year, I remember reading in the papers where some foreigner, a cook in some New York hotel, won over a hundred thousand dollars on a sweepstakes ticket."

"And you're not that cook. You've been talking yourself blue in the face about winning in baseball pools almost as long as I can remember. And what have you won? What?"

"Didn't I win twenty-five dollars on a baseball pool last year?"

"Yes, and how much did you spend buying tickets during the year?"

"Gee, give a man a chance."

"Give you a chance! That's all I've ever given you."

"Have it your way then. But three years ago Tom Foley, who runs a car on Western Avenue, won five hundred, didn't he? If he can have luck like that, what's to stop me from having it?"

"You're not Tom Foley."

"Aw, Ma!" O'Dell whined, causing Gerry to glance at him quickly in disgust.

"I can't be listening to all your nonsense, George. I got to see that the boys get ready for tonight," she said when they had finished their tea and dessert.

"Gee, Ma, are you sure you can't come?" Gerry said as she arose from the table, a small, broad, fat-cheeked woman in her forties whose stomach was swollen out.

"Gerald, your mother isn't feeling up to snuff this evening. But I'll be thinking of you, speaking, and saying a little prayer to the Lord that you'll win the prize. Your mother knows that her son is going to take the prize, and she'll be just as happy whether she hears you or not, just as long as you telephone me the minute you get out of the hall," the mother said.

"Ma, can I go?" the sister asked.

"You got to stay home with your mother," the father said while Gerry kissed Mrs. O'Dell goodbye and left.

II

Mrs. O'Dell sat knitting baby socks in the dining room, and the daughter was bent over her school books at the table. The father entered the cramped room and asked his wife for some money. She slowly arose and waddled to their bedroom. She drew a two-dollar bill from a large leather pocketbook and handed it to him.

"George, I get spells. I'm afraid," she said.

"Don't worry, Martha. Gerry is a chip off the old block, and he has the makings of a fine orator. Why, he already orates better than a lot of lawyers and politicians I've heard," he said.

"It's not that, George. I'm too old now and this one is going to be a harder ordeal than when I was younger and had the others. Oh, George, I'm afraid! I can't bear to think of leaving you and the children without their mother."

Worried, he gently patted her back, tenderly caressed her unkempt black hair.

"I feel as if I can't carry the load inside of me. And my back gets so sore. I had a dream last night, and it's a premonition. I fear I shan't be pulling through. Oh, George, hold me, kiss me like you used to a long time ago! I can't bear it, the thought of dying and leaving you with an infant baby."

She sobbed in his arms. Holding her, he felt as if paralyzed. He sensed in her the mystery of woman which enabled them to bring forth a man's child. He was filled with respect, awed into speechlessness. He kissed her, clasped her tightly, his feelings reverential. He thought of how they were going along now, and of how they were past knowing and feeling again what they had known and felt in those first burning days of their marriage. Now it was just having sympathy with each other, being used to one another, having their family, their duties, and the obligations which they had to meet together, the feeling of liking, more than loving, each other, and wanting to be proud of their kids. He kissed her again.

Michael called his dad from the doorway. The parents blushed with embarrassment. They turned their heads aside. The father gruffly told his son that he was coming. He kissed his wife a final goodbye.

III

It was a muggy, misty March evening. Walking to the streetcar line with his son, O'Dell turned memories of other times over and over in his mind. He remembered his courtship and the days when he was younger and had worked nights, and of how at this time, on this kind of a night, he would be driving his car along Ashland Avenue. He wished that it were still those days and that he were young instead of a motorman rapidly getting old as his family was beginning to grow up. It was strange now to think of himself in other days, to think of what he had been, to realize how he had not at all known what life had in store for himself and his young bride. And now they both knew. And just to think that there had been a time when this boy, Michael, beside him had not been born, and neither had Gerry. Gerry had once been in his mother's womb just as the latest newcomer was at this very moment. He remembered the coming of his three children, Martha's shrieks and agonies, his own apprehensions and worries, the helpless feeling that had come over him, the drowsy tiredness on Martha's face after each delivery. He was afraid for it to happen all over again, afraid that this new one was going to mean trouble. *Death!* He wished that it were over with. Yes, and he wished that he were a young motorman again, instead of being pretty close on toward the declining years of middle age. He shook his head wistfully thinking of how now, for years, day after day, he had driven streetcars. And he had been driving them before the boy at his side was born, and even before Gerry had been on the way. Gerry had turned out fine, but not just exactly what he had imagined Gerry would be. Ah, nothing in life turned out just as a man imagined that it would turn out. And this new one? When it would be Gerry's age, he and Martha, if the Lord spared them both, they would be old. He trembled at the thought of this new one, and it turned his mind to thoughts of the years, of death, the end of them both.

"Mickey, you always want to be good to your mother. Help her all you can while you've got her, because you'll never realize how much she means to you until she's gone," he said.

"Yes, Dad," the boy dutifully replied, the father's words merely giving him the feeling that the old man was just preaching a little in order to hear himself talk.

"You won't have her with you always, you know."

They boarded a streetcar and stood on the rear platform talking with the conductor, who was a friend of Mr. O'Dell's. O'Dell told his friend where they were going and why. The conductor told O'Dell that one of his girls was a smart one like that, too, and she had just won a prize button in school for writing. But anyway, that girl of his, she was a great kid, and a smart one, too. Then they had to get off at Sixty-third Street and change for an eastbound car.

IV

O'Dell became increasingly timid as the car approached the school auditorium of Mary Our Mother. He tried to force a feeling of reassurance upon himself, thinking that he was just as good as any man, telling himself that he was a freeborn American who earned his living by honest work. He had just as much right as any man to come to this contest and hear his own boy whom he was educating out of his hard-earned money. He was an honest man, and work was honorable, and what if he was a motorman and some of the fathers of Gerry's classmates were higher up on the ladder than he? No, there was no need of his being ashamed. America was a democratic country. Still, he was shy. He knew that he would feel out of place. But he was proud of his son, and he knew that Gerry was going to win out over the sons of richer fathers, and . . . he felt that he just wouldn't be in place, and that maybe he shouldn't have come.

And he realized that Gerry, instead of waiting for him and Michael, had gone ahead. Gerry, he suddenly felt, was ashamed of him. He argued with himself that the boy had had to get there early, and that, anyway, he had been nervous about the contest and restless, like a colt before the start of a race. But still, no, he could not rid his mind of that thought.

He noticed other people on the sidewalk, walking in the same direction as he, and he heard them talking. Some of them sounded like parents, and he was sure that many of them must be the fathers and mothers of boys who went to Mary Our Mother. Did any of them, he wondered, have thoughts such as he? Well, before this evening was over they were all going to know about Gerald O'Dell.

And at home, there was Martha, her body big and swollen. He wished that she had come along. And she was at home, knitting away. He was responsible for her condition, and if he had curbed himself, well, they wouldn't be having this worry and this danger, and all the expense and sacrifice that it would involve, and she would be at his side, and they would both be so proud and happy, hearing Gerry win with his oration. How good it would be to have Martha at his side, both of them hearing the whole auditorium applaud her boy, her own flesh and blood. And she would not be granted this pleasure. He could just see her at home, knitting, silent, afraid. And she was going to be hurt, and this new child was going to be, maybe, so hard at her age, and oh, God forbid that she should die.

In front of the auditorium, he saw boys of varying ages, some only a year or so older than his Michael, other lads of seventeen and eighteen in long pants. He looked about to see if Gerry were among them, but he wasn't. He would like to tell them who he was, the father of Gerry O'Dell.

"Mike, here we are," he said in an attempt to be whimsical.

He handed two complimentary tickets to the lad collecting them at the door, and in a humble mood he followed the usher to seats in the center of the auditorium. He looked shyly about the lighted hall, seeing a confusion of strange faces, the people moving down the aisles to seats, and he was excited and expectant. He wanted it to begin. He glanced up toward the stage, with the stand and a row of chairs in front of the drawn red curtain. The boys, judges, and the honored guests, including a number of priests, some of whom might be Gerry's teachers, would all sit in those chairs. And again he felt out of place, humbly so. He felt that in the auditorium there must be the fathers of many of Gerry's classmates, men who had gone so much further in the world than he had, men who could afford to send their sons to good colleges.

He remembered the sight of the lads outside, and it caused him to think of how Gerry must have an entire life closed out to his father and mother, a life they could never get their little fingers on. He glanced sidewise at Michael, who was awkwardly twisting in his seat and looking about at faces with a boy's alive and curious eyes. And what did he see? What? Michael, too, and the girl, they had their lives that were closed to their father and mother, and as they grew older they would both drift further and further away.

"Like it, Mickey?" he asked, wanting to get close to his son, to be like a pal with him.

Michael smiled, muttered an absorbed uhuh.

"Some day you'll be going to the school here, too, and maybe, like Gerry, you'll be winning oratorical contests and prizes."

"I'd rather be on the football team."

"Maybe you can do both."

Michael smiled frankly, and the father suddenly found his mood dissipating under the smile. He did not feel himself to be such a stranger to Michael.

V

He was conscious of the movement of people, priests in the rear, the hall filling up, and he guessed that it was going to start. Suddenly the orchestra began a scratchy prelude, and O'Dell told himself that it must be fine music.

Like those around him, he sat quiet, a little hushed. Glad, too, that it was starting. He waited, entertained but anxious, through the elocution contests, when first-year students recited pieces. The junior contest followed, and four boys delivered famous orations. O'Dell thought that the tall boy who delivered a speech of Senator Hoar's defending the retention of the Philippine Islands had been the best. All of them had been good, but his boy would be better. And that was what he was waiting for.

He heard more music, idly reflecting that the priests here at Mary Our Mother must be giving the boys a good education. Anxiety was working within him like a pump. Right after the music Gerry would speak. He gripped and clasped his hands. Michael stirred. He tapped him, whispering to be quiet and to act well-mannered. The music, carried through by violins, seemed like the distant sounds of a waterfall, and they lulled within him. Dreamily he visualized Gerry speaking, imagined the lad's future as a great lawyer, and he thought of how boys in oratorical contests such as this one would, in years to come, be delivering the famous speeches and orations of Senator Gerald O'Dell. Gerald O'Dell, his son, the boy whose education had cost him sacrifices.

And now Gerry, small and freckled, was on the platform. He seemed so calm, as if there was not a worry in his head. He stood there, straight, dignified, and, ah, but wouldn't he be a pride to his father in the years to come. He was speaking. O'Dell leaned forward, listening attentively as his son's deep and full voice carried down the auditorium.

So the first step is, what is the Constitution?

O'Dell was in a spell, completely under the sway of his son's words, and he nodded his head as Gerry's voice rose in the final introductory statement which suggested that the United States and the Constitution are inseparable, and that without one there could not be the other.

And to all of us who are true Americans, our Constitution is sacred, the creed of those rights which are guaranteed to every one of us as an enduring pledge of our liberties.

Gerry spoke without halt, retaining not only the absorbed attention of his father but also of nearly everyone in the auditorium. He continued, declaiming that the defense of the Constitution, and of the principles which it embodied, was a sacred duty to be held inviolable, and that he who did not, nor would not, uphold these principles did not deserve to be called an American. He added that he who holds public office and willingly betrays his trust cannot be called an American. But in his talk he was not primarily interested in such men, even though they wantonly betrayed their public trust. He was concerned with something more vital, the betrayal of the fundamental principles on which the Constitution was founded, that of States' rights, individual liberty. And men, men in public affairs, were, because of ignorance or perversity or even malice, seeking to destroy that principle by advocating the passage of a Federal Maternity Act and a law establishing a Federal Education Department. These men wanted to abolish child labor by an act of Congress, even though the Constitution did not grant this prerogative to Congress.

O'Dell smiled when the boy quoted the late Champ Clark.[1]

If the groups seeking Federal assistance would put their burdens on the state legislatures where they belong, Congress would have time for the work which, under the Constitution, belongs to Congress.

Continuing, Gerry referred to this tendency toward centralization, seeking to prove that it was unjustified. And then, with cleanly contrived gestures and a rising voice, he concluded:

Should we allow our rights to be taken from us? No! Wherever this tendency to centralization shows its serpentine head, we shall fight it, because it is a menace to us, to everyone who is a liberty-loving American, and we must fight this menace. And defending our liberties, we shall take a slogan from some recent words of a Cabinet member,

---

[1] *Champ Clark:* (1850–1921) Democratic Congressman from Missouri and Speaker of the House; he was widely admired for his wit and forcefulness as an orator.

Herbert Hoover: [2] *"It is time to decentralize." Our fore-*
fathers, Washington, Jefferson, and Madison, fought to
give us our rights. Shall we let them be stripped away from
us? Never! We will defend our rights. We will raise our
voices until we are heard and our voices resound. Yes, we
will even shout: It is time to decentralize.

Gerry O'Dell bowed to the audience. He turned and
walked to his place among the others on the stage, while
the applause thundered. The father clapped himself weary,
restraining strong impulses to shout and stamp his feet.
Tears welled in his eyes. He smiled with a simple and child-
like joy. Unable to check himself, he turned to the man on
his left and said:

"That's my boy."

"Smart lad."

The remaining speeches in the senior oratorical contest
seemed dull and uninteresting to him. His boy had it all
over these other lads. And he felt himself justified in these
impressions when the judges announced their decision,
and amid a second strong burst of clapping Gerald O'Dell
was announced the winner of the gold medal in the Senior
Oratorical Contest. O'Dell rushed out to a drugstore to
telephone the news to Martha. Then he and Michael went
back. The tag end of the crowd was filtering out. Boys
were coming out in groups, standing, talking, dispersing
with the crowd. He searched for Gerry. Gerry would certainly have waited. A boy came out. It was Gerry. No! He
searched again. Gerry must be inside, being congratulated.
He went in, but found the stage empty. Gerry must have
gone. He told himself that Gerry had known that his father
would wait to see him, congratulate him, buy him a treat,
and that then they would go home together. And Gerry
had not waited. He still looked anxiously about at the disappearing faces. Where was he? He asked a boy in a lingering group of students if any of them had seen Gerald
O'Dell. They hadn't. He said that he was Gerald's father.

[2] *Herbert Hoover:* Secretary of Commerce 1921–1928, during the
Republican administrations of Harding and Coolidge; in 1922 he published *American Individualism*, a statement of his social philosophy.
In 1929 he became the nation's thirty-first President, and at the time
this story was written (1935) Hoover's administration was believed
by many to be responsible for the Depression.

They said Gerald had spoken well and deserved his victory. He stood with Michael. Only a few scattered groups remained in front of the hall. Feeling blank, he told himself, yes, Gerry had gone. He solemnly led Michael away, both of them silent. He asked himself why Gerry hadn't waited, and he knew the answer to his question.

precinct captain

I

☐ O'Malley was a stocky man in his forties, with a solid, brick-like face, thinning reddish hair, and narrow blue eyes. He had an air about him. He walked, he talked, he sat, he stood, he gesticulated with an air of authority. He was always playing his role in public, the role of a man who had been in the political game for twenty years. The fruits of his public service were a job as deputy sheriff in the county building and the title of precinct captain in his neighborhood near South Shore Drive and Seventy-first Street.

The primary fight put O'Malley on the spot. In the previous election, he had gone around and told all his people to vote for Kline for Governor. He had said that Kline was as fine a man as they would ever find in public life in the whole state of Illinois. He told them that Kline had a fine record. He said that it showed you what a fine country America was when it would elect a Jew. Many of his voters were Irish, and he told them that the Irish and the Jews had to stick together. Look what happened to the Irish in the old country. And look what happened to the Jews in, where was it, Jerusalem? Anyway, look what happened to them. He had thus argued that the Irish had to vote for Kline for Governor because he was a fine man, because he

"Precinct Captain" from *The Short Stories of James T. Farrell*, copyright 1937, 1964 by James T. Farrell. Reprinted by permission of the publisher, Vanguard Press, Inc.

had a fine record, because he was a good Democrat, because the Party and the organization were behind him, and because it was a fine thing for the Irish and the Jews to stick together. If the Irish voted for a Jew, the Jews would return the compliment by voting for a mick. And to Jewish voters in his precinct he had said that they had to come out and stand by a man of their own race and repay him for his public service rendered to them, and to all of the people.

Now, O'Malley was in the hole. All those whom he had lined up to vote for Kline had now to be lined up to cast their ballots for Anderson against Kline. It was a hot primary fight, and the organization needed every vote it could garner in the entire county because Kline was certain to roll up a large downstate plurality. O'Malley was working night and day, ringing doorbells, rapping on doors, trying to compose letters to his voters, handing out cards and cigars, hiring one gang of kids and young men to put Anderson literature into mailboxes and another group to take Kline literature out of the same mailboxes.

Easter Sunday came two days before the primary election. He was still busy, with more people to see, more cards to dispose of, more Kline literature to be destroyed, more Anderson literature to be distributed. The organization was fighting for big spoils, and the machine was built up of such rank-and-file corporals as himself. They had to do the producing. If they didn't, the machine was sunk and they were sunk with it. In every ward the Kline people were putting together an organization. If they won, they could have their own ward committeemen, their own precinct captains, and then, where would O'Malley be? He had to hop to it, and he was doing the hopping. He went to an early Mass on Easter Sunday, received Holy Communion, and then, after a quick breakfast, he was out working. He had to see a printer and arrange for the printing of more cards and for the mimeographing of a letter for distribution to the voters on Tuesday morning. He had sat up almost all of Saturday night composing this letter. It told the Democratic voters of the precinct that their friend and neighbor was Patrick J. Connolly. He had served them long and well. He had guarded the public interest as if it were his own property. He had never turned a deaf ear to their needs and their appeals. And now Patrick J. Connolly needed them as they had needed him. He needed their votes so that he could be returned as ward committeeman, in which capacity he would continue to serve them as he had done in the past. O'Malley was pleased with this letter of his. It convinced him that the big-shots down in the City Hall weren't the only fellows who knew a trick or two. None of them could have written a better letter, a letter that would win more votes than his would. But it had been hard work. He had gone to confession, and after midnight he could not eat, drink, even take a sip of water. He had done the job, though. After arranging with the printer, he had his rounds to make. The ballot was so long, and he had to give instructions to the people on how to vote, what names to skip on it, what men to vote for. It was a tough job, and no matter how long he spent explaining the ballot, he still could not be sure that the idea had been put across. And some of his voters were so damn dumb! They might vote for Anderson, but not for Connolly. They might give a vote to some of the traitors on the ticket who had waited until their names were printed on the organization's list on the ballot before they had changed and come out for Kline. Ah, yes, his job was all grief during an election fight.

About four o'clock, tired and weary, he got around to the Doyles. The Doyles were nice people, and he was glad he had met them. He knew that Mr. Doyle must have once been a well-to-do man. He acted and talked like a gentleman. Now he was having hard times and the breaks had gone against him. And the boy, he was all right, too, a fine chap. They were poor because of hard times, and too proud to go on relief. He was going to try and see what he could do for them by way of getting a job for Doyle if he could manage it. The Doyles were the kind of people you called the worthy poor.

He walked in on them in their one-room furnished apartment over a store. The apartment gave the sense of overcrowding, and the furniture was old and scratched. It seemed almost to breathe out a feeling of its own unlivableness. O'Malley smiled and handed a box of candy to Mrs. Doyle, a fat, beefy-armed, bovine woman. He pulled out cigars for Doyle, a tall, thin, graying man whose blue trousers were frayed at the pocket and their narrow, worn cuffs were out of style. He also handed two cigars to the son.

"Well, Mildred, here's the best precinct captain in Chicago," Doyle said as Mrs. Doyle was dusting off the best chair for O'Malley.

"No, just the most worn out," O'Malley said.

"You poor man, you must be so tired. Here, let me make you a cup of coffee," Mrs. Doyle said.

"Please don't, Mrs. Doyle. I only got a minute. There's still a long list of people I got to see," he said.

"You work so hard. It'll be a shame if everybody doesn't turn out and vote for you," she said.

"You don't think they will?" he asked, his brows beetling in worry.

"Certainly they will," Doyle quickly said.

"Don't be giving me heart failure, Mrs. Doyle. After all, a man of my advanced age can't take too much," O'Malley said, smiling grimly.

"It looks good, huh, O'Malley?" said the twenty-five-year-old son, a rather emaciated, characterless young chap with badly decayed teeth.

"I think I got it pretty much set. Now, how have you folks got the people managed in this building?"

"Skipper, you needn't worry about this building. Say, it's in your vest pocket," Doyle said.

"That's the way I like to hear you talk," O'Malley said, smiling and lighting a cigar while Doyle and his son puffed on theirs.

"Mr. O'Malley, are you sure you wouldn't take a cup of coffee? It'll only take a minute to make it for you," Mrs. Doyle said maternally.

"No, thanks. Now, about this fellow across the hall, the Polack?"

"I'm getting up at six in the morning to see him. He's hard to catch," Mrs. Doyle said.

"Be sure and do it. We got to get every vote we can. We got a fight on our hands this time."

"You'll win. Everybody else in the building is going to vote for Anderson. And you know, Mr. O'Malley, there was somebody around putting folders for Kline in the mailboxes."

"There was?" he exclaimed, glancing angrily at Mrs. Doyle. "Say, I'll bet he was one of these birds with a fishhook for a nose."

"But wait until you hear the rest of the story. I spoke to him. He asked me who I was for. I said, why I was for Kline. But now wait a minute until I tell you all of the story, Mr. O'Malley. I said that I was for Kline and so was everybody else in the building. I said that I had talked to them for Kline, so he put his folders in the mailboxes, and I asked him for more. He gave me some. I said, 'Oh, Mister, give me a lot more. I want to give these to all of my friends in the neighborhood.' So I got a great big pile of Kline literature. And right after I saw that he was gone, I took the stuff out of the boxes and threw the whole shebang into the garbage can," Mrs. Doyle said.

"Good for you! Good for you, Mrs. Doyle! If all people were like you folks here, I'll tell you, my job would be a good deal easier than it is and I wouldn't be getting early gray hairs from worry."

"Say, what the hell, Skipper! Don't have such a low opinion of yourself. You're the best precinct captain in Chicago," Doyle said ingratiatingly.

"I only wish I was," O'Malley said with almost histrionic dejection.

"Why, of course you are, Mr. O'Malley," Mrs. Doyle said.

"Sure, but let me tell you something. Roosevelt's the best precinct captain we got."

"My, but isn't he a wonderful man!" Mrs. Doyle exclaimed.

"He's a real bird, all right, fine man. He's done a lot for the people and the country," Doyle said.

"Best president we had since Woodrow Wilson," young Doyle said.

"You're damn tootin', he is! Damn tootin'! And he's the best precinct captain we got. But I ain't worried none about putting him over in my precinct in the fall. What I'm worried about is the primary election this Tuesday. Now, are you sure you got everybody in the building all set?"

"Oh, yes, of course. There isn't one Kline person in the whole building," Mrs. Doyle said.

"Here's the way I handle them. I say that, of course, now, Kline is a fine man. He's governor. A fine man. Sure. But so is Anderson. Anderson is a fine man, and he is the one we got to put over. Kline has that Oriental strain in him that's in his blood. He's not one of us, and he doesn't understand our problems."

"Say, Mr. Doyle, you ought to have my job. You're a smart man. That's the ticket, and I'm going to use that line myself. Say, I wish everybody in my precinct was like you. And you got mostly Irish in this building, haven't you?"

"Yes, Irish and Catholic."

"Of course, there is the Polish man across the way, and Mrs. Hirsch. I don't like her. She's too dirty, and, say, she would talk a leg off you. Now the other day—"

"Who's she for?" O'Malley interrupted.

"Why, Anderson, of course."

"Well, tell her to stay that way. And don't forget to nail the Polack," O'Malley said.

"Of course, I will," Mrs. Doyle said.

"You know, folks, I can't understand an Irishman who would vote for Kline after what he done to us. It was us who put him in, and then he is a turncoat. Why, four years ago I went around and told everybody to vote for him. Why, I got out a bigger vote for Kline in this precinct than I ever got out for anybody except Roosevelt. The Irish didn't go against him because he's a Jew. And what does he do? He turns on us," O'Malley said, his words and tone giving expression to a puzzled, wounded feeling.

"He gave us the can, didn't he? But he ain't got a chance, has he?" the son said.

"Not a chance of a snowball in hell if all the others around the city get out the vote the way I'll do it. Now, take that big apartment building down the street here in the next block. There must be a hundred voters in that buildin'. Well, I got every Democratic vote in the joint," O'Malley proudly said.

"Good for you," Mrs. Doyle said.

"The woman who works in the renting office there, I spoke to her and lined her up. So when some dame comes around for Kline, why, this woman, she says to the Kline dame, she says that the tenants in the buildin' have just gotten sick and tired of everybody and his brother comin' around about votin' and puttin' cards in the boxes. She says to the Kline dame that she can't let anybody else go around botherin' and annoyin' her tenants, because if she does, a lot of them will move out on her. So this Kline dame, she is dumb. You know, she ain't never been in politics and thinks she can come in and lick somebody like myself who has been in the political game all my life. She's dumb, see! She asks the woman, are her tenants for Kline. The woman says of course they are, sure, because everybody is. She takes the Kline literature from this dumb dame and throws it all in the ash-can, just the same as you did, Mrs. Doyle."

"That was clever," Doyle said.

"You ought to meet that woman. She's a fine woman," said O'Malley.

"Well, she helped. And in this game, every little bit helps," the son said profoundly.

"You're a smart young fellow. Every little bit, every vote does count. Every one. And to think of how many votes I swung to Kline four years ago. For him to go and turn his back on the organization and the people that made him, bitin' the hand that fed him. Well, don't worry! I'm cookin' the goose for him in my precinct. We don't waste our time with traitors to us when we're the fellows that made them somebody," O'Malley said vindictively.

"Mr. O'Malley, I'm just so certain that Anderson will get the nomination," Mrs. Doyle said.

"So am I. But we can't take any chances. Every vote counts. Now, are you sure you got every voter in this here buildin'?"

"It's in the bag," the son said.

"Yes, we guarantee it," Doyle said.

"All of the people have promised me already, except that man across the hall, the Polish one. I'm getting up in the morning to make sure of him," Mrs. Doyle said.

"That's the way I like to hear you talk. And if we win, I won't forget how helpful you've been to me," O'Malley said.

"We're doing everything we can," Mrs. Doyle said.

"That's the ticket," O'Malley said.

"And, Mr. O'Malley, what about election day?" Doyle nervously asked.

"Here, I brought these sample ballots," O'Malley said, arising and pulling out long pink-sheeted ballots, one of which he spread out upon the narrow dining-room table. "Now, I got this all marked up just right." The family gathered around him. He became official and almost coldly professional. His tone of voice changed. "You can all study this after I go, and I'm gonna leave some of these here for you to show to the people in the buildin' and to get them to study it. Now watch me carefully. See, you start here with Anderson's name at the top of the ticket. Now you go straight down until you get to Hogan for sheriff. You skip him. Any man that would turn on his friends the way Hogan did, he doesn't deserve a vote. Coming out yesterday and sayin' he was for Kline like he did on us. Be sure to skip Hogan, and tell your friends in the buildin' here to. And then you go straight down the list, Kaczmarski, Moran, Cogan, Connell, and then, here, you skip Schulman for county clerk. See, I got it here, and there's no X after Schulman's name. He is another one who turned his coat and betrayed his friends and the organization. And now here, don't forget, Connolly. See, right here! Tell all your people, absolutely, to mark an X after Connolly's name. See it, for ward committeeman. When you mention Connolly, you say: 'Your ward committeeman.' You see, what good is it going to do us if we get in the top of the ticket but don't get our own man, our own friend and neighbor, in for ward committeeman? So, don't forget it. Above all else, we got to get Connolly in," O'Malley said.

"Of course," Mrs. Doyle said with assurance.

"Now it should all be clear. See how they are marked with an X, and then, I got rings around the names of those you skip, like Hogan. You won't forget this and go votin' for the men I got ringed, will you?"

"Holy Moses, no!" Doyle said.

"You can study this sample ballot carefully after I go. And you know, you can take these into the booths with you when you vote, in order to see how to vote. We just got the rulin' on that, and it's O.K. to take sample ballots into the booth."

"We'll study it, Skipper, and show the neighbors what to do," Doyle said.

"If you're sure you can do that, you'll save me a lot of valuable time," said O'Malley.

"Of course we can. And we're glad to do it. You poor man, you must be so tired," said Mrs. Doyle.

"Well, I've been doing this for twenty years. I'm used to it, but, golly, a man does get tired toward the end of a hot primary fight," O'Malley said.

"And what about election day, Mr. O'Malley?" Mrs. Doyle asked.

"I've just been demonstratin' it to you, and I thought you all said you got the dope straight?" O'Malley asked, his expression changing.

"Yes, we understand that. But what I meant is, what time should we come to vote and, you know, Mr. O'Malley, you said something about your wanting us working around the polls, because you said we were so helpful to you," Mrs. Doyle tactfully said.

"Sure, you come around at six, and I'll get you fixed up."

"We'll be there," said Doyle.

"Then, if we win, as I fully expect to, well, as I just said, I don't forget them that sticks with me. If I did, I wouldn't be worthy of the name of O'Malley."

"Oh, we know it. And Mr. O'Malley, you look so tired, haven't you the time for a cup of coffee?" said Mrs. Doyle.

"Gee, no, I spent more time talkin' than I meant to. I'm so busy. I got to get these cards distributed," he said, taking out a stack of Connolly cards and giving some to Mrs. Doyle.

"You better leave a little more than that. I can distribute them," Mrs. Doyle said.

"Ah, that's the way to hear you talk," O'Malley said, handing her additional cards.

Leaving more cigars, he went out, followed by profuse farewells from all of the Doyles.

II

"He's such a nice man," said Mrs. Doyle.

"He's a sketch," the son said.

"We don't care what he is, as long as he gets us a job," said Doyle.

"I wonder? Maybe it would have been better for us if we had gone for Anderson, but let Arty here be a Kline man. Then we might have gotten somewhere either way," Mrs. Doyle said.

"Catch me voting for a Jew," the son said.

"Listen, Arty, we don't care what he is, if he gives us a job. We want to get a job for one of us, or we can't go on! We can't be such choosers," said Doyle.

"Here, he brought this candy, and it's filling. If you watch it, Papa, so the sweets don't get in your teeth, and you do the same, Arty, it's filling," said Mrs. Doyle.

"I can't eat chocolates, not with these molars I got," the son said, as his father took a chocolate and chewed it carefully.

"I'm glad that he didn't take the coffee. We hardly have any canned milk left," Mrs. Doyle said.

"Yes, we'll vote for Kline, Anderson, or the Devil himself for a job," Doyle said.

"That's why I talked like I did, about the people here. You know, some of them won't talk to me if I say Anderson. They're Republicans. But we might as well let him think that we're doing everything in our power," Mrs. Doyle said, eating a chocolate.

"Yes, and we'll give him our votes. Golly, I hope that we put Anderson over," Doyle said, grabbing a caramel.

"We got to! If we don't, we won't be anywheres," said Mrs. Doyle while the son enviously watched his parents eating the candy, his tongue playing around in his decayed teeth.

"Damn it, I meant to pray for Anderson's success this morning at Mass, and I forgot to," Doyle said.

"You would! You're just like an absent-minded professor," said Mrs. Doyle.

"Couldn't help it. I meant to. And I can still pray until Tuesday," said Doyle.

"Well, I think that the Lord will provide for us by electing Anderson so you can get a job," Mrs. Doyle said, dividing the last two pieces of candy with her husband.

"And after election, Tuesday, we can get a swell meal. We'll have five dollars each. And, Ma, I think that we can spare ourselves a movie. Shirley Temple will be at the show that night," Doyle said.

"But, Pa, we'll have to watch that money. You know, the agent told us last month that he was giving us our last chance. If we get evicted, we got to have a little something, or where will we sleep?" said Mrs. Doyle.

"Damn it, damn it, Anderson has got to get in," said Doyle, pacing the floor nervously.

for discussion

1. Situational irony exists when the actual outcome of a situation sharply contradicts the imagined or anticipated outcome. Modern realistic authors have made much use of such ironic reversals in order to bring literature closer to the actual character of life. How might a more sentimental author than Farrell have ended "The Oratory Contest"? What perspective on American society is gained through Farrell's ironic ending?

2. We have dramatic irony when a character in a narrative, confident of an imagined or anticipated outcome, makes statements that mean something different to him from what they mean to the reader who has been cued by the author to the likely outcome. Farrell employs dramatic irony in his characterization of both Gerry O'Dell and his father, but he does so to reveal quite different kinds of failure. Which details of Gerry's speech are, without his realizing it, particularly ironic? What failures are exposed by Gerry's victory?

3. In what way does Mr. Doyle's "nervously" asking Mr. O'Malley, "What about election day?" prepare the reader for the final scene in "Precinct Captain"? (Notice that Mrs. Doyle repeats her husband's question.)

4. The situational and dramatic ironies in "Precinct Captain" are directed at specific individuals. But what is the broader, more far-reaching criticism conveyed through Farrell's irony? For example, what is the reader to make of O'Malley's description of Mr. Doyle as a former gentleman (p. 223) in relation to Doyle's behavior in the story's final scene?

born 1905

LEON SURMELIAN

☐ *Leon Surmelian was born in 1905 on ancient
Armenian land under Turkish rule. He was reared in an
educated family; his father was a pharmacist. As a child
Surmelian showed literary promise and became a
protégé of the Armenian poet Tekeyan. But the course
of his life was suddenly and violently diverted in 1915 by
the holocaust in which the Turks massacred more than a
million Armenians. Surmelian escaped the terror that
fell upon his Armenian village, and fled with other
survivors to the city of Trebizond. Several years later,
sickened by the hatred and injustice he had experienced,
he left the Old World for the New. He arrived in
America in 1921, a sixteen-year-old orphan, almost
penniless and unable to speak a word of English.*

*Interested in agriculture and science as well as
literature, Surmelian enrolled at Kansas State University,
where he earned a bachelor's degree. For a number of
years he worked as a free-lance journalist. More recently
he has been a teacher of writing at California State
College in Los Angeles.*

*Surmelian's boyhood memories of the old country
and the terrible massacre were the subject of his first
book, the autobiographical narrative* I Ask You, Ladies
and Gentlemen, *published in 1945. His strong attachment
to the Armenian past is also evident in his 1964
translation of* Daredevils of Sassoun, *the Armenian folk
epic poem, and in his 1968 collection of Armenian
folktales titled* Apples of Immortality. *But Surmelian has
not sentimentalized the Armenian past: he remembers
both its tragedies and its accomplishments; he does not
forget the centuries of intolerance that weighed so
heavily upon the Armenians' effort to preserve their
culture. From this vantage point, Surmelian has sensitively
examined his adopted land and calculated its strengths
and weaknesses. A direct witness of persecution in the
Old World, Surmelian has warmed to the opportunity*

for harmonious human relations in the openness and prosperity of American life. But deeply influenced by Armenian religious idealism, he has also been troubled by the hypocrisy and materialism in American life. Thus, his writing possesses the kind of double focus often found in authors who stand somewhere between two worlds.

Surmelian's only novel, 98.6°, was published in 1950.

m. farid

☐ He was a fat swarthy man wearing conservative English clothes and a black bowler hat, a gold chain hanging on his ample vest, and with so foreign an appearance that I walked up to him and introduced myself when the weekly student assembly was over and we were coming out of the auditorium. I had not seen him at the meetings of the International Club. He turned out to be an Egyptian, and his name was Mohammed Farid.

"*Turkje biliorsun?*" I said.

"No, I can't speak Turkish," he said. "Just a few words. How long have you been here?"

"This is my third year. I am a junior. You are new?"

"Yes. I am still feeling my way about, getting oriented."

"You'll like this university," I said. "You've come to a good school."

"It has a good reputation. I heard about it in England."

That pleased me. Its fame had reached England. He said he attended an English engineering college before coming to America. He took a card from his wallet, jotted down his address on it with a gold pencil, and asked me to have dinner with him. "It's nice to meet someone from my part of the world," he said.

I did not know how friendly I wanted to get with a

"M. Farid" by Leon Surmelian. Reprinted by permission of the author.

man called Mohammed,[1] even though on the card his name was simply "M. Farid."

La ilah ill'Allah, Mohammed rassoul Allah, "There is no God but Allah and Mohammed is his prophet," were to me terrible words, and my father had refused to recite them as a boy, preferring death to the renunciation of his Christian faith, and had miraculously survived the massacre of the Armenians in his town.

But this Mohammed with his bowler hat and English accent looked harmless enough, and I thought I'd risk a dinner with him. I tried to be diplomatic. I thought a man like him might be useful in saving Armenian and Greek lives in Egypt if there was an outbreak of Mussulman fanaticism and armed mobs attacked foreigners and infidels, as had happened in the past. The Arab world was aflame, and I knew how strong was the Pan-Islamic movement among certain intellectuals and the rank and file of the Turkish people in a country that had abolished the Sultanate and Caliphate but was reintroducing the teaching of Islam in the schools, and where violent Islamic sentiments, linked with Pan-Turkism, were by no means dead. They had the tacit support of some government leaders.

Farid lived in the home of a professor of engineering, who opened the door when I rang the bell and took me to a room upstairs. A Moslem living in a Christian home— that in itself was something unusual for me. To the American professor, Farid was just another foreign student and renting him a room made for "international goodwill and understanding." This professor would probably call a mosque a Moslem church, but I was still fighting the Crusades, and to me Farid was somebody who had wandered to America from the enemy camp.

The Egyptian had been reading his Arabic newspapers. I saw daggers and snakes in that familiar script, so strange in Nebraska, so out of place. This was the real thing and not the Shrine version of it.

---

[1] *Mohammed:* The narrator, an Armenian, is here calling attention to the religious basis of the hostility between the Armenians (who are Christians) and the Turks (who are Moslems, or followers of Mohammed).

"Make yourself comfortable," he said, offering me a chair. "I've asked a friend to join us—an Arab from Palestine. I think you'll enjoy meeting him."

I wondered. What was this, a Moslem invasion? There were already two students from Pakistan who passed around propaganda pamphlets written by Indian apologists of Islam. One of these authors, a Dr. Sir Mohammed something, writing in an impressive scholarly style, and even with a certain poetic grace, went so far as to say that there is no fundamental difference between Christianity and Islam, but I knew better. The Pakistanis talked about the essential principles of Islam being democracy, freedom, tolerance, social justice, and progress, and were engaged in a missionary activity in Brighton, holding out the ideal of Pan-Islamism as the cure for all the ills of the modern world, which made me smile. Meanwhile there were bloody riots in India and the Moslems there massacred the Hindus. The Hindus, I was glad to read in the papers, struck back. Nonviolence might work against the British, but not against the sword of Mohammed.

A family portrait on Farid's dresser attracted my attention. As I was looking at it, he said, "That's my brother in London with his English wife and children."

How could an English woman marry a Moslem? She looked happy too. As a family picture it was charming, but its implications disturbed me. She had probably adopted her husband's faith, as Islamic law required. I wanted to tell him an Armenian woman would never marry a Moslem voluntarily; we had lived with the Turks more than a thousand years but there was never any intermarriage between Turks and Armenians, except by force, and if such a tragedy happened the woman ceased being Armenian. That's how we managed to preserve our Christian faith.

On his bedside table Farid had two large Arabic volumes.

"They are dream books," he said, when I glanced through them. "Rather valuable. They belonged to my father, and before him to his father. Books like this aren't printed any more."

"You believe in dreams?" I said.

"Don't you? This is a very wise old book. You tell me your dreams and we'll look them up in this book and find out what they mean," he added smiling.

"I'm afraid my dreams are a little too dirty," I said, smiling myself.

He did not smile again. Something about his manner indicated that for a Moslem he was strict in morals, if not a prude, and I liked this quality in him. Of course I myself was above such oriental superstitions. I was reading Freud and Jung.

Presently his friend came in. He was younger, about my age, light-skinned, with short curly black hair, and spoke perfect English through his Bedouin nose. His name was Jelal Ahmed. And Ahmed is another variation of Mohammed.

"My father's name was Jelal for a while, when he was made a Turk after his parents were massacred and he pretended to have become a Moslem until he escaped," I told them.

"The Armenians have suffered much," said Farid. "We like them in Egypt. Perhaps you know that at one time we had an Armenian prime minister in Egypt, Nubar Pasha. There is a monument to him in Alexandria."

I was glad to hear him mention Nubar Pasha, who reformed and modernized Egypt and presided at the opening of the Suez Canal.

"Nubar Pasha introduced many improvements in your country," I said.

"He was an excellent administrator," said Farid.

Ahmed also spoke a few words of sympathy, and praised the Armenians in Palestine for not siding with the Zionists during the Arab-Jewish war, and for not taking up arms against the Arabs in Syria and Lebanon when the French tried to "bribe" them and provoke them against the Arabs, he said, when the Arabs demanded independence. He mentioned the names of some Armenian students in the American University of Beirut he had attended for two years.

Farid took us to a good restaurant, and it struck me as strange that I should be dining with two Moslems. In Turkey my family had no social relations with Moslems; the barrier of religion was too great even after the republican reforms, and I went to an Armenian and not a Turkish school. Armenian history was a forbidden subject, but it was taught secretly when none of our Turkish teachers appointed by the government were present, and if one or two suspected something was going on in their absence they closed their eyes to it when they pocketed their *bakshish*.[2] Ironically, it was here in Nebraska that I met Arabs for the first time, and was dining with Moslems for the first time. I broke bread with them, as it were, to forget our past differences and the Arab-Armenian wars. But it was impossible for me to say "Mohammed," and I called the Egyptian by his last name and the Palestinian by his first name, to avoid calling him Ahmed, although Jelal brought back my father's ghastly memories of Shabin Karahisar.[3] They called me Valadian.

After dinner we went to a movie. Farid was an ardent movie fan. By the time I returned to my room I was their friend. They ate, walked, smiled, or laughed like me. We had so many thoughts and sentiments in common that I almost forgot they were Moslem Arabs.

From that day on I was their constant companion. Jelal was Americanized in Beirut and I didn't mind it too much when I saw a Koran in his room. He probably brought it with him for sentimental reasons and, if he ever read it, he read it secretly. I never saw him doing his *namaz*, the chief prayer of Moslems, recited five times daily. He wore a hat.[4] He was studying agricultural engineering to teach Palestine Arabs American methods of farming. He wanted the Arabs to catch up with the Zionists, as he always called the Israelis. Zionists had bombed his family out of Ramleh, and he was waiting for the second round with Jews.

Jelal's father, once a rich landowner, was a refugee in Jordan. Evidently the father made great sacrifices to have

---

[2] *bakshish* (bak·shāsh′): a tip or present.

[3] *Shabin Karahisar:* the name of a village and its surrounding area in Anatolia, a region in central Turkey densely populated by Armenians before the 1915 massacre.

[4] *He ... hat:* a mark of Western influence, as opposed to wearing a fez, the cap traditionally worn by Moslems.

his son study in America. I took him to be an Arab gentle-man of the old school. He had refused to sell any of his land to the Zionists, though they had offered him large sums for it. Jelal's grandfather had been a schoolteacher and an official of the Turkish ministry of education when Palestine was part of Turkey. Sometimes the check Jelal expected from his father did not come, which put him in a difficult position, but Farid was glad to loan him the money he needed. I understood father and son were very close, and Jelal was his family's hope, and perhaps of many other displaced Arabs, for a better life through the American technical and scientific skills he was acquiring in Brighton. It touched me. Moslem-wise, Jelal never mentioned his mother and sisters and the womenfolk, but it was my im-pression they were all very dear to him and he was dear to them, and they were bound together by affectionate family ties. Just like us, I thought.

Jelal was a good student, and made himself so likable that he became president of the International Club, while the only office I managed to get elected to in this organ-ization was that of marshal, to which I gave its more mili-tary meaning when, standing erect like a soldier, I swore the new members in. I voted for Jelal as president.

Farid was so shy that I could not drag him to any meet-ing or lecture or party with me, and he would not even join the International Club. He was too self-conscious. He thought everybody would be looking at him and see how ungainly he was in appearance. He exercised regularly with a couple of dumbbells he kept in his closet and claimed to be all muscle, but he was built somewhat on the proportions of King Farouk,[5] though with his short wiry hair and thick lips, he looked much more Egyptian than the king, who is, if I am not mistaken, largely of Albanian descent.

Farid was no scholar. I tried to help him with his les-sons, and he studied hard enough, but it was tough going. He wanted to specialize in geology. He lived on the income of his cotton plantations in Egypt and was probably the richest student on the campus. In a pinch, foreign students

[5] King Farouk: King of Egypt (1936–52), renowned for his fatness.

could borrow from him. He was generous with his money and always picked up the check.

I took Farid and Jelal to Dean Miller's home for a Christmas dinner, and I was always glad to introduce them to my friends. Jelal got around, made speeches in Brighton churches, presenting the Arab side of the complicated Palestine question, and soon he had his own circle of American friends. Everybody liked Jelal, and I thought he and the Egyptian were inseparable friends, but he fell out with Farid, and they stopped seeing each other. Neither would tell me what happened. I tried to bring them together, without success.

"For the love of Allah tell me what happened," I said to Farid. "Why don't you want to see him any more?"

"Very well, I'll tell you. He has been using black magic on me."

"Black magic!" I exclaimed. "You aren't serious. Jelal wouldn't harm anyone, and least of all a fellow-Arab."

"I was never more serious in my life. I know him better than you do. He is perfectly capable of it.

"So you believe in black magic? Don't be funny."

"I'm not being funny. I caught him just in time." He snapped his fingers. "Don't mention him to me any more. You can be friends with him if you like. I'm through. Valadian, sometimes you're so innocent. Jelal is a snake in the grass."

I would not even repeat to Jelel what Farid told me. It was the most absurd thing I had heard, and I could not convince the Egyptian with his ancient dream books that his fears were imaginary, there is no scientific basis whatever for such superstitions. The old East still lingered in Farid, despite his English clothes and college textbooks, and I tried to root the dark Sudan out of his mind. I figured that if an Armenian could reform and modernize the whole of Egypt there was no reason why I couldn't reform one Egyptian and make him forget his *jinn* and the Evil Eye.

He decided to move from his room, and asked me to help him find another room. He was too timid to look for a room by himself, and I went around with him and noticed how he suffered under the gaze of landladies who had rooms to let and glanced, doubtfully, at his hair and swarthy features, and said the room was already rented, or they wanted to rent it to a woman, or found some other excuse for not renting it to him.

Nothing was said between us, but I realized it would not be easy for him to rent a desirable room or apartment, and he was very particular. In the end he had to be satisfied with a two-room apartment in an old rooming house near the campus where by a sort of gentlemen's agreement only Indian, Filipino, and other oriental students lived. It was a depressing place. He did not have to share, really, this voluntary segregation, and I was sure to find a better apartment for him, but he felt freer and more comfortable in this rooming house. He furnished his new quarters with oriental rugs and silks.

"This looks like a pasha's penthouse," I said.

"I am a pasha," he said with his shy smile.

I did not know he belonged to one of the most influential families in Egypt. I urged him to pass himself off as a prince, and on occasion, much to his discomfort, I introduced him as "Prince Farid" and pretended to be his secretary. On Sundays we cooked *pilaf*,[6] green beans, or okra, with lamb, and other Near Eastern dishes in his kitchenette and played backgammon. He wanted me to go to Egypt with him and manage his properties there. He talked of forming a company and prospecting for oil in the Sinai peninsula and other areas of Egypt. My economic future would be assured, he said. And I could marry a pretty Armenian girl in Egypt.

I was already doing some managing. I helped him make his purchases in local stores and acted as his guide and companion—and meanwhile I enlightened him on America and the West.

"But I don't trust Western women," he said. "My brother was lucky, his wife is an exception. My experiences with Western women have been rather unfortunate, and they took me, as Americans say, for a ride. They care for nothing but money and good times."

However, he was quite taken up with his chemistry

[6] *pilaf:* a rice dish popular throughout the Near and Middle East.

teacher, an unmarried woman about his age, I supposed, getting to be an old maid, but not unattractive, and it tickled my funnybone when I saw them dining together in the town's best restaurant. On her birthday he gave her an expensive present, and I suggested she would make a good wife for him. She was quiet, plump, and did not have a Ph.D.

Farid would not tell me his age, but I took him to be about thirty—so much older than I that he was a mature, portly man in my eyes. My own youth was passing; I was twenty-one, going on twenty-two, and I hadn't started to live yet. I was missing so much for lack of money, perhaps the most important part of my American education. I could not afford to take a girl to dinner, to travel a bit and see America, to enjoy life as Farid was doing. He took weekend trips to Omaha or Kansas City and came back with a box of his favorite candy, chocolate cherries. These were mysterious trips, but I had my suspicions, and sometimes I did not know he had been away until I saw a new box of chocolate cherries in his apartment. He had a sweet tooth. When I questioned him, discreetly, about these weekend trips, the color deepened in his face and he changed the subject.

Indian and Filipino students living in the same building with Farid often gathered in his apartment. Their rooms were quite bare in comparison, although one or two Indians were reputed to be rich. I liked the Filipinos, always dapper, always well barbered, and decidedly Western in their thinking: the Spanish Catholic and American influence, I thought. They danced with bamboo sticks during our International Club programs, and they were equally adept at what seemed to be the courtly dances of old Spain, and the Filipino records they played on Farid's phonograph had nothing Malayan or oriental in them. It was rich Western music, that aroused visions of balls in the palaces of Spanish governors, and I wanted to visit Manila, which seemed to be a modern Western metropolis in the Far East. These dignified little men worked their way through college as houseboys, and I enjoyed their company. In Europe I had never seen Filipinos.

But the Indians were always arguing with me about

America and the West. In general I loathed Asia with its ignorance, its miseries, its cruelties, its mysticism, and the Taj Mahal was not enough to make me change my opinion about India. The leader of these Indian students—ten of them—was Dr. Chandra, a brilliant chocolate-brown biochemist doing graduate work. He had a string of degrees from India and American universities, all of which were printed on his card, and he spoke in a soft velvety voice which changed to a snarl when the subject of Western civilization vs. Eastern came up, and more specifically the civilization of India, which he considered superior to that of the West. Dr. Chandra spoke not only as an Indian, but as an Asian patriot, and saw nothing good in the West. He said he would take nothing from America except the knowledge he needed in his specialty, "and how to use the machine guns and our own atomic bombs," as he put it.

"Look at America," said Dr. Chandra. "Here is the perfection of your Western civilization. Twenty-five million Americans have been classified as borderline mental cases by the United States Army. In India, we put the emphasis on what is permanent, and we don't work ourselves to death or a mental breakdown. Americans are such hypocrites. I though I came to the land of the Declaration of Independence, but do you know, my dear, that I was beaten up and thrown out of a train in this wonderful America of yours when I refused to ride a Jim Crow car in the great state of Georgia? That I couldn't get a haircut in Chicago; that there are restaurants in this town that will not serve me? You can travel from one end of India to the other and no one will hold you up and rob you or kill you, and I can assure you, my dear, that you'd be safer there than in the streets of any American city."

"How about your caste system?" I countered. "Aren't there millions of untouchables in India? Don't you treat them worse than Negroes are treated in this country? Don't tell me about the glories of Indian civilization. You were ruled by a few thousand British soldiers, all four hundred million of you."

"If we spat on them we could drown them all. We bided our time, and our day has come. In five years India will be the third greatest power on earth and will hold the balance between America and Russia. And if we have to choose between America and Russia, it will not be America."

"Russia is part of Western civilization," I said. "Russia is Europe. You're contradicting yourself. You're not against the industrialization of India, are you? You don't want millions of Indians to continue starving and living in filth. Who will save India? Yogis and snake-charmers? Or the machines created by the West? You've to choose between *Karma* [7] and production."

I spoke as the commissar of common sense. Farid took no part in these arguments, and let me slug it out with his Indian guests, and particularly with this America-hater, though I could not blame him for feeling about America the way he did, after the indignities he had suffered because of his dark skin. I never mentioned my own experience in a small-town barbershop, when I was mistaken for a Mexican. Thank God I did not have to live in this building and I could eat in any restaurant in Brighton.

One day my Egyptian friend said to me, "You are going to churches all the time. Why don't you take me with you? Why are you so surprised? I'd like it very much."

"Okay," I said. "Next Sunday we'll go to the Congregational church, and I'll introduce you as His Royal Highness, Prince Farid of Egypt."

On our way to church I told him about the Christian religion and answered his questions as best I could.

"We recognize Christ as a prophet," he said, "and honor him for it."

"Christ wasn't just a prophet," I said. "He was the Son of God, and He was God. He was divine, in human form. We believe like you that there is only one God, but our God is a trinity—the Father, the Son, and the Holy Spirit. Sounds complicated, doesn't it? I can't say I understand it very well myself. We Christians accept these things with faith rather than reason."

"Christ was the son of Mary and Joseph?"

"Of Mary, but not of Joseph. He was born by what we

---

[7] *Karma:* a supernatural conception of fate that is one of the central doctrines of Hinduism and Buddhism.

call the Immaculate Conception. Joseph had nothing to do with it. Joseph was a good man, a carpenter by trade. Christ always said, 'My father in heaven.' "

Farid listened carefully to what I said, though I didn't think it made much sense to him. I tried to explain the doctrine of free will, or as much as I knew about it, and told him according to our religion man is free to choose between good and evil and is responsible for his acts. His fate is not written on his forehead.

"That's why Christian nations have made so much progress compared to Mohammedans. When you have free will, and your fate is not determined in advance by some supernatural force, you can do much to improve your lot. Take Turkey. As long as Islam was a powerful force in Turkey and the only way of life for Turks—and your religion more than ours is a way of life—the Turks were lethargic and fell behind their Christian subjects. The Turks realized they had to have science or perish as a nation. The only science that was acceptable to them at first was medical science, besides military science. Doctors were as necessary for their armies as generals. So you might say the new republican Turkey began in the medical school of Istanbul, where my father also studied. We believe man is master of his own destiny, and not a slave to his kismet, or to dark supernatural forces."

I did not directly refer to black magic, but I was working on him. I granted that Islam is a more simple and perhaps logical religion than Christianity—designed, originally, for the primitive people of the desert, as my instructor of medieval history used to say in Cyprus. He used to dramatize the rise and military conquests of Islam— how it spread like wildfire among rude backward peoples, but could make no headway among Christians and superior pagans, and maintained its solidarity among the peoples it conquered by the sword by making apostasy from Islam punishable by death.

And much for the same reason, I thought on our way to church, Islam is spreading today among the blacks of Africa, to whom it does give a certain pride and dignity as human beings, and admits them into the family of Mohammedan nations. And then of course Islam does not deny these new converts a man's right to have four wives and an unlimited number of concubines. That's a talking point with the *mullahs* [8] preaching among the bookless blacks—the *kitabsiz*—in Africa south of the Sahara.

"I'll tell you what Christianity is in one word: love. Forget the Trinity, the Immaculate Conception, free will, and all that stuff. Christians are still quarreling over what Christ meant, or the Apostles meant, or the Fathers of the Church meant. There has been and still is a lot of interpretation in our religion. But all of our theologians and interpreters agree on one thing: love.

"To us, Farid, God is love. Ours is not a religion to be spread or maintained by the sword. It champions the weak against the strong, the poor against the rich. We don't have Dar-ul-Islam and Dar-el-Harb. For us the world isn't divided into two, the country of peace on one side, for the believers, and the country of war on the other side, for the infidels—for Giaours [9] like myself. It's peace and love for all. Christ said, love your enemies. If they strike you on one cheek, turn them the other. Resist not evil, by evil means, that is. That's the whole thing in a nutshell. Of course we Christians don't live up to it. It's not the fault of our religion that Christians kill, hate, have prejudices. If everybody practiced Christ's teachings there would be no wars, and Chandra wouldn't be thrown out of a train or refused service in a restaurant, and Egyptians wouldn't be robbed by Western companies controlling the traffic on the Suez Canal."

It was a long speech. As we entered the Congregational church I remembered that Sunday when, wearing my diplomatic trousers, I was afraid to step inside this white limestone building and wondered now if my Egyptian friend was holding his breath as I did then. We sat in the last pew, for I knew he would attract attention if we walked down the aisle and I wanted to save him the pain of being stared at. I was relaxed, I felt at home in this Protestant church, and the old fears and prejudices were

[8] *mullahs* (mŏŏl'əs): Moslem teachers.
[9] *Giaours:* Turkish word for unbelievers or non-Moslems, especially Christians.

gone. Did I really find the soul of America in this small-town church, with its atmosphere of Old America I was so partial to? I hesitated to answer this question, fond as I was of the Congregational church and recognizing the part it played in my Americanization, the sense of belonging it gave me. The "soullessness" of America used to bother me in those days and now I had to admit I was less concerned with it; this "soullessness" was not peculiar to America but a sign of the modern industrial age spreading to other parts of the world, although here the contact between soul and soil was not fully established yet. The Armenian words were alike too: "hoq" for soul, "hogh" for soil. As always, I found myself drawn to the Puritans,[10] those tough theocrats, and I thought maybe some atavistic connection in me with the Paulicians, the Armenian sect that originated in the region of Shabin Karahisar and which may be said to be the first Puritan movement in Christendom and the forerunner of modern Protestantism, has something to do with the affinity for American Puritans. But another side of me resisted the Protestant Ethic,[11] and I knew I was still enamored with the vow of holy poverty, still a monk at heart. I could not rid myself of the conviction that the real purity lies in purposeful poverty. What my mind approved my heart rejected. I was disappointed in the Puritans for not measuring up to their own moral code. I wished they were as indifferent to the world's goods, and as bird and flower loving as St. Francis of Assisi.

Farid wanted to show himself as being broadminded, and with all his superstitions I knew he was a man of good will. I saw him following the simple service of the church with respectful attention, sitting or standing with me in the last row. I tried to appear a better Christian than I was, singing the hymns and bowing my head in silent prayer with the rest of the congregation. When the service was over he begged me not to introduce him to anyone and we

[10] *Puritans:* The New England Puritans were, for the most part, Congregationalists.
[11] *the Protestant Ethic:* a discipline of hard work and thrift that many historians and economists regard as one of the main sources of modern capitalism.

slipped out of the church before Dr. Smith took his position by the door and began shaking hands.

"Well, how did you like it?" I asked him.

"It was very interesting . . . different from what I thought it would be," Farid said thoughtfully.

I was absorbed in my own thoughts, and we walked under the wide-branching elms that lined the main street, Holtz Avenue, without speaking for some moments. A wild idea occurred to me—Christians and Moslems uniting and becoming as friendly as Farid and I were, now. I thought it would open a new chapter in the history of the world and bring East and West closer together. If Islam is in need of reform, so is Christianity, I said to myself. There are some good things in the Koran also, not so different from our Christian ethics, and no Christian can quarrel with what Mohammed said about charity and benevolence, for instance. I thought we should forget the past and find a common ground of cooperation with the three or four hundred million Moslems of the world. I saw myself at the head of a movement to unite Moslems and Christians— Christians speaking in mosques, Moslems in churches, during an annual brotherhood week set aside for that purpose, and myself addressing the biggest crowds of all, from Cairo to Karachi.

Maybe that Indian apologist of Islam wasn't so far off the mark. A man could be a Moslem and still be a good man, like Farid, and like Jelal.

My Egyptian friend dropped out of college before graduating and I lost track of him after a brief correspondence. Years later I met Jelal in California. He was buying seeds and machinery for an agricultural project in the Gaza strip, where he worked as a representative of the United Nations refugee commission, and was a young man of some consequence among Arabs. We spent a few days together driving up and down the Coast and remembering our college days in Nebraska.

"Have you heard from Farid?" I asked him. "I wonder what happened to him?"

"Don't you know?" said Jelal. "Farid became a Christian and married an Armenian girl."

for discussion

1. Does the narrator of "M. Farid" speak more typically as an Armenian or as an American? Or does he speak as both?

2. What evidence in the story indicates that the narrator is finding it hard to define his loyalties?

3. The picture of American life drawn by the narrator reveals both its positive and negative features. What are they?

PART 3

ETHNIC WRITING COMES OF AGE

INTRODUCTION

☐ The 1940's stand as a kind of watershed for ethnic
writing in America. During that decade Ralph Ellison
and Melvin Tolson enlarged the scope of their art, Saul
Bellow and J. F. Powers published their first books,
Bernard Malamud and James Baldwin made their obscure
first appearances in print. Behind them were two
generations of earlier ethnic writers whose work had
only on rare occasions reached beyond sentimental
public appeals or shrill social protest. Ahead of them was
the opportunity to break through these restrictions on
their art. By the 1950's a sizable group of ethnic writers
had accepted the challenge of making the fullest artistic
use of their ethnic materials. This new generation peers
from its ethnic vantage points into the larger, more
pervasive, endlessly complicated questions that inform
human experience in our time.

During the 1950's and 1960's ethnic literature
became an integral part of American literature. In
striking contrast to the "special" status accorded such
earlier ethnic writers as Langston Hughes and Richard
Wright, many ethnic writers now achieve widespread
public acceptance. Major literary honors, like the National
Book Award and membership in the National Institute of
Arts and Letters, are regularly bestowed upon them. No
longer exotic novelties, ethnic writers are the nation's
writers. Thus, *ethnic* joins *region, social class,* and *literary
school* as a term describing a principal source of our
national literature. Just as the origins of Hawthorne and
Faulkner are regional, just as Benjamin Franklin and
Sinclair Lewis derive from the middle class, just as
Stephen Crane and Hemingway emerge from the realistic
movement, the sources of an Ellison or a Malamud are
ethnic. Whatever their origins, however, all become
identifiably American writers by virtue of the insight and
the art with which they probe the larger meanings of their
local materials. Together they succeed in giving their
material a shape and significance that extend its meaning

to the larger community outside their own.

At their artistic best, ethnic writers are neither ambassadors of good will nor voices of alienation and protest. At their best, ethnic writers do not narrowly conceive their stories and poems as instruments of social change to be valued chiefly in terms of doctrinal correctness and cultural impact. Rather, they attach primary importance to the mastery of their art as the means of seeing further into their ethnic experience. A growing number of ethnic writers now know that they must extend their vision to its furthest limits, to a perception of the uncertainty and the ambiguity that frame all human behavior and make easy judgments impossible. These writers find the expression of social and psychological truths to be a complicated venture, demanding total investment of their imaginative and linguistic talents. But through the honesty and the art of their portrayals, writers like Ellison and Malamud manage to reveal the essential humanity of ethnic life without blurring its distinguishing features. They have earned a national audience by looking deeply enough into the ethnic experience in America to discover aches, confusions, and triumphs that are elemental properties of the twentieth century.

On the other hand, ethnic literature in America has come of age at a time when Americans have been made increasingly aware of their diversity. The conventional belief that American cultural unity is both possible and desirable was sharply questioned during the 1960's. Many social critics have denied that the American "melting pot" has ever become a reality. And owing to the intense ethnic consciousness of that decade, the "melting pot" ideal has also been judged undesirable by ethnic spokesmen anxious to preserve their cultural integrity.

Ethnic writers have found their way into the American literary mainstream at a time when the stream has commenced to overflow its familiar boundaries and when social forces are at work that may alter the composition and even the direction of the stream. As America moves into the last decades of the twentieth century, both the society and its literature are undergoing change. America's ethnic communities are major determinants of that change. And ethnic writers presently occupy a position of comparable influence as American literature tries, through new acts of the imagination, to find the enduring unities of American life in the very facts of its unceasing variety.

PHILIP ROTH

☐ *Philip Roth was born in Newark, New Jersey, in 1933. He was educated in Newark's public schools, at Bucknell University, and at the University of Chicago. His first book,* Goodbye, Columbus, *was published in 1959, comprising a novelette—the title story—and five short stories.* Goodbye, Columbus *earned Roth the National Book Award for fiction in 1960. He has since published three novels:* Letting Go *in 1962,* When She Was Good *in 1967, and* Portnoy's Complaint *in 1969.*

Roth is more than a generation removed from the world of the Jewish immigrant to America, the world depicted by Abraham Cahan. And Roth seems equally remote from the militant, left-wing protest writers of the thirties. Unlike such "proletarian" authors as Michael Gold and Albert Halper, Roth is deeply preoccupied with the Jewishness of his fictional characters. The characters in his stories are unmistakably American Jews in their speech and points of view. But unlike the earliest Jewish writers in America, Roth never idealizes his characters. He refuses to beautify their behavior or to rationalize their motives. Whatever coarseness or opportunism or folly he detects in their natures remains —together with their virtues—as the emblem of their humanity. Jews provide Roth with specific forms of general human conduct; Jewishness for him is the familiar material out of which he is able to shape and dramatize his conceptions of life.

Roth denies that, as a writer of fiction, he is under any obligation to make his stories serve the particular social interests of the Jewish community. As an artist dedicated only to serving the deepest insights afforded by real and imagined experience, he refuses to delete or to disguise even those actions of his characters which appear to confirm the stereotypes fostered by anti-Semites. Thus, paradoxically, the sternest criticism of Roth's widely acclaimed stories comes from members

*of the Jewish-American community. This criticism
compels Roth to ask the fundamental question often
neglected by earlier ethnic writers—to whom is the
artist responsible and for whom does he speak?*

writing about jews

☐ Ever since some of my first stories were published in
1959 in a volume called *Goodbye, Columbus,* my work has
been attacked from certain pulpits and in certain periodicals as dangerous, dishonest, and irresponsible. I have read
editorials and articles in Jewish community newspapers
condemning these stories for ignoring the accomplishments
of Jewish life, or, as Rabbi Emanuel Rackman recently
told a convention of the Rabbinical Council of America,
for creating a "distorted image of the basic values of
Orthodox Judaism," and even, he went on, for denying the
non-Jewish world the opportunity of appreciating "the
overwhelming contributions which Orthodox Jews are
making in every avenue of modern endeavor. . . ." Among
the letters I receive from readers, there have been a number written by Jews accusing me of being anti-Semitic and
"self-hating," or, at the least, tasteless; they argue or imply
that the sufferings of the Jews throughout history, culminating in the murder of six million by the Nazis, have
made certain criticisms of Jewish life insulting and trivial.
Furthermore, it is charged that such criticism as I make of
Jews—or apparent criticism—is taken by anti-Semites as
justification for their attitudes, as "fuel" for their fires,
particularly as it is a Jew himself who seemingly admits
to habits and behavior that are not exemplary, or even
normal and acceptable. When I speak before Jewish audiences, invariably there have been people who have come

An edited version of "Writing About Jews" by Philip Roth from
Commentary, December 1963, copyright © 1963 by the American Jewish Committee. Reprinted by permission of *Commentary.*

up to me afterward to ask, "Why don't you leave us alone? Why don't you write about the Gentiles?"—"Why must you be so critical?"—"Why do you disapprove of us so?" —this last question asked as often with incredulity as with anger; and often when asked by people a good deal older than myself, asked as of an erring child by a loving but misunderstood parent.

It is difficult, if not impossible, to explain to some of the people claiming to have felt my teeth sinking in, that in many instances they haven't been bitten at all. Not always, but frequently, what readers have taken to be my disapproval of the lives lived by Jews seems to have to do more with their own moral perspective than with the one they would ascribe to me: at times they see wickedness where I myself had seen energy or courage or spontaneity; they are ashamed of what I see no reason to be ashamed of, and defensive where there is no cause for defense.

Not only do they seem to me often to have cramped and untenable notions of right and wrong, but looking at fiction as they do—in terms of "approval" and "disapproval" of Jews, "positive" and "negative" attitudes toward Jewish life—they are likely not to see what it is that the story is really about.[1]

This was central to the question raised—and urgently —when a story of mine, "Defender of the Faith," appeared in the *New Yorker* in April 1959. The story is told by Nathan Marx, an Army sergeant just rotated back to Missouri from combat duty in Germany, where the war has ended. As soon as he arrives, he is made First Sergeant in a training company, and immediately is latched onto by a young recruit who tries to use his attachment to the sergeant to receive kindnesses and favors. His attachment, as he sees it, is that they are both Jews. As the story progresses, what the recruit, Sheldon Grossbart, comes to demand are not mere considerations, but privileges to which Marx does not think he is entitled. The story is about one man who uses his own religion, and another's uncertain conscience, for selfish ends; but mostly it is

---

[1] In the first publication of this essay, the author discussed here his story of "Epstein."

about this other man, the narrator, who because of the ambiguities of being a member of his particular religion, is involved in a taxing, if mistaken, conflict of loyalties.

I don't now, however, and didn't while writing, see Marx's problem as nothing more than "Jewish": confronting the limitations of charity and forgiveness in one's nature—having to draw a line between what is merciful and what is just—trying to distinguish between apparent evil and the real thing, in one's self and others—these are problems for most people, regardless of the level at which they are perceived or dealt with. Yet, though the moral complexities are not exclusively characteristic of the experience of being a Jew, I never for a moment considered that the characters in the story should be anything other than Jews. Someone else might have written a story embodying the same themes, and similar events perhaps, and had at its center Negroes or Irishmen; for me there was no choice. Nor was it a matter of making Grossbart a Jew and Marx a Gentile, or vice versa; telling half the truth would have been much the same here as telling a lie. Most of those jokes beginning, "Two Jews were walking down the street," lose a little of their punch if one of the Jews, or both, are disguised as Englishmen or Republicans. Similarly, to have made any serious alteration in the Jewish factuality of "Defender of the Faith" as it began to fill itself out in my imagination, would have so unsprung the tensions I felt in the story that I would no longer have had left a story that I wanted to tell, or one I believed myself able to.

Some of my critics must wish that this had happened, for in going ahead and writing this story about Jews, what else did I do but confirm an anti-Semitic stereotype? But to me the story confirms something different, if no less painful to its readers. To me Grossbart is not something we can dismiss solely as an anti-Semitic stereotype; he is a Jewish fact. If people of bad intention or weak judgment have converted certain facts of Jewish life into a stereotype of The Jew, that does not mean that such facts are no longer important in our lives, or that they are taboo for the writer of fiction. Literary investigation may even be a way to redeem the facts, to give them the weight and value that they should have in the world, rather than the disproportionate significance they probably have for some misguided or vicious people.

Sheldon Grossbart, the character I imagined as Marx's antagonist, has his seed in fact. He is not meant to represent The Jew, or Jewry, nor does the story indicate that it is the writer's intention that he be so understood by the reader. Grossbart is depicted as a single blundering human being, one with force, self-righteousness, cunning, and on occasion, even a little disarming charm; he is depicted as a man whose lapses of integrity seem to him so necessary to his survival as to convince him that such lapses are actually committed in the name of integrity. He has been able to work out a system whereby his own sense of responsibility can suspend operation, what with the collective guilt of the others having become so immense as to have seriously altered the conditions of trust in the world. He is presented not as the stereotype of The Jew, but as a Jew who acts like the stereotype, offering back to his enemies their vision of him, answering the punishment with the crime. Given the particular kinds of denials, humiliations, and persecutions that the nations have practiced on their Jews, it argues for far too much nobility to deny not only that Jews like Grossbart exist, but to deny that the temptations of Grossbartism exist in many who perhaps have more grace, or will, or are perhaps only more cowed, than the simple frightened soul that I imagined weeping with fear and disappointment at the end of the story. Grossbart is not The Jew; but he is a fact of Jewish experience and well within the range of its moral possibilities.

And so is his adversary, Marx, who is, after all, the story's central character, its consciousness and its voice. He is a man who calls himself a Jew more tentatively than does Grossbart; he is not sure what it means, means for him, for he is not unintelligent or without conscience; he is dutiful, almost to a point of obsession, and confronted by what are represented to him as the needs of another Jew, he does not for a while know what to do. He moves back and forth from feelings of righteousness to feelings of betrayal, and only at the end, when he truly does betray the trust that Grossbart tries to place in him, does he commit what he has hoped to all along: an act he can believe to be honorable.

Marx does not strike me, nor any of the readers I heard from, as unlikely, incredible, "made-up"; the verisimilitude of the characters and their situation was not what was called into question. In fact, an air of convincingness that the story was believed to have, caused a number of people to write to me, and the *New Yorker*, and the Anti-Defamation League,[2] protesting its publication.

Here is one of the letters I received after the story was published:

> Mr. Roth:
> With your one story, "Defender of the Faith," you have done as much harm as all the organized anti-Semitic organizations have done to make people believe that all Jews are cheats, liars, connivers. Your one story makes people—the general public —forget all the great Jews who have lived, all the Jewish boys who served well in the armed services, all the Jews who live honest hard lives the world over. . . .

Here is one received by the *New Yorker:*

> Dear Sir:
> . . . We have discussed this story from every possible angle and we cannot escape the conclusion that it will do irreparable damage to the Jewish people. We feel that this story presented a distorted picture of the average Jewish soldier and are at a loss to understand why a magazine of your fine reputation should publish such a work which lends fuel to anti-Semitism.
> Clichés like "this being Art" will not be acceptable. A reply will be appreciated.

[2] *Anti-Defamation League:* An offshoot of B'nai B'rith, the American Jewish service organization, the Anti-Defamation League was founded in 1913 to oppose anti-Semitism in America and to defend Jews against bigotry and discrimination.

Here is a letter received by the Anti-Defamation League, who out of the pressure of the public response, telephoned to ask if I wanted to talk to them. The strange emphasis of the invitation, I thought, indicated the discomfort they felt at having to pass on—or believing they had to pass on—messages such as this:

Dear ———,
What is being done to silence this man? Medieval Jews would have known what to do with him. . . .

The first two letters I quoted were written by Jewish laymen, the last by a rabbi and educator in New York City, a man of prominence in the world of Jewish affairs.

The rabbi was later to communicate directly with me. He did not mention that he had already written the Anti-Defamation League to express regret over the decline of medieval justice, though he was careful to point out at the conclusion of his first letter his reticence in another quarter. I believe I was supposed to take it as an act of mercy: "I have not written to the editorial board of the *New Yorker*," he told me. "I do not want to compound the sin of informing. . . ."

Informing—there was the charge so many of the correspondents had made, even when they did not want to make it openly to me, or to themselves. I had informed on the Jews. I had told the Gentiles what apparently it would otherwise have been possible to keep secret from them: that the perils of human nature afflict the members of our minority. That I had also informed them it was possible for there to be such a Jew as Nathan Marx did not seem to bother anybody; if I said earlier that Marx did not strike my correspondents as unlikely, it is because he didn't strike them at all. He might as well not have been there. Of the letters that I read, only one even mentioned Marx and only to point out that I was no less blameworthy for portraying the Sergeant as "a white Jew" as he was described by my correspondent, a kind of Jewish Uncle Tom.

But even if Marx were that and only that, a white Jew, and Grossbart only a black one, did it in any way follow that because I had examined the relationship between them

—another concern central to the story which drew barely a comment from my correspondents—that I had then advocated that Jews be denationalized, deported, persecuted, murdered? Well, no. Whatever the rabbi may believe privately, he did not indicate to me that he thought I was an anti-Semite. There was a suggestion, however, and a grave one, that I had acted like a fool. "You have earned the gratitude," he wrote, "of all who sustain their anti-Semitism on such conceptions of Jews as ultimately led to the murder of six million in our time."

Despite the sweep there at the end of the sentence, the charge made is actually up at the front: I "earned the gratitude. . . ." But of whom? I would put it less dramatically, but maybe more exactly: of those who are predisposed to misread the story—out of bigotry, ignorance, malice, or even innocence. If I did earn their gratitude, it was because they failed to see, even to look for, what I was talking about. . . . Such conceptions of Jews as anti-Semites hold, then, and as they were able to confirm by misunderstanding my story, are the same, the rabbi goes on to say, as those which "ultimately led to the murder of six million in our time."

"Ultimately"? Is that not a gross simplification of the history of the Jews and the history of Hitler's Germany? People hold serious grudges against one another, vilify one another, deliberately misunderstand one another, and tell lies about one another, but they do not always, as a consequence, *murder* one another, as the Germans murdered the Jews, and as other Europeans allowed the Jews to be murdered, or even helped the slaughter along. Between prejudice and persecution there is usually, in civilized life, a barrier constructed by the individual's convictions and fears, and the community's laws, ideals, and values. What "ultimately" caused this barrier to disappear in Germany cannot be explained only in terms of anti-Semitic misconceptions; surely what must also be understood here is the intolerability of Jewry, on the one hand, and its usefulness, on the other, to the Nazi ideology and dream.

By simplifying the Nazi-Jewish relationship, by making *prejudice* appear to be the primary cause of annihilation, the rabbi is able to make the consequences of publishing

"Defender of the Faith" in the *New Yorker* seem very grave indeed. He doesn't appear to be made at all anxious, however, by the consequences of his own position. For what he is suggesting is that some subjects must not be written about, or brought to public attention, because it is possible for them to be misunderstood by people with weak minds or malicious instincts. Thus he consents to put the malicious and weak-minded in a position of determining the level at which open communication on these subjects will take place. This is not fighting anti-Semitism, but submitting to it; that is, submitting to a restriction of consciousness as well as communication because being conscious and being candid is too risky.

In his letter the rabbi calls my attention to the famous madman who shouts "Fire!" in "a crowded theater." He leaves me to complete the analogy myself: by publishing "Defender of the Faith" in the *New Yorker:* (1) I am shouting; (2) I am shouting "Fire!"; (3) there is no fire; (4) all this is happening in the equivalent of "a crowded theater." The crowded theater: there is the risk. I should agree to sacrifice the freedom that is essential to my vocation, and even to the general well-being of the culture, because—because of what? "The crowded theater" has absolutely no relevance to the situation of the Jew in America today. It is a grandiose delusion. It is not a metaphor describing a cultural condition, but a revelation of the nightmarish visions that must plague people as demoralized as the rabbi appears to be: rows endless, seats packed, lights out, doors too few and too small, panic and hysteria just under the skin. . . . No wonder he says to me finally, "Your story—in Hebrew—in an Israeli magazine or newspaper—would have been judged exclusively from a literary point of view." That is, ship it off to Israel. But please don't tell it here, now.

Why? So that "they" will not commence persecuting Jews again? If the barrier between prejudice and persecution collapsed in Germany, this is hardly reason to contend that no such barrier exists in our country. And if it should ever begin to appear to be crumbling, then we must do what is necessary to strengthen it. But not by putting on a good face; not by refusing to admit to the intricacies and impossibilities of Jewish lives; not by pretending that Jews have existences less in need of, less deserving of, honest attention than the lives of their neighbors; not by making Jews invisible. The solution is not to convince people to like Jews so as not to want to kill them; it is to let them know that they cannot kill them even if they despise them. And how to let them know? Surely repeating over and over to oneself, "It can happen here," does little to prevent "it" from happening. Moreover, ending persecution involves more than stamping out persecutors. It is necessary, too, to learn certain responses to them. All the tolerance of persecution that has seeped into the Jewish character—the adaptability, the patience, the resignation, the silence, the self-denial—must be squeezed out, until the only response there is to *any* restriction of liberties is "No, I refuse."

The chances are that there will always be some people who will despise Jews, just so long as they continue to call themselves Jews; and, of course, we must keep an eye on them. But if some Jews are dreaming of a time when they will be accepted by Christians as Christians accept one another—if *this* is why certain Jewish writers should be silent—it may be that they are dreaming of a time that cannot be, and of a condition that does not exist, this side of one's dreams. Perhaps even the Christians don't accept one another as they are imagined to in that world from which Jews may believe themselves excluded solely because they are Jews. Nor are the Christians going to feel toward Jews what one Jew may feel toward another. The upbringing of the alien does not always alert him to the whole range of human connections which exists between the liaisons that arise out of clannishness, and those that arise—or fail to—out of deliberate exclusion. Like those of most men, the lives of Jews no longer take place in a world that is just *landsmen* [3] and enemies. The cry "Watch out for the *goyim!*" [4] at times seems more the expression of an unconscious wish than of a warning: Oh that they were out there, so that we could be together in here! A rumor of persecution, a taste of exile, might even bring

---

[3] *landsmen* (lonts′mən): Yiddish for "fellow Jews."
[4] *goyim* (goi′əm): Yiddish for "any non-Jews."

with it that old world of feelings and habits—something to replace the new world of social accessibility and moral indifference, the world which tempts all our promiscuous instincts, and where one cannot always figure out what a Jew is that a Christian is not.

Jews are people who are not what anti-Semites say they are. That was once a statement out of which a man might begin to construct an identity for himself; now it does not work so well, for it is difficult to act counter to the ways people expect you to act when fewer and fewer people define you by such expectations. The success of the struggle against the defamation of Jewish character in this country has itself made more pressing the need for a Jewish self-consciousness that is relevant to this time and place, where neither defamation nor persecution are what they were elsewhere in the past. Surely, for those Jews who choose to continue to call themselves Jews, and find reason to do so, there are courses to follow to prevent it from ever being 1933 again that are more direct, reasonable, and dignified than beginning to act as though it already is 1933—*or as though it always is.* But the death of all those Jews seems to have taught my correspondent, a rabbi and a teacher, little more than to be discreet, to be foxy, to say this but not that. It has taught him nothing other than how to remain a victim in a country where he does not have to live like one if he chooses. How pathetic. And what an insult to the dead. Imagine: sitting in New York in the 1960's and piously summoning up "the six million" to justify one's own timidity.

Timidity—and paranoia. It does not occur to the rabbi that there are Gentiles who will read the story intelligently. The only Gentiles the rabbi can imagine looking into the *New Yorker* are those who hate Jews and those who don't know how to read very well. If there are others, they can get along without reading about Jews. For to suggest that one translate one's stories into Hebrew and publish them in Israel, is to say, in effect: "There is nothing in our lives we need to tell the Gentiles about, unless it has to do with how well we manage. Beyond that, it's none of their business. We are important to no one but ourselves, which is as it should be (or better be) anyway." But to indicate that moral crisis is something to be hushed up is not, of course, to take the prophetic line; [5] nor is it a rabbinical point of view that Jewish life is of no significance to the rest of mankind.

Even given his own kinds of goals, however, the rabbi is not very farsighted or imaginative. What he fails to see is that the stereotype as often arises from ignorance as from malice; deliberately keeping Jews out of the imagination of Gentiles, for fear of the bigots and their stereotyping minds, is really to invite the invention of stereotypical ideas. A book like Ralph Ellison's *Invisible Man*, for instance, seems to me to have helped many whites who are not anti-Negro, but who do hold Negro stereotypes, to surrender simple-minded notions about Negro life. Just as there are Jews who feel that my books do nothing for the Jewish cause, so there are Negroes, I am led to understand, who feel that Mr. Ellison's work has done little for the Negro cause and probably has harmed it. But that seems to place the Negro cause somewhat outside the cause of truth and justice. That many blind people are still blind, does not mean that Mr. Ellison's book gives off no light. Certainly those of us who are willing to be taught, and who needed to be, have been made by *Invisible Man* less stupid than we were about Negro lives, including those lives that a bigot would point to as affirming his own half-baked, inviolable ideas.

But it is the treachery of the bigot that the rabbi appears to be worried about and that he presents to me, to himself, and probably to his congregation, as the major cause for concern. Frankly, I think those are just the old words coming out, when the right buttons are pushed. Can he actually believe that on the basis of my story anyone is going to start a pogrom, or keep a Jew out of medical school, or even call some Jewish schoolchild a kike? The rabbi is entombed in his nightmares and fears; but that is not the whole of it. He is also hiding something. Much of this disapproval of "Defender of the Faith" because of its effect upon Gentiles seems to me a cover-up for what is really objected to, what is immediately painful—and that is its direct effect

[5] *the prophetic line:* the position of the ancient Hebrew prophets.

upon certain Jews. "You have hurt a lot of people's feelings because you have revealed something they are ashamed of." That is the letter the rabbi did not write, but should have. I would have argued then that there are things of more importance—even to these Jews—than those feelings that have been hurt, but at any rate he would have confronted me with a genuine fact, with something I was actually responsible for, and which my conscience would have had to deal with, as it does.

For the record, all the letters that came in about "Defender of the Faith," and that I saw, were from Jews. Not one of those people whose gratitude the rabbi believes I earned, wrote to say, "Thank you," nor was I invited to address any anti-Semitic organizations. When I did begin to receive speaking invitations, they were from Jewish ladies' groups, Jewish community centers, and from all sorts of Jewish organizations, large and small.

And I think this bothers the rabbi, too. On the one hand, some Jews are hurt by my work; but on the other, some are interested. At the rabbinical convention I mentioned earlier, Rabbi Emanuel Rackman, a professor of political science at Yeshiva University, reported to his colleagues that certain Jewish writers were "assuming the mantle of self-appointed spokesmen and leaders for Judaism." To support this remark he referred to a symposium held in Israel . . . at which I was present; as far as I know, Rabbi Rackman was not. If he had been there, he would have heard me make it quite clear that I did not want to, did not intend to, and was not able to, speak *for* American Jews; I surely did not deny, and no one questioned the fact, that I spoke *to* them, and hopefully to others as well. The competition that Rabbi Rackman imagines himself to be engaged in hasn't to do with who will presume to lead the Jews; it is really a matter of who, in addressing them, is going to take them more seriously—strange as that may sound—with who is going to see them as something more than part of the mob in a crowded theater, more than helpless and threatened and in need of reassurance that they are as "balanced" as anyone else. The question really is, who is going to address men and women like men and women, and who like children. If there are Jews who have begun to find the stories the novelists tell more provocative and pertinent than the sermons of some of the rabbis, perhaps it is because there are regions of feeling and consciousness in them which cannot be reached by the oratory of self-congratulation and self-pity.

Fiction is not written to affirm the principles and beliefs that everybody seems to hold, nor does it seek to guarantee us of the appropriateness of our feelings. The world of fiction, in fact, frees us from the circumscriptions that the society places upon feeling; one of the greatnesses of the art is that it allows both the writer and the reader to respond to experience in ways not always available in day-to-day conduct; or if they are available, they are not possible, or manageable, or legal, or advisable, or even necessary to the business of living. We may not even know that we have such a range of feelings and responses *until* we have come into contact with the work of fiction. This does not mean that either reader or writer no longer brings any moral judgment to bear upon human action. Rather, we judge at a different level of our being, for not only are we judging with the aid of new feelings, but without the necessity of having to act upon judgment, or even to be judged for our judgment. Ceasing for a while to be upright citizens, we drop into another layer of consciousness. And this dropping, this expansion of moral consciousness, this exploration of moral fantasy, is of considerable value to a man and to society.

for discussion

1. Roth says that the problems with which he dealt in his story "Defender of the Faith" were "problems for most people" as well as being distinctively Jewish problems. How does he justify these seemingly contradictory claims?

2. What is meant by the reference to Sergeant Nathan Marx as "a kind of Jewish Uncle Tom"?

3. What human traits motivate the criticism Roth received?

4. Much of Roth's essay is given over to explicit rebuttal of his critics, but he also manages to suggest the qualities that readers must possess if they are truly to understand the stories they read. What are these qualities of the good reader of fiction?

5. What, according to Roth, is the function of the writer of stories? Why does he require the large measure of freedom that Roth demands?

born 1914

RALPH ELLISON

☐ *Ralph Ellison and Richard Wright were close friends,*
and they fought for many of the same causes during the
early years of their friendship, which began in 1937.
But Ellison never committed himself to Wright's view
that the Negro writer is first a Negro and second a writer
whose pen is most properly used as an instrument of
social change. Ellison's primary commitment is to the
art of fiction.

In 1945, after service in the Merchant Marine during
the second World War, Ellison moved from New York
to the more detached setting of a college of the arts in
Vermont, where he began to write Invisible Man. *Since*
then, he has steadily insisted that the true writer must
know the difference between his social and his artistic
responsibilities. He has bent his full effort to the writing
of stories that untangle the deepest and most elusive
complications of American civilization. Ellison seeks,
with unusual dedication, to translate his experience as a
black American into literary art. The stories resulting
from that effort show rare truthfulness and great
imaginative power.

Ellison describes the Oklahoma where he was raised
in the years between the first World War and the
Depression as a community "still characterized by
frontier attitudes." This frontier community provided
enough freedom to produce Ellison's qualified faith in
the American dream of an entirely open society. And
from its fluidity and "strange mixture," he gained a
lasting sense of the complexity of the American
experience—its curious blending of innocence and
sophistication, of malice and high-mindedness. These
awarenesses have influenced Ellison's literary career; for
both his stories and his essays reveal a skepticism of all
stereotypes—liberal and reactionary alike—and a related
desire to honestly illuminate the puzzling features of
American life. He reports that he found "the greatest

*difficulty for a Negro writer was the problem of revealing
what he truly felt, rather than serving up what Negroes
were supposed to feel, and were encouraged to feel."*

Since the appearance of Invisible Man *in 1952, Ellison
has published a collection of his essays,* Shadow and
Act *(1964).*

hidden name and complex fate

A Writer's Experience in the United States °

☐ In *Green Hills of Africa,* Ernest Hemingway reminds
us that both Tolstoy and Stendhal had seen war, that Flaubert had seen a revolution and the Commune,[1] that Dostoievsky had been sent to Siberia and that such experiences
were important in shaping the art of these great masters.
And he goes on to observe that "writers are forged in injustice as a sword is forged." He declined to describe the
many personal forms which injustice may take in this
chaotic world—who would be so mad as to try?—nor does
he go into the personal wounds which each of these writers sustained. Now, however, thanks to his brother and
sister, we do know something of the injustice in which he
himself was forged, and this knowledge has been added to
what we have long known of Hemingway's artistic temper.

In the end, however, it is the quality of his art which is
primary. It is the art which allows the wars and revolutions
which he knew, and the personal and social injustice which
he suffered, to lay claims upon our attention; for it was

° Address delivered at the Library of Congress, January 6, 1964.
[1] *the Commune:* the socialistic government that ruled Paris briefly
in 1871.

through his art that they achieved their most enduring meaning. It is a matter of outrageous irony, perhaps, but in literature the great social clashes of history no less than the painful experience of the individual are secondary to the meaning which they take on through the skill, the talent, the imagination and personal vision of the writer who transforms them into art. Here they are reduced to more manageable proportions; here they are imbued with humane values; here, injustice and catastrophe become less important in themselves than what the writer makes of them. This is *not* true, however, of the writer's struggle with that recalcitrant angel called Art; and it was through *this* specific struggle that Ernest Hemingway became *Hemingway* (now refined to a total body of transcendent work, after forty years of being endlessly dismembered and resurrected, as it continues to be, in the styles, the themes, the sense of life and literature of countless other writers). And it was through this struggle with form that he became the master, the culture hero, whom we have come to know and admire.

It was suggested that it might be of interest if I discussed here this evening some of my notions of the writer's experience in the United States; hence I have evoked the name of Hemingway, not by way of inviting far-fetched comparisons but in order to establish a perspective, a set of assumptions from which I may speak, and in an attempt to avoid boring you by emphasizing those details of racial hardship which for some forty years now have been evoked whenever writers of my own cultural background have essayed their experience in public.

I do this *not* by way of denying totally the validity of these by now stylized recitals, for I have shared and still share many of their detailed injustices—what Negro can escape them?—but by way of suggesting that they are, at least in a discussion of a writer's experience, as *writer*, as artist, somewhat beside the point.

For we select neither our parents, our race nor our nation; these occur to us out of the love, the hate, the circumstances, the fate, of others. But we *do* become writers out of an act of will, out of an act of choice; a dim, confused

and ofttimes regrettable choice, perhaps, but choice nevertheless. And what happens thereafter causes all those experiences which occurred before we began to function as
writers to take on a special quality of uniqueness. If this
does not happen then as far as writing goes, the experiences have been misused. If we do not make of them a
value, if we do not transform them into forms and images
of meaning which they did not possess before, then we
have failed as artists.

Thus for a writer to insist that his personal suffering is
of special interest in itself, or simply because he belongs to
a particular racial or religious group, is to advance a claim
for special privileges which members of his group who are
not writers would be ashamed to demand. The kindest
judgment one can make of this point of view is that it reveals a sad misunderstanding of the relationship between
suffering and art. Thomas Mann and André Gide have told
us much of this, and there are critics, like Edmund Wilson,
who have told of the connection between the wound and
the bow.[2]

As I see it, it is through the process of making artistic
forms—plays, poems, novels—out of one's experience that
one becomes a writer, and it is through this process, this
struggle, that the writer helps give meaning to the experience of the group. And it is the process of mastering the
discipline, the techniques, the fortitude, the culture, through
which this is made possible that constitutes the writer's real
experience as *writer*, as artist. If this sounds like an argument for the artist's withdrawal from social struggles, I
would recall to you W. H. Auden's comment to the effect
that:

> In our age, the mere making of a work of art is itself
> a political act. So long as artists exist, making what
> they please, and think they ought to make, even if
> it is not terribly good, even if it appeals to only a
> handful of people, they remind the Management of
> something managers need to be reminded of,

[2] *the wound and the bow:* the theory that creative power derives
from physical or emotional suffering.

namely, that the managed are people with faces, not anonymous members, that *Homo Laborans* is also *Homo Ludens*. . . .[3]

Without doubt, even the most *engagé* [4] writers—and I refer to true artists, not to artists *manqués* [5]—begin their careers in play and puzzlement, in dreaming over the details of the world in which they become conscious of themselves.

Let Tar Baby, that enigmatic figure from Negro folklore, stand for the world. He leans, black and gleaming, against the wall of life utterly noncommittal under our scrutiny, our questioning, starkly unmoving before our naïve attempts at intimidation. Then we touch him playfully and before we can say *Sonny Liston!* we find ourselves stuck. Our playful investigations become a labor, a fearful struggle, an *agon*.[6] Slowly we perceive that our task is to learn the proper way of freeing ourselves to develop, in other words, technique.

Sensing this, we give him our sharpest attention, we question him carefully, we struggle with more subtlety; while he, in his silent way, holds on, demanding that we perceive the necessity of calling him by his true name as the price of our freedom. It is unfortunate that he has so many, many "true names"—all spelling chaos; and in order to discover even one of these we must first come into the possession of our own names. For it is through our names that we first place ourselves in the world. Our names, being the gift of others, must be made our own.

Once while listening to the play of a two-year-old girl who did not know she was under observation, I heard her saying over and over again, at first with questioning and then with sounds of growing satisfaction, "I am Mimi Livisay? . . . I am Mimi Livisay. I *am* Mimi Livisay. . . . I am *Mimi* Li-visay! I am Mimi. . . ."

[3] *Homo Laborans . . . Homo Ludens:* Man the worker is also man who delights in play.

[4] *engagé* (áng·gä·zhā′): in this context, *engagé* means "politically committed."

[5] *manqués* (máng·kā′): in wish but not in fact; in intention but not in achievement.

[6] *agon:* in Greek drama, a conflict or verbal contest between two main characters.

And in deed and in fact she was—or became so soon thereafter, by working playfully to establish the unity between herself and her name.

For many of us this is far from easy. We must learn to wear our names within all the noise and confusion of the environment in which we find ourselves; make them the center of all of our associations with the world, with man and with nature. We must charge them with all our emotions, our hopes, hates, loves, aspirations. They must become our masks and our shields and the containers of all those values and traditions which we learn and/or imagine as being the meaning of our familial past.

And when we are reminded so constantly that we bear, as Negroes, names originally possessed by those who owned our enslaved grandparents, we are apt, especially if we are potential writers, to be more than ordinarily concerned with the veiled and mysterious events, the fusions of blood, the furtive couplings, the business transactions, the violations of faith and loyalty, the assaults; yes, and the unrecognized and unrecognizable loves through which our names were handed down unto us.

So charged with emotion does this concern become for some of us, that we have, earlier, the example of the followers of Father Divine [7] and, now, the Black Muslims, discarding their original names in rejection of the blood-stained, the brutal, the sinful images of the past. Thus they would declare new identities, would clarify a new program of intention and destroy the verbal evidence of a willed and ritualized discontinuity of blood and human intercourse.

Not all of us, actually only a few, seek to deal with our names in this manner. We take what we have and make of them what we can. And there are even those who know where the old broken connections lie, who recognize their relatives across the chasm of historical denial and the artificial barriers of society, and who see themselves as bearers of many of the qualities which were admirable in the original sources of their common line (Faulkner has made much of this); and I speak here not of mere forgiveness, nor of

[7] *Father Divine:* the name taken by George Baker, who built a large social and religious movement in the 1920's and 1930's by promising to make the world a "heaven" for his followers.

obsequious insensitivity to the outrages symbolized by the denial and the division, but of the conscious acceptance of the harsh realities of the human condition, of the ambiguities and hypocrisies of human history as they have played themselves out in the United States.

Perhaps, taken in aggregate, these European names (sometimes with irony, sometimes with pride, but always with personal investment) represent a certain triumph of the spirit, speaking to us of those who rallied, reassembled and transformed themselves and who under dismembering pressures refused to die. "Brothers and sisters," I once heard a Negro preacher exhort, "let us make up our faces before the world, and our names shall sound throughout the land with honor! For we ourselves are our *true* names, not their epithets! So let us, I say, Make Up Our Faces and Our Minds!"

Perhaps my preacher had read T. S. Eliot,[8] although I doubt it. And in actuality, it was unnecessary that he do so, for a concern with names and naming was very much a part of that special area of American culture from which I come, and it is precisely for this reason that this example should come to mind in a discussion of my own experience as a writer.

Undoubtedly, writers begin their *conditioning* as manipulators of words long before they become aware of literature—certain Freudians would say at the breast. Perhaps. But if so, that is far too early to be of use at this moment. Of this, though, I am certain: that despite the misconceptions of those educators who trace the reading difficulties experienced by large numbers of Negro children in Northern schools to their Southern background, these children are, in *their* familiar South, facile manipulators of words. I know, too, that the Negro community is deadly in its ability to create nicknames and to spot all that is ludicrous in an unlikely name or that which is incongruous in conduct. Names are not qualities; nor are words, in this particular sense, actions. To assume that they are could cost one his life many times a day. Language skills depend

---

[8] *T. S. Eliot:* "There will be time, there will be time/ To prepare a face to meet the faces that you meet . . ." ("The Love Song of J. Alfred Prufrock").

to a large extent upon a knowledge of the details, the manners, the objects, the folkways, the psychological patterns, of a given environment. Humor and wit depend upon much the same awareness, and so does the suggestive power of names.

"A small brown bowlegged Negro with the name 'Franklin D. Roosevelt Jones' might sound like a clown to someone who looks at him from the outside," said my friend Albert Murray, "but on the other hand he just might turn out to be a hell of a fireside operator.[9] He might just lie back in all of that comic juxtaposition of names and manipulate you deaf, dumb and blind—and you not even suspecting it, because you're thrown out of stance by his name! There you are, so dazzled by the F.D.R. image —which you *know* you can't see—and so delighted with your own superior position that you don't realize that it's *Jones* who must be confronted."

Well, as you must suspect, all of this speculation on the matter of names has a purpose, and now, because it is tied up so ironically with my own experience as a writer, I must turn to my own name.

For in the dim beginnings, before I ever thought consciously of writing, there was my own name, and there was, doubtless, a certain magic in it. From the start I was uncomfortable with it, and in my earliest years it caused me much puzzlement. Neither could I understand what a poet was, nor why, exactly, my father had chosen to name me after one. Perhaps I could have understood it perfectly well had he named me after his own father, but that name had been given to an older brother who died and thus was out of the question. But why hadn't he named me after a hero, such as Jack Johnson, or a soldier like Colonel Charles Young, or a great seaman like Admiral Dewey, or an educator like Booker T. Washington, or a great orator and abolitionist like Frederick Douglass? Or again, why hadn't he named me (as so many Negro parents had done) after President Teddy Roosevelt?

Instead, he named me after someone called Ralph

[9] *a fireside operator:* President Roosevelt (1933–45) made persuasive use of radio broadcasting in his "fireside chats" with the American people.

Waldo Emerson, and then, when I was three, he died. It was too early for me to have understood his choice, although I'm sure he must have explained it many times, and it was also too soon for me to have made the connection between my name and my father's love for reading. Much later, after I began to write and work with words, I came to suspect that he was aware of the suggestive powers of names and of the magic involved in naming.

I recall an odd conversation with my mother during my early teens in which she mentioned their interest in, of all things, prenatal culture! But for a long time I actually knew only that my father read a lot, and that he admired this remote Mr. Emerson, who was something called a "poet and philosopher"—so much so that he named his second son after him.

I knew, also, that whatever his motives, the combination of names he'd given me caused me no end of trouble from the moment when I could talk well enough to respond to the ritualized question which grownups put to very young children. Emerson's name was quite familiar to Negroes in Oklahoma during those days when World War I was brewing, and adults, eager to show off their knowledge of literary figures, and obviously amused by the joke implicit in such a small brown nubbin of a boy carrying around such a heavy moniker, would invariably repeat my first two names and then to my great annoyance, they'd add "Emerson."

And I, in my confusion, would reply, "No, no, I'm not Emerson; he's the little boy who lives next door." Which only made them laugh all the louder. "Oh no," they'd say, "*you're* Ralph Waldo Emerson," while I had fantasies of blue murder.

For a while the presence next door of my little friend, Emerson, made it unnecessary for me to puzzle too often over this peculiar adult confusion. And since there were other Negro boys named Ralph in the city, I came to suspect that there was something about the combination of names which produced their laughter. Even today I know of only one other Ralph who had as much comedy made out of his name, a campus politician and deep-voiced orator whom I knew at Tuskegee, who was called in friendly ribbing, *Ralph Waldo Emerson Edgar Allan Poe*, spelled Powe. This must have been quite a trial for him, but I had been initiated much earlier.

During my early school years the name continued to puzzle me, for it constantly evoked in the faces of others some secret. It was as though I possessed some treasure or some defect, which was invisible to my own eyes and ears; something which I had but did not *possess*, like a piece of property in South Carolina, which was mine but which I could not have until some future time. I recall finding, about this time, while seeking adventure in back alleys—which possess for boys a superiority over playgrounds like that which kitchen utensils possess over toys designed for infants—a large photographic lens. I remember nothing of its optical qualities, of its speed or color correction, but it gleamed with crystal mystery and it was beautiful.

Mounted handsomely in a tube of shiny brass, it spoke to me of distant worlds of possibility. I played with it, looking through it with squinted eyes, holding it in shafts of sunlight, and tried to use it for a magic lantern. But most of this was as unrewarding as my attempts to make the music come from a phonograph record by holding the needle in my fingers.

I could burn holes through newspapers with it, or I could pretend that it was a telescope, the barrel of a cannon, or the third eye of a monster—*I* being the monster—but I could do nothing at all about its proper function of making images; nothing to make it yield its secret. But I could not discard it.

Older boys sought to get it away from me by offering knives or tops, agate marbles or whole zoos of grass snakes and horned toads in trade, but I held on to it. No one, not even the white boys I knew, had such a lens, and it was my own good luck to have found it. Thus I would hold on to it until such time as I could acquire the parts needed to make it function. Finally I put it aside and it remained buried in my box of treasures, dusty and dull, to be lost and forgotten as I grew older and became interested in music.

I had reached by now the grades where it was necessary to learn something about Mr. Emerson and what he had written, such as the "Concord Hymn" and the essay "Self-

Reliance," and in following his advice,[10] reduced the "Waldo" to a simple and, I hoped, mysterious "W," and in my own reading I avoided his works like the plague. I could no more deal with my name—I shall never really master it—than I could find a creative use for my lens. Fortunately there were other problems to occupy my mind. Not that I forgot my fascination with names, but more about that later.

Negro Oklahoma City was starkly lacking in writers. In fact, there was only Roscoe Dungee, the editor of the local Negro newspaper and a very fine editorialist in that valuable tradition of personal journalism which is now rapidly disappearing; a writer who in his emphasis upon the possibilities for justice offered by the Constitution anticipated the anti-segregation struggle by decades. There were also a few reporters who drifted in and out, but these were about all. On the level of *conscious* culture the Negro community was biased in the direction of music.

These were the middle and late twenties, remember, and the state was still a new frontier state. The capital city was one of the great centers for southwestern jazz, along with Dallas and Kansas City. Orchestras which were to become famous within a few years were constantly coming and going. As were the blues singers—Ma Rainey and Ida Cox, and the old bands like that of King Oliver. But best of all, thanks to Mrs. Zelia N. Breaux, there was an active and enthusiastic school music program through which any child who had the interest and the talent could learn to play an instrument and take part in the band, the orchestra, the brass quartet. And there was a yearly operetta and a chorus and a glee club. Harmony was taught for four years and the music appreciation program was imperative. European folk dances were taught throughout the Negro school system, and we were also taught complicated patterns of military drill.

I tell you this to point out that although there were no incentives to write, there was ample opportunity to re-

---

[10] *his advice:* In "Self-Reliance" Emerson says, "There is a time in every man's education when he arrives at the conviction that envy is ignorance; that imitation is suicide. . . ." Emerson's central doctrine in the essay is "Trust thyself."

ceive an artistic discipline. Indeed, once one picked up an instrument it was difficult to escape. If you chafed at the many rehearsals of the school band or orchestra and were drawn to the many small jazz groups, you were likely to discover that the jazzmen were apt to rehearse far more than the school band; it was only that they seemed to enjoy themselves better and to possess a freedom of imagination which we were denied at school. And one soon learned that the wild, transcendent moments which occurred at dances or "battles of music," moments in which memorable improvisations were ignited, depended upon a dedication to a discipline which was observed even when rehearsals had to take place in the crowded quarters of Halley Richardson's shoeshine parlor. It was not the place which counted, although a large hall with good acoustics was preferred, but what one did to perfect one's performance.

If this talk of musical discipline gives the impression that there were no forces working to nourish one who would one day blunder, after many a twist and turn, into writing, I am misleading you. And here I might give you a longish lecture on the Ironies and Uses of Segregation. When I was a small child there was no library for Negroes in our city; and not until a Negro minister invaded the main library did we get one. For it was discovered that there was no law, only custom, which held that we could not use these public facilities. The results were the quick renting of two large rooms in a Negro office building (the recent site of a pool hall), the hiring of a young Negro librarian, the installation of shelves and a hurried stocking of the walls with any and every book possible. It was, in those first days, something of a literary chaos.

But how fortunate for a boy who loved to read! I started with the fairy tales and quickly went through the junior fiction; then through the Westerns and the detective novels, and very soon I was reading the classics— only I didn't know it. There were also the Haldeman Julius Blue Books, which seem to have floated on the air down from Girard, Kansas; the syndicated columns of O. O. McIntyre, and the copies of *Vanity Fair* and the *Literary Digest* which my mother brought home from work—how could I ever join uncritically in the heavy-handed attacks on the so-called Big Media which have become so common today?

There were also the pulp magazines and, more important, that other library which I visited when I went to help my adopted grandfather, J. D. Randolph (my parents had been living in his rooming house when I was born), at his work as custodian of the law library of the Oklahoma State Capitol. Mr. Randolph had been one of the first teachers in what became Oklahoma City; and he'd also been one of the leaders of a group who walked from Gallatin, Tennessee, to the Oklahoma Territory. He was a tall man, as brown as smoked leather, who looked like the Indians with whom he'd herded horses in the early days.

And while his status was merely the custodian of the law library, I was to see the white legislators come down on many occasions to question him on points of law, and often I was to hear him answer without recourse to the uniform rows of books on the shelves. This was a thing to marvel at in itself, and the white lawmakers did so, but even more marvelous, ironic, intriguing, haunting— call it what you will—is the fact that the Negro who knew the answers was named after Jefferson Davis.[11] What Tennessee lost, Oklahoma was to gain, and after gaining it (a gift of courage, intelligence, fortitude, and grace), used it only in concealment and, one hopes, with embarrassment.

So, let us, I say, make up our faces and our minds!

In the loosely structured community of that time, knowledge, news of other ways of living, ancient wisdom, the latest literary fads, hate literature—for years I kept a card warning Negroes away from the polls, which had been dropped by the thousands from a plane which circled over the Negro community—information of all kinds, found its level, catch-as-catch can, in the minds of those who were receptive to it. Not that there was no conscious structuring—I read my first Shaw and Maupassant, my

[11] *Jefferson Davis:* president of the Confederate States during the Civil War.

first Harvard Classics in the home of a friend whose parents were products of that stream of New England education which had been brought to Negroes by the young and enthusiastic white teachers who staffed the schools set up for the freedmen after the Civil War. These parents were both teachers and there were others like them in our town.

But the places where a rich oral literature was truly functional were the churches, the schoolyards, the barbershops, the cotton-picking camps; places where folklore and gossip thrived. The drug store where I worked was such a place, where on days of bad weather the older men would sit with their pipes and tell tall tales, hunting yarns and homely versions of the classics. It was here that I heard stories of searching for buried treasure and of headless horsemen, which I was told were my own father's versions told long before. There were even recitals of popular verse, "The Shooting of Dan McGrew," and, along with these, stories of Jesse James, of Negro outlaws and black United States marshals, of slaves who became the chiefs of Indian tribes and of the exploits of Negro cowboys. There was both truth and fantasy in this, intermingled in the mysterious fashion of literature.

Writers, in their formative period, absorb into their consciousness much that has no special value until much later, and often much which is of no special value even then—perhaps, beyond the fact that it throbs with affect and mystery and in it "time and pain and royalty in the blood" are suspended in imagery. So, long before I thought of writing, I was claimed by weather, by speech rhythms, by Negro voices and their different idioms, by husky male voices and by the high shrill singing voices of certain Negro women, by music; by tight spaces and by wide spaces in which the eyes could wander; by death, by newly born babies, by manners of various kinds, company manners and street manners; the manners of white society and those of our own high society; and by interracial manners; by street fights, circuses and minstrel shows; by vaudeville and moving pictures, by prize fights and foot races, baseball games and football matches. By spring floods and blizzards, catalpa worms and jack rabbits;

honeysuckle and snapdragons (which smelled like old cigar butts); by sunflowers and hollyhocks, raw sugar cane and baked yams; pigs' feet, chili and blue haw ice cream. By parades, public dances and jam sessions, Easter sunrise ceremonies and large funerals. By contests between fire-and-brimstone preachers and by presiding elders who got "laughing-happy" when moved by the spirit of God.

I was impressed by expert players of the "dozens" [12] and certain notorious bootleggers of corn whiskey. By jazz musicians and fortunetellers and by men who did anything well; by strange sicknesses and by interesting brick or razor scars; by expert cursing vocabularies as well as by exalted praying and terrifying shouting, and by transcendent playing or singing of the blues. I was fascinated by old ladies, those who had seen slavery and those who were defiant of white folk and black alike; by the enticing walks of prostitutes and by the limping walks affected by Negro hustlers, especially those who wore Stetson hats, expensive shoes with well-starched overalls, usually with a diamond stickpin (when not in hock) in their tieless collars as their gambling uniforms.

And there were the blind men who preached on corners, and the blind men who sang the blues to the accompaniment of washboard and guitar; and the white junkmen who sang mountain music, and the famous hucksters of fruit and vegetables.

And there was the Indian-Negro confusion. There were Negroes who were part Indian and who lived on reservations, and Indians who had children who lived in towns as Negroes, and Negroes who were Indians and traveled back and forth between the groups with no trouble. And Indians who were as wild as wild Negroes and others who were as solid and as steady as bankers. There were the teachers, too, inspiring teachers and villainous teachers who chased after the girl students, and

[12] the "dozens": a verbal game played by Negroes, originating in slave times as a way of teaching and practicing the self-control necessary for survival when one has no rights. The winner of the game is the one with the most "cool": he takes abuse without becoming visibly upset, and returns it so subtly and cleverly that his attacker is left helplessly discomfited.

certain female teachers who one wished would chase after young male students. And a handsome old principal of military bearing who had been blemished by his classmates at West Point when they discovered on the eve of graduation that he was a Negro. There were certain Jews, Mexicans, Chinese cooks, a German orchestra conductor and an English grocer who owned a Franklin touring car. And certain Negro mechanics—"Cadillac Slim," "Sticks" Walker, Buddy Bunn and Oscar Pitman—who had so assimilated the automobile that they seemed to be behind a steering wheel even as they walked the streets or danced with girls. And there were the whites who despised us and the others who shared our hardships and our joys.

There is much more, but this is sufficient to indicate some of what was present even in a segregated community to form the background of my work, my sense of life.

And now comes the next step. I went to Tuskegee to study music, hoping to become a composer of symphonies and there, during my second year, I read *The Waste Land* and that, although I was then unaware of it, was the real transition to writing.

Mrs. L. C. McFarland had taught us much of Negro history in grade school and from her I'd learned of the New Negro Movement of the twenties, of Langston Hughes, Countee Cullen, Claude McKay, James Weldon Johnson and the others. They had inspired pride and had given me a closer identification with poetry (by now, oddly enough, I seldom thought of my hidden name), but with music so much on my mind it never occurred to me to try to imitate them. Still I read their work and was excited by the glamour of the Harlem which emerged from their poems and it was good to know that there were Negro writers.—Then came *The Waste Land*.

I was much more under the spell of literature than I realized at the time. *Wuthering Heights* had caused me an agony of unexpressible emotion and the same was true of *Jude the Obscure*, but *The Waste Land* seized my mind. I was intrigued by its power to move me while eluding my understanding. Somehow its rhythms were often closer to those of jazz than were those of the Negro poets, and even though I could not understand then, its range of allusion was as mixed and as varied as that of Louis Armstrong. Yet there were its discontinuities, its changes of pace and its hidden system of organization which escaped me.

There was nothing to do but look up the references in the footnotes to the poem, and thus began my conscious education in literature.

For this, the library at Tuskegee was quite adequate and I used it. Soon I was reading a whole range of subjects drawn upon by the poet, and this led, in turn, to criticism and to Pound and Ford Madox Ford, Sherwood Anderson and Gertrude Stein, Hemingway and Fitzgerald and "round about 'til I was come" back to Melville and Twain—the writers who are taught and doubtlessly overtaught today. Perhaps it was my good luck that they were not taught at Tuskegee, I wouldn't know. But at the time I was playing, having an intellectually interesting good time.

Having given so much attention to the techniques of music, the process of learning something of the craft and intention of modern poetry and fiction seemed quite familiar. Besides, it was absolutely painless because it involved no deadlines or credits. Even then, however, a process which I described earlier had begun to operate. The more I learned of literature in this conscious way, the more the details of my background became transformed. I heard undertones in remembered conversations which had escaped me before, local customs took on a more universal meaning, values which I hadn't understood were revealed; some of the people whom I had known were diminished while others were elevated in stature. More important, I began to see my own possibilities with more objective, and in some ways, more hopeful eyes.

The following summer I went to New York seeking work, which I did not find, and remained there, but the personal transformation continued. Reading had become a conscious process of growth and discovery, a method of reordering the world. And that world had widened considerably.

At Tuskegee I had handled manuscripts which Prokofiev had given to Hazel Harrison, a Negro concert pianist who taught there and who had known him in Europe, and through Miss Harrison I had become aware of Prokofiev's symphonies. I had also become aware of the radical movement in politics and art, and in New York had begun reading the work of André Malraux,[13] not only the fiction but chapters from his *Psychology of Art*. And in my search for an expression of modern sensibility in the works of Negro writers I discovered Richard Wright. Shortly thereafter I was to meet Wright, and it was at his suggestion that I wrote both my first book review and my first short story. These were fatal suggestions.

For although I had tried my hand at poetry while at Tuskegee, it hadn't occurred to me that I might write fiction, but once he suggested it, it seemed the most natural thing to try. Fortunately for me, Wright, then on the verge of his first success, was eager to talk with a beginner and I was able to save valuable time in searching out those works in which writing was discussed as a craft. He guided me to Henry James's prefaces, to Conrad, to Joseph Warren Beach and to the letters of Dostoievsky. There were other advisers and other books involved, of course, but what is important here is that I was consciously concerned with the art of fiction, that almost from the beginning I was grappling quite consciously with the art through which I wished to realize myself. And this was not done in isolation; the Spanish Civil War was now in progress and the Depression was still on. The world was being shaken up, and through one of those odd instances which occur to young provincials in New York, I was to hear Malraux make an appeal for the Spanish Loyalists at the same party where I first heard the folk singer Leadbelly perform. Wright and I were there seeking money for the magazine which he had come to New York to edit.

Art and politics; a great French novelist and a Negro folk singer; a young writer who was soon to publish *Uncle Tom's Children*; and I who had barely begun to study his craft. It is such accidents, such fortuitous meetings, which count for so much in our lives. I had never

---

[13] *André Malraux:* then one of France's leading left-wing novelists; more recently a leading art historian and the Minister of Culture in France.

dreamed that I would be in the presence of Malraux, of whose work I became aware on my second day in Harlem when Langston Hughes suggested that I read *Man's Fate* and *Days of Wrath* before returning them to a friend of his. And it is this fortuitous circumstance which led to my selecting Malraux as a literary "ancestor," whom, unlike a relative, the artist is permitted to choose. There was in progress at the time all the agitation over the Scottsboro boys and the Herndon Case,[14] and I was aware of both. I had to be; I myself had been taken off a freight train at Decatur, Alabama, only three years before while on my way to Tuskegee. But while I joined in the agitation for their release, my main energies went into learning to write.

I began to publish enough, and not too slowly, to justify my hopes for success, and as I continued, I made a most perplexing discovery; namely, that for all his conscious concern with technique, a writer did not so much create the novel as he was created *by* the novel. That is, one did not make an arbitrary gesture when one sought to write. And when I say that the novelist is created by the novel, I mean to remind you that fictional techniques are not a mere set of objective tools, but something much more intimate: a way of feeling, of seeing and of expressing one's sense of life. And the process of *acquiring* technique is a process of modifying one's responses, of learning to see and feel, to hear and observe, to evoke and evaluate the images of memory and of summoning up and directing the imagination; of learning to conceive of human values in the ways which have been established by the great writers who have developed and extended the art. And perhaps the writer's greatest freedom, as artist, lies precisely in his possession of technique; for it is through

[14] *the Scottsboro boys and the Herndon Case:* In Scottsboro, Alabama, eight blacks, who had been charged with the rape of two white women, were convicted and sentenced to death in 1931. The case received much national attention and was reviewed three times by the U.S. Supreme Court because it was so obviously tied to the issue of racial prejudice. In 1932 a nineteen-year-old Negro named Angelo Herndon led a hunger march of unemployed workers and their families to the courthouse in Atlanta, Georgia. He was arrested, charged with violating an 1866 statute, and given a long-term sentence on a chain gang. After much legal dispute, the U.S. Supreme Court set aside Herndon's conviction.

technique that he comes to possess and express the meaning of his life.

Perhaps at this point it would be useful to recapitulate the route—perhaps as mazelike as that of *Finnegan's Wake* —which I have been trying to describe; that which leads from the writer's discovery of a sense of purpose, which is that of becoming a writer, and then the involvement in the passionate struggle required to master a bit of technique, and then, as this begins to take shape, the disconcerting discovery that it is *technique* which transforms the individual before he is able in turn to transform it. And in that personal transformation he discovers something else: he discovers that he has taken on certain obligations, that he must not embarrass his chosen form, and that in order to avoid this he must develop taste. He learns—and this is most discouraging—that he is involved with values which turn in their *own* way, and not in the ways of politics, upon the central issues affecting his nation and his time. He learns that the American novel, from its first consciousness of itself as a literary form, has grappled with the meaning of the American experience; that it has been aware and has sought to define the nature of that experience by addressing itself to the specific details, the moods, the landscapes, the cityscapes, the tempo of American change. And that it has borne, at its best, the full weight of that burden of conscience and consciousness which Americans inherit as one of the results of the revolutionary circumstances of our national beginnings.

We began as a nation not through the accidents of race or religion or geography (Robert Penn Warren has dwelled on these circumstances) but when a group of men, *some* of them political philosophers, put down, upon what we now recognize as being quite sacred papers, their conception of the nation which they intended to establish on these shores. They described, as we know, the obligations of the state to the citizen, of the citizen to the state; they committed themselves to certain ideas of justice, just as they committed us to a system which would guarantee all of its citizens equality of opportunity.

I need not describe the problems which have arisen from these beginnings. I need only remind you that the contradiction between these noble ideals and the actualities of our conduct generated a guilt, an unease of spirit, from the very beginning, and that the American novel at its best has always been concerned with this basic moral predicament. During Melville's time and Twain's, it was an implicit aspect of their major themes; by the twentieth century and after the discouraging and traumatic effect of the Civil War and the Reconstruction, it had gone underground, had become *understated*. Nevertheless it did not disappear completely and it is to be found operating in the work of Henry James as well as in that of Hemingway and Fitzgerald. And then (and as one who believes in the impelling moral function of the novel and who believes in the moral seriousness of the form) it pleases me no end that it comes into explicit statement again in the works of Richard Wright and William Faulkner, writers who lived close to moral and political problems which would not stay put underground.

I go into these details not to recapitulate the history of the American novel but to indicate the trend of thought which was set into motion when I began to discover the nature of that process with which I was actually involved. Whatever the opinions and decisions of critics, a novelist must arrive at his own conclusions as to the meaning and function of the form with which he is engaged, and these are, in all modesty, some of mine.

In order to orient myself I also began to learn that the American novel had long concerned itself with the puzzle of the one-and-the-many; the mystery of how each of us, despite his origin in diverse regions, with our diverse racial, cultural, religious backgrounds, speaking his own diverse idiom of the American language in his own accent, is, nevertheless, American. And with this concern with the implicit pluralism of the country and with the composite nature of the ideal character called "the American," there goes a concern with gauging the health of the American promise, with depicting the extent to which it was being achieved, being made manifest in our daily conduct.

And with all of this there still remained the specific concerns of literature. Among these is the need to keep literary standards high, the necessity of exploring new possibilities of language which would allow it to retain that flexibility and fidelity to the common speech which has been its glory since Mark Twain. For me this meant learning to add to it the wonderful resources of Negro American speech and idiom and to bring into range as fully and eloquently as possible the complex reality of the American experience as it shaped and was shaped by the lives of my own people.

Notice that I stress as "fully" as possible, because I would no more strive to write great novels by leaving out the complexity of circumstances which go to make up the Negro experience and which alone go to make the obvious injustice bearable, than I would think of preparing myself to become President of the United States simply by studying Negro American history or confining myself to studying those laws affecting civil rights.

For it seems to me that one of the obligations I took on when I committed myself to the art and form of the novel was that of striving for the broadest range, the discovery and articulation of the most exalted values. And I must squeeze these from the life which I know best. (A highly truncated impression of that life I attempted to convey to you earlier.)

If all this sounds a bit heady, remember that I did not destroy that troublesome middle name of mine, I only suppressed it. Sometimes it reminds me of my obligations to the man who named me.

It is our fate as human beings always to give up some good things for other good things, to throw off certain bad circumstances only to create others. Thus there is a value for the writer in trying to give as thorough a report of social reality as possible. Only by doing so may we grasp and convey the cost of change. Only by considering the broadest accumulation of data may we make choices that are based upon our own hard-earned sense of reality. Speaking from my own special area of American culture, I feel that to embrace uncritically values which are extended to us by others is to reject the validity, even the sacredness, of our own experience. It is also to forget that the small share of reality which each of our diverse groups is able to snatch from the whirling chaos of history belongs not to the group alone, but to all of us. It is a property and a witness which can be ignored only to the danger of the entire nation.

I could suppress the name of my namesake out of respect for the achievements of its original bearer but I cannot escape the obligation of attempting to achieve some of the things which he asked of the American writer. As Henry James suggested, being an American is an arduous task, and for most of us, I suspect, the difficulty begins with the name.

for discussion

1. What is the "perspective" on writing that Ellison establishes at the very beginning of his essay? At what other points in the development of his argument about the true relation between art and life does Ellison restate this perspective?

2. What are "those details of racial hardship" that Ellison elects to ignore? Why does he choose to set these details aside?

3. What is Ellison driving at when he says figuratively (p. 272) that we must "come into the possession of our own names" before we can discover the "names" of the world?

4. In what way was Ellison's own name something of value to him, even before he knew who Ralph Waldo Emerson was?

5. How does Ellison resolve the difficult question of the ethnic writer's double identity as a Negro and as an American? As an artist, is his loyalty to neither race nor nation, to either one or the other, or to both?

born 1924

JAMES BALDWIN

☐ *James Baldwin, born in Harlem in 1924, was the first child of a mother who subsequently married and bore eight more children. While hardly more than a child himself, Baldwin was obliged to help raise his half-brothers and half-sisters. His stepfather worked in a bottling plant during the week and preached in some* of Harlem's "store-front" churches on Sunday. Throughout most of his youth, Baldwin knew real poverty, and his relations with his stepfather were always painfully strained. However, one of his teachers in the Harlem junior high school he attended was Countee Cullen. And it was Baldwin's three years at De Witt Clinton High School in the Bronx that first brought him regularly, via the subway, out of the Harlem ghetto. In these public schools, a succession of black and white teachers recognized Baldwin's literary promise and early gave him the praise essential to a young writer.

During the six years following his graduation from high school in 1942, Baldwin spent much of his time in the unconventional surroundings of New York's Greenwich Village. He held briefly a variety of menial jobs: porter, elevator operator, factory and shipyard worker, dishwasher and waiter. But by 1943 he had decided to make an all-out effort to become a writer; he was already at work then on his first novel, not to be published for another decade. In 1944 a friend took him to Richard Wright's apartment in Brooklyn, where the unknown, twenty-year-old Baldwin described his book to the famous author of Native Son. Impressed by Baldwin's talent, Wright helped him secure a writing fellowship. In the mid-1940's Baldwin's essays began to appear in important political and literary magazines; and in 1948 he published his first short story.

Although launched as a writer, Baldwin still found himself experiencing the everyday humiliations of life in a segregated society. In 1948 he left America for Paris, intending never to return. But during the next nine years Baldwin discovered in Europe a new perspective on his native land: he saw more deeply into himself as a Negro, as an American, and as a human being. The novel he had begun as a Harlem teen-ager was completed in the Swiss Alps and published in 1953 as Go Tell It on the Mountain. Baldwin also published the book of essays Notes of a Native Son (1955) and another novel, Giovanni's Room (1956), before returning to America in 1957.

Baldwin continues to spend much of his time in other

*countries, and he has spoken out against white America
more unhesitatingly and angrily than any other black
writer of comparable stature. However, as a writer, he
has remained acutely aware of his "roots" in a familiar
world that he understands. "The danger of being an
expatriate," Baldwin told an interviewer in Istanbul, "is
that you are very likely to find yourself living, in effect,
nowhere." Despite extended periods of foreign residence,
Baldwin has frequently declared his abiding sense of
American identity.*

the discovery of what it means
to be an american

☐ "It is a complex fate to be an American," Henry James observed, and the principal discovery an American writer makes in Europe is just how complex this fate is. America's history, her aspirations, her peculiar triumphs, her even more peculiar defeats, and her position in the world— yesterday and today—are all so profoundly and stubbornly unique that the very word "America" remains a new, almost completely undefined and extremely controversial proper noun. No one in the world seems to know exactly what it describes, not even we motley millions who call ourselves Americans.

I left America because I doubted my ability to survive the fury of the color problem here. (Sometimes I still do.) I wanted to prevent myself from becoming *merely* a Negro; or, even, merely a Negro writer. I wanted to find out in what way the *specialness* of my experience could be made to connect me with other people instead of dividing me from them. (I was as isolated from Negroes as I was from whites, which is what happens when a Negro begins, at bottom, to believe what white people say about him.)

In my necessity to find the terms on which my experience could be related to that of others, Negroes and whites, writers and non-writers, I proved, to my astonishment, to be as American as any Texas G.I. And I found my experience was shared by every American writer I knew in Paris. Like me, they had been divorced from their origins, and it turned out to make very little difference that the origins of white Americans were European and mine were African—they were no more at home in Europe than I was.

The fact that I was the son of a slave and they were the sons of free men meant less, by the time we confronted each other on European soil, than the fact that we were both searching for our separate identities. When we had found these, we seemed to be saying, why, then, we would no longer need to cling to the shame and bitterness which had divided us so long.

It became terribly clear in Europe, as it never had been here, that we knew more about each other than any European ever could. And it also became clear that, no matter where our fathers had been born, or what they had endured, the fact of Europe had formed us both, was part of our identity and part of our inheritance.

I had been in Paris a couple of years before any of this became clear to me. When it did, I, like many a writer before me upon the discovery that his props have all been knocked out from under him, suffered a species of breakdown and was carried off to the mountains of Switzerland. There, in that absolutely alabaster landscape, armed with two Bessie Smith records and a typewriter, I began to try to re-create the life that I had first known as a child and from which I had spent so many years in flight.

It was Bessie Smith, through her tone and her cadence, who helped me to dig back to the way I myself must have spoken when I was a pickaninny, and to remember the things I had heard and seen and felt. I had buried them very deep. I had never listened to Bessie Smith in America (in the same way that, for years, I would not touch watermelon), but in Europe she helped to reconcile me to being a "nigger."

I do not think that I could have made this reconciliation here. Once I was able to accept my role—as distinguished, I must say, from my "place"—in the extraordinary drama which is America, I was released from the illusion that I hated America.

The story of what can happen to an American Negro writer in Europe simply illustrates, in some relief, what can happen to any American writer there. It is not meant, of course, to imply that it happens to them all, for Europe can be very crippling, too; and, anyway, a writer, when he has made his first breakthrough, has simply won a crucial skirmish in a dangerous, unending and unpredictable battle. Still, the breakthrough is important, and the point is that an American writer, in order to achieve it, very often has to leave this country.

The American writer, in Europe, is released, first of all, from the necessity of apologizing for himself. It is not until he *is* released from the habit of flexing his muscles and proving that he is just a "regular guy" that he realizes how crippling this habit has been. It is not necessary for him, there, to pretend to be something he is not, for the artist does not encounter in Europe the same suspicion he encounters here. Whatever the Europeans may actually think of artists, they have killed enough of them off by now to know that they are as real—and as persistent—as rain, snow, taxes or businessmen.

Of course, the reason for Europe's comparative clarity concerning the different functions of men in society is that European society has always been divided into classes in a way that American society never has been. A European writer considers himself to be part of an old and honorable tradition—of intellectual activity, of letters—and his choice of a vocation does not cause him any uneasy wonder as to whether or not it will cost him all his friends. But this tradition does not exist in America.

On the contrary, we have a very deep-seated distrust

of real intellectual effort (probably because we suspect that it will destroy, as I hope it does, that myth of America to which we cling so desperately). An American writer fights his way to one of the lowest rungs on the American social ladder by means of pure bull-headedness and an indescribable series of odd jobs. He probably *has* been a "regular fellow" for much of his adult life, and it is not easy for him to step out of that lukewarm bath.

We must, however, consider a rather serious paradox: though American society is more mobile than Europe's, it is easier to cut across social and occupational lines there than it is here. This has something to do, I think, with the problem of status in American life. Where everyone has status, it is also perfectly possible, after all, that no one has. It seems inevitable, in any case, that a man may become uneasy as to just what his status is.

But Europeans have lived with the idea of status for a long time. A man can be as proud of being a good waiter as of being a good actor, and, in neither case, feel threatened. And this means that the actor and the waiter can have a freer and more genuinely friendly relationship in Europe than they are likely to have here. The waiter does not feel, with obscure resentment, that the actor has "made it," and the actor is not tormented by the fear that he may find himself, tomorrow, once again a waiter.

This lack of what may roughly be called social paranoia causes the American writer in Europe to feel—almost certainly for the first time in his life—that he can reach out to everyone, that he is accessible to everyone and open to everything. This is an extraordinary feeling. He feels, so to speak, his own weight, his own value.

It is as though he suddenly came out of a dark tunnel and found himself beneath the open sky. And, in fact, in Paris, I began to see the sky for what seemed to be the first time. It was borne in on me—and it did not make me feel melancholy—that this sky had been there before I was born and would be there when I was dead. And it was up to me, therefore, to make of my brief opportunity the most that could be made.

I was born in New York, but have lived only in pockets

of it. In Paris, I lived in all parts of the city—on the Right Bank and the Left, among the bourgeoisie and among *les misérables,* and knew all kinds of people, from pimps and prostitutes in Pigalle to Egyptian bankers in Neuilly. This may sound extremely unprincipled or even obscurely immoral: I found it healthy. I love to talk to people, all kinds of people, and almost everyone, as I hope we still know, loves a man who loves to listen.

This perpetual dealing with people very different from myself caused a shattering in me of preconceptions I scarcely knew I held. The writer is meeting in Europe people who are not American, whose sense of reality is entirely different from his own. They may love or hate or admire or fear or envy this country—they see it, in any case, from another point of view, and this forces the writer to reconsider many things he had always taken for granted. This reassessment, which can be very painful, is also very valuable.

This freedom, like all freedom, has its dangers and its responsibilities. One day it begins to be borne in on the writer, and with great force, that he is living in Europe as an American. If he were living there as a European, he would be living on a different and far less attractive continent.

This crucial day may be the day on which an Algerian taxi-driver tells him how it feels to be an Algerian in Paris. It may be the day on which he passes a café terrace and catches a glimpse of the tense, intelligent and troubled face of Albert Camus. Or it may be the day on which someone asks him to explain Little Rock and he begins to feel that it would be simpler—and, corny as the words may sound, more honorable—to *go* to Little Rock than sit in Europe, on an American passport, trying to explain it.

This is a personal day, a terrible day, the day to which his entire sojourn has been tending. It is the day he realizes that there are no untroubled countries in this fearfully troubled world; that if he has been preparing himself for anything in Europe, he has been preparing himself—for America. In short, the freedom that the American writer finds in Europe brings him, full circle, back to himself, with the responsibility for his development where it always was: in his own hands.

Even the most incorrigible maverick has to be born somewhere. He may leave the group that produced him— he may be forced to—but nothing will efface his origins, the marks of which he carries with him everywhere. I think it is important to know this and even find it a matter for rejoicing, as the strongest people do, regardless of their station. On this acceptance, literally, the life of a writer depends.

The charge has often been made against American writers that they do not describe society, and have no interest in it. They only describe individuals in opposition to it, or isolated from it. Of course, what the American writer is describing is his own situation. But what is *Anna Karenina* describing if not the tragic fate of the isolated individual, at odds with her time and place?

The real difference is that Tolstoy was describing an old and dense society in which everything seemed—to the people in it, though not to Tolstoy—to be fixed forever. And the book is a masterpiece because Tolstoy was able to fathom, and make us see, the hidden laws which really governed this society and made Anna's doom inevitable.

American writers do not have a fixed society to describe. The only society they know is one in which nothing is fixed and in which the individual must fight for his identity. This is a rich confusion, indeed, and it creates for the American writer unprecedented opportunities.

That the tensions of American life, as well as the possibilities, are tremendous is certainly not even a question. But these are dealt with in contemporary literature mainly compulsively; that is, the book is more likely to be a symptom of our tension than an examination of it. The time has come, God knows, for us to examine ourselves, but we can only do this if we are willing to free ourselves of the myth of America and try to find out what is really happening here.

Every society is really governed by hidden laws, by unspoken but profound assumptions on the part of the people, and ours is no exception. It is up to the American writer to find out what these laws and assumptions are.

In a society much given to smashing taboos without thereby managing to be liberated from them, it will be no easy matter.

It is no wonder, in the meantime, that the American writer keeps running off to Europe. He needs sustenance for his journey and the best models he can find. Europe has what we do not have yet, a sense of the mysterious and inexorable limits of life, a sense, in a word, of tragedy. And we have what they sorely need: a new sense of life's possibilities.

In this endeavor to wed the vision of the Old World with that of the New, it is the writer, not the statesman, who is our strongest arm. Though we do not wholly believe it yet, the interior life is a real life, and the intangible dreams of people have a tangible effect on the world.

for discussion

1. What does Baldwin mean by "that myth of America to which we cling so desperately"? Why does he think it necessary for the writer to free himself from the myth of America?

2. What parallel does Baldwin discover between the Algerian taxi-driver's experience in Paris and his own in New York? What "reassessment" of America is forced upon him by the recognition of this parallel?

3. In what ways does the "life of a writer" depend upon his "acceptance" of his "origins"?

1900–1966

MELVIN B. TOLSON

☐ Melvin Tolson had already accomplished much—as
a man and as a poet—when his first book of poems,
Rendezvous with America, appeared in 1944. By that
time his achievements were well known within the
black American community. However, the last two
decades of Tolson's life were his most productive and
successful years. They were years of growing national and
international recognition for Tolson. In 1947 he was
appointed Poet Laureate of Liberia, and in 1952 he was
honored by Poetry Magazine. His poems were printed
in such journals as the Atlantic Monthly and included in
important anthologies. Influential American poets like
Robert Frost, William Carlos Williams, and Allen Tate
urged wider attention to Tolson's writings. It was
principally Tolson's last two books that evoked this
critical acclaim.

In 1953 Tolson published his dramatic ode Libretto
for the Republic of Liberia, and in 1965 Harlem Gallery
appeared. These profoundly Afro-American works move
far beyond both the genteel performances of the Harlem
Renaissance and the raw anger of the social protest
writers. In these two books Tolson made the fullest use
of his extraordinarily comprehensive experience and
historical imagination. These books also show him
straining his vast learning and command of poetic craft
as he experimented with new ways of expressing how
the black man's past operates upon his present and his
future. Tolson's later work brilliantly combines the
exotic and the commonplace, the heroic and the
grotesque, the tragic and the comic. He fuses these
extremes into an intricate vision of black people so
unwaveringly true that it also becomes an exploration of
mankind in general.

At the time of his death in 1966, Tolson was Avalon
Professor of the Humanities at Tuskegee Institute in
Alabama.

the sea-turtle and the shark

Strange but true is the story
of the sea-turtle and the shark—
the instinctive drive of the weak to survive
in the oceanic dark.
Driven,
riven
by hunger
from abyss to shoal,
sometimes the shark swallows
the sea-turtle whole.

The sly reptilian marine
withdraws,
into the shell
of his undersea craft,
his leathery head and the rapacious claws
that can rip
a rhinoceros' hide
or strip
a crocodile to fare-thee-well;
now,
inside the shark,
the sea-turtle begins the churning seesaws
of his descent into pelagic hell;
then . . . *then,*
with ravenous jaws
that can cut sheet steel scrap,
the sea-turtle gnaws
. . . and gnaws . . . and gnaws . . .
his way in a way that appalls—
his way to freedom,
beyond the vomiting dark,
beyond the stomach walls
of the shark.

abraham lincoln of rock spring farm

I

Along the Wilderness Road, through Cumberland Gap,[1]
The black ox hours limped toward Sunday's sun,
Across a buff clay belt with scrawls of stone,
Where bird and beast quailed in the bosom brush
From February's fang and claw; the stars,
Blue white, like sheer icicles, spired aglow
As if the three wise men barged in the East
Or priests in sackcloth balked the Scourge of God.

Foursquare by the rite of arm and heart and law,
The scrubby log cabin dared the compass points
Of Rock Spring farm,[2] man's world, God's universe,
The babel of the circumstance and era.
The frozen socket of its window stared
Beyond the spayed crabapple trees, to where
The skulls of hills, the skeletons of barrens,[3]
Lay quiet as time without the watch's tick.

Not knowing muck and star would vie for him,
The man Tom sank upon an ax-split stool,

"Abraham Lincoln of Rock Spring Farm" by Melvin B. Tolson from
Soon, One Morning, edited by Herbert Hill, published by Alfred A.
Knopf, Inc. Reprinted by permission of Ruth Tolson.

[1] *Along the Wilderness Road . . . :* In 1782 Abraham Lincoln's grandfather moved his family from Virginia to Kentucky. He followed the
arduous Wilderness Trail that had been marked out by Daniel Boone,
a trail leading down the Shenandoah Valley to Lexington and around
to Cumberland Gap in Tennessee, then northwest into Kentucky.
Tolson has telescoped the time of that long, difficult journey and the
time of Lincoln's birth at Rock Spring farm in Kentucky on Sunday,
February 12, 1809.

[2] *Rock Spring farm:* Thomas Lincoln married Nancy Hanks in 1806.
In 1808 they moved to a small farm near Nolin's Creek. According to
Carl Sandburg, "It was called the Rock Spring farm because at the
foot of one of its sloping hills the rocks curved in like the beginning
of a cave . . . a ledge of rock formed a beckoning roof with room for
people to stand under; and at the heart of it, for its center, was a
never-ending flow of clear, cool water."

[3] *barrens:* poor farmland made up of clay, stones, and thick under-
brush.

Hands fisted, feet set wide to brace the spirit,
Big shoulders shoved, dark hazel eyes glazed by
Grotesqueries of flame that yawled and danced
Up, up, the stick-clay chimney. While fire imps combed
The black and bristling hair, the acids of thoughts
Made of the orby [4] face an etching-plate.

II

Near pyrotechnic logs, the purling kettle,
Aunt Peggy [5] puffed her pipe on God's rich time:
A granny at a childbed on the border,
Where head and backbone answered the tomahawk.
Her wise old eyes had seen a hundred Nancys
In travail tread the dark winepress alone;
Her wise old hands had plucked a stubborn breed
Into the outer world of pitch and toss.

The cabin that her myth and mission entered
Became a castle in which Aunt Peggy throned
A dynasty of grunts and nods and glances.
The nest, the barn, the hovel had schooled her in
The ABC of motherhood, and somehow
She'd lost her ego in the commonweal:
She sensed so accurately a coming child
That rakes dubbed her the St. Bernard of Sex!

And now her keyhole look explored Tom Lincoln
Beneath the patched homespun, the hue and cry
Of malice,[6] until she touched his loneliness,
The taproot that his fiber gave no tongue.
Then, lulling the wife, troubled in flesh and mind,
She eased the sack quilts higher and mused the while:

[4] *orby:* round.
[5] *Aunt Peggy:* "One morning in February of this year, 1809, Tom Lincoln came out of his cabin to the road, stopped a neighbor and asked him to tell 'the granny woman,' Aunt Peggy Walters, that Nancy would need help soon" (Carl Sandburg, *Abraham Lincoln*). A "granny woman" was a frontier midwife. Aunt Peggy was not related to the Lincolns.
[6] *malice:* Tom Lincoln had the reputation of being idle and unambitious.

There's but one way of coming into the world,
And seven times seventy ways of leaving it!

III

The woman Nancy, like a voyager sucked
Into the sea's whale belly by a wreck,
Buoyed to the surface air of consciousness
And clutched the solace of her corn-husk bed.
Her dark face, sharped in forehead, cheekbone, chin,
Cuddled in dark brown hair; her eyes waxed grayer
With wonder of the interlude: her beauty
And courage choked Aunt Peggy's hyperbole!

Out of the fog of pain, the bog of bygones,
The bag of cabin cant and tavern tattle,
She picked the squares to piece tomorrow's quilt:
She puzzled now, as then, about her father [7]
Who let wild Lucy Hanks bundle and carry
Flesh of his flesh beyond the Cumberland Gap:
A strange roof is no roof when imps of fear
Pilfer the fatherless in blossom time.

Year in, year out, the daughter tinkered with
The riddle of her birth; the mother chided
The woman Nancy as she had the child,
"Hush thee, hush thee, thy father's a gentleman."
The butt of bawd, grand jury, Sunday bonnet, [8]
Lucy, driven, taught her daughter the Word,
And Nancy, driven, taught her son the Word, [9]
And Abraham, driven, taught his people the Word!

[7] *her father:* Nancy Hanks was born in Virginia in 1784. Her
mother, Lucy Hanks, was unmarried, and brought her infant with her
down the Wilderness Road to Kentucky.

[8] *The butt of bawd ... :* For some time after her arrival in Kentucky, Lucy Hanks was talked about as "too free and easy"; on one
occasion, a grand jury "named her to be investigated for immoral
tendencies." Later, however, she married and reared a large, highly
respectable family.

[9] *And Nancy, driven ... :* Sandburg relates that Nancy "was sad
with sorrows like dark stars in blue mist." But he adds, "The hope
was burned deep in her that beyond the harsh clay paths, the everyday scrubbing, washing, patching, fixing, the babble and the gabble
of today, there are pastures and purple valleys of song."

IV

The man Tom bit his fingernails, then rammed
His pockets with the hector hands that gave
Raw timber the shape of cabinet and coffin,
And in his lame speech said: "Aunt Peggy, listen.
Now that our Nancy's time is come, I'm haunted
By my own nothingness. Why breed nobodies?"
He tapped the dirt floor with the iron-capped boot
That aided fist and skull in border fights.

Aunt Peggy counseled: "Tom, you say the say
Poor Joseph probably said in that low stable
Ere Jesus came into this mishmash world."
She paused, then boxed the ears of cynicism:
"It's true, down in the barnyard, blood speaks loud,
Among the hogs, the chickens, the cows, the horses;
But, when it comes to Man, who knows, who knows
What greatness feeds down in the lowliest mother?"

The man Tom turned and spat: his naked surmise
Ranged out and out. Aunt Peggy's innermost said:
"Your father Abraham,[10] bred like Daniel Boone,
Conquered a land with gun and ax and plow,
Baptized it in his blood! I say, I've said,
What's in a baby is God Almighty's business;
How the elders wring it out is worry enough!
The best, the worst—it's all, all human nature."

V

The tavern, Tom remembered, the New Year's Eve,
The clubfoot scholar bagged in Old World clothes,
With arrowy eyes and a hoary mushroom beard.
An Oxford don, he hymned the Bastille's fall
In spite of the hair-hung sword; his betters set
Him free to hail new truths in new lands, where

[10] *Abraham:* Abraham Lincoln's grandfather, for whom he was
named.

He seined with slave and master, knave and priest,
And out of all fished up the rights of man:

"As Citizen Lincoln asks, 'What's human nature?'
His full mug says a clear mind puts the question
Which ties the fogey scholar in a knot!
My new idea fed to his new baby
Would fetch the New World and the New Year peace!
The sum of anything unriddles the riddle:
The child whose wet nurse is the mother-of-all
Grows like a pine unmarked by rock or wind.

"To make a New World and a New Year, Plato
And Jesus begged the boon of little children!
Now Citizen Lincoln asks, 'What's human nature?'
It's what we elders have: no baby has it.
It's what our good and bad graft on the neutral.
It's what our rulers feed the boy and girl.
It's what society garbs nature in.
It's a misnomer: call it *human nurture!*"

VI

Aunt Peggy hovered closer, with flawless rites
Grown lyrical from habit: muffled pain sounds
Dragged from the bed of cleated poles; she hawed
Tom Lincoln, as one turns a nag aside,
Then swooped her way, even as a setting hen
Carves a dictatorship from yard to nest.
And Tom again was squeezed into a cell
Whose inmates were the ghosts of unsuccess.

Later his memories climbed a gala peak,
His Nancy's infare [11] that ran riotous:
The bear meat, venison, wild turkey, duck,
The maple sugar hanging for the whiskey,
The red ham, gourds of syrup, bowls of honey,
The wood coal pit with brown and juicy sheep,

[11] *infare:* a Kentucky wedding celebration.

The guzzling, fiddling, guttling [12] monkeyshining:
A continent sprawled between that day and this!

A havenot on the frontier is no havenot;
A Crusoe without Friday has no conscience:
Yet Tom's grub living gnawed him like the teeth
Of slavery, land titles, melancholy.
He, like his forebears, visioned a Promised Land
And tidied ways and means to fly the barrens
That doomed the flesh to peck, to patch, to pinch,
And wrung the soul of joy and beauty dry.

VII

The black ox hours limped by, and day crawled after.
White prongs of ice, like dinosaur fangs, gleamed in
The cavernous mouth of Rock Spring; snowbirds shivered
And chirped rebellion; a cow with jags and gaps
Chewed emptily; hogs squealed in hunger fits;
And scrags of dogs huddled against the chimney,
Which shoveled smoke dust into the throats and noses
Of ragged winds kicking up snow in the desert.

Nancy lay white, serene, like virgin milk
After the udder's fury in the pail.
Beneath the sack quilts and the bearskin robe,
In yellow petticoat and linsey shirt,
The baby snuggled at her breast and gurgled—
An anonymity of soft red wrinkles.
Aunt Peggy, hovering, grinned, "He's Sabbath-born.
Remember . . . Sunday—it's red-letter day!"

Like ax and helve, like scythe and snath, the bond
Held Tom and Nancy: she smiled at his halt smile,
His titan's muss in picking up the baby.
Tom frowned and spat, then gulped, "He's legs! All legs!"
Aunt Peggy beamed, "Long legs can eat up miles."
Tom gloomed, "The hands—look at the axman's hands!"
And Nancy mused, "The Hankses' dream, the Lincolns',
Needs such a man to hew and blaze the way."

[12] *guttling:* overeating.

1. In "The Sea-Turtle and the Shark," the description of the sea-turtle's "rapacious claws/ that can rip/ a rhinoceros' hide/ or strip/ a crocodile to fare-thee-well" ends with an ironic understatement. What is the effect of this understatement on the reader? How does the understatement help the reader to establish the narrator's attitude toward the sea-turtle?

2. The first stanza of "Abraham Lincoln of Rock Spring Farm" mixes fact and heroic legend. Which of the images in this stanza define the physical hardships that preceded Lincoln's birth? Which images also suggest the imminent birth of a hero? What kind of hero?

3. In the fourth and fifth parts of the poem, what topics form a kind of debate? Does Tom Lincoln think his unborn child likely to become "somebody"? What are the viewpoints of Aunt Peggy and the radical scholar from Oxford on the forces that produce exceptional men?

4. How would you respond to the claim of another reader that neither of these poems by Tolson deals with the experience of black people?

born 1917

GWENDOLYN BROOKS

☐ *Gwendolyn Brooks was born in Kansas, but was raised and educated in Chicago. For most of her life Chicago has been her home, and much of her poetry grows out of her intimate knowledge of the city's black community. As a poet, she allows neither sentimentality nor social anger to distort her honest observations and precise use of language. In her work, personal experience and social problems are regularly transmuted into art.*

Gwendolyn Brooks's first collection of poems, A Street in Bronzeville, *was published in 1945. It was followed in 1949 by* Annie Allen, *which won her the Pulitzer Prize for poetry. Her other books of verse are* The Bean Eaters *(1960),* Selected Poems *(1963), and*

In the Mecca (*1968*). *She has also written a novel,* Maud Martha, *published in 1953. Gwendolyn Brooks has received numerous awards for outstanding literary accomplishment.*

southeast corner°

The School of Beauty's a tavern now.
The Madam is underground.
Out at Lincoln, among the graves
Her own is early found.
Where the thickest, tallest monument
Cuts grandly into the air
The Madam lies, contentedly.
Her fortune, too, lies there,
Converted into cool hard steel
And bright red velvet lining;
While over her tan impassivity
Shot silk is shining.

° *Southeast Corner:* This poem is one of a group titled "A Street in Bronzeville." Bronzeville is the author's name for the black ghetto on Chicago's South Side; Lincoln is the cemetery where Bronzeville's dead are buried.

the white troops had their orders
but the negroes looked like men

They had supposed their formula was fixed.
They had obeyed instructions to devise
A type of cold, a type of hooded gaze.
But when the Negroes came they were perplexed.
These Negroes looked like men. Besides, it taxed
Time and the temper to remember those
Congenital iniquities that cause
Disfavor of the darkness. Such as boxed
Their feelings properly, complete to tags— [1]
A box for dark men and a box for Other—
Would often find the contents had been scrambled.
Or even switched. Who really gave two figs?
Neither the earth nor heaven ever trembled.
And there was nothing startling in the weather.

for discussion

1. In "Southeast Corner," how do the title and first line, taken together, help to define both the local and the more universal meanings of the poem?

2. Is there any indication that "The White Troops" are carrying out a specific task? What "orders" do they appear to have received? How does the dramatic situation presented in the poem contribute to its impact and meaning?

[1] *tags:* dog tags; metal disks used to identify men in the armed forces.

born 1914

OWEN DODSON

☐ *Owen Dodson was born in Brooklyn, New York, and
was educated in its public schools. He received his
higher education in New England, at Bates College in
Maine and at Yale University. As a writer, teacher, and
theater director, Dodson has traveled widely in this
country and in Europe. He has been receptive to many
kinds of artistic influence, and has labored long to perfect
his mastery of the several literary forms in which he
works. Accordingly, although Dodson writes about the
experience and the traditions of the Negro, he does so
in a style that reflects the cosmopolitan range of his
human and artistic concerns.*

*Dodson is the author of poems, short stories, novels,
and plays. His first book of poems,* Powerful Long Ladder,
was published in 1946; and in 1951 he published a novel,
Boy at the Window. *Dodson's plays have been performed
throughout America and in England. As a dramatist, he
has also collaborated with composers in the writing of
song cycles, pageants, and operas.*

open letter

Brothers, let us discover our hearts again,
Permitting the regular strong beat of humanity there
To propel the likelihood of other terror to an exit.

For at last it is nearly ended: the daily anguish needles
Probing in our brains when alarms crust the air
And planes stab over us.

(Tears screamed from our eyes,
Animals moaned for death, gardens were disguised,
Stumps strained to be whole again.)

For at last it is nearly ended, grass
Will be normal, hillsides
Pleased with boys roaming their bellies.

All the mourning children
Will understand the long word, hallelujah,
Each use for joy will light for them.

The torn souls and broken bodies will be restored,
Primers circulate for everlasting peace,
The doors to hope swung open.

Brothers, let us enter that portal for good
When peace surrounds us like a credible universe.
Bury that agony, bury this hate, take our black hands in
    yours.

definition

Everyone says: fate is a bad number,
Should be jailed and put on bread and water.
Fate has drilled into the spirit's bone,
And all our marrow has leaked out.

They talk of fate as they talk of God and Devil;
Something like a storm between mountains
Or tigers or whales or tornadoes,
Something like the chemistry of air.

"Definition" from *Powerful Long Ladder*, copyright 1946 by Owen
Dodson. Reprinted by permission of the publisher, Farrar, Straus &
Giroux, Inc.

Fate is ourselves awake and asleep,
Fighting in the sky or armies in the earth,
Speeches, treaties, elections, hopes of heaven,
Preparations for hell. Fate is the collection plate

Of our sins and our loves—variety of coins,
Stored away or stolen by those fakirs
Who blame the plus or minus of our condition
On God or Devil or the sound of the sea.

for discussion

1. In "Open Letter," what is "it" that the speaker says in the second stanza "is nearly ended"? What meaning does *discover* (first line) have in addition to its more obvious sense of "find"?

2. In what way does the physical setting of "Open Letter" tend to universalize the specifically racial gesture with which the poem ends?

3. "Definition" offers two views of fate in sharply contrasting terms. What image of fate is defined in the first two stanzas, and how does it operate upon the opposed conception of fate that is defined in the two concluding stanzas?

born 1913

ROBERT HAYDEN

☐ Robert Hayden was born in 1913 in Detroit, where he attended public schools and Wayne State University. He earned his master's degree at the University of Michigan, twice winning the Hopwood Award there for his poetry. For more than twenty years Hayden was a member of the English Department at Fisk University in Nashville, Tennessee. In 1969 he became a professor of English at the University of Michigan.

Hayden's literary career has evolved without fanfare,

but it has been a genuinely successful one. He has continued to win awards, including a Ford Foundation grant that permitted him to spend a year in Mexico; his poems have been printed in national periodicals and have frequently been anthologized. Hayden's first book of poems, Heart-Shape in the Dust, was published in 1940. In 1948 he collaborated with Myron O'Higgins in writing The Lion and the Archer; and in 1955 Hayden's Figure of Time appeared. His fourth volume of poetry, A Ballad of Remembrance, was issued in England in 1962. This book won the Grand Prize for Poetry at the First World Festival of Negro Arts, held in 1965 in Dakar, Senegal. Hayden's Selected Poems was published in 1966. In 1967 he edited Kaleidoscope: Poems by American Negro Poets.

Much of Hayden's poetry stems directly from his compelling interest in Negro history and folklore, but he has said that "he sees no reason why a Negro poet should be limited to 'racial utterance' or to having his writing judged by standards different from those applied to the work of other poets." Now in mid-career, Hayden has matured slowly but surely as a poet, carefully refining old poems even while beginning more ambitious ones. His original use of ethnic materials and his firm control of technique have culminated in a body of poems that have enriched modern American literature.

No longer throne of a goddess [1] to whom we pray,
no longer the bubble house of childhood's
tumbling Mother Goose man,[2]

The emphatic moon ascends—
the brilliant challenger of rocket experts,
the white hope of communications men.

Some I love who are dead
were watchers of the moon and knew its lore;
planted seeds, trimmed their hair,

Pierced their ears for gold hoop earrings
as it waxed or waned.
It shines tonight upon their graves.

And burned in the garden of Gethsemane,[3]
its light made holy by the dazzling tears
with which it mingled.

And spread its radiance on the exile's path
of Him who was The Glorious One,[4]
its light made holy by His holiness.

Already a mooted goal and tomorrow perhaps
an arms base, a livid sector,
the full moon dominates the dark.

[1] *goddess:* Many ancient peoples—including the Greeks and Romans—identified the moon with a goddess.
[2] *Mother Goose man:* a reference to the old nursery rhyme which begins, "The man in the moon/ Came tumbling down/ And asked his way to Norwich. . . ."
[3] *Gethsemane:* the place of Christ's agony and betrayal. See *Matthew* 26.
[4] *The Glorious One:* one of the titles given to Bahá'u'lláh, prophet of the Bahá'í religion.

homage to the empress of the blues °

Because there was a man somewhere in a candystripe silk
shirt, gracile and dangerous as a jaguar and because a
woman moaned for him in sixty-watt gloom and mourned
him Faithless Love Twotiming Love Oh Love Oh Careless
Aggravating Love,

> She came out on the stage in yards of pearls, emerging
> like a favorite scenic view, flashed her golden smile
> and sang.

Because grey laths began somewhere to show from underneath torn hurdygurdy lithographs of dollfaced heaven;
and because there were those who feared alarming fists of
snow on the door and those who feared the riot-squad of
statistics,

> She came out on the stage in ostrich feathers, beaded
> satin, and shone that smile on us and sang.

for discussion

1. On its most literal level, "Full Moon" surveys some historical changes that have ocurred in the moon's identity. How many such changes does the poem describe?
2. In what sense does the poem's last line state a function of the moon that has been characteristic of all its different identities? Why does the speaker call the moon a "brilliant challenger" and a "white hope," terms which suggest prize fighting?

3. The two stanzas of "Homage to the Empress of the Blues" are strikingly similar. In how many actual details do they run parallel with each other? What is the effect of such duplication?

° *Empress of the Blues:* Blues is a form of music originated by black Americans. The themes of blues songs are melancholy and tragic, but blues also possess both the humor and the warmth that make suffering more endurable. Bessie Smith, the greatest blues singer of the 1920's and 1930's, is often referred to as "Empress of the Blues."

MARGARET DANNER

☐ *Margaret Danner has lived most of her life in Chicago. She attended Roosevelt and Loyola universities in that city. By the mid-1940's she had won local recognition as a poet; and in 1952 she reached a national audience when her three-poem sequence "Far from Africa" was published in* Poetry: A Magazine of Verse. *Margaret Danner later served as an assistant editor of that famous magazine, and in 1960 she became the first Poet in Residence at Wayne State University in Detroit.*

As a young writer, Margaret Danner was drawn to the classical world of European art and literature. Since 1950, however, she has been far more responsive to her African heritage. Much of Margaret Danner's poetry celebrates her faith in Africa's future and her excited discovery of the distinctive art that Africa has already inspired. But her poetry also expresses sensitively the complicated personal tensions that arise inevitably from shared cultural loyalties.

Margaret Danner published her Impressions of African Art Forms *in 1961,* To Flower *in 1963,* Poem Counterpoem *(with Dudley Randall) in 1966, and* Iron Lace *in 1968. In addition to her printed verse, Margaret Danner has exercised another direct influence on her contemporaries—whether in Chicago or Detroit, her home has been a fertile meeting place and school for young black artists.*

a sparrow is a bird

Why would a robin think that a sparrow
was made to fly in a narrow line and tug
at the bugs and worms that a robin struts

away from with dislike? Be but a scavenger? A sparrow too
is a bird and who can tell a bird when to fly
or teach him why he must observe a place? Stay in it?

The minute a sparrow is hatched he's a bird
and he girds his loins and determines
to eat any kind of vermin he pleases.

And breezes around everywhere and if
there must be a tiff or a cherry
or very choice worm, although he didn't begin it,
he will fight back, hoping to eventually win it.

"A Sparrow Is a Bird" by Margaret Danner, published in *Poem Counterpoem* by Broadside Press in 1966. Reprinted by permission of the author.

this is an african worm

This is an African worm
but then a worm in any land
is still a worm.

It will not stride, run, stand up
before the butterflies, who
have passed their worm-like state.

"This Is an African Worm" by Margaret Danner, published in *Poem Counterpoem* by Broadside Press in 1966. Reprinted by permission of the author.

It must keep low, not lift its head.
I've had the dread experience, I know.
A worm can do no thing but crawl.

Crawl, and wait.

for discussion

1. Notice that the four stanzas of "A Sparrow Is a Bird" are arranged in a pattern of question and answer. What is the tone of the questions and their answer? How does the poet's use of understatement throughout the poem help to establish the speaker's tone and point of view?

2. *Worm* is a common word with an apparently obvious meaning. Consequently, the reader may not immediately see the range of its meanings in "This Is an African Worm." Check the meanings of this word in a dictionary and show which of them are relevant to the poem's total meaning.

born 1914

DUDLEY RANDALL

☐ *Dudley Randall was born in 1914 in Washington, D.C., but Detroit has been his home for most of his life. He attended Detroit's public schools, worked on a factory production line, graduated from Wayne State University, and received a master's degree at the University of Michigan. For the past two decades he has been a librarian, and recently has taught American Negro literature at the University of Michigan and has been Poet in Residence at the University of Detroit.*

Randall possesses a versatile literary talent; he is a translator, editor, and publisher as well as a poet. He has translated Russian, French, and Latin poetry. In 1967 he and Margaret Burroughs edited For Malcolm, *a collection of "poems on the life and the death of Malcolm X." And in 1969 Randall edited* Black Poetry, *an anthology* of modern Negro poetry. As a publisher, Randall is an independent and accurate judge of new work who has helped to launch the careers of several promising black writers. The Broadside Press, which he founded in 1965, is one of America's most important new outlets for black literature. Randall's own poems, stories, and essays have appeared in various periodicals and anthologies. His first book of poems, Poem Counterpoem (1966), was a collaboration with Margaret Danner. Cities Burning, Randall's second book, was published in 1968.

Whether as poet, editor, or publisher, Randall has shown his awareness of the accumulated injustices that are the central fact of the black American's life. However, Randall is also challenged by the mysteries of imagination and craft that are the central fact of the poet's life. Randall's dedication to the shaping of experience into verses that ring true as poetry is matched by his dedication to the struggle for equal rights. In his own work and in much of the work he publishes, he has demonstrated that these two goals can be reconciled.

booker t. and w. e. b.°

"It seems to me," said Booker T.,
"It shows a mighty lot of cheek
To study chemistry and Greek
When Mister Charlie needs a hand
To hoe the cotton on his land,
And when Miss Ann looks for a cook,
Why stick your nose inside a book?"

° *Booker T. and W. E. B.*: Booker T. Washington (1856–1915) and William Edward Burghardt Du Bois (1868–1963). Du Bois was a Harvard Ph.D., a college professor, and one of the founders of the

"I don't agree," said W. E. B.
"If I should have the drive to seek
Knowledge of chemistry or Greek,
I'll do it. Charles and Miss can look
Another place for hand or cook.
Some men rejoice in skill of hand,
And some in cultivating land,
But there are others who maintain
The right to cultivate the brain."

"It seems to me," said Booker T.,
"That all you folks have missed the boat
Who shout about the right to vote,
And spend vain days and sleepless nights
In uproar over civil rights.
Just keep your mouths shut, do not grouse,
But work, and save, and buy a house."

"I don't agree," said W. E. B.,
"For what can property avail
If dignity and justice fail?
Unless you help to make the laws,
They'll steal your house with trumped-up clause.
A rope's as tight, a fire as hot,
No matter how much cash you've got.
Speak soft, and try your little plan,
But as for me, I'll be a man."

"It seems to me," said Booker T.—

"I don't agree,"
Said W. E. B.

NAACP. He provided militant leadership for the movement that demanded immediate full civil rights for the Negro. Even before 1900
he opposed Washington's strategy of delaying the struggle for equal
rights in favor of pursuing economic progress through vocational training. He opposed Washington's belief that through patient self-improvement the Negro would be allowed to exercise the civil rights
that were already his legally. But Du Bois and Washington were not
enemies; they disagreed over the choice of tactics, but their objectives
were essentially the same. Near the end of his life, Du Bois said, "I
never thought Washington was a bad man; I believed him to be sin-
cere, though wrong."

1. What is the difference in the actual speech of the two characters in Randall's poem? What differences of temperament and philosophy are hinted at by their ways of talking?

2. The poem contains much repetition of language and rhythm, and it also appears to end inconclusively. How do these details help to establish the general nature of the debate between the two men?

3. Is the debate in the poem a new one or an old one? Are such opposed viewpoints likely to occur among other people, in different circumstances, in different times and places?

born 1917

SAMUEL ALLEN

☐ *Samuel Allen, who uses the penname Paul Vesey, was born in 1917 in Columbus, Ohio. He was educated at Fisk University, where his writing teacher was James Weldon Johnson. Allen next took a law degree at Harvard University. Later, under the GI Bill, he studied at the Sorbonne in Paris. There he met Richard Wright, who helped him to publish his poems. Allen lived in Europe between 1948 and 1955; his first book of poems was printed in Germany in a bilingual English-German edition. Titled* Ivory Tusks: Poems of an Afro-American, *it appeared in 1956.*

In addition to his European travels, Allen has made long visits to Africa and Latin America. He has published essays on both African and Afro-American literature, and was the editor of the book Pan-Africanism Reconsidered *(1962). As an attorney, Allen has been occupied in public service, first as Assistant General Counsel in the United States Information Agency and then in the Community Relations Service of the Department of Justice. In 1968 Allen became a member of the faculty at Tuskegee Institute, where he succeeded Melvin B. Tolson as Avalon Professor of Humanities.*

to satch
(or american gothic) °

Sometimes I feel like I will *never* stop
Just go on forever
Till one fine mornin
I'm gonna reach up and grab me a handfulla stars
Swing out my long lean leg
And whip three hot strikes burnin down the heavens
And look over at God and say
How about that!

for discussion

1. What significance do you find in the absence of internal punctuation from "To Satch"?

2. Which features of the legendary hero are attributed to Satch in the poem?

"To Satch (or American Gothic)" by Paul Vesey. Reprinted by permission of the author (Samuel W. Allen).

° *Satch:* LeRoy (Satchel) Paige was born in 1906 and began pitching for a black baseball team in 1924, twenty-three years before Jackie Robinson became the first black man given the opportunity to play major league baseball. Satch's active career spanned about forty years; it is estimated that he pitched nearly three thousand games over many seasons in which he was virtually unbeatable. The brilliance and length of his pitching career have made him legendary in his own time. In 1962 he is reported to have declared, "Maybe I'll pitch forever."

Gothic: in art history, an irregular style that mixes grandeur with grotesqueness; primitive or unschooled; a picturesque ruin of great antiquity.

M. CARL HOLMAN

☐ *Carl Holman was born in 1919 in Mississippi, but he grew up in St. Louis, Missouri. He attended public schools there, then ran an elevator, worked as a machine operator, delivered parcels, and waited in the job lines of the Depression. Holman left St. Louis to study at Lincoln University in Missouri, and later earned graduate degrees at the University of Chicago and Yale University. At Chicago he won the Fiske Poetry Prize in 1944 and received a fellowship for advanced study and creative writing.*

Holman has been a professor of English at Hampton Institute in Virginia and at Clark College in Atlanta, Georgia. He was also, for a time, editor of the weekly Atlanta Inquirer. *More recently, he has been an information officer for the United States Commission on Civil Rights in Washington, D.C. Although Holman's poems have been printed in notable journals and anthologies, they have not yet been collected into a book.*

mr. z

Taught early that his mother's skin was the sign of error,
He dressed and spoke the perfect part of honor;
Won scholarships, attended the best schools,
Disclaimed kinship with jazz and spirituals;
Chose prudent, raceless views for each situation,
Or when he could not cleanly skirt dissension,
Faced up to the dilemma, firmly seized
Whatever ground was Anglo-Saxonized.

"Mr. Z" by M. Carl Holman. Reprinted by permission of the author.

In diet, too, his practice was exemplary:
Of pork in its profane forms he was wary;
Expert in vintage wines, sauces and salads,
His palate shrank from cornbread, yams and collards.

He was as careful whom he chose to kiss:
His bride had somewhere lost her Jewishness,
But kept her blue eyes; an Episcopalian
Prelate proclaimed them matched chameleon.
Choosing the right addresses, here, abroad,
They shunned those places where they might be barred;
Even less anxious to be asked to dine
Where hosts catered to kosher accent or exotic skin.

And so he climbed, unclogged by ethnic weights,
An airborne plant, flourishing without roots.
Not one false note was struck—until he died:
His subtly grieving widow could have flayed
The obit writers, ringing [1] crude changes on a clumsy
    phrase:
"One of the most distinguished members of his race."

for discussion

1. What is a eulogy? Is the poem "Mr. Z" a eulogy? Cite the lines which support your answer.
2. What evidence do you find that the poet is being ironic?
3. At which aspects of Mr. Z's behavior is the speaker's irony directed?

4. How intense is the satire of Mr. Z? Is he mildly or harshly satirized?

[1] *ringing:* introducing or inserting.

KARL SHAPIRO

☐ *Karl Shapiro was born in Baltimore, Maryland, and
educated at the University of Virginia and at The Johns
Hopkins University. He has been a professor at several
colleges, most recently at the universities of Nebraska,
Illinois, and California. He was the editor of two of
America's foremost literary magazines,* Poetry *and*
Prairie Schooner. *And he has argued his views on poetry
and contemporary culture in such books as* Beyond
Criticism *(1953),* In Defense of Ignorance *(1960), and*
To Abolish Children *(1968).*

*Shapiro is, however, best known as a poet. Starting
with* Poems *in 1935, he published* Person, Place and Thing
and The Place of Love *in 1942,* V-Letter *in 1944,* Essay
on Rime *in 1945,* Trial of a Poet *in 1947,* Poems of a Jew
in 1958, The Bourgeois Poet *in 1964, and* White-Haired
Lover *in 1968. Shapiro's* Selected Poems *also appeared in
1968. He has been elected to the National Institute of
Arts and Letters and made a Fellow in American Letters
at the Library of Congress. Shapiro has won many awards
for his poetry, including the Pulitzer Prize in 1945.*

*Shapiro is a second-generation American Jew for
whom being a Jew is a matter neither of religion nor of
nationality. His Jewishness is the awareness that one's
identity is imposed upon him by others and that survival
is always difficult, but that one must nevertheless affirm
the value of life in such a world. For Shapiro, the
experience of Jewishness is fundamentally the condition
of all mankind. He defines the modern Jew as "man in all
his raw potentiality," still undefeated "after everything
that can happen has happened." It is in this general spirit
that Shapiro has said "the undercurrent of most of my
poems is the theme of the Jew."*

my grandmother

My grandmother moves to my mind in context of sorrow
And, as if apprehensive of near death, in black;
Whether erect in chair, her dry and corded throat harangued
    by grief,
Or at ragged book bent in Hebrew prayer,
Or gentle, submissive, and in tears to strangers;
Whether in sunny parlor or back of drawn blinds.

Though time and tongue made any love disparate,
On daguerreotype with classic perspective
Beauty I sigh and soften at is hers.
I pity her life of deaths, the agony of her own,
But most that history moved her through
Stranger lands and many houses,
Taking her exile for granted, confusing
The tongues and tasks of her children's children.

travelogue for exiles

Look and remember. Look upon this sky;
Look deep and deep into the sea-clean air,
The unconfined, the terminus of prayer.
Speak now and speak into the hallowed dome.
What do you hear? What does the sky reply?
The heavens are taken: this is not your home.

Look and remember. Look upon this sea;
Look down and down into the tireless tide.
What of a life below, a life inside,
A tomb, a cradle in the curly foam?
The waves arise; sea-wind and sea agree
The waters are taken: this is not your home.

Look and remember. Look upon this land,
Far, far across the factories and the grass.
Surely, there, surely, they will let you pass.
Speak then and ask the forest and the loam.
What do you hear? What does the land command?
The earth is taken: this is not your home.

for discussion

1. As the pronoun in the title "My Grandmother" suggests, the speaker is as central to the meaning of the poem as his grandmother. With nearly all the descriptive details referring to the grandmother, how is the speaker established as a controlling presence in the poem?

2. In what ways are the two parts of this irregular sonnet connected?

3. What qualities of the modern world endow the specifically Jewish grief in "My Grandmother" and "Travelogue for Exiles" with more universal meaning?

born 1920
HOWARD NEMEROV

☐ *Howard Nemerov was born in 1920 in New York City where he lived until he entered Harvard University, from which he graduated in 1941. He returned to New England in 1948 as a teacher of literature at Bennington College in Vermont. Since 1966 he has taught at Brandeis University in Massachusetts. Nemerov is a poet, novelist, and literary critic whose work has circulated widely in magazines like the* New Yorker *and the* Atlantic, *in political weeklies like the* Nation, *and in the intellectual quarterly journals.*

His first book of poems, The Image and the Law, *was published in 1947. It was followed by* Guide to the Ruins *in 1950,* The Salt Garden *in 1955,* Mirrors and Windows *in 1958,* New and Selected Poems *in 1960,* The Next Room of the Dream *in 1962, and* The Blue Swallows *in 1967. The verse plays* Cain *and* Endor *appeared in 1959 and 1961. Nemerov's novels are* The Melodramatists *(1949),* Federigo, or The Power of Love *(1954), and* The Homecoming Game *(1957). He has also published a volume of short stories,* A Commodity of Dreams *(1959).* Poetry and Fiction, *a collection of Nemerov's literary essays, appeared in 1963. Nemerov is a member of the National Institute of Arts and Letters and the American Academy of Arts and Sciences, and has received many other honors.*

Native to New York City and an adopted New Englander, Nemerov is a kind of Jewish Puritan whose gaze is focused upon the aches and the puzzles of human experience. He is a meditative poet of both the city and the countryside who penetrates deeply into the perilous, always altering lives of men. As a writer, Nemerov is committed to seeing the world truthfully and to finding the means of accurately stating what he sees. The objects of Nemerov's vision sometimes evoke doubt and disgust, sometimes joy and faith; they always evoke his determination to see further into life's mysteriousness. Nemerov believes that the "responsibility of poetry" is to clarify the "great primary human drama" of birth, discovery, and death to which all men are called.

a song of degrees °

Though the road lead nowhere
I have followed the road
In its blind turnings, its descents
And the long levels where the emptiness ahead
Is inescapably seen.

I have cried for justice, I have cried
For mercy, now I desire neither.
A man may grow strong in his wandering,
His foot strong as a wheel
Turning the endless road.

Foot and hand hardened to horn,
Nose but a hook of bone, and eyes
Not liquid now but stone—I
To myself violent, fiercely exult
In Zion everywhere.

° *A Song of Degrees:* Fifteen of the Psalms in the Bible (120–34) bear this title, sometimes translated "A Song of Ascents." It is believed that these fifteen Psalms were sung by pilgrims retracing the ascending path from the Babylonian captivity to Jerusalem.

debate with the rabbi

You've lost your religion, the Rabbi said.
    It wasn't much to keep, said I.
You should affirm the spirit, said he,

And the communal solidarity.
　　I don't feel so solid, I said.

We are the people of the Book, the Rabbi said.
　　Not of the phone book, said I.
Ours is a great tradition, said he,
And a wonderful history.
　　But history's over, I said.

We Jews are creative people, the Rabbi said.
　　Make something, then, said I.
In science and in art, said he,
Violinists and physicists have we.
　　Fiddle and physic indeed, I said.

Stubborn and stiff-necked man! the Rabbi cried.
　　The pain you give me, said I.
Instead of bowing down, said he,
You go on in your obstinacy.
　　We Jews are that way, I replied.

for discussion

1. In "A Song of Degrees," what contrasting emotions are expressed by the speaker?

2. Under what circumstances may a man "grow strong in his wandering"? How do you account for the exultant note on which the poem ends?

3. In "Debate with the Rabbi," what test does the second speaker consistently apply to his religion? How would you describe the "turn" or the development which occurs in the poem's final stanza?

1911–1962

HYAM PLUTZIK

☐ *Hyam Plutzik, born in 1911 in Brooklyn, New York, was raised and educated in Connecticut. He received his bachelor's degree from Trinity College in Hartford in 1932 and his master's from Yale University in 1940. In between, he worked as a reporter on newspapers in Brooklyn and Newark during the Depression years. Plutzik taught literature at the University of Rochester from 1945 until his death in 1962.*

At first, Plutzik's poems appeared rather quietly in university quarterlies, but their merit was recognized. He won the Cook Prize for poetry at Yale and was honored by the National Institute of Arts and Letters. Plutzik's first book of poems, Aspects of Proteus, *was published in 1949, followed a decade later by* Apples from Shinar. *A third volume, the long narrative poem* Horatio, *was published in 1961. Plutzik was thoroughly at home in the many traditions of English and American poetry, but his familiarity with them never diluted or cooled the intensely personal quality of his own poetry. Rather, mastery of these traditions enabled him to give form to his experience and to discover its correspondences with the experience of other people.*

after looking into a book belonging to my great-grandfather, eli eliakim plutzik

I am troubled by the blank fields, the speechless graves.
Since the names were carved upon wood, there is no word
For the thousand years that shaped this scribbling fist
And the eyes staring at strange places and times
Beyond the veldt dragging to Poland.
Lovers of words make simple peace with death,
At last demanding, to close the door to the cold,
Only *Here lies someone.*
Here lie no one and no one, your fathers and mothers.

portrait

Notice with what careful nonchalance
He tries to be a Jew casually,
To ignore the monster, the mountain—
A few thousand years of history.

Of course he personally remembers nothing,
And the world has forgotten the older objections—
The new ones not being socially acceptable:
Hangdogs, hiding in the privies and alleys of the mind.

It is agreed
That he of all men has gained the right to his soul
(Though like the others he no longer believes in one).
He lives in his own house under his oak.
He stands by his car, shod in decently-grained leather.
He is smiling. His hair is peacefully in place.
His suit is carefully pressed; his cravat harmonious.

Whose father, it is whispered, stubbornly cried old clothes
    and bric-a-brac,
He of all men, might yet be master of self, all self-
    possession,
Were it not (how gauche and incredible!) for the one ill-
    fitting garment—
The historical oversight in the antique wardrobe—
The shirt, the borrowed shirt,
The Greek shirt.

Notice how even when at ease he is somehow anxious,
Like a horse who whiffs smoke somewhere nearby faintly.
Notice with what nonchalance,
The magazine in his hand and the casual cigarette to his
    lips,
He wears a shirt by Nessus.[1]

for discussion

1. In what sense is "history" the common theme of both poems by Plutzik? Contrast the attitude toward the past in "After Looking into a Book" with the one in "Portrait."
2. What does the Greek shirt in "Portrait" symbolize? Why is it described as "ill-fitting" and "borrowed"?

3. Does the subject of Plutzik's "Portrait" resemble M. Carl Holman's "Mr. Z"?

[1] *Nessus:* in Greek mythology, the centaur killed by the hero Heracles. Before he died, Nessus set in motion his revenge. The plan involved the gift to Heracles of a poisoned garment which, when he put it on, burned him to death.

born 1914

DAVID IGNATOW

☐ *David Ignatow has been a lifelong resident of New York City. He was born in Brooklyn in 1914, was educated in the public schools of New York, and for a time was a businessman there. Ignatow never attended college; he learned from his own reading of European and American literature. He read Flaubert and the great Russian novelists; he was influenced by Whitman and Dreiser, by William Carlos Williams and Hemingway. But he also learned from New York and from the ample Jewish culture in the city.*

Ignatow has edited a poetry magazine; he has been a teacher of writing at Columbia University, Vassar College, and the City University of New York. It is, however, the writing of poetry that is the true center of his life. Through the years his poems have been printed in such magazines as Poetry, *the* Nation, *and the* New Yorker. *Ignatow's first book,* Poems, *was published in 1948. It was followed by* The Gentle Weight Lifter *in 1955,* Say Pardon *in 1961,* Figures of the Human *in 1964, and* Rescue the Dead *in 1968. Ignatow's* Poems: 1934–1969, *which fully represents his long devotion to the art of poetry, was published in 1970. He has received several high honors, among them the Poetry Society's Shelley Award and a Guggenheim Fellowship.*

europe and america

My father brought the emigrant bundle
of desperation and worn threads,
that in anxiety as he stumbles
tumble out distractedly;
while I am bedded upon soft green money
that grows like grass. Thus,
between my father who lives on a bed of anguish
for his daily bread, and I who tear money
at leisure by the roots,
where I lie in sun or shade,
a vast continent of breezes, storms to him,
shadows, darkness to him, small lakes,
difficult channels to him, and hills,
mountains to him, lie between us.

My father comes of a hell
where bread and man have been kneaded
and baked together. You have heard the scream
as the knife fell; while I have slept
as guns pounded on the shore.

to nowhere

I carry my keys like a weapon,
their points bunched together
and held outwards in the palm

for a step too close behind me
as I approach the subway through the dark.
Drunks are swaying against walls,
hopped-up men are leaning over
and dancing together crazily
and clapping hands, their faces twitching.
Quiet ones lounge against the wall watching.
They look for the weakness
in a man where they can jump him
and my keys are sure sign.
I walk as I always do, quickly,
my face set straight ahead
as I pretend not to see or hear,
busy on a mission to nowhere.

for discussion

1. In "Europe and America," what differences between those two worlds are established by the narrator?

2. Which detail of his father's world noted by the speaker suggests that he and his father are Jewish? What do you conclude from the absence of any other details that might serve to indicate their specific ethnic identity?

3. What is the general setting of "To Nowhere"? What kinds of human behavior emerge in such a setting?

born 1914

RALPH ELLISON

☐ *On the strength of his novel* Invisible Man, *the essays now collected in* Shadow and Act, *and a few short stories, Ralph Ellison has become one of the chief American prose writers of the 1950's and 1960's. He has lectured and taught in many of the nation's leading universities and throughout the world. The list of his honors grows steadily longer. It is not until the nature of Ellison's literary achievement is grasped that one may understand how such a relatively small body of work has aroused so much acclaim.*

By the mid-1940's Ellison had rejected the claim that a Negro fiction writer is primarily an agent of social reform, that he is inevitably the spokesman of his people's protests, that his stories are to be judged first in terms of the doctrines they contain. Indeed, Invisible Man *is, in part, a dramatic demonstration of the way in which doctrinaire protests obscure precisely those individual areas of thought and feeling that literary art seeks to reveal.*

Ellison shows that people are "invisible" when they are perceived abstractly as types or races. His stories compel us to see that when a person is only perceived as a Negro—whether by friends or enemies—he is flattened out into a caricature and stripped of his humanity. Ellison fastens so surely on the manner in which the realities of black life in white America are hidden by illusions that his figurative description of the Negro as an invisible man has become one of the central metaphors of our time. But he also demonstrates the power of great fiction writers to make "visible" the myriad complications of actual human behavior.

☐ When Todd came to, he saw two faces suspended above him in a sun so hot and blinding that he could not tell if they were black or white. He stirred, feeling a pain that burned as though his whole body had been laid open to the sun which glared into his eyes. For a moment an old fear of being touched by white hands seized him. Then the very sharpness of the pain began slowly to clear his head. Sounds came to him dimly. *He done come to.* Who are they? he thought. *Naw he ain't, I coulda sworn he was white.* Then he heard clearly,

"You hurt bad?"

Something within him uncoiled. It was a Negro sound.

"He's still out," he heard.

"Give 'im time. . . . Say, son, you hurt bad?"

Was he? There was that awful pain. He lay rigid, hearing their breathing and trying to weave a meaning between them and his being stretched painfully upon the ground. He watched them warily, his mind traveling back over a painful distance. Jagged scenes, swiftly unfolding as in a movie trailer,[1] reeled through his mind, and he saw himself piloting a tailspinning plane and landing and falling from the cockpit and trying to stand. Then, as in a great silence, he remembered the sound of crunching bone and, now, looking up into the anxious faces of an old Negro man and a boy from where he lay in the same field, the memory sickened him and he wanted to remember no more.

"How you feel, son?"

Todd hesitated, as though to answer would be to admit an inacceptable weakness. Then, "It's my ankle," he said.

"Which one?"

"The left."

With a sense of remoteness he watched the old man

"Flying Home" by Ralph Ellison from *The Best Short Stories of World War II*, edited by Charles Fenton, copyright © 1944 by Ralph Ellison. Reprinted by permission of William Morris Agency, Inc.

[1] *movie trailer:* a brief film clip showing selected scenes from a full-length movie; the preview of a coming attraction.

bend and remove his boot, feeling the pressure ease.

"That any better?"

"A lot. Thank you."

He had the sensation of discussing someone else, that his concern was with some far more important thing, which for some reason escaped him.

"You done broke it bad," the old man said. "We have to get you to a doctor."

He felt that he had been thrown into a tailspin. He looked at his watch; how long had he been here? He knew there was but one important thing in the world, to get the plane back to the field before his officers were displeased.

"Help me up," he said. "Into the ship."

"But it's broke too bad. . . ."

"Give me your arm!"

"But, son. . . ."

Clutching the old man's arm he pulled himself up, keeping his left leg clear, thinking, "I'd never make him understand," as the leather-smooth face came parallel with his own.

"Now, let's see."

He pushed the old man back, hearing a bird's insistent shrill. He swayed, giddily. Blackness washed over him, like infinity.

"You best sit down."

"No, I'm OK."

"But, son. You jus' gonna make it worse. . . ."

It was a fact that everything in him cried out to deny, even against the flaming pain in his ankle. He would have to try again.

"You mess with that ankle they have to cut your foot off," he heard.

Holding his breath, he started up again. It pained so badly that he had to bite his lips to keep from crying out and he allowed them to help him down with a pang of despair.

"It's best you take it easy. We gon' git you a doctor."

Of all the luck, he thought. Of all the rotten luck, now I have done it. The fumes of high-octane gasoline clung in the heat, taunting him.

"We kin ride him into town on old Ned," the boy said.

Ned? He turned, seeing the boy point toward an ox team, browsing where the buried blade of a plow marked the end of a furrow. Thoughts of himself riding an ox through the town, past streets full of white faces, down the concrete runways of the airfield made swift images of humiliation in his mind. With a pang he remembered his girl's last letter. "Todd," she had written, "I don't need the papers to tell me you had the intelligence to fly. And I have always known you to be as brave as anyone else. The papers annoy me. Don't you be contented to prove over and over again that you're brave or skillful just because you're black, Todd. I think they keep beating that dead horse because they don't want to say why you boys are not yet fighting.[2] I'm really disappointed, Todd. Anyone with brains can learn to fly, but then what. What about using it, and who will you use it for? I wish, dear, you'd write about this. I sometimes think they're playing a trick on us. It's very humiliating. . . ." He whipped cold sweat from his face, thinking, What does she know of humiliation? She's never been down South. *Now* the humiliation would come. When you must have them judge you, knowing that they never accept your mistakes as your own, but hold it against your whole race—that was humiliation. Yes, and humiliation was when you could never be simply yourself; when you were always a part of this old black ignorant man. Sure, he's all right. Nice and kind and helpful. But he's not you. Well, there's one humiliation I can spare myself.

"No," he said, "I have orders not to leave the ship. . . ."

"Aw," the old man said. Then turning to the boy, "Teddy, then you better hustle down to Mister Graves and get him to come. . . ."

"No, wait!" he protested before he was fully aware. Graves might be white. "Just have him get word to the field, please. They'll take care of the rest."

He saw the boy leave, running.

"How far does he have to go?"

---

[2] *not yet fighting:* During the second World War (1941–45) U.S. governmental and military authorities made the token gesture of recruiting and training a black flying squadron, but delayed sending it into action along with other American flying units.

"Might' nigh a mile."

He rested back, looking at the dusty face of his watch. But now they know something has happened, he thought. In the ship there was a perfectly good radio, but it was useless. The old fellow would never operate it. That buzzard knocked me back a hundred years, he thought. Irony danced within him like the gnats circling the old man's head. With all I've learned I'm dependent upon this "peasant's" sense of time and space. His leg throbbed. In the plane, instead of time being measured by the rhythms of pain and a kid's legs, the instruments would have told him at a glance. Twisting upon his elbows he saw where dust had powdered the plane's fuselage, feeling the lump form in his throat that was always there when he thought of flight. It's crouched there, he thought, like the abandoned shell of a locust. I'm naked without it. Not a machine, a suit of clothes you wear. And with a sudden embarrassment and wonder he whispered, "It's the only dignity I have. . . ."

He saw the old man watching, his torn overalls clinging limply to him in the heat. He felt a sharp need to tell the old man what he felt. But that would be meaningless. If I tried to explain why I need to fly back, he'd think I was simply afraid of white officers. But it's more than fear . . . a sense of anguish clung to him like the veil of sweat that hugged his face. He watched the old man, hearing him humming snatches of a tune as he admired the plane. He felt a furtive sense of resentment. Such old men often came to the field to watch the pilots with childish eyes. At first it had made him proud; they had been a meaningful part of a new experience. But soon he realized they did not understand his accomplishments and they came to shame and embarrass him, like the distasteful praise of an idiot. A part of the meaning of flying had gone, then, and he had not been able to regain it. If I were a prize fighter I would be more human, he thought. Not a monkey doing tricks, but a man. They were pleased simply that he was a Negro who could fly, and that was not enough. He felt cut off from them by age, by understanding, by sensibility, by technology and by his need to measure himself against the mirror of other men's appreciation. Somehow he felt be-

trayed, as he had when as a child he grew to discover that
his father was dead. Now, for him, any real appreciation
lay with his white officers; and with them he could never
be sure. Between ignorant black men and condescending
whites, his course of flight seemed mapped by the nature
of things away from all needed and natural landmarks.
Under some sealed orders, couched in ever more technical
and mysterious terms, his path curved swiftly away from
both the shame the old man symbolized and the cloudy
terrain of white man's regard. Flying blind, he knew but
one point of landing and there he would receive his wings.
After that the enemy would appreciate his skill and he
would assume his deepest meaning, he thought sadly,
neither from those who condescended nor from those who
praised without understanding, but from the enemy who
would recognize his manhood and skill in terms of hate. . . .

He sighed, seeing the oxen making queer, prehistoric
shadows against the dry brown earth.

"You just take it easy, son," the old man soothed. "That
boy won't take long. Crazy as he is about airplanes."

"I can wait," he said.

"What kinda airplane you call this here'n?"

"An Advanced Trainer," he said, seeing the old man
smile. His fingers were like gnarled dark wood against the
metal as he touched the low-slung wing.

" 'Bout how fast can she fly?"

"Over two hundred an hour."

"Lawd! That's so fast I bet it don't seem like you
moving!"

Holding himself rigid, Todd opened his flying suit. The
shade had gone and he lay in a ball of fire.

"You mind if I take a look inside? I was always curious
to see. . . ."

"Help yourself. Just don't touch anything."

He heard him climb upon the metal wing, grunting.
Now the questions would start. Well, so you don't have to
think to answer. . . .

He saw the old man looking into the cockpit, his eyes
bright as a child's.

"You must have to know a lot to work all these here
things."

He was silent, seeing him step down and kneel beside him.

"Son, how come you want to fly way up there in the air?"

Because it's the most meaningful act in the world . . . because it makes me less like you, he thought.

But he said: "Because I like it, I guess. It's as good a way to fight and die as I know."

"Yeah? I guess you right," the old man said. "But how long you think before they gonna let you all fight?"

He tensed. This was the question all Negroes asked, put with the same timid hopefulness and longing that always opened a greater void within him than that he had felt beneath the plane the first time he had flown. He felt light-headed. It came to him suddenly that there was something sinister about the conversation, that he was flying unwillingly into unsafe and uncharted regions. If he could only be insulting and tell this old man who was trying to help him to shut up!

"I bet you one thing. . . ."

"Yes?"

"That you was plenty scared coming down."

He did not answer. Like a dog on a trail the old man seemed to smell out his fears and he felt anger bubble within him.

"You sho' scared *me*. When I seen you coming down in that thing with it a-rollin' and a-jumpin' like a pitchin' hoss, I thought sho' you was a goner. I almost had me a stroke!"

He saw the old man grinning. "Ever'thin's been happening round here this morning, come to think of it."

"Like what?" he asked.

"Well, first thing I know, here come two white fellers looking for Mister Rudolph, that's Mister Graves' cousin. That got me worked up right away. . . ."

"Why?"

"Why? 'Cause he done broke outta the crazy house, that's why. He liable to kill somebody," he said. "They oughta have him by now though. Then here *you* come. First I think it's one of them white boys. Then doggone if you don't fall outa there. Lawd, I'd done heard about you boys but I haven't never *seen* one o' you-all. Cain't tell you how it felt to see somebody what look like me in a air-plane!"

The old man talked on, the sound streaming around Todd's thoughts like air flowing over the fuselage of a flying plane. You were a fool, he thought, remembering how before the spin the sun had blazed, bright against the billboard signs beyond the town, and how a boy's blue kite had bloomed beneath him, tugging gently in the wind like a strange, odd-shaped flower. He had once flown such kites himself and tried to find the boy at the end of the invisible cord. But he had been flying too high and too fast. He had climbed steeply away in exultation. Too steeply, he thought. And one of the first rules you learn is that if the angle of thrust is too steep the plane goes into a spin. And then, instead of pulling out of it and going into a dive you let a buzzard panic you. A lousy buzzard!

"Son, what made all that blood on the glass?"

"A buzzard," he said, remembering how the blood and feathers had sprayed back against the hatch. It had been as though he had flown into a storm of blood and blackness.

"Well, I declare! They's lots of 'em around here. They after dead things. Don't eat nothing what's alive."

"A little bit more and he would have made a meal out of me," Todd said grimly.

"They bad luck all right. Teddy's got a name for 'em, calls 'em 'jimcrows,' " the old man laughed.

"It's a damned good name."

"They the damnedest birds. Once I seen a hoss all stretched out like he was sick, you know. So I hollers, 'Gid up from there, suh!' Just to make sho! An, doggone, son, if I don't see two ole jimcrows come flying right up outa that hoss's insides! Yessuh! The sun was shinin' on 'em and they couldn't a been no greasier if they'd been eating barbecue!"

Todd thought he would vomit, his stomach quivered.

"You made that up," he said.

"Nawsuh! Saw him just like I see you."

"Well, I'm glad it was you."

"You see lots a funny things down here, son."

"No, I'll let you see them," he said.

"By the way, the white folks round here don't like to see you boys up there in the sky. They ever bother you?"

"No."

"Well, they'd like to."

"Someone always wants to bother someone else," Todd said. "How do you know?"

"I just know."

"Well," he said defensively, "no one has bothered us."

Blood pounded in his ears as he looked away into space. He tensed, seeing a black spot in the sky and strained to confirm what he could not clearly see.

"What does that look like to you?" he asked excitedly.

"Just another bad luck, son."

Then he saw the movement of wings with disappointment. It was gliding smoothly down, wings outspread, tail feathers gripping the air, down swiftly—gone behind the green screen of trees. It was like a bird he had imagined there, only the sloping branches of the pines remained, sharp against the pale stretch of sky. He lay barely breathing and stared at the point where it had disappeared, caught in a spell of loathing and admiration. Why did they make them so disgusting and yet teach them to fly so well? *It's like when I was up in heaven* he heard, starting.

The old man was chuckling, rubbing his stubbed chin.

"What did you say?"

"Sho', I died and went to heaven . . . maybe by time I tell you about it they be done come after you."

"I hope so," he said wearily.

"You boys ever sit around and swap lies?"

"Not often. Is this going to be one?"

"Well, I ain't so sho', on account of it took place when I was dead."

The old man paused, "That wasn't no lie 'bout the buzzards, though."

"All right," he said.

"Sho' you want to hear 'bout heaven?"

"Please," he answered, resting his head upon his arm.

"Well, I went to heaven and right away started to sproutin' me some wings. Six foot ones, they was. Just like them the white angels had. I couldn't hardly believe it. I was so glad that I went off on some clouds by myself and tried 'em out. You know, 'cause I didn't want to make a fool outa myself the first thing. . . ."

It's an old tale, Todd thought. Told me years ago. Had forgotten. But at least it will keep him from talking about buzzards.

He closed his eyes, listening.

". . . First thing I done was to git up on a low cloud and jump off. And doggone, boy, if them wings didn't work! First I tried the right; then I tried the left; then I tried 'em both together. Then, Lawd, I started to move on out among the folks. I let 'em see me. . . ."

He saw the old man gesturing flight with his arms, his face full of mock pride as he indicated an imaginary crowd, thinking, *It'll be in the newspapers,* as he heard, ". . . so I went and found me some colored angels—somehow I didn't believe I was an angel 'til I seen a real black one, ha, yes! Then I was sho'— but they tole me I better come down 'cause us colored folks had to wear a special kin'a harness when we flew. That was how come *they* wasn't flyin'. Oh yes, an' you had to be extra strong for a black man even, to fly with one of them harnesses. . . ."

This is a new turn, Todd thought, what's he driving at?

"So I said to myself, I ain't gonna be bothered with no harness! Oh naw! 'Cause if God let you sprout wings you oughta have sense enough not to let nobody make you wear something what gits in the way of flyin'. So I starts to flyin'. Hecks, son," he chuckled, his eyes twinkling, "you know I had to let eve'ybody know that old Jefferson could fly good as anybody else. And I could too, fly smooth as a bird! I could even loop-the-loop—only I had to make sho' to keep my long white robe down roun' my ankles. . . ."

Todd felt uneasy. He wanted to laugh at the joke, but his body refused, as of an independent will. He felt as he had as a child when after he had chewed a sugar-coated pill which his mother had given him, she had laughed at his efforts to remove the terrible taste.

". . . Well," he heard. "I was doing all right 'til I got to speeding. Found out I could fan up a right strong breeze, I could fly so fast. I could do all kin'sa stunts too. I started flying up to the stars and divin' down and zooming roun' the moon. Man, I like to scare the devil outa some ole white angels. I was raisin' hell. Not that I meant any harm, son. But I was just feeling good. It was so good to know I was free at last. I accidently knocked the tips offa some stars and they tell me I caused a storm and a coupla lynchings down here in Macon County—though I swear I believe them boys what said that was making up lies on me. . . ."

He's mocking me, Todd thought angrily. He thinks it's a joke. Grinning down at me . . . His throat was dry. He looked at his watch; why the hell didn't they come? Since they had to, why? *One day I was flying down one of them heavenly streets.* You got yourself into it, Todd thought. Like Jonah in the whale.

"Justa throwin' feathers in everybody's face. An' ole Saint Peter called me in. Said, 'Jefferson, tell me two things, what you doin' flyin' without a harness; an' how come you flyin' so fast?' So I tole him I was flyin' without a harness 'cause it got in my way, but I couldn'ta been flyin' so fast, 'cause I wasn't usin' but one wing. Saint Peter said, 'You wasn't flyin' with but *one* wing?' 'Yessuh,' I says, scaredlike. So he says, 'Well, since you got sucha extra fine pair of wings you can leave off yo' harness awhile. But from now on none of that there one-wing flyin', 'cause you gittin' up too damn much speed!'"

And with one mouth full of bad teeth you're making too damned much talk, thought Todd. Why don't I send him after the boy? His body ached from the hard ground and seeking to shift his position he twisted his ankle and hated himself for crying out.

"It gittin' worse?"

"I . . . I twisted it," he groaned.

"Try not to think about it, son. That's what I do."

He bit his lip, fighting pain with counter pain as the voice resumed its rhythmical droning. Jefferson seemed caught in his own creation.

". . . After all that trouble I just floated roun' heaven in slow motion. But I forgot like colored folks will do and got to flyin' with one wing agin. This time I was restin' my ole broken arm and got to flyin' fast enough to shame the devil. I was comin' so fast, Lawd, I got myself called befo' ole Saint Peter agin. He said, 'Jeff, didn't I warn you 'bout that speedin'?' 'Yessuh,' I says, 'but it was an accident.' He looked at me sad-like and shook his head and I knowed I was gone. He said, 'Jeff, you and that speedin' is a danger to the heavenly community. If I was to let you keep on flyin', heaven wouldn't be nothin' but uproar. Jeff, you got to go!' Son, I argued and pleaded with that old white man, but it didn't do a bit of good. They rushed me straight to them pearly gates and gimme a parachute and a map of the state of Alabama. . . ."

Todd heard him laughing so that he could hardly speak, making a screen between them upon which his humiliation glowed like fire.

"Maybe you'd better stop a while," he said, his voice unreal.

"Ain't much more," Jefferson laughed. "When they gimme the parachute ole Saint Peter ask me if I wanted to say a few words before I went. I felt so bad I couldn't hardly look at him, specially with all them white angels standin' around. Then somebody laughed and made me mad. So I tole him, 'Well, you done took my wings. And you puttin' me out. You got charge of things so's I can't do nothin' about it. But you got to admit just this: While I was up here I was the flyinest sonofabitch what ever hit heaven!' "

At the burst of laughter Todd felt such an intense humiliation that only great violence would wash it away. The laughter which shook the old man like a boiling purge set up vibrations of guilt within him which not even the intricate machinery of the plane would have been adequate to transform and he heard himself screaming, "Why do you laugh at me this way?"

He hated himself at that moment, but he had lost control. He saw Jefferson's mouth fall open, "What—?"

"Answer me!"

His blood pounded as though it would surely burst his temples and he tried to reach the old man and fell, screaming, "Can I help it because they won't let us actually fly? Maybe we are a bunch of buzzards feeding on a dead horse, but we can hope to be eagles, can't we? *Can't we?*"

He fell back, exhausted, his ankle pounding. The saliva was like straw in his mouth. If he had the strength he would strangle this old man. This grinning, gray-headed clown who made him feel as he felt when watched by the white officers at the field. And yet this old man had neither power, prestige, rank nor technique. Nothing that could rid him of this terrible feeling. He watched him, seeing his face struggle to express a turmoil of feeling.

"What you mean, son? What you talking 'bout . . . ?"

"Go away. Go tell your tales to the white folks."

"But I didn't mean nothing like that . . . I . . . I wasn't tryin' to hurt your feelings. . . ."

"Please. Get the hell away from me!"

"But I didn't, son. I didn't mean all them things a-tall."

Todd shook as with a chill, searching Jefferson's face for a trace of the mockery he had seen there. But now the face was somber and tired and old. He was confused. He could not be sure that there had ever been laughter there, that Jefferson had ever really laughed in his whole life. He saw Jefferson reach out to touch him and shrank away, wondering if anything except the pain, now causing his vision to waver, was real. Perhaps he had imagined it all.

"Don't let it get you down, son," the voice said pensively.

He heard Jefferson sigh wearily, as though he felt no more than he could say. His anger ebbed, leaving only the pain.

"I'm sorry," he mumbled.

"You just wore out with pain, was all. . . ."

He saw him through a blur, smiling. And for a second he felt the embarrassed silence of understanding flutter between them.

"What you was doin' flyin' over this section, son? Wasn't you scared they might shoot you for a crow?"

Todd tensed. Was he being laughed at again? But before he could decide the pain shook him and a part of him was lying calmly behind the screen of pain that had fallen between them, recalling the first time he had ever seen a plane. It was as though an endless series of hangars had been shaken ajar in the air base of his memory and from each, like a young wasp emerging from its cell, arose the memory of a plane.

The first time I ever saw a plane I was very small and planes were new in the world. I was four-and-a-half and the only plane that I had ever seen was a model suspended from the ceiling of the automobile exhibit at the State Fair. But I did not know that it was only a model. I did not know how large a real plane was, nor how expensive. To me it was a fascinating toy, complete in itself, which my mother said could only be owned by rich little white boys. I stood rigid with admiration, my head straining backwards as I watched the gray little plane describing arcs above the gleaming tops of the automobiles. And I vowed that, rich or poor, some day I would own such a toy. My mother had to drag me out of the exhibit, and not even the merry-go-round, the Ferris wheel, or the racing horses could hold my attention for the rest of the Fair. I was too busy imitating the tiny drone of the plane with my lips, and imitating with my hands the motion, swift and circling, that it made in flight.

After that I no longer used the pieces of lumber that lay about our back yard to construct wagons and autos ... now it was used for airplanes. I built bi-planes, using pieces of board for wings, a small box for the fuselage, another piece of wood for the rudder. The trip to the fair had brought something new into my small world. I asked my mother repeatedly when the Fair would come back again. I'd lie in the grass and watch the sky and each flighting bird became a soaring plane. I would have been good a year just to have seen a plane again. I became a nuisance to everyone with my questions about airplanes. But planes were new to the old folks, too, and there was little that they could tell me. Only my uncle knew some of the answers. And better still, he could carve propellers from pieces of wood that would whirl rapidly in the wind, wobbling noisily upon oiled nails.

I wanted a plane more than I'd wanted anything; more than I wanted the red wagon with rubber tires, more than the train that ran on a track with its train of cars. I asked my mother over and over again:

"Mamma?"

"What do you want, boy?" she'd say.

"Mamma, will you get mad if I ask you?" I'd say.

"What do you want now, I ain't got time to be answering a lot of fool questions. What you want?"

"Mamma, when you gonna get me one . . . ?" I'd ask.

"Get you one what?" she'd say.

"You know, Mamma; what I been asking you. . . ."

"Boy," she'd say, "if you don't want a spanking you better come on 'n tell me what you talking about so I can get on with my work."

"Aw, Mamma, you know. . . ."

"What I just tell you?" she'd say.

"I mean when you gonna buy me a airplane."

"AIRPLANE! Boy, is you crazy? How many times I have to tell you to stop that foolishness. I done told you them things cost too much. I bet I'm gon' wham the living daylight out of you if you don't quit worrying me 'bout them things!"

But this did not stop me, and a few days later I'd try all over again.

Then one day a strange thing happened. It was spring and for some reason I had been hot and irritable all morning. It was a beautiful spring. I could feel it as I played barefoot in the backyard. Blossoms hung from the thorny black locust trees like clusters of fragrant white grapes. Butterflies flickered in the sunlight above the short new dew-wet grass. I had gone in the house for bread and butter and coming out I heard a steady unfamiliar drone. It was unlike anything I had ever heard before. I tried to place the sound. It was no use. It was a sensation like that I had when searching for my father's watch, heard ticking unseen in a room. It made me feel as though I had forgotten to perform some task that my mother had ordered . . . then I located it, overhead. In the sky, flying quite low and about a hundred yards off was a plane! It came so slowly that it seemed barely to move. My mouth hung wide; my bread and butter fell into the dirt. I wanted to jump up and down and cheer. And when the idea struck I trembled with excitement: "Some little white boy's plane's done flew away and all I got to do is stretch out my hands and it'll be mine!" It was a little plane like that at the Fair, flying no higher than the eaves of our roof. Seeing it come steadily forward I felt the world grow warm with promise. I opened *the screen and climbed over it and clung there, waiting. I would catch the plane as it came over and swing down fast and run into the house before anyone could see me. Then no one could come to claim the plane. It droned nearer. Then when it hung like a silver cross in the blue directly above me I stretched out my hand and grabbed. It was like sticking my finger through a soap bubble. The plane flew on, as though I had simply blown my breath after it. I grabbed again, frantically, trying to catch the tail. My fingers clutched the air and disappointment surged tight and hard in my throat. Giving one last desperate grasp, I strained forward. My fingers ripped from the screen. I was falling. The ground burst hard against me. I drummed the earth with my heels and when my breath returned, I lay there bawling.*

My mother rushed through the door.

"What's the matter, chile! What on earth is wrong with you?"

"It's gone! It's gone!"

"What gone?"

"The airplane...."

"Airplane?"

"Yessum, jus' like the one at the Fair.... I ... I tried to stop it an' it kep' right on going...."

"When, boy?"

"Just now," I cried through my tears.

"Where it go, boy, what way?"

"Yonder, there...."

She scanned the sky, her arms akimbo and her check-ered apron flapping in the wind as I pointed to the fading plane. Finally she looked down at me, slowly shaking her head.

"It's gone! It's gone!" I cried.

"Boy, is you a fool?" she said. "Don't you see that there's a real airplane 'stead of one of them toy ones?"

"Real ... ?" I forgot to cry. "Real?"

"Yass, real. Don't you know that thing you reaching for is bigger'n a auto? You here trying to reach for it and I bet it's flying 'bout two hundred miles higher'n this roof." She was disgusted with me. "You come on in this house before somebody else sees what a fool you done turned out to be.

You must think these here li'l ole arms of your'n is mighty long. . . ."

I was carried into the house and undressed for bed and the doctor was called. I cried bitterly, as much from the disappointment of finding the plane so far beyond my reach as from the pain.

When the doctor came I heard my mother telling him about the plane and asking if anything was wrong with my mind. He explained that I had had a fever for several hours. But I was kept in bed for a week and I constantly saw the plane in my sleep, flying just beyond my finger tips, sailing so slowly that it seemed barely to move. And each time I'd reach out to grab it I'd miss and through each dream I'd hear my grandma warning:

> *"Young man, young man*
> *Yo' arm's too short*
> *To box with God. . . ."*

"Hey, son!"

At first he did not know where he was and looked at the old man pointing, with blurred eyes.

"Ain't that one of you-all's airplanes coming after you?"

As his vision cleared he saw a small black shape above a distant field, soaring through waves of heat. But he could not be sure and with the pain he feared that somehow a horrible recurring fantasy of being split in twain by the whirling blades of a propeller had come true.

"You think he sees us?" he heard.

"See? I hope so."

"He's coming like a bat outa hell!"

Straining, he heard the faint sound of a motor and hoped it would soon be over.

"How you feeling?"

"Like a nightmare," he said.

"Hey, he's done curved back the other way!"

"Maybe he saw us," he said. "Maybe he's gone to send out the ambulance and ground crew." And, he thought with despair, maybe he didn't even see us.

"Where did you send the boy?"

"Down to Mister Graves," Jefferson said. "Man what owns this land."

"Do you think he phoned?"

Jefferson looked at him quickly.

"Aw sho'. Dabney Graves is got a bad name on accounta them killings but he'll call though. . . ."

"What killings?"

"Them five fellers . . . ain't you heard?" he asked with surprise.

"No."

"Everybody knows 'bout Dabney Graves, especially the colored. He done killed enough of us."

Todd had the sensation of being caught in a white neighborhood after dark.

"What did they do?" he asked.

"Thought they was men," Jefferson said. "An' some he owed money, like he do me. . . ."

"But why do you stay here?"

"You black, son."

"I know, but. . . ."

"You have to come by the white folks, too."

He turned away from Jefferson's eyes, at once consoled and accused. And I'll have to come by them soon, he thought with despair. Closing his eyes, he heard Jefferson's voice as the sun burned blood red upon his lids.

"I got nowhere to go," Jefferson said, "an' they'd come after me if I did. But Dabney Graves is a funny fellow. He's all the time making jokes. He can be mean as hell, then he's liable to turn right around and back the colored against the white folks. I seen him do it. But me, I hates him for that more'n anything else. 'Cause just as soon as he gits tired helping a man he don't care what happens to him. He just leaves him stone cold. And then the other white folks is double hard on anybody he done helped. For him it's just a joke. He don't give a hilla beans for nobody —but hisself. . . ."

Todd listened to the thread of detachment in the old man's voice. It was as though he held his words at arm's length before him to avoid their destructive meaning.

"He'd just as soon do you a favor and then turn right around and have you strung up. Me, I stays outa his way 'cause down here that's what you gotta do."

If my ankle would only ease for a while, he thought. The closer I spin toward the earth the blacker I become, flashed through his mind. Sweat ran into his eyes and he was sure that he would never see the plane if his head continued whirling. He tried to see Jefferson, what it was that Jefferson held in his hand. It was a little black man, another Jefferson! A little black Jefferson that shook with fits of belly-laughter while the other Jefferson looked on with detachment. Then Jefferson looked up from the thing in his hand and turned to speak but Todd was far away, searching the sky for a plane in a hot dry land on a day and age he had long forgotten. He was going mysteriously with his mother through empty streets where black faces peered from behind drawn shades and someone was rapping at a window and he was looking back to see a hand and a frightened face frantically beckoning from a cracked door and his mother was looking down the empty perspective of the street and shaking her head and hurrying him along and at first it was only a flash he saw and a motor was droning as through the sun-glare he saw it gleaming silver as it circled and he was seeing a burst like a puff of white smoke and hearing his mother yell, Come along, boy, I got no time for them fool airplanes, I got no time, and he saw it a second time, the plane flying high, and the burst appeared suddenly and fell slowly, billowing out and sparkling like fireworks and he was watching and being hurried along as the air filled with a flurry of white pin-wheeling cards that caught in the wind and scattered over the rooftops and into the gutters and a woman was running and snatching a card and reading it and screaming and he darted into the shower, grabbing as in winter he grabbed for snowflakes and bounding away at his mother's, Come on here, boy! Come on, I say! and he was watching as she took the card away seeing her face grow puzzled and turning taut as her voice quavered, "Niggers Stay From The Polls," and died to a moan of terror as she saw the eyeless sockets of a white hood staring at him from the card and above he saw the plane spiraling gracefully, agleam in the sun like a fiery sword. And seeing it soar he was caught, transfixed between a terrible horror and a horrible fascination.

The sun was not so high now, and Jefferson was calling and gradually he saw three figures moving across the curving roll of the field.

"Look like some doctors, all dressed in white," said Jefferson.

They're coming at last, Todd thought. And he felt such a release of tension within him that he thought he would faint. But no sooner did he close his eyes than he was seized and he was struggling with three white men who were forcing his arms into some kind of coat. It was too much for him, his arms were pinned to his sides and as the pain blazed in his eyes, he realized that it was a strait jacket. What filthy joke was this?

"That oughta hold him, Mister Graves," he heard.

His total energies seemed focused in his eyes as he searched their faces. That was Graves, the other two wore hospital uniforms. He was poised between two poles of fear and hate as he heard the one called Graves saying,

"He looks kinda purty in that there suit, boys. I'm glad you dropped by."

"This boy ain't crazy, Mister Graves," one of the others said. "He needs a doctor, not us. Don't see how you led us way out here anyway. It might be a joke to you, but your cousin Rudolph liable to kill somebody. White folks or niggers don't make no difference. . . ."

Todd saw the man turn red with anger. Graves looked down upon him, chuckling.

"This nigguh belongs in a strait jacket, too, boys. I knowed that the minit Jeff's kid said something 'bout a nigguh flyer. You all know you cain't let the nigguh git up that high without his going crazy. The nigguh brain ain't built right for high altitudes. . . ."

Todd watched the drawling red face, feeling that all the unnamed horror and obscenities that he had ever imagined stood materialized before him.

"Let's git outa here," one of the attendants said.

Todd saw the other reach toward him, realizing for the first time that he lay upon a stretcher as he yelled,

"Don't put your hands on me!"

They drew back, surprised.

"What's that you say, nigguh?" asked Graves.

He did not answer and thought that Graves's foot was aimed at his head. It landed in his chest and he could hardly breathe. He coughed helplessly, seeing Graves's lips stretch taut over his yellow teeth and tried to shift his head. It was as though a half-dead fly was dragging slowly across his face and a bomb seemed to burst within him. Blasts of hot, hysterical laughter tore from his chest, causing his eyes to pop and he felt that the veins in his neck would surely burst. And then a part of him stood behind it all, watching the surprise in Graves's red face and his own hysteria. He thought he would never stop, he would laugh himself to death. It rang in his ears like Jefferson's laughter and he looked for him, centering his eyes desperately upon his face, as though somehow he had become his sole salvation in an insane world of outrage and humiliation. It brought a certain relief. He was suddenly aware that although his body was still contorted it was an echo that no longer rang in his ears. He heard Jefferson's voice with gratitude.

"Mister Graves, the Army done tole him not to leave his airplane."

"Nigguh, Army or no, you gittin' off my land! That airplane can stay 'cause it was paid for by taxpayers' money. But you gittin' off. An' dead or alive, it don't make no difference to me."

Todd was beyond it now, lost in a world of anguish.

"Jeff," Graves said, "you and Teddy come and grab holt. I want you to take this here black eagle over to that nigguh airfield and leave him."

Jefferson and the boy approached him silently. He looked away, realizing and doubting at once that only they could release him from his overpowering sense of isolation.

They bent for the stretcher. One of the attendants moved toward Teddy.

"Think you can manage it, boy?"

"I think I can, suh," Teddy said.

"Well, you better go behind then, and let yo' pa go ahead so's to keep that leg elevated."

He saw the white men walking ahead as Jefferson and the boy carried him along in silence. Then they were pausing and he felt a hand wiping his face, then he was moving again. And it was as though he had been lifted out of his isolation, back into the world of men. A new current of communication flowed between the man and boy and himself. They moved him gently. Far away he heard a mockingbird liquidly calling. He raised his eyes, seeing a buzzard poised unmoving in space. For a moment the whole afternoon seemed suspended and he waited for the horror to seize him again. Then like a song within his head he heard the boy's soft humming and saw the dark bird glide into the sun and glow like a bird of flaming gold.

for discussion

1. What contrast is drawn in the story between Todd and Jefferson? What are Todd's attitudes toward the old man? How are Todd's attitudes altered by his "rescue"?

2. What is the literal meaning of the title? In what other, rather ironic, sense has Todd flown home? What is the home or destination toward which Todd has been directing his life, a "course of flight" between and beyond "ignorant black men and condescending whites"?

3. Would you agree or disagree with the interpretation that the meaning of "Flying Home" is Todd's realization that ultimately he is only at home among his own people and that "black is beautiful"? Why?

born 1924
JAMES BALDWIN

☐ *James Baldwin's autobiographical essays, social criticism, and fiction shade into each other, and are not easily separated. Since his return to America, there have been two more volumes of Baldwin's essays on the personal and social consequences of racism:* Nobody Knows My Name *(1961) and* The Fire Next Time *(1963). His two plays,* The Amen Corner *and* Blues for Mr. Charlie, *also explore the private and the public miseries of life in a segregated society.*

At times Baldwin has been one of the black community's fiercest critics of white America; at other times his primary loyalty has been to his art. And, as a short story writer and novelist, he moved into the foreground of American fiction during the 1960's. His first two novels, published during his residence in France, have been followed by Another Country (1962) and Tell Me How Long the Train's Been Gone (1968). In 1965 Baldwin published a collection of his short stories, Going to Meet the Man.

One of the keys to Baldwin's conception of literature is his early outburst against "protest" novels like Harriet Beecher Stowe's Uncle Tom's Cabin and Richard Wright's Native Son. When arguing that such works of fiction turn the Negro into an abstraction and strip him of his humanity, Baldwin acknowledges the undeniable complexity of all human experience. As a young writer, Baldwin learned that "writing was not simply the act of writing—that it was something else, something much harder. Which is to tell the truth." At their best, Baldwin's stories are governed only by this desire to see all there is to see.

the rockpile

☐ Across the street from their house, in an empty lot between two houses, stood the rockpile. It was a strange place to find a mass of natural rock jutting out of the ground; and someone, probably Aunt Florence,[1] had once told them that the rock was there and could not be taken away because without it the subway cars underground

[1] *Aunt Florence:* The characters in "The Rockpile" are the same ones that appear in Baldwin's first novel, Go Tell It on the Mountain.

would fly apart, killing all the people. This, touching on some natural mystery concerning the surface and the center of the earth, was far too intriguing an explanation to be challenged, and it invested the rockpile, moreover, with such mysterious importance that Roy felt it to be his right, not to say his duty, to play there.

Other boys were to be seen there each afternoon after school and all day Saturday and Sunday. They fought on the rockpile. Sure-footed, dangerous, and reckless, they rushed each other and grappled on the heights, sometimes disappearing down the other side in a confusion of dust and screams and upended, flying feet. "It's a wonder they don't kill themselves," their mother said, watching sometimes from the fire escape. "You children stay away from there, you hear me?" Though she said "children," she was looking at Roy, where he sat beside John on the fire escape. "The good Lord knows," she continued, "I don't want you to come home bleeding like a hog every day the Lord sends." Roy shifted impatiently, and continued to stare at the street, as though in this gazing he might somehow acquire wings. John said nothing. He had not really been spoken to: he was afraid of the rockpile and of the boys who played there.

Each Saturday morning John and Roy sat on the fire escape and watched the forbidden street below. Sometimes their mother sat in the room behind them, sewing, or dressing their younger sister, or nursing the baby, Paul. The sun fell across them and across the fire escape with a high, benevolent indifference; below them, men and women, and boys and girls, sinners all, loitered; sometimes one of the church-members passed and saw them and waved. Then, for the moment that they waved decorously back, they were intimidated. They watched the saint, man or woman, until he or she had disappeared from sight. The passage of one of the redeemed made them consider, however vacantly, the wickedness of the street, their own latent wickedness in sitting where they sat; and made them think of their father, who came home early on Saturdays and who would soon be turning this corner and entering the dark hall below them.

But until he came to end their freedom, they sat, watching and longing above the street. At the end of the street nearest their house was the bridge which spanned the Harlem River and led to a city called the Bronx; which was where Aunt Florence lived. Nevertheless, when they saw her coming, she did not come from the bridge, but from the opposite end of the street. This, weakly, to their minds, she explained by saying that she had taken the subway, not wishing to walk, and that, besides, she did not live in *that* section of the Bronx. Knowing that the Bronx was across the river, they did not believe this story ever, but, adopting toward her their father's attitude, assumed that she had just left some sinful place which she dared not name, as, for example, a movie palace.

In the summertime boys swam in the river, diving off the wooden dock, or wading in from the garbage-heavy bank. Once a boy, whose name was Richard, drowned in the river. His mother had not known where he was; she had even come to their house, to ask if he was there. Then, in the evening, at six o'clock, they had heard from the street a woman screaming and wailing; and they ran to the windows and looked out. Down the street came the woman, Richard's mother, screaming, her face raised to the sky and tears running down her face. A woman walked beside her, trying to make her quiet and trying to hold her up. Behind them walked a man, Richard's father, with Richard's body in his arms. There were two white policemen walking in the gutter, who did not seem to know what should be done. Richard's father and Richard were wet, and Richard's body lay across his father's arms like a cotton baby. The woman's screaming filled all the street; cars slowed down and the people in the cars stared; people opened their windows and looked out and came rushing out of doors to stand in the gutter, watching. Then the small procession disappeared within the house which stood beside the rockpile. Then, *"Lord, Lord, Lord!"* cried Elizabeth, their mother, and slammed the window down.

One Saturday, an hour before his father would be coming home, Roy was wounded on the rockpile and brought screaming upstairs. He and John had been sitting on the fire escape and their mother had gone into the kitchen to sip tea with Sister McCandless. By and by Roy became bored and sat beside John in restless silence; and John began drawing into his schoolbook a newspaper advertisement which featured a new electric locomotive. Some friends of Roy passed beneath the fire escape and called him. Roy began to fidget, yelling down to them through the bars. Then a silence fell. John looked up. Roy stood looking at him.

"I'm going downstairs," he said.

"You better stay where you is, boy. You know Mama don't want you going downstairs."

"I be right *back*. She won't even know I'm gone, less you run and tell her."

"I ain't *got* to tell her. What's going to stop her from coming in here and looking out the window?"

"She's talking," Roy said. He started into the house.

"But Daddy's going to be home soon!"

"I be back before *that*. What you all the time got to be so *scared* for?" He was already in the house and he now turned, leaning on the windowsill, to swear impatiently, "I be back in *five* minutes."

John watched him sourly as he carefully unlocked the door and disappeared. In a moment he saw him on the sidewalk with his friends. He did not dare to go and tell his mother that Roy had left the fire escape because he had practically promised not to. He started to shout, *Remember, you said five minutes!* but one of Roy's friends was looking up at the fire escape. John looked down at his schoolbook: he became engrossed again in the problem of the locomotive.

When he looked up again he did not know how much time had passed, but now there was a gang fight on the rockpile. Dozens of boys fought each other in the harsh sun: clambering up the rocks and battling hand to hand, scuffed shoes sliding on the slippery rock; filling the bright air with curses and jubilant cries. They filled the air, too, with flying weapons: stones, sticks, tin cans, garbage, whatever could be picked up and thrown. John watched in a kind of absent amazement—until he remembered that Roy was still downstairs, and that he was one of the boys on the rockpile. Then he was afraid; he could not see his brother among the figures in the sun; and he stood up, leaning over the fire-escape railing. Then Roy appeared from the other side of the rocks; John saw that his shirt was torn; he was laughing. He moved until he stood at the very top of the rockpile. Then, something, an empty tin can, flew out of the air and hit him on the forehead, just above the eye. Immediately, one side of Roy's face ran with blood, he fell and rolled on his face down the rocks. Then for a moment there was no movement at all, no sound, the sun, arrested, lay on the street and the sidewalk and the arrested boys. Then someone screamed or shouted; boys began to run away, down the street, toward the bridge. The figure on the ground, having caught its breath and felt its own blood, began to shout. John cried, "Mama! Mama!" and ran inside.

"Don't fret, don't fret," panted Sister McCandless as they rushed down the dark, narrow, swaying stairs, "don't fret. Ain't a boy been born don't get his knocks every now and again. *Lord!*" They hurried into the sun. A man had picked Roy up and now walked slowly toward them. One or two boys sat silent on their stoops; at either end of the street there was a group of boys watching. "He ain't hurt bad," the man said, "wouldn't be making this kind of noise if he was hurt real bad."

Elizabeth, trembling, reached out to take Roy, but Sister McCandless, bigger, calmer, took him from the man and threw him over her shoulder as she once might have handled a sack of cotton. "God bless you," she said to the man, "God bless you, son." Roy was still screaming. Elizabeth stood behind Sister McCandless to stare at his bloody face.

"It's just a flesh wound," the man kept saying, "just broke the skin, that's all." They were moving across the sidewalk, toward the house. John, not now afraid of the staring boys, looked toward the corner to see if his father was yet in sight.

Upstairs, they hushed Roy's crying. They bathed the blood away, to find, just above the left eyebrow, the jagged, superficial scar. "Lord, have mercy," murmured Elizabeth, "another inch and it would've been his eye." And she looked with apprehension toward the clock. "Ain't it the truth," said Sister McCandless, busy with bandages and iodine.

"When did he go downstairs?" his mother asked at last.

Sister McCandless now sat fanning herself in the easy chair, at the head of the sofa where Roy lay, bound and silent. She paused for a moment to look sharply at John. John stood near the window, holding the newspaper advertisement and the drawing he had done.

"We was sitting on the fire escape," he said. "Some boys he knew called him."

"When?"

"He said he'd be back in five minutes."

"Why didn't you tell me he was downstairs?"

He looked at his hands, clasping his notebook, and did not answer.

"Boy," said Sister McCandless, "you hear your mother a-talking to you?"

He looked at his mother. He repeated:

"He said he'd be back in five minutes."

"He said he'd be back in five minutes," said Sister McCandless with scorn, "don't look to me like that's no right answer. You's the man of the house, you supposed to look after your baby brothers and sisters—you ain't supposed to let them run off and get half-killed. But I expect," she added, rising from the chair, dropping the cardboard fan, "your Daddy'll make you tell the truth. Your Ma's way too soft with you."

He did not look at her, but at the fan where it lay in the dark red, depressed seat where she had been. The fan advertised a pomade for the hair and showed a brown woman and her baby, both with glistening hair, smiling happily at each other.

"Honey," said Sister McCandless, "I got to be moving along. Maybe I drop in later tonight. I don't reckon you going to be at Tarry Service tonight?"

Tarry Service was the prayer meeting held every Saturday night at church to strengthen believers and prepare the church for the coming of the Holy Ghost on Sunday.

"I don't reckon," said Elizabeth. She stood up; she and Sister McCandless kissed each other on the cheek. "But you be sure to remember me in your prayers."

"I surely will do that." She paused, with her hand on the doorknob, and looked down at Roy and laughed. "Poor little man," she said, "reckon he'll be content to sit on the fire escape *now*."

Elizabeth laughed with her. "It sure ought to be a lesson to him. You don't reckon," she asked nervously, still smiling, "he going to keep that scar, do you?"

"Lord, no," said Sister McCandless, "ain't nothing but a scratch. I declare, Sister Grimes, you worse than a child. Another couple of weeks and you won't be able to *see* no scar. No, you go on about your housework, honey, and thank the Lord it weren't no worse." She opened the door; they heard the sound of feet on the stairs. "I expect that's the Reverend," said Sister McCandless, placidly, "I *bet* he going to raise Cain."

"Maybe it's Florence," Elizabeth said. "Sometimes she get here about this time." They stood in the doorway, staring, while the steps reached the landing below and began again climbing to their floor. "No," said Elizabeth then, "that ain't her walk. That's Gabriel."

"Well, I'll just go on," said Sister McCandless, "and kind of prepare his mind." She pressed Elizabeth's hand as she spoke and started into the hall, leaving the door behind her slightly ajar. Elizabeth turned slowly back into the room. Roy did not open his eyes, or move; but she knew that he was not sleeping; he wished to delay until the last possible moment any contact with his father. John put his newspaper and his notebook on the table and stood, leaning on the table, staring at her.

"It wasn't my fault," he said. "I couldn't stop him from going downstairs."

"No," she said, "you ain't got nothing to worry about. You just tell your Daddy the truth."

He looked directly at her, and she turned to the window, staring into the street. What was Sister McCandless saying? Then from her bedroom she heard Delilah's thin wail and she turned, frowning, looking toward the bedroom and toward the still open door. She knew that John was watching her. Delilah continued to wail, she thought, angrily, *Now that girl's getting too big for that*, but she feared that Delilah would awaken Paul and she hurried into the bedroom. She tried to soothe Delilah back to sleep. Then she heard the front door open and close—too loud, Delilah raised her voice, with an exasperated sigh Elizabeth picked the child up. Her child and Gabriel's, her children and Gabriel's: Roy, Delilah, Paul. Only John was nameless and a stranger, living, unalterable testimony to his mother's days in sin.

"What happened?" Gabriel demanded. He stood, enormous, in the center of the room, his black lunchbox dangling from his hand, staring at the sofa where Roy lay. John stood just before him, it seemed to her astonished vision just below him, beneath his fist, his heavy shoe. The child stared at the man in fascination and terror—when a girl down home she had seen rabbits stand so paralyzed before the barking dog. She hurried past Gabriel to the sofa, feeling the weight of Delilah in her arms like the weight of a shield, and stood over Roy, saying:

"Now, ain't a thing to get upset about, Gabriel. This boy sneaked downstairs while I had my back turned and got hisself hurt a little. He's alright now."

Roy, as though in confirmation, now opened his eyes and looked gravely at his father. Gabriel dropped his lunchbox with a clatter and knelt by the sofa.

"How you feel, son? Tell your Daddy what happened."

Roy opened his mouth to speak and then, relapsing into panic, began to cry. His father held him by the shoulder.

"You don't want to cry. You's Daddy's little man. Tell your Daddy what happened."

"He went downstairs," said Elizabeth, "where he didn't have no business to be, and got to fighting with them bad boys playing on that rockpile. That's what happened and it's a mercy it weren't nothing worse."

He looked up at her. "Can't you let this boy answer me for hisself?"

Ignoring this, she went on, more gently: "He got cut on the forehead, but it ain't nothing to worry about."

"You call a doctor? How you know it ain't nothing to worry about?"

"Is you got money to be throwing away on doctors? No, I ain't called no doctor. Ain't nothing wrong with my eyes that I can't tell whether he's hurt bad or not. He got a fright more'n anything else, and you ought to pray God it teaches him a lesson."

"You got a lot to say *now*," he said, "but I'll have *me* something to say in a minute. I'll be wanting to know when all this happened, what you was doing with your eyes *then*." He turned back to Roy, who had lain quietly sobbing eyes wide open and body held rigid: and who now, at his father's touch, remembered the height, the sharp, sliding rock beneath his feet, the sun, the explosion of the sun, his plunge into darkness and his salty blood; and recoiled, beginning to scream, as his father touched his forehead. "Hold still, hold still," crooned his father, shaking, "hold still. Don't cry. Daddy ain't going to hurt you, he just wants to see this bandage, see what they've done to his little man." But Roy continued to scream and would not be still and Gabriel dared not lift the bandage for fear of hurting him more. And he looked at Elizabeth in fury: "Can't you put that child down and help me with this boy? John, take your baby sister from your mother—don't look like neither of you got good sense."

John took Delilah and sat down with her in the easy chair. His mother bent over Roy, and held him still, while his father, carefully—but still Roy screamed—lifted the bandage and stared at the wound. Roy's sobs began to lessen. Gabriel readjusted the bandage. "You see," said Elizabeth, finally, "he ain't nowhere near dead."

"It sure ain't your fault that he ain't dead." He and Elizabeth considered each other for a moment in silence. "He came mightly close to losing an eye. Course, his eyes ain't as big as your'n, so I reckon you don't think it matters so much." At this her face hardened; he smiled. "Lord, have mercy," he said, "you think you ever going to learn to do right? Where was you when all this happened? Who let him go downstairs?"

"Ain't nobody let him go downstairs, he just went. He got a head just like his father, it got to be broken before it'll bow. I was in the kitchen."

"Where was Johnnie?"

"He was in here."

"Where?"

"He was on the fire escape."

"Didn't he know Roy was downstairs?"

"I reckon."

"What you mean, you reckon? He ain't got your big eyes for nothing, does he?" He looked over at John. "Boy, you see your brother go downstairs?"

"Gabriel, ain't no sense in trying to blame Johnnie. You know right well if you have trouble making Roy behave, he ain't going to listen to his brother. He don't hardly listen to me."

"How come you didn't tell your mother Roy was downstairs?"

John said nothing, staring at the blanket which covered Delilah.

"Boy, you hear me? You want me to take a strap to you?"

"No, you ain't," she said. "You ain't going to take no strap to this boy, not today you ain't. Ain't a soul to blame for Roy's lying up there now but you—you because you done spoiled him so that he thinks he can do just anything and get away with it. I'm here to tell you that ain't no way to raise no child. You don't pray to the Lord to help you do better than you been doing, you going to live to shed bitter tears that the Lord didn't take his soul today." And she was trembling. She moved, unseeing, toward John and took Delilah from his arms. She looked back at Gabriel, who had risen, who stood near the sofa, staring at her. And she found in his face not fury alone, which would not have surprised her; but hatred so deep as to become insupportable in its lack of personality. His eyes were struck alive, unmoving, blind with malevolence—she felt, like the pull of the earth at her feet, his longing to witness her perdition. Again, as though it might be propitiation, she moved the child in her arms. And at this his eyes changed, he looked at Elizabeth, the mother of his children, the helpmeet given by the Lord. Then her eyes clouded; she moved to leave the room; her foot struck the lunchbox lying on the floor.

"John," she said, "pick up your father's lunchbox like a good boy."

She heard, behind her, his scrambling movement as he left the easy chair, the scrape and jangle of the lunchbox as he picked it up, bending his dark head near the toe of his father's heavy shoe.

for discussion

1. What is the underlying reason for Gabriel's rejection of John and his doting attention to Roy?

2. How does the fact that Gabriel is "the Reverend" help to explain the hatred he displays to John and Elizabeth? Describe the two Elizabeths he sees.

3. Define the irony in the situation which finds John an obviously more dutiful son than Roy.

4. What age-old conflict rages within Gabriel with respect to his oldest sons? What universal problems and desires are implicit in a character who does not know the identity of his true father?

born 1937

WILLIAM MELVIN KELLEY

☐ *William Melvin Kelley, born in 1937 in New York City, grew up in one of its white immigrant neighborhoods. He was educated at a good private school in the New York area and then at Harvard, where one of his writing teachers was Archibald MacLeish. Kelley received several important honors and fellowships in the years immediately following his graduation from Harvard. His stories began to appear in print in 1959, and his talent was promptly acknowledged. His first novel,* A Different Drummer, *was published in 1962; it was followed two years later by* Dancers on the Shore, *a collection of his stories.*

Kelley's early work reflects the highly integrationist orientation of his early life and education. For example, in the preface to Dancers on the Shore, *Kelley states that he is "not a sociologist or a politician or a spokesman." "Such people," he said, "try to give answers. A writer, I think, should ask questions. He should depict people, not*

*symbols or ideas disguised as people." At this stage
of his career, Kelley described himself as an American
Negro writer.*

*However, Kelley's subsequent novels—*A Drop of
Patience *(1965),* Dem *(1967), and* Dunfords Travels
Everywheres *(1970)—reveal both his disillusionment with
America and the rediscovery of his blackness. He writes
now as a bitterly satiric black interpreter of white social
values and as an experimental artist seeking literary
ways to reunite the black American and the black African.*

a visit to grandmother

☐ Chig knew something was wrong the instant his father
kissed her. He had always known his father to be the warm-
est of men, a man so kind that when people ventured tim-
idly into his office, it took only a few words from him to
make them relax, and even laugh. Doctor Charles Dunford
cared about people.

But when he had bent to kiss the old lady's black face,
something new and almost ugly had come into his eyes:
fear, uncertainty, sadness, and perhaps even hatred.

Ten days before in New York, Chig's father had decided suddenly he wanted to go to Nashville to attend his
college class reunion, twenty years out. Both Chig's brother
and sister, Peter and Connie, were packing for camp and
besides were too young for such an affair. But Chig was
seventeen, had nothing to do that summer, and his father
asked if he would like to go along. His father had given
him additional reasons: "All my running buddies got their
diplomas and were snapped up by them crafty young gals,
and had kids within a year—now all those kids, some of
them gals, are your age."

The reunion had lasted a week. As they packed for home, his father, in a far too offhand way, had suggested they visit Chig's grandmother. "We this close. We might as well drop in on her and my brothers."

So, instead of going north, they had gone farther south, had just entered her house. And Chig had a suspicion now that the reunion had been only an excuse to drive south, that his father had been heading to this house all the time.

His father had never talked much about his family, with the exception of his brother, GL, who seemed part con man, part practical joker and part Don Juan; he had spoken of GL with the kind of indulgence he would have shown a cute, but ill-behaved and potentially dangerous, five-year-old.

Chig's father had left home when he was fifteen. When asked why, he would answer: "I wanted to go to school. They didn't have a Negro high school at home, so I went up to Knoxville and lived with a cousin and went to school."

They had been met at the door by Aunt Rose, GL's wife, and ushered into the living room. The old lady had looked up from her seat by the window. Aunt Rose stood between the visitors.

The old lady eyed his father. "Rose, who that? Rose?" She squinted. She looked like a doll, made of black straw, the wrinkles in her face running in one direction like the head of a broom. Her hair was white and coarse and grew out straight from her head. Her eyes were brown—the whites, too, seemed light brown—and were hidden behind thick glasses, which remained somehow on a tiny nose. "That Hiram?" That was another of his father's brothers. "No, it ain't Hiram; too big for Hiram." She turned then to Chig. "Now that man, he look like Eleanor, Charles's wife, but Charles wouldn't never send my grandson to see me. I never even heard from Charles." She stopped again.

"It Charles, Mama. That who it is." Aunt Rose, between them, led them closer. "It Charles come all the way from New York to see you, and brung little Charles with him."

The old lady stared up at them. "Charles? Rose, that really Charles?" She turned away, and reached for a handkerchief in the pocket of her clean, ironed, flowered housecoat, and wiped her eyes. "God have mercy. Charles." She spread her arms up to him, and he bent down and kissed her cheek. That was when Chig saw his face, grimacing. She hugged him; Chig watched the muscles in her arms as they tightened around his father's neck. She half rose out of her chair. "How are you, son?"

Chig could not hear his father's answer.

She let him go, and fell back into her chair, grabbing the arms. Her hands were as dark as the wood, and seemed to become part of it. "Now, who that standing there? Who that man?"

"That's one of your grandsons, Mama." His father's voice cracked. "Charles Dunford, junior. You saw him once, when he was a baby, in Chicago. He's grown now."

"I can see that, boy!" She looked at Chig squarely. "Come here, son, and kiss me once." He did. "What they call you? Charles too?"

"No, ma'am, they call me Chig."

She smiled. She had all her teeth, but they were too perfect to be her own. "That's good. Can't have two boys answering to Charles in the same house. Won't nobody at all come. So you that little boy. You don't remember me, do you. I used to take you to church in Chicago, and you'd get up and hop in time to the music. You studying to be a preacher?"

"No, ma'am. I don't think so. I might be a lawyer."

"You'll be an honest one, won't you?"

"I'll try."

"Trying ain't enough! You be honest, you hear? Promise me. You be honest like your daddy."

"All right. I promise."

"Good. Rose, where's GL at? Where's that thief? He gone again?"

"I don't know, Mama." Aunt Rose looked embarrassed. "He say he was going by his liquor store. He'll be back."

"Well, then where's Hiram? You call up those boys, and get them over here—now! You got enough to eat? Let me go see." She started to get up. Chig reached out his hand. She shook him off. "What they tell you about me, Chig? They tell you I'm all laid up? Don't believe it. They don't know nothing about old ladies. When I want help, I'll let you know. Only time I'll need help getting anywheres is when I dies and they lift me into the ground."

She was standing now, her back and shoulders straight. She came only to Chig's chest. She squinted up at him. "You eat much? Your daddy ate like two men."

"Yes, ma'am."

"That's good. That means you ain't nervous. Your mama, she ain't nervous. I remember that. In Chicago, she'd sit down by a window all afternoon and never say nothing, just knit." She smiled. "Let me see what we got to eat."

"I'll do that, Mama." Aunt Rose spoke softly. "You haven't seen Charles in a long time. You sit and talk."

The old lady squinted at her. "You can do the cooking if you promise it ain't because you think I can't."

Aunt Rose chuckled. "I know you can do it, Mama."

"All right. I'll just sit and talk a spell." She sat again and arranged her skirt around her short legs.

Chig did most of the talking, told all about himself before she asked. His father only spoke when he was spoken to, and then, only one word at a time, as if by coming back home, he had become a small boy again, sitting in the parlor while his mother spoke with her guests.

When Uncle Hiram and Mae, his wife, came they sat down to eat. Chig did not have to ask about Uncle GL's absence; Aunt Rose volunteered an explanation: "Can't never tell where the man is at. One Thursday morning he left here and next thing we knew, he was calling from Chicago, saying he went up to see Joe Louis fight. He'll be here though; he ain't as young and foot-loose as he used to be." Chig's father had mentioned driving down that GL was about five years older than he was, nearly fifty.

Uncle Hiram was somewhat smaller than Chig's father; his short-cropped kinky hair was half gray, half black. One spot, just off his forehead, was totally white. Later, Chig found out it had been that way since he was twenty. Mae (Chig could not bring himself to call her Aunt) was a good deal younger than Hiram, pretty enough so that Chig would have looked at her twice on the street. She was a honey-colored woman, with long eye lashes. She was wearing a white sheath.

At dinner, Chig and his father sat on one side, opposite Uncle Hiram and Mae; his grandmother and Aunt Rose sat at the ends. The food was good; there was a lot and Chig ate a lot. All through the meal, they talked about the family as it had been thirty years before, and particularly about the young GL. Mae and Chig asked questions; the old lady answered; Aunt Rose directed the discussion, steering the old lady onto the best stories; Chig's father laughed from time to time; Uncle Hiram ate.

"Why don't you tell them about the horse, Mama?" Aunt Rose, over Chig's weak protest, was spooning mashed potatoes onto his plate. "There now, Chig."

"I'm trying to think." The old lady was holding her fork halfway to her mouth, looking at them over her glasses. "Oh, you talking about that crazy horse GL brung home that time."

"That's right, Mama." Aunt Rose nodded and slid another slice of white meat on Chig's plate.

Mae started to giggle. "Oh, I've heard this. This is funny, Chig."

The old lady put down her fork and began: Well, GL went out of the house one day with an old, no-good chair I wanted him to take over to the church for a bazaar, and he met up with this man who'd just brung in some horses from out West. Now, I reckon you can expect one swindler to be in every town, but you don't rightly think there'll be two, and God forbid they should ever meet—but they did, GL and his chair, this man and his horses. Well, I wished I'd-a been there; there must-a been some mighty high-powered talking going on. That man with his horses, he told GL them horses was half-Arab, half-Indian, and GL told that man the chair was an antique he'd stole from some rich white folks. So they swapped. Well, I was a-looking out the window and seen GL dragging this animal to the house. It looked pretty gentle and its eyes was most closed and its feet was shuffling.

"GL, where'd you get that thing?" I says.

"I swapped him for that old chair, Mama," he says. "And made myself a bargain. This is even better than Papa's horse."

Well, I'm a-looking at this horse and noticing how he be looking more and more wide awake every minute, sort of warming up like a teakettle until, I swears to you, that horse is blowing steam out its nose.

"Come on, Mama," GL says, "come on and I'll take you for a ride." Now George, my husband, God rest his tired soul, he'd brung home this white folks' buggy which had a busted wheel and fixed it and was to take it back that day and GL says: "Come on, Mama, we'll use this fine buggy and take us a ride."

"GL," I says, "no, we ain't. Them white folks'll burn us alive if we use their buggy. You just take that horse right on back." You see, I was sure that boy'd come by that animal ungainly.

"Mama, I can't take him back," GL says.

"Why not?" I says.

"Because I don't rightly know where that man is at," GL says.

"Oh," I says. "Well, then I reckon we stuck with it." And I turned around to go back into the house because it was getting late, near dinner time, and I was cooking for ten.

"Mama," GL says to my back. "Mama, ain't you coming for a ride with me?"

"Go on, boy. You ain't getting me inside kicking range of that animal." I was eying that beast and it was boiling hotter all the time. I reckon maybe that man had drugged it. "That horse is wild, GL," I says.

"No, he ain't. He ain't. That man say he is buggy and saddle broke and as sweet as the inside of a apple."

My oldest girl, Essie, had-a come out on the porch and she says: "Go on, Mama. I'll cook. You ain't been out the house in weeks."

"Sure, come on, Mama," GL says. "There ain't nothing to be fidgety about. This horse is gentle as a rose petal." And just then that animal snorts so hard it sets up a little dust storm around its feet.

"Yes, Mama," Essie says, "you can see he gentle." Well,

I looked at Essie and then at that horse because I didn't think we could be looking at the same animal. I should-a figured how Essie's eyes ain't never been so good.

"Come on, Mama," GL says.

"All right," I says. So I stood on the porch and watched GL hitching that horse up to the white folks' buggy. For a while there, the animal was pretty quiet, pawing a little, but not much. And I was feeling a little better about riding with GL behind that crazy-looking horse. I could see how GL was happy I was going with him. He was scurrying around that animal buckling buckles and strapping straps, all the time smiling, and that made me feel good.

Then he was finished, and I must say, that horse looked mighty fine hitched to that buggy and I knew anybody what climbed up there would look pretty good too. GL came around and stood at the bottom of the steps, and took off his hat and bowed and said: "Madam," and reached out his hand to me and I was feeling real elegant like a fine lady. He helped me up to the seat and then got up beside me and we moved out down our alley. And I remember how colored folks come out on their porches and shook their heads, saying: "Lord now, will you look at Eva Dunford, the fine lady! Don't she look good sitting up there!" And I pretended not to hear and sat up straight and proud.

We rode on through the center of town, up Market Street, and all the way out where Hiram is living now, which in them days was all woods, there not being even a farm in sight and that's when that horse must-a first realized he weren't at all broke or tame or maybe thought he was back out West again, and started to gallop.

"GL," I says, "now you ain't joking with your mama, is you? Because if you is, I'll strap you purple if I live through this."

Well, GL was pulling on the reins with all his meager strength, and yelling, "Whoa, you. Say now, whoa!" He turned to me just long enough to say, "I ain't fooling with you, Mama. Honest!"

I reckon that animal weren't too satisfied with the road, because it made a sharp right turn just then, down into a gulley and struck out across a hilly meadow. "Mama," GL yells. "Mama, do something!"

I didn't know what to do, but I figured I had to do something so I stood up, hopped down onto the horse's back and pulled it to a stop. Don't ask me how I did that; I reckon it was that I was a mother and my baby asked me to do something, is all.

"Well, we walked that animal all the way home; sometimes I had to club it over the nose with my fist to make it come, but we made it, GL and me. You remember how tired we was, Charles?"

"I wasn't here at the time." Chig turned to his father and found his face completely blank, without even a trace of a smile or a laugh.

"Well, of course you was, son. That happened in . . . in . . . it was a hot summer that year and—"

"I left here in June of that year. You wrote me about it."

The old lady stared past Chig at him. They all turned to him; Uncle Hiram looked up from his plate.

"Then you don't remember how we all laughed?"

"No, I don't, Mama. And I probably wouldn't have laughed. I don't think it was funny." They were staring into each other's eyes.

"Why not, Charles?"

"Because in the first place, the horse was gained by fraud. And in the second place, both of you might have been seriously injured or even killed." He broke off their stare and spoke to himself more than to any of them: "And if I'd done it, you would've beaten me good for it."

"Pardon?" The old lady had not heard him; only Chig had heard.

Chig's father sat up straight as if preparing to debate. "I said that if I had done it, if I had done just exactly what GL did, you would have beaten me good for it, Mama." He was looking at her again.

"Why did you say that, son?" She was leaning toward him.

"Don't you know? Tell the truth. It can't hurt me now." His voice cracked, but only once. "If GL and I did something wrong, you'd beat me first and then be too damn tired to beat him. At dinner, he'd always get seconds and I wouldn't. You'd do things with him, like ride in that buggy, but if I wanted you to do something for me, you were always too busy." He paused and considered whether to say what he finally did say: "I cried when I left here. Nobody loved me, Mama. I cried all the way up to Knoxville. That was the last time I ever cried in my life."

"Oh, Charles." She started to get up, to come around the table to him.

He stopped her. "It's too late."

"But you don't understand."

"What don't I understand? I understood then; I understand now."

Tears now traveled down the lines of her face, but when she spoke, her voice was clear. "I thought you knew. I had ten children. I had to give all of them what they needed most." She nodded. "I paid more mind to GL. I had to. GL could-a ended up swinging if I hadn't. But you was smarter. You was more growed up than GL when you was five and he was ten, and I tried to show you that by letting you do what you wanted to do."

"That's not true, Mama. You know it. GL was light-skinned and had good hair and looked almost white and you loved him for that."

"Charles, no. No, son. I didn't love any one of you more than any other."

"That can't be true." His father was standing now, his fists clenched tight. "Admit it, Mama . . . please!" Chig looked at him, shocked; the man was actually crying.

"It may not-a been right what I done, but I ain't no liar." Chig knew she did not really understand what had happened, what he wanted of her. "I'm not lying to you, Charles."

Chig's father had gone pale. He spoke very softly. "You're about thirty years too late, Mama." He bolted from the table. Silverware and dishes rang and jumped. Chig heard him hurrying up to their room.

They sat in silence for awhile and then heard a key in the front door. A man with a new, lacquered straw hat came in. He was wearing brown and white two-tone shoes with very pointed toes and a white summer suit. "Say now! Man! I heard my brother was in town. Where he at? Where that rascal?"

He stood in the doorway, smiling broadly, an engaging, open, friendly smile, the innocent smile of a five-year-old.

for discussion

1. The narrator presents much of the story through Chig's eyes. What does this device contribute to the full meaning of the story? Does it seem likely that Chig has been importantly affected by his visit to grandmother?
2. Is there any evidence in grandmother's account of the runaway horse which might support her claim that she favored GL only because he required more of her affection than Charles did?

3. Which of Doctor Dunford's charges suggests that his tragic misunderstanding of his mother's feelings toward him was a direct consequence of his having been raised in a racially segregated society?

1913–1966

DELMORE SCHWARTZ

☐ *Delmore Schwartz was born in Brooklyn in 1913, and all his life the big city remained his natural setting. He graduated from New York University in 1935, and then attended Harvard for two years. A widely read, sensitive, witty cosmopolitan, Schwartz was a brilliant example of the urban intellectual. He was an editor of both* Partisan Review *and the* New Republic, *two of America's most sophisticated journals. He taught at Harvard, Princeton, and Syracuse universities. But foremost he was a writer of stories, poems, and essays.*

Schwartz's first book, In Dreams Begin Responsibilities *(1938), contains a play and poetry in addition to the title story. It was followed by the poetic drama* Shenandoah *(1941). In his book* Genesis *(1943), Schwartz relates in prose and poetry the background of a child born to a*

Jewish immigrant family in America just before the first World War. Schwartz published two collections of his stories, The World Is a Wedding (1948) and Successful Love (1961). He also published two volumes of poetry, Vaudeville for a Princess (1950) and Summer Knowledge: New and Selected Poems, 1938–1958 (1959). Schwartz won the Bollingen Prize for poetry in 1959 and several other major distinctions.

Schwartz's writings exhibit full identification with his Jewishness, on the one hand, and his no less genuine attachment to the American scene, on the other. But, as a writer, he never functioned narrowly as a spokesman for the Jew or the American. As both a Jew and a native of metropolitan America, Schwartz acquired an especially acute consciousness of what it means to be marginal, anonymous, and terribly vulnerable. He spoke with painful authority of the loneliness and despair that pervade so much of modern industrial society. His own name—"Delmore" so oddly assorting with "Schwartz"— always reminded him of the nightmarish incongruities that compose reality. As both a Jew and an American, he was alerted to the progressive isolation of modern men from their past and felt their resulting susceptibility to confusion and anxiety.

Ultimately, Schwartz's fiction grows out of the sometimes agonizing, sometimes comic results of exaggerated self-consciousness. His heroes are driven to merciless contemplation of themselves and the modern situation. Schwartz cherished the example of Joyce, Mann, Proust, Rimbaud, and other great writers of the twentieth century. Like them he struggled to impose at least imaginative order upon the whirl of contemporary experience.

in dreams begin responsibilities °

I

☐ I think it is the year 1909. I feel as if I were in a motion picture theater, the long arm of light crossing the darkness and spinning, my eyes fixed on the screen. This is a silent picture as if an old Biograph one, in which the actors are dressed in ridiculously old-fashioned clothes, and one flash succeeds another with sudden jumps. The actors too seem to jump about and walk too fast. The shots themselves are full of dots and rays, as if it were raining when the picture was photographed. The light is bad.

It is Sunday afternoon, June 12th, 1909, and my father is walking down the quiet streets of Brooklyn on his way to visit my mother. His clothes are newly pressed and his tie is too tight in his high collar. He jingles the coins in his pockets, thinking of the witty things he will say. I feel as if I had by now relaxed entirely in the soft darkness of the theater; the organist peals out the obvious and approximate emotions on which the audience rocks unknowingly. I am anonymous, and I have forgotten myself. It is always so when one goes to the movies, it is, as they say, a drug.

My father walks from street to street of trees, lawns, and houses, once in a while coming to an avenue on which a street-car skates and gnaws, slowly progressing. The conductor, who has a handle-bar mustache, helps a young lady wearing a hat like a bowl with feathers on to the car. She lifts her long skirts slightly as she mounts the steps. He leisurely makes change and rings his bell. It is obviously Sunday, for everyone is wearing Sunday clothes,

° Schwartz drew his title from W. B. Yeats's *Responsibilities,* a book of poems first published in 1914, with the epigraph 'In dreams begins responsibility."

and the street-car's noises emphasize the quiet of the holiday. Is not Brooklyn the City of Churches? The shops are closed and their shades drawn, but for an occasional stationery store or drug-store with great green balls in the window.

My father has chosen to take this long walk because he likes to walk and think. He thinks about himself in the future and so arrives at the place he is to visit in a state of mild exaltation. He pays no attention to the houses he is passing, in which the Sunday dinner is being eaten, nor to the many trees which patrol each street, now coming to their full leafage and the time when they will room the whole street in cool shadow. An occasional carriage passes, the horse's hooves falling like stones in the quiet afternoon, and once in a while an automobile, looking like an enormous upholstered sofa, puffs and passes.

My father thinks of my mother, of how nice it will be to introduce her to his family. But he is not yet sure that he wants to marry her, and once in a while he becomes panicky about the bond already established. He reassures himself by thinking of the big men he admires who are married: William Randolph Hearst, and William Howard Taft, who has just become President of the United States.

My father arrives at my mother's house. He has come too early and so is suddenly embarrassed. My aunt, my mother's sister, answers the loud bell with her napkin in her hand, for the family is still at dinner. As my father enters, my grandfather rises from the table and shakes hands with him. My mother has run upstairs to tidy herself. My grandmother asks my father if he has had dinner, and tells him that Rose will be downstairs soon. My grandfather opens the conversation by remarking on the mild June weather. My father sits uncomfortably near the table, holding his hat in his hand. My grandmother tells my aunt to take my father's hat. My uncle, twelve years old, runs into the house, his hair tousled. He shouts a greeting to my father, who has often given him a nickel, and then runs upstairs. It is evident that the respect in which my father is held in this household is tempered by a good deal of mirth. He is impressive, yet he is very awkward.

II

Finally my mother comes downstairs, all dressed up, and my father being engaged in conversation with my grandfather becomes uneasy, not knowing whether to greet my mother or continue the conversation. He gets up from the chair clumsily and says "hello" gruffly. My grandfather watches, examining their congruence, such as it is, with a critical eye, and meanwhile rubbing his bearded cheek roughly, as he always does when he reflects. He is worried; he is afraid that my father will not make a good husband for his oldest daughter. At this point something happens to the film, just as my father is saying something funny to my mother; I am awakened to myself and my unhappiness just as my interest was rising. The audience begins to clap impatiently. Then the trouble is cared for but the film has been returned to a portion just shown, and once more I see my grandfather rubbing his bearded cheek and pondering my father's character. It is difficult to get back into the picture once more and forget myself, but as my mother giggles at my father's words, the darkness drowns me.

My father and mother depart from the house, my father shaking hands with my gra. father once more, out of some unknown uneasiness. I stir uneasily also, slouched in the hard chair of the theater. Where is the older uncle, my mother's older brother? He is studying in his bedroom upstairs, studying for his final examination at the College of the City of New York, having been dead of rapid pneumonia for the last twenty-one years. My mother and father walk down the same quiet streets once more. My mother is holding my father's arm and telling him of the novel which she has been reading; and my father utters judgments of the characters as the plot is made clear to him. This is a habit which he very much enjoys, for he feels the utmost superiority and confidence when he approves and condemns the behavior of other people. At times he feels moved to utter a brief "Ugh," whenever the story becomes what he would call sugary. This tribute is paid to his manliness. My mother feels satisfied by the interest which she has awakened; she is showing my father how intelligent she is, and how interesting.

They reach the avenue, and the street-car leisurely arrives. They are going to Coney Island this afternoon, although my mother considers that such pleasures are inferior. She has made up her mind to indulge only in a walk on the boardwalk and a pleasant dinner, avoiding the riotous amusements as being beneath the dignity of so dignified a couple.

My father tells my mother how much money he has made in the past week, exaggerating an amount which need not have been exaggerated. But my father has always felt that actualities somehow fall short. Suddenly I begin to weep. The determined old lady who sits next to me in the theater is annoyed and looks at me with an angry face, and being intimidated, I stop. I drag out my handkerchief and dry my face, licking the drop which has fallen near my lips. Meanwhile I have missed something, for here are my mother and father alighting at the last stop, Coney Island.

III

They walk toward the boardwalk, and my father commands my mother to inhale the pungent air from the sea. They both breathe in deeply, both of them laughing as they do so. They have in common a great interest in health, although my father is strong and husky, my mother frail. Their minds are full of theories of what is good to eat and not good to eat, and sometimes they engage in heated discussions of the subject, the whole matter ending in my father's announcement, made with a scornful bluster, that you have to die sooner or later anyway. On the boardwalk's flagpole, the American flag is pulsing in an intermittent wind from the sea.

My father and mother go to the rail of the boardwalk and look down on the beach where a good many bathers are casually walking about. A few are in the surf. A peanut whistle pierces the air with its pleasant and active whine, and my father goes to buy peanuts. My mother remains at the rail and stares at the ocean. The ocean seems merry to her; it pointedly sparkles and again and again the pony waves are released. She notices the children digging in the wet sand, and the bathing costumes of the girls who are her own age. My father returns with the peanuts. Overhead the sun's lightning strikes and strikes, but neither of them is at all aware of it. The boardwalk is full of people dressed in their Sunday clothes and idly strolling. The tide does not reach as far as the boardwalk, and the strollers would feel no danger if it did. My mother and father lean on the rail of the boardwalk and absently stare at the ocean. The ocean is becoming rough; the waves come in slowly, tugging strength from far back. The moment before they somersault, the moment when they arch their backs so beautifully, showing green and white veins amid the black, that moment is intolerable. They finally crack, dashing fiercely upon the sand, actually driving, full force downward, against the sand, bouncing upward and forward, and at last petering out into a small stream which races up the beach and then is recalled. My parents gaze absentmindedly at the ocean, scarcely interested in its harshness. The sun overhead does not disturb them. But I stare at the terrible sun which breaks up sight, and the fatal, merciless, passionate ocean, I forget my parents. I stare fascinated and finally, shocked by the indifference of my father and mother, I burst out weeping once more. The old lady next to me pats me on the shoulder and says "There, there, all of this is only a movie, young man, only a movie," but I look up once more at the terrifying sun and the terrifying ocean, and being unable to control my tears, I get up and go to the men's room, stumbling over the feet of the other people seated in my row.

IV

When I return, feeling as if I had awakened in the morning sick for lack of sleep, several hours have apparently passed and my parents are riding on the merry-go-round. My father is on a black horse, my mother on a white one, and they seem to be making an eternal circuit for the single purpose of snatching the nickel rings which are attached to the arm of one of the posts. A hand-organ is playing; it is one with the ceaseless circling of the merry-go-round.

For a moment it seems that they will never get off the merry-go-round because it will never stop. I feel like one who looks down on the avenue from the fiftieth story of a building. But at length they do get off; even the music of the hand-organ has ceased for a moment. My father has acquired ten rings, my mother only two, although it was my mother who really wanted them.

They walk on along the boardwalk as the afternoon descends by imperceptible degrees into the incredible violet of dusk. Everything fades into a relaxed glow, even the ceaseless murmuring from the beach, and the revolutions of the merry-go-round. They look for a place to have dinner. My father suggests the best one on the boardwalk and my mother demurs, in accordance with her principles.

However they do go to the best place, asking for a table near the window, so that they can look out on the boardwalk and the mobile ocean. My father feels omnipotent as he places a quarter in the waiter's hand as he asks for a table. The place is crowded and here too there is music, this time from a kind of string trio. My father orders dinner with a fine confidence.

As the dinner is eaten, my father tells of his plans for the future, and my mother shows with expressive face how interested she is, and how impressed. My father becomes exultant. He is lifted up by the waltz that is being played, and his own future begins to intoxicate him. My father tells my mother that he is going to expand his business, for there is a great deal of money to be made. He wants to settle down. After all, he is twenty-nine, he has lived by himself since he was thirteen, he is making more and more money, and he is envious of his married friends when he visits them in the cozy security of their homes, surrounded, it seems, by the calm domestic pleasures, and by delightful children, and then, as the waltz reaches the moment when all the dancers swing madly, then, then with awful daring, then he asks my mother to marry him, although awkwardly enough and puzzled, even in his excitement, at how he had arrived at the proposal, and she, to make the whole business worse, begins to cry, and my father looks nervously about, not knowing at all what to do now, and my mother says: "It's all I've wanted from the moment I saw you," sobbing, and he finds all of this very difficult, scarcely to his taste, scarcely as he had thought it would be, on his long walks over Brooklyn Bridge in the revery of a fine cigar, and it was then that I stood up in the theater and shouted: "Don't do it. It's not too late to change your minds, both of you. Nothing good will come of it, only remorse, hatred, scandal, and two children whose characters are monstrous." The whole audience turned to look at me, annoyed, the usher came hurrying down the aisle flashing his searchlight, and the old lady next to me tugged me down into my seat, saying: "Be quiet. You'll be put out, and you paid thirty-five cents to come in." And so I shut my eyes because I could not bear to see what was happening. I sat there quietly.

V

But after awhile I begin to take brief glimpses, and at length I watch again with thirsty interest, like a child who wants to maintain his sulk although offered the bribe of candy. My parents are now having their picture taken in a photographer's booth along the boardwalk. The place is shadowed in the mauve light which is apparently necessary. The camera is set to the side on its tripod and looks like a Martian man. The photographer is instructing my parents in how to pose. My father has his arm over my mother's shoulder, and both of them smile emphatically. The photographer brings my mother a bouquet of flowers to hold in her hand but she holds it at the wrong angle. Then the photographer covers himself with the black cloth which drapes the camera and all that one sees of him is one protruding arm and his hand which clutches the rubber ball which he will squeeze when the picture is finally taken. But he is not satisfied with their appearance. He feels with certainty that somehow there is something wrong in their pose. Again and again he issues from his hidden place with new directions. Each suggestion merely makes matters worse. My father is becoming impatient. They try a seated pose. The photographer explains that he has pride, he is not interested in all of this for the money, he wants to make beautiful pictures. My father says: "Hurry up, will you? We haven't got all night." But the photographer only scurries about apologetically, and issues new directions. The photographer charms me. I approve of him with all my heart, for I know just how he feels, and as he criticizes each revised pose according to some unknown idea of rightness, I become quite hopeful. But then my father says angrily: "Come on, you've had enough time, we're not going to wait any longer." And the photographer, sighing unhappily, goes back under his black covering, holds out his hand, says: "One, two, three, Now!", and the picture is taken, with my father's smile turned to a grimace and my mother's bright and false. It takes a few minutes for the picture to be developed and as my parents sit in the curious light they become quite depressed.

VI

They have passed a fortune-teller's booth, and my mother wishes to go in, but my father does not. They begin to argue about it. My mother becomes stubborn, my father once more impatient, and then they begin to quarrel, and what my father would like to do is walk off and leave my mother there, but he knows that that would never do. My mother refuses to budge. She is near to tears, but she feels an uncontrollable desire to hear what the palm-reader will say. My father consents angrily, and they both go into a booth which is in a way like the photographer's, since it is draped in black cloth and its light is shadowed. The place is too warm, and my father keeps saying this is all nonsense, pointing to the crystal ball on the table. The fortune-teller, a fat, short woman, garbed in what is supposed to be Oriental robes, comes into the room from the back and greets them, speaking with an accent. But suddenly my father feels that the whole thing is intolerable; he tugs at my mother's arm, but my mother refuses to budge. And then, in terrible anger, my father lets go of my mother's arm and strides out, leaving my mother stunned. She moves to go after my father, but the fortune-teller holds her arm tightly and begs her not to do so, and I in my seat am shocked more than can ever be said, for I feel as if I were walking a tight-rope a hundred feet over a circus-audience and suddenly the rope is showing signs of breaking, and I get up from my seat and begin to shout once more the first words I can think of to communicate my terrible fear and once more the usher comes hurrying down the aisle flashing his searchlight, and the old lady pleads with me, and the shocked audience has turned to stare at me, and I keep shouting: "What are they doing? Don't they know what they are doing? Why doesn't my mother go after my father? If she does not do that, what will she do? Doesn't my father know what he is doing?" But the usher has seized my arm and is dragging me away, and as he does so, he says: "What are *you* doing? Don't you know that you can't do whatever you want to do? Why should a young man like you, with your whole life before you, get hysterical like this? Why don't you *think* of what you're doing? You can't act like this even if other people aren't around! You will be sorry if you do not do what you should do, you can't carry on like this, it is not right, you will find that out soon enough, everything you do matters too much," and he said that dragging me through the lobby of the theater into the cold light, and I woke up into the bleak winter morning of my twenty-first birthday, the windowsill shining with its lip of snow, and the morning already begun.

for discussion

1. This story is in the form of a dream, and twentieth-century men have become highly aware that dreams often reveal the fears and conflicts which are masked during their waking hours. What do we learn about the narrator both from the details of his dream and from his responses to those details?

2. Point out some of the unusual language that helps to establish the dream atmosphere of the story. What is gained through Schwartz's having written the story almost entirely in the present tense?

3. The story's most original narrative device is its presentation of the dreamer as a spectator at a silent film in a movie house. How well does this device represent the actual state of dreaming? How well does the device help to characterize the specific fears and conflicts of the narrator?

born 1915

SAUL BELLOW

☐ *Saul Bellow was born in Quebec, Canada, two years after his parents had emigrated there from Russia. Until Bellow was nine, he lived in one of the oldest and most impoverished sections of Montreal. In 1924 the family moved to Chicago, where Bellow attended public schools. From 1933 to 1935 Bellow studied at the University of Chicago. He spent the next two years at nearby Northwestern University, from which he graduated in 1937 with honors in anthropology and sociology. But after only a brief period of graduate study at the University of Wisconsin, Bellow turned from formal study of the social sciences to the writing of fiction. In 1941 his first published story appeared in the* Partisan Review. *During his long career as a writer, however, Bellow has usually remained close to the university scene as a professor of humanities at the universities of Minnesota and Chicago.*

Although Bellow's first two novels, Dangling Man *(1944) and* The Victim *(1947), received little attention initially, he has since earned a high position among the major American novelists of the past three decades. He won the National Book Award for both* The Adventures of Augie March *(1953) and* Herzog *(1964). His other novels are* Henderson the Rain King *(1959) and* Mr. Sammler's Planet *(1970). Two volumes of his stories—* Seize the Day *(1956) and* Mosby's Memoirs *(1968)— have been published, and his play* The Last Analysis *(1965) was produced on Broadway. The consistent excellence of Bellow's literary accomplishments has won him many distinctions, among them a Guggenheim Fellowship and* membership in the National Institute of Arts and Letters.

Born in the New World, Bellow nevertheless preserves a rich awareness of the Old World from which his Jewish immigrant parents came. He has translated into English such great Yiddish writers as Sholom Aleichem and Isaac Bashevis Singer; and in 1963 he edited Great Jewish Short Stories. Thus Bellow is clearly linked, in important ways, to Jewish culture. But that culture is more the vehicle than the object of his art. Being a Jew in the neighborhoods, schools, and businesses of the modern American city has equipped Bellow with the means of seeing and expressing the quality of human experience in an advanced industrial civilization. In this often unprecedented world, where physical appearances and public beliefs are blurred by ceaseless change, the experience of being a lonely outsider is no longer an uncommon one. An increasing number of people feel like rootless, persecuted wanderers in their own land. Thus, no longer exotic, the "Jews" in Bellow's stories speak and act like "representative men."

Bellow regards writing as a difficult art precisely because human life is now undergoing such profound transformations. What, he asks, has the writer "to say about the 'crisis of our civilization' "? In an essay published in 1967, he says that "writers cannot simply continue in the old way," and he asks questions that are central to the understanding of his stories: "What can be said now? What is truly relevant? What can art signify? What core of significance endures through all the changes we have experienced?"

a father-to-be

☐ The strangest notions had a way of forcing themselves into Rogin's mind. Just thirty-one and passable-looking, with short black hair, small eyes, but a high, open forehead, he was a research chemist, and his mind was generally serious and dependable. But on a snowy Sunday evening while this stocky man, buttoned to the chin in a Burberry coat and walking in his preposterous gait—feet turned outward—was going toward the subway, he fell into a peculiar state.

He was on his way to have supper with his fiancée. She had phoned him a short while ago and said, "You'd better pick up a few things on the way."

"What do we need?"

"Some roast beef, for one thing. I bought a quarter of a pound coming home from my aunt's."

"Why a quarter of a pound, Joan?" said Rogin, deeply annoyed. "That's just about enough for one good sandwich."

"So you have to stop at a delicatessen. I had no more money."

He was about to ask, "What happened to the thirty dollars I gave you on Wednesday?" but he knew that would not be right.

"I had to give Phyllis money for the cleaning woman," said Joan.

Phyllis, Joan's cousin, was a young divorcée, extremely wealthy. The two women shared an apartment.

"Roast beef," he said, "and what else?"

"Some shampoo, sweetheart. We've used up all the shampoo. And hurry, darling, I've missed you all day."

"And I've missed you," said Rogin, but to tell the truth he had been worrying most of the time. He had a younger brother whom he was putting through college. And his mother, whose annuity wasn't quite enough in these days of inflation and high taxes, needed money, too. Joan had debts he was helping her to pay, for she wasn't working. She was looking for something suitable to do. Beautiful, well educated, aristocratic in her attitude, she couldn't clerk in a dime store; she couldn't model clothes (Rogin thought this made girls vain and stiff, and he didn't want her to); she couldn't be a waitress or a cashier. What could she be? Well, something would turn up, and meantime Rogin hesitated to complain. He paid her bills—the dentist, the department store, the osteopath, the doctor, the psychiatrist. At Christmas, Rogin almost went mad. Joan bought him a velvet smoking jacket with frog fasteners, a beautiful pipe, and a pouch. She bought Phyllis a garnet brooch, an Italian silk umbrella, and a gold cigarette holder. For other friends, she bought Dutch pewter and Swedish glassware. Before she was through, she had spent five hundred dollars of Rogin's money. He loved her too much to show his suffering. He believed she had a far better nature than his. She didn't worry about money. She had a marvelous character, always cheerful, and she really didn't need a psychiatrist at all. She went to one because Phyllis did and it made her curious. She tried too much to keep up with her cousin, whose father had made millions in the rug business.

While the woman in the drugstore was wrapping the shampoo bottle, a clear idea suddenly arose in Rogin's thoughts: Money surrounds you in life as the earth does in death. Superimposition is the universal law. Who is free? No one is free. Who has no burdens? Everyone is under pressure. The very rocks, the waters of the earth, beasts, men, children—everyone has some weight to carry. This idea was extremely clear to him at first. Soon it became rather vague, but it had a great effect nevertheless, as if someone had given him a valuable gift. (Not like the velvet smoking jacket he couldn't bring himself to wear, or the pipe it choked him to smoke.) The notion that all were under pressure and affliction, instead of saddening him, had the opposite influence. It put him in a wonderful mood. It was extraordinary how happy he became and, in addition, clear-sighted. His eyes all at once were opened to what was around him. He saw with delight how the druggist and the woman who wrapped the shampoo bottle were smiling and flirting, how the lines of worry in her face went over into lines of cheer and the druggist's receding gums did not hinder his kidding and friendliness. And in the delicatessen, also, it was amazing how much Rogin noted and what happiness it gave him simply to be there.

Delicatessens on Sunday night, when all other stores are shut, will overcharge you ferociously, and Rogin would normally have been on guard, but he was not tonight, or scarcely so. Smells of pickle, sausage, mustard, and smoked fish overjoyed him. He pitied the people who would buy the chicken salad and chopped herring; they could do it only because their sight was too dim to see what they were getting—the fat flakes of pepper on the chicken, the soppy herring, mostly vinegar-soaked stale bread. Who would buy them? Late risers, people living alone, waking up in the darkness of the afternoon, finding their refrigerators empty, or people whose gaze was turned inward. The roast beef looked not bad, and Rogin ordered a pound.

While the storekeeper was slicing the meat, he yelled at a Puerto Rican kid who was reaching for a bag of chocolate cookies, "Hey, you want to pull me down the whole display on yourself? You, *chico*, wait a half a minute." This storekeeper, though he looked like one of Pancho Villa's bandits, the kind that smeared their enemies with syrup and staked them down on anthills, a man with toad-like eyes and stout hands made to clasp pistols hung around his belly, was not so bad. He was a New York man, thought Rogin—who was from Albany himself—a New York man toughened by every abuse of the city, trained to suspect everyone. But in his own realm, on the board behind the counter, there was justice. Even clemency.

The Puerto Rican kid wore a complete cowboy outfit—a green hat with white braid, guns, chaps, spurs, boots, and gauntlets—but he couldn't speak any English. Rogin unhooked the cellophane bag of hard circular cookies and gave it to him. The boy tore the cellophane with his teeth and began to chew one of those dry chocolate discs. Rogin recognized his state—the energetic dream of childhood. Once, he, too, had found these dry biscuits delicious. It would have bored him now to eat one.

What else would Joan like? Rogin thought fondly.

Some strawberries? "Give me some frozen strawberries. No, raspberries, she likes those better. And heavy cream. And some rolls, cream cheese, and some of those rubber-looking gherkins."

"What rubber?"

"Those, deep green, with eyes. Some ice cream might be in order, too."

He tried to think of a compliment, a good comparison, an endearment, for Joan when she'd open the door. What about her complexion? There was really nothing to compare her sweet, small, daring, shapely, timid, defiant, loving face to. How difficult she was, and how beautiful!

As Rogin went down into the stony, odorous, metallic, captive air of the subway, he was diverted by an unusual confession made by a man to his friend. These were two very tall men, shapeless in their winter clothes, as if their coats concealed suits of chain mail.

"So, how long have you known me?" said one.

"Twelve years."

"Well, I have an admission to make," he said. "I've decided that I might as well. For years I've been a heavy drinker. You didn't know. Practically an alcoholic."

But his friend was not surprised, and he answered immediately, "Yes, I did know."

"You knew? Impossible! How could you?"

Why, thought Rogin, as if it could be a secret! Look at that long, austere, alcohol-washed face, that drink-ruined nose, the skin by his ears like turkey wattles, and those whiskey-saddened eyes.

"Well, I did know, though."

"You couldn't have. I can't believe it." He was upset, and his friend didn't seem to want to soothe him. "But it's all right now," he said. "I've been going to a doctor and taking pills, a new revolutionary Danish discovery. It's a miracle. I'm beginning to believe they can cure you of anything and everything. You can't beat the Danes in science. They do everything. They turned a man into a woman."

"That isn't how they stop you from drinking, is it?"

"No. I hope not. This is only like aspirin. It's super-aspirin. They call it the aspirin of the future. But if you use it, you have to stop drinking."

Rogin's illuminated mind asked of itself while the human tides of the subway swayed back and forth, and cars linked and transparent like fish bladders raced under the streets: How come he thought nobody would know what everybody couldn't help knowing? And, as a chemist, he asked himself what kind of compound this new Danish drug might be, and started thinking about various inventions of his own, synthetic albumen, a cigarette that lit itself, a cheaper motor fuel. Ye gods, but he needed money! As never before. What was to be done? His mother was growing more and more difficult. On Friday night, she had neglected to cut up his meat for him, and he was hurt. She had sat at the table motionless, with her long-suffering face, severe, and let him cut his own meat, a thing she almost never did. She had always spoiled him and made his brother envy him. But what she expected now! Oh, Lord, how he had to pay, and it had never even occurred to him formerly that these things might have a price.

Seated, one of the passengers, Rogin recovered his calm, happy, even clairvoyant state of mind. To think of money was to think as the world wanted you to think; then you'd never be your own master. When people said they wouldn't do something for love or money, they meant that love and money were opposite passions and one the enemy of the other. He went on to reflect how little people knew about this, how they slept through life, how small a light the light of consciousness was. Rogin's clean, snub-nosed face shone while his heart was torn with joy at these deeper thoughts of our ignorance. You might take this drunkard as an example, who for long years thought his closest friends never suspected he drank. Rogin looked up and down the aisle for this remarkable knightly symbol, but he was gone.

However, there was no lack of things to see. There was a small girl with a new white muff; into the muff a doll's head was sewn, and the child was happy and affectionately vain of it, while her old man, stout and grim, with a huge scowling nose, kept picking her up and resettling her in the seat, as if he were trying to change her into something else. Then another child, led by her mother, boarded the car, and this other child carried the very same doll-faced muff, and this greatly annoyed both parents. The woman, who looked like a difficult, contentious woman, took her daughter away. It seemed to Rogin that each child was in love with its own muff and didn't even see the other, but it was one of his foibles to think he understood the hearts of little children.

A foreign family next engaged his attention. They looked like Central Americans to him. On one side the mother, quite old, dark-faced, white-haired, and worn out; on the other a son with the whitened, porous hands of a dishwasher. But what was the dwarf who sat between them —a son or a daughter? The hair was long and wavy and the cheeks smooth, but the shirt and tie were masculine. The overcoat was feminine, but the shoes—the shoes were a puzzle. A pair of brown oxfords with an outer seam like a man's, but Baby Louis heels like a woman's—a plain toe like a man's, but a strap across the instep like a woman's. No stockings. That didn't help much. The dwarf's fingers were beringed, but without a wedding band. There were small grim dents in the cheeks. The eyes were puffy and concealed, but Rogin did not doubt that they could reveal strange things if they chose and that this was a creature of remarkable understanding. He had for many years owned De la Mare's *Memoirs of a Midget*. Now he took a resolve; he would read it. As soon as he had decided, he was free from his consuming curiosity as to the dwarf's sex and was able to look at the person who sat beside him.

Thoughts very often grow fertile in the subway, because of the motion, the great company, the subtlety of the rider's state as he rattles under streets and rivers, under the foundations of great buildings, and Rogin's mind had already been strangely stimulated. Clasping the bag of groceries from which there rose odors of bread and pickle spice, he was following a train of reflections, first about the chemistry of sex determination, the X and Y chromosomes, hereditary linkages, the uterus, afterward about his brother as a tax exemption. He recalled two dreams of the night before. In one, an undertaker had offered to cut his hair, and he had refused. In another, he had been carrying a woman on his head. Sad dreams, both! Very sad! Which was the woman—Joan or Mother? And the undertaker—his lawyer? He gave a deep sigh, and by force of habit began to put together his synthetic albumen that was to revolutionize the entire egg industry.

Meanwhile, he had not interrupted his examination of the passengers and had fallen into a study of the man next to him. This was a man whom he had never in his life seen before but with whom he now suddenly felt linked through all existence. He was middle-aged, sturdy, with clear skin and blue eyes. His hands were clean, well formed, but Rogin did not approve of them. The coat he wore was a fairly expensive blue check such as Rogin would never have chosen for himself. He would not have worn blue suède shoes, either, or such a faultless hat, a cumbersome felt animal of a hat encircled by a high, fat ribbon. There are all kinds of dandies, not all of them are of the flaunting kind; some are dandies of respectability, and Rogin's fellow passenger was one of these. His straight-nosed profile was handsome, yet he had betrayed his gift, for he was flat-looking. But in his flat way he seemed to warn people that he wanted no difficulties with them, he wanted nothing to do with them. Wearing such blue suède shoes, he could not afford to have people treading on his feet, and he seemed to draw about himself a circle of privilege, notifying all others to mind their own business and let him read his paper. He was holding a *Tribune*, and perhaps it would be overstatement to say that he was reading. He was holding it.

His clear skin and blue eyes, his straight and purely Roman nose—even the way he sat—all strongly suggested one person to Rogin: Joan. He tried to escape the comparison, but it couldn't be helped. This man not only looked like Joan's father, whom Rogin detested; he looked like Joan herself. Forty years hence, a son of hers, provided she had one, might be like this. A son of hers? Of such a son, he himself, Rogin, would be the father. Lacking in dominant traits as compared with Joan, his heritage would not appear. Probably the children would resemble her. Yes, think forty years ahead, and a man like this, who sat by him knee to knee in the hurtling car among their fellow creatures, unconscious participants in a sort of great carnival of transit—such a man would carry forward what had been Rogin.

This was why he felt bound to him through all existence. What were forty years reckoned against eternity! Forty years were gone, and he was gazing at his own son. Here he was. Rogin was frightened and moved. "My son! My son!" he said to himself, and the pity of it almost made him burst into tears. The holy and frightful work of the masters of life and death brought this about. We were their instruments. We worked toward ends we thought were our own. But no! The whole thing was so unjust. To suffer, to labor, to toil and force your way through the spikes of life, to crawl through its darkest caverns, to push through the worst, to struggle under the weight of economy, to make money—only to become the father of a fourth-rate man of the world like this, so flat-looking, with his ordinary, clean, rosy, uninteresting, self-satisfied, fundamentally bourgeois face. What a curse to have a dull son! A son like this, who could never understand his father. They had absolutely nothing, but nothing, in common, he and this neat, chubby, blue-eyed man. He was so pleased, thought Rogin, with all he owned and all he did and all he was that he could hardly unfasten his lip. Look at that lip, sticking up at the tip like a little thorn or egg tooth.[1] He wouldn't give anyone the time of day. Would this perhaps be general forty years from now? Would personalities be chillier as the world aged and grew colder? The inhumanity of the next generation incensed Rogin. Father and son had no sign to make to each other. Terrible! Inhuman! What a vision of existence it gave him. Man's personal aims were nothing, illusion. The life force occupied each of us in turn in its progress toward its own fulfillment, trampling on our individual humanity, using us for its own ends like mere dinosaurs or bees, exploiting love heartlessly, making us engage in the social process, labor, struggle for money, and submit to the law of pressure, the universal law of layers, superimposition!

What the blazes am I getting into? Rogin thought. To be the father of a throwback to *her* father. The image of

[1] *egg tooth:* a hard, pointed spur on the beak tip of embryo birds by which they break through the eggshell.

this white-haired, gross, peevish old man with his ugly selfish blue eyes revolted Rogin. This was how his grandson would look. Joan, with whom Rogin was now more and more displeased, could not help that. For her, it was inevitable. But did it have to be inevitable for him? Well, then, Rogin, you fool, don't be a damned instrument. Get out of the way!

But it was too late for this, because he had already experienced the sensation of sitting next to his own son, his son and Joan's. He kept staring at him, waiting for him to say something, but the presumptive son remained coldly silent though he must have been aware of Rogin's scrutiny. They even got out at the same stop—Sheridan Square. When they stepped to the platform, the man, without even looking at Rogin, went away in a different direction in his detestable blue-checked coat, with his rosy, nasty face.

The whole thing upset Rogin very badly. When he approached Joan's door and heard Phyllis's little dog Henri barking even before he could knock, his face was very tense. "I won't be used," he declared to himself. "I have my own right to exist." Joan had better watch out. She had a light way of bypassing grave questions he had given earnest thought to. She always assumed no really disturbing thing would happen. He could not afford the luxury of such a carefree, debonair attitude himself, because he had to work hard and earn money so that disturbing things would *not* happen. Well, at the moment this situation could not be helped, and he really did not mind the money if he could feel that she was not necessarily the mother of such a son as his subway son or entirely the daughter of that awful, obscene father of hers. After all, Rogin was not himself so much like either of his parents, and quite different from his brother.

Joan came to the door, wearing one of Phyllis's expensive housecoats. It suited her very well. At first sight of her happy face, Rogin was brushed by the shadow of resemblance; the touch of it was extremely light, almost figmentary, but it made his flesh tremble.

She began to kiss him, saying, "Oh, my baby. You're covered with snow. Why didn't you wear your hat? It's all over its little head"—her favorite third-person endearment.

"Well, let me put down this bag of stuff. Let me take off my coat," grumbled Rogin, and escaped from her embrace. Why couldn't she wait making up to him? "It's so hot in here. My face is burning. Why do you keep the place at this temperature? And that damned dog keeps barking. If you didn't keep it cooped up, it wouldn't be so spoiled and noisy. Why doesn't anybody ever walk him?"

"Oh, it's not really so hot here! You've just come in from the cold. Don't you think this housecoat fits me better than Phyllis? Especially across the hips. She thinks so, too. She may sell it to me."

"I hope not," Rogin almost exclaimed.

She brought a towel to dry the melting snow from his short black hair. The flurry of rubbing excited Henri intolerably, and Joan locked him up in the bedroom, where he jumped persistently against the door with a rhythmic sound of claws on the wood.

Joan said, "Did you bring the shampoo?"

"Here it is."

"Then I'll wash your hair before dinner. Come."

"I don't want it washed."

"Oh, come on," she said, laughing.

Her lack of consciousness of guilt amazed him. He did not see how it could be. And the carpeted, furnished, lamp-lit, curtained room seemed to stand against his vision. So that he felt accusing and angry, his spirit sore and bitter, but it did not seem fitting to say why. Indeed, he began to worry lest the reason for it all slip away from him.

They took off his coat and his shirt in the bathroom, and she filled the sink. Rogin was full of his troubled emotions; now that his chest was bare he could feel them even more distinctly inside, and he said to himself, I'll have a thing or two to tell her pretty soon. I'm not letting them get away with it. "Do you think," he was going to tell her, "that I alone was made to carry the burden of the whole world on me? Do you think I was born just to be taken advantage of and sacrificed? Do you think I'm just a natural resource, like a coal mine, or oil well, or fishery, or the like? Remember, that I'm a man is no reason why I should be loaded down. I have a soul in me no bigger or stronger than yours.

"Take away the externals, like the muscles, deeper voice, and so forth, and what remains? A pair of spirits, practically alike. So why shouldn't there also be equality? I can't always be the strong one."

"Sit here," said Joan, bringing up a kitchen stool to the sink. "Your hair's gotten all matted."

He sat with his breast against the cool enamel, his chin on the edge of the basin, the green, hot, radiant water reflecting the glass and the tile, and the sweet, cool, fragrant juice of the shampoo poured on his head. She began to wash him.

"You have the healthiest-looking scalp," she said. "It's all pink."

He answered, "Well, it should be white. There must be something wrong with me."

"But there's absolutely nothing wrong with you," she said, and pressed against him from behind, surrounding him, pouring the water gently over him until it seemed to him that the water came from within him, it was the warm fluid of his own secret loving spirit overflowing into the sink, green and foaming, and the words he had rehearsed he forgot, and his anger at his son-to-be disappeared altogether, and he sighed, and said to her from the water-filled hollow of the sink, "You always have such wonderful ideas, Joan. You know? You have a kind of instinct, a regular gift."

for discussion

1. In what way does the narrator indicate to the reader, at the beginning of the story and elsewhere, that he intends to report Rogin's innermost experience?

2. What do we learn about the inner Rogin? What fears gnaw at him? Which details of his environment most oppress him?

3. One characteristic of the traditional story is that its conflicts are in some way resolved and its hero is brought—by the story's end—to some heightened awareness or deepened understanding of himself and his world. Such stories reflect worlds that seem familiar and understandable, to the reader if not always to the characters. How well does the conclusion of "A Father-to-Be" fit these traditional requirements of narrative fiction?

4. Which features of contemporary life does Bellow's story capture best?

BERNARD MALAMUD

☐ *Bernard Malamud was born in Brooklyn in 1914. He was educated in New York's public schools, and received a bachelor's degree from The City College of New York in 1936. He later earned a master's degree at Columbia University. During the 1940's, Malamud was a teacher in the evening classes of the New York high schools. His first published stories appeared in 1943. But it was not until the following decade, while he was a professor at Oregon State University, that Malamud gained wide recognition. His first two novels,* The Natural *(1952) and* The Assistant *(1957), were unmistakable literary triumphs; and in 1959 he won the National Book Award for his first book of short stories,* The Magic Barrel *(1958).*

Malamud returned to the East in 1961 to join the faculty of Bennington College. His next novel, A New Life, *was published the same year. It was followed by a second book of stories,* Idiots First *(1963). Malamud won a second National Book Award for his fourth novel,* The Fixer, *published in 1966. In 1969 Malamud issued* Pictures of Fidelman: An Exhibition, *which added three new episodes in the life of Arthur Fidelman to the three included in the two earlier collections of his stories. Malamud is a member of the National Institute of Arts and Letters, and has been awarded many other honors. He stands with Bellow, Salinger, and Roth as a leader of the highly influential school of Jewish writers in modern American fiction.*

Malamud's stories occupy a world midway between the natural and the supernatural; they join the real to the ideal and link material facts to spiritual hopes. One premise of his stories is the uncertainty and the suffering that are unavoidable conditions of human existence. The other premise is the human will to believe and endure, which enables Malamud's heroes to accept the world and perhaps to transcend it. His heroes are frequently the victims of cruel circumstances whose lives are redeemed through their struggle to preserve their faith in what is right and good against the doubts and defeats of ordinary life. The fate which dogs Malamud's heroes is man's fate, but it is mysteriously subject to miraculous developments which defy common sense explanation.

The Jewish immigrant community out of which Malamud came provides him with the tragic sense of life, the moral code, the folklore, and the verbal gestures that he puts to original imaginative use. Jewishness is Malamud's metaphor for a suffering humanity still able to love and to trust.

the magic barrel

☐ Not long ago there lived in uptown New York, in a small, almost meager room, though crowded with books, Leo Finkle, a rabbinical student in the Yeshivah University. Finkle, after six years of study, was to be ordained in June and had been advised by an acquaintance that he might find it easier to win himself a congregation if he were married. Since he had no present prospects of marriage, after two tormented days of turning it over in his mind, he called in Pinye Salzman, a marriage broker whose two-line advertisement he had read in the *Forward*.[1]

The matchmaker appeared one night out of the dark fourth-floor hallway of the graystone rooming house where Finkle lived, grasping a black, strapped portfolio that had been worn thin with use. Salzman, who had been long in the business, was of slight but dignified build, wearing an old hat, and an overcoat too short and tight for him. He

[1] *Forward*: the *Jewish Daily Forward*, the most widely read Yiddish-language newspaper in America.

smelled frankly of fish, which he loved to eat, and although he was missing a few teeth, his presence was not displeasing, because of an amiable manner curiously contrasted with mournful eyes. His voice, his lips, his wisp of beard, his bony fingers were animated, but give him a moment of repose and his mild blue eyes revealed a depth of sadness, a characteristic that put Leo a little at ease although the situation, for him, was inherently tense.

He at once informed Salzman why he had asked him to come, explaining that his home was in Cleveland, and that but for his parents, who had married comparatively late in life, he was alone in the world. He had for six years devoted himself almost entirely to his studies, as a result of which, understandably, he had found himself without time for a social life and the company of young women. Therefore he thought it the better part of trial and error—of embarrassing fumbling—to call in an experienced person to advise him on these matters. He remarked in passing that the function of the marriage broker was ancient and honorable, highly approved in the Jewish community, because it made practical the necessary without hindering joy. Moreover, his own parents had been brought together by a matchmaker. They had made, if not a financially profitable marriage—since neither had possessed any worldly goods to speak of—at least a successful one in the sense of their everlasting devotion to each other. Salzman listened in embarrassed surprise, sensing a sort of apology. Later, however, he experienced a glow of pride in his work, an emotion that had left him years ago, and he heartily approved of Finkle.

The two went to their business. Leo had led Salzman to the only clear place in the room, a table near a window that overlooked the lamp-lit city. He seated himself at the matchmaker's side but facing him, attempting by an act of will to suppress the unpleasant tickle in his throat. Salzman eagerly unstrapped his portfolio and removed a loose rubber band from a thin packet of much-handled cards. As he flipped through them, a gesture and sound that physically hurt Leo, the student pretended not to see and gazed steadfastly out the window. Although it was still February, winter was on its last legs, signs of which he had for the first time in years begun to notice. He now observed the round white moon, moving high in the sky through a cloud menagerie, and watched with half-open mouth as it penetrated a huge hen, and dropped out of her like an egg laying itself. Salzman, though pretending through eyeglasses he had just slipped on, to be engaged in scanning the writing on the cards, stole occasional glances at the young man's distinguished face, noting with pleasure the long, severe scholar's nose, brown eyes heavy with learning, sensitive yet ascetic lips, and a certain, almost hollow quality of the dark cheeks. He gazed around at shelves upon shelves of books and let out a soft, contented sigh.

When Leo's eyes fell upon the cards, he counted six spread out in Salzman's hand.

"So few?" he asked in disappointment.

"You wouldn't believe me how much cards I got in my office," Salzman replied. "The drawers are already filled to the top, so I keep them now in a barrel, but is every girl good for a new rabbi?"

Leo blushed at this, regretting all he had revealed of himself in a curriculum vitae he had sent to Salzman. He had thought it best to acquaint him with his strict standards and specifications, but in having done so, felt he had told the marriage broker more than was absolutely necessary.

He hesitantly inquired, "Do you keep photographs of your clients on file?"

"First comes family, amount of dowry, also what kind promises," Salzman replied, unbuttoning his tight coat and settling himself in the chair. "After comes pictures, rabbi."

"Call me Mr. Finkle. I'm not yet a rabbi."

Salzman said he would, but instead called him doctor, which he changed to rabbi when Leo was not listening too attentively.

Salzman adjusted his horn-rimmed spectacles, gently cleared his throat and read in an eager voice the contents of the top card:

"Sophie P. Twenty-four years. Widow one year. No children. Educated high school and two years college. Father promises eight thousand dollars. Has wonderful wholesale business. Also real estate. On the mother's side comes teachers, also one actor. Well known on Second Avenue."

Leo gazed up in surprise. "Did you say a widow?"

"A widow don't mean spoiled, rabbi. She lived with her husband maybe four months. He was a sick boy she made a mistake to marry him."

"Marrying a widow has never entered my mind."

"This is because you have no experience. A widow, especially if she is young and healthy like this girl, is a wonderful person to marry. She will be thankful to you the rest of her life. Believe me, if I was looking now for a bride, I would marry a widow."

Leo reflected, then shook his head.

Salzman hunched his shoulders in an almost imperceptible gesture of disappointment. He placed the card down on the wooden table and began to read another:

"Lily H. High school teacher. Regular. Not a substitute. Has savings and new Dodge car. Lived in Paris one year. Father is successful dentist thirty-five years. Interested in professional man. Well Americanized family. Wonderful opportunity."

"I knew her personally," said Salzman. "I wish you could see this girl. She is a doll. Also very intelligent. All day you could talk to her about books and theyater and what not. She also knows current events."

"I don't believe you mentioned her age?"

"Her age?" Salzman said, raising his brows. "Her age is thirty-two years."

Leo said after a while, "I'm afraid that seems a little too old."

Salzman let out a laugh. "So how old are you, rabbi?"

"Twenty-seven."

"So what is the difference, tell me, between twenty-seven and thirty-two? My own wife is seven years older than me. So what did I suffer?—Nothing. If Rothschild's a daughter wants to marry you, would you say on account her age, no?"

"Yes," Leo said dryly.

Salzman shook off the no in the yes. "Five years don't mean a thing. I give you my word that when you will live with her for one week you will forget her age. What does it mean five years—that she lived more and knows more than somebody who is younger? On this girl, God bless her, years are not wasted. Each one that it comes makes better the bargain."

"What subject does she teach in high school?"

"Languages. If you heard the way she speaks French, you will think it is music. I am in the business twenty-five years, and I recommend her with my whole heart. Believe me, I know what I'm talking, rabbi."

"What's on the next card?" Leo said abruptly.

Salzman reluctantly turned up the third card:

"Ruth K. Nineteen years. Honor student. Father offers thirteen thousand cash to the right bridegroom. He is a medical doctor. Stomach specialist with marvelous practice. Brother-in-law owns own garment business. Particular people."

Salzman looked as if he had read his trump card.

"Did you say nineteen?" Leo asked with interest.

"On the dot."

"Is she attractive?" He blushed. "Pretty?"

Salzman kissed his finger tips. "A little doll. On this I give you my word. Let me call the father tonight and you will see what means pretty."

But Leo was troubled. "You're sure she's that young?"

"This I am positive. The father will show you the birth certificate."

"Are you positive there isn't something wrong with her?" Leo insisted.

"Who says there is wrong?"

"I don't understand why an American girl her age should go to a marriage broker."

A smile spread over Salzman's face.

"So for the same reason you went, she comes."

Leo flushed. "I am pressed for time."

Salzman, realizing he had been tactless, quickly explained. "The father came, not her. He wants she should have the best, so he looks around himself. When we will locate the right boy he will introduce him and encourage. This makes a better marriage than if a young girl without experience takes for herself. I don't have to tell you this."

"But don't you think this young girl believes in love?" Leo spoke uneasily.

Salzman was about to guffaw but caught himself and said soberly, "Love comes with the right person, not before."

Leo parted dry lips but did not speak. Noticing that Salzman had snatched a glance at the next card, he cleverly asked, "How is her health?"

"Perfect," Salzman said, breathing with difficulty. "Of course, she is a little lame on her right foot from an auto accident that it happened to her when she was twelve years, but nobody notices on account she is so brilliant and also beautiful."

Leo got up heavily and went to the window. He felt curiously bitter and upbraided himself for having called in the marriage broker. Finally, he shook his head.

"Why not?" Salzman persisted, the pitch of his voice rising.

"Because I detest stomach specialists."

"So what do you care what is his business? After you marry her do you need him? Who says he must come every Friday night in your house?"

Ashamed of the way the talk was going, Leo dismissed Salzman, who went home with heavy, melancholy eyes.

Though he had felt only relief at the marriage broker's departure, Leo was in low spirits the next day. He explained it as arising from Salzman's failure to produce a suitable bride for him. He did not care for his type of clientele. But when Leo found himself hesitating whether to seek out another matchmaker, one more polished than Pinye, he wondered if it could be—his protestations to the contrary, and although he honored his father and mother —that he did not, in essence, care for the matchmaking institution? This thought he quickly put out of mind yet found himself still upset. All day he ran around in the woods—missed an important appointment, forgot to give out his laundry, walked out of a Broadway cafeteria without paying and had to run back with the ticket in his hand; had even not recognized his landlady in the street when she passed with a friend and courteously called out, "A good evening to you, Doctor Finkle." By nightfall, however, he had regained sufficient calm to sink his nose into a book and there found peace from his thoughts.

Almost at once there came a knock on the door. Before Leo could say enter, Salzman, commercial cupid, was standing in the room. His face was gray and meager, his expression hungry, and he looked as if he would expire on his feet. Yet the marriage broker managed, by some trick of the muscles, to display a broad smile.

"So good evening. I am invited?"

Leo nodded, disturbed to see him again, yet unwilling to ask the man to leave.

Beaming still, Salzman laid his portfolio on the table. "Rabbi, I got for you tonight good news."

"I've asked you not to call me rabbi. I'm still a student."

"Your worries are finished. I have for you a first-class bride."

"Leave me in peace concerning this subject." Leo pretended lack of interest.

"The world will dance at your wedding."

"Please, Mr. Salzman, no more."

"But first must come back my strength," Salzman said weakly. He fumbled with the portfolio straps and took out of the leather case an oily paper bag, from which he extracted a hard, seeded roll and a small, smoked white fish. With a quick motion of his hand he stripped the fish out of its skin and began ravenously to chew. "All day in a rush," he muttered.

Leo watched him eat.

"A sliced tomato you have maybe?" Salzman hesitantly inquired.

"No."

The marriage broker shut his eyes and ate. When he had finished he carefully cleaned up the crumbs and rolled up the remains of the fish, in the paper bag. His spectacled eyes roamed the room until he discovered, amid some piles of books, a one-burner gas stove. Lifting his hat he humbly asked, "A glass tea you got, rabbi?"

Conscience-stricken, Leo rose and brewed the tea. He served it with a chunk of lemon and two cubes of lump sugar, delighting Salzman.

After he had drunk his tea, Salzman's strength and good spirits were restored.

"So tell me, rabbi," he said amiably, "you considered some more the three clients I mentioned yesterday?"

"There was no need to consider."

"Why not?"

"None of them suits me."

"What then suits you?"

Leo let it pass because he could give only a confused answer.

Without waiting for a reply, Salzman asked, "You remember this girl I talked to you—the high school teacher?"

"Age thirty-two?"

But, surprisingly, Salzman's face lit in a smile. "Age twenty-nine."

Leo shot him a look. "Reduced from thirty-two?"

"A mistake," Salzman avowed. "I talked today with the dentist. He took me to his safety deposit box and showed me the birth certificate. She was twenty-nine years last August. They made her a party in the mountains where she went for her vacation. When her father spoke to me the first time I forgot to write the age and I told you thirty-two, but now I remember this was a different client, a widow."

"The same one you told me about? I thought she was twenty-four?"

"A different. Am I responsible that the world is filled with widows?"

"No, but I'm not interested in them, nor for that matter, in school teachers."

Salzman pulled his clasped hands to his breast. Looking at the ceiling he devoutly exclaimed, "Yiddishe kinder,[2] what can I say to somebody that he is not interested in high school teachers? So what then you are interested?"

Leo flushed but controlled himself.

"In what else will you be interested," Salzman went on, "if you not interested in this fine girl that she speaks

___

[2] *Yiddishe kinder* (yi′dish·ə kin′dər): "Jewish children," an exclamation of impatience.

four languages and has personally in the bank ten thousand dollars? Also her father guarantees further twelve thousand. Also she has a new car, wonderful clothes, talks on all subjects, and she will give you a first-class home and children. How near do we come in our life to paradise?"

"If she's so wonderful, why wasn't she married ten years ago?"

"Why?" said Salzman with a heavy laugh. "—Why? Because she is *partikiler*.[3] This is why. She wants the *best*."

Leo was silent, amused at how he had entangled himself. But Salzman had aroused his interest in Lily H., and he began seriously to consider calling on her. When the marriage broker observed how intently Leo's mind was at work on the facts he had supplied, he felt certain they would soon come to an agreement.

Late Saturday afternoon, conscious of Salzman, Leo Finkle walked with Lily Hirschorn along Riverside Drive. He walked briskly and erectly, wearing with distinction the black fedora he had that morning taken with trepidation out of the dusty hat box on his closet shelf, and the heavy black Saturday coat he had thoroughly whisked clean. Leo also owned a walking stick, a present from a distant relative, but quickly put temptation aside and did not use it. Lily, petite and not unpretty, had on something signifying the approach of spring. She was au courant,[4] animatedly, with all sorts of subjects, and he weighed her words and found her surprisingly sound—score another for Salzman, whom he uneasily sensed to be somewhere around, hiding perhaps high in a tree along the street, flashing the lady signals with a pocket mirror; or perhaps a cloven-hoofed Pan,[5] piping nuptial ditties as he danced his invisible way before them, strewing wild buds on the walk and purple grapes in their path, symbolizing fruit of a union, though there was of course still none.

Lily startled Leo by remarking, "I was thinking of Mr.

---

[3] *partikiler* (pär·tik′i·lār): particular.

[4] *au courant* (ō coor·an′): French for "well informed."

[5] *Pan:* a Greek nature god, represented as part man and part goat, who was a pursuer of women. He was unpredictable, a trickster who was alternately playful and frightening, a creator of "panic."

Salzman, a curious figure, wouldn't you say?"

Not certain what to answer, he nodded.

She bravely went on, blushing, "I for one am grateful for his introducing us. Aren't you?"

He courteously replied, "I am."

"I mean," she said with a little laugh—and it was all in good taste, or at least gave the effect of being not in bad —"do you mind that we came together so?"

He was not displeased with her honesty, recognizing that she meant to set the relationship aright, and understanding that it took a certain amount of experience in life, and courage, to want to do it quite that way. One had to have some sort of past to make that kind of beginning.

He said that he did not mind. Salzman's function was traditional and honorable—valuable for what it might achieve, which, he pointed out, was frequently nothing.

Lily agreed with a sigh. They walked on for a while and she said after a long silence, again with a nervous laugh, "Would you mind if I asked you something a little bit personal? Frankly, I find the subject fascinating." Although Leo shrugged, she went on half embarrassedly, "How was it that you came to your calling? I mean was it a sudden passionate inspiration?"

Leo, after a time, slowly replied, "I was always interested in the Law."

"You saw revealed in it the presence of the Highest?"

He nodded and changed the subject. "I understand that you spent a little time in Paris, Miss Hirschorn?"

"Oh, did Mr. Salzman tell you, Rabbi Finkle?" Leo winced but she went on, "It was ages ago and almost forgotten. I remember I had to return for my sister's wedding."

And Lily would not be put off. "When," she asked in a trembly voice, "did you become enamored of God?"

He stared at her. Then it came to him that she was talking not about Leo Finkle, but of a total stranger, some mystical figure, perhaps even passionate prophet that Salzman had dreamed up for her—no relation to the living or dead. Leo trembled with rage and weakness. The trickster had obviously sold her a bill of goods, just as he had him, who'd expected to become acquainted with a young lady of twenty-nine, only to behold, the moment he laid eyes upon her strained and anxious face, a woman past thirty-five and aging rapidly. Only his self control had kept him this long in her presence.

"I am not," he said gravely, "a talented religious person," and in seeking words to go on, found himself possessed by shame and fear. "I think," he said in a strained manner, "that I came to God not because I loved Him, but because I did not."

This confession he spoke harshly because its unexpectedness shook him.

Lily wilted. Leo saw a profusion of loaves of bread go flying like ducks high over his head, not unlike the winged loaves by which he had counted himself to sleep last night. Mercifully, then, it snowed, which he would not put past Salzman's machinations.

He was infuriated with the marriage broker and swore he would throw him out of the room the minute he reappeared. But Salzman did not come that night, and when Leo's anger had subsided, an unaccountable despair grew in its place. At first he thought this was caused by his disappointment in Lily, but before long it became evident that he had involved himself with Salzman without a true knowledge of his own intent. He gradually realized—with an emptiness that seized him with six hands—that he had called in the broker to find him a bride because he was incapable of doing it himself. This terrifying insight he had derived as a result of his meeting and conversation with Lily Hirschorn. Her probing questions had somehow irritated him into revealing—to himself more than her—the true nature of his relationship to God, and from that it had come upon him, with shocking force, that apart from his parents, he had never loved anyone. Or perhaps it went the other way, that he did not love God so well as he might, because he had not loved man. It seemed to Leo that his whole life stood starkly revealed and he saw himself for the first time as he truly was—unloved and loveless. This bitter but somehow not fully unexpected revelation brought him to a point of panic, controlled only by extraordinary effort. He covered his face with his hands and cried.

The week that followed was the worst of his life. He did not eat and lost weight. His beard darkened and grew ragged. He stopped attending seminars and almost never opened a book. He seriously considered leaving the Yeshivah, although he was deeply troubled at the thought of the loss of all his years of study—saw them like pages torn from a book, strewn over the city—and at the devastating effect of this decision upon his parents. But he had lived without knowledge of himself, and never in the Five Books [6] and all the Commentaries—mea culpa [7]—had the truth been revealed to him. He did not know where to turn, and in all this desolating loneliness there was no *to whom*, although he often thought of Lily but not once could bring himself to go downstairs and make the call. He became touchy and irritable, especially with his landlady, who asked him all manner of personal questions; on the other hand, sensing his own disagreeableness, he waylaid her on the stairs and apologized abjectly, until mortified, she ran from him. Out of this, however, he drew the consolation that he was a Jew and that a Jew suffered. But gradually, as the long and terrible week drew to a close, he regained his composure and some idea of purpose in life: to go on as planned. Although he was imperfect, the ideal was not. As for his quest of a bride, the thought of continuing afflicted him with anxiety and heartburn, yet perhaps with this new knowledge of himself he would be more successful than in the past. Perhaps love would now come to him and a bride to that love. And for this sanctified seeking who needed a Salzman?

The marriage broker, a skeleton with haunted eyes, returned that very night. He looked, withal, the picture of frustrated expectancy—as if he had steadfastly waited the week at Miss Lily Hirschorn's side for a telephone call that never came.

Casually coughing, Salzman came immediately to the point: "So how did you like her?"

[6] *Five Books:* the first five books of the Old Testament.
[7] *mea culpa:* Latin for "my fault."

Leo's anger rose and he could not refrain from chiding the matchmaker: "Why did you lie to me, Salzman?"

Salzman's pale face went dead white, the world had snowed on him.

"Did you not state that she was twenty-nine?" Leo insisted.

"I give you my word—"

"She was thirty-five, if a day. *At least* thirty-five."

"Of this don't be too sure. Her father told me—"

"Never mind. The worst of it was that you lied to her."

"How did I lie to her, tell me?"

"You told her things about me that weren't true. You made me out to be more, consequently less than I am. She had in mind a totally different person, a sort of semi-mystical Wonder Rabbi."

"All I said, you was a religious man."

"I can imagine."

Salzman sighed. "This is my weakness that I have," he confessed. "My wife says to me I shouldn't be a salesman, but when I have two fine people that they would be wonderful to be married, I am so happy that I talk too much." He smiled wanly. "This is why Salzman is a poor man."

Leo's anger left him. "Well, Salzman, I'm afraid that's all."

The marriage broker fastened hungry eyes on him.

"You don't want any more a bride?"

"I do," said Leo, "but I have decided to seek her in a different way. I am no longer interested in an arranged marriage. To be frank, I now admit the necessity of pre-marital love. That is, I want to be in love with the one I marry."

"Love?" said Salzman, astounded. After a moment he remarked, "For us, our love is our life, not for the ladies. In the ghetto they—"

"I know, I know," said Leo. "I've thought of it often. Love, I have said to myself, should be a by-product of living and worship rather than its own end. Yet for myself I find it necessary to establish the level of my need and fulfill it."

Salzman shrugged but answered, "Listen, rabbi, if you

want love, this I can find for you also. I have such beautiful clients that you will love them the minute your eyes will see them."

Leo smiled unhappily. "I'm afraid you don't understand."

But Salzman hastily unstrapped his portfolio and withdrew a manila packet from it.

"Pictures," he said, quickly laying the envelope on the table.

Leo called after him to take the pictures away, but as if on the wings of the wind, Salzman had disappeared.

March came. Leo had returned to his regular routine. Although he felt not quite himself yet—lacked energy— he was making plans for a more active social life. Of course it would cost something, but he was an expert in cutting corners; and when there were no corners left he would make circles rounder. All the while Salzman's pictures had lain on the table, gathering dust. Occasionally as Leo sat studying, or enjoying a cup of tea, his eyes fell on the manila envelope, but he never opened it.

The days went by and no social life to speak of developed with a member of the opposite sex—it was difficult, given the circumstances of his situation. One morning Leo toiled up the stairs to his room and stared out the window at the city. Although the day was bright his view of it was dark. For some time he watched the people in the street below hurrying along and then turned with a heavy heart to his little room. On the table was the packet. With a sudden relentless gesture he tore it open. For a half-hour he stood by the table in a state of excitement, examining the photographs of the ladies Salzman had included. Finally, with a deep sigh he put them down. There were six, of varying degrees of attractiveness, but look at them long enough and they all became Lily Hirschorn: all past their prime, all starved behind bright smiles, not a true personality in the lot. Life, despite their frantic yoohoo-ings, had passed them by; they were pictures in a brief-case that stank of fish. After a while, however, as Leo attempted to return the photographs into the envelope, he found in it another, a snapshot of the type taken by a machine for a quarter. He gazed at it a moment and let out a cry.

Her face deeply moved him. Why, he could at first not say. It gave him the impression of youth—spring flowers, yet age—a sense of having been used to the bone, wasted; this came from the eyes, which were hauntingly familiar, yet absolutely strange. He had a vivid impression that he had met her before, but try as he might he could not place her although he could almost recall her name, as if he had read it in her own handwriting. No, this couldn't be; he would have remembered her. It was not, he affirmed, that she had an extraordinary beauty—no, though her face was attractive enough; it was that *something* about her moved him. Feature for feature, even some of the ladies of the photographs could do better; but she leaped forth to his heart—had *lived*, or wanted to—more than just wanted, perhaps regretted how she had lived—had somehow deeply suffered: it could be seen in the depths of those reluctant eyes, and from the way the light enclosed and shone from her, and within her, opening realms of possibility: this was her own. Her he desired. His head ached and eyes narrowed with the intensity of his gazing, then as if an obscure fog had blown up in the mind, he experienced fear of her and was aware that he had received an impression, somehow, of evil. He shuddered, saying softly, it is thus with us all. Leo brewed some tea in a small pot and sat sipping it without sugar, to calm himself. But before he had finished drinking, again with excitement he examined the face and found it good: good for Leo Finkle. Only such a one could understand him and help him seek whatever he was seeking. She might, perhaps, love him. How she had happened to be among the discards in Salzman's barrel he could never guess, but he knew he must urgently go find her.

Leo rushed downstairs, grabbed up the Bronx telephone book, and searched for Salzman's home address. He was not listed, nor was his office. Neither was he in the Manhattan book. But Leo remembered having written down the address on a slip of paper after he had read Salzman's advertisement in the "personals" column of the *Forward*. He ran up to his room and tore through his papers, without luck. It was exasperating. Just when he needed the matchmaker he was nowhere to be found. Fortunately Leo remembered to look in his wallet. There on a card he found his name written and a Bronx address. No phone number was listed, the reason—Leo now recalled—he had originally communicated with Salzman by letter. He got on his coat, put a hat on over his skull cap and hurried to the subway station. All the way to the far end of the Bronx he sat on the edge of his seat. He was more than once tempted to take out the picture and see if the girl's face was as he remembered it, but he refrained, allowing the snapshot to remain in his inside coat pocket, content to have her so close. When the train pulled into the station he was waiting at the door and bolted out. He quickly located the street Salzman had advertised.

The building he sought was less than a block from the subway, but it was not an office building, nor even a loft, nor a store in which one could rent office space. It was a very old tenement house. Leo found Salzman's name in pencil on a soiled tag under the bell and climbed three dark flights to his apartment. When he knocked, the door was opened by a thin, asthmatic, gray-haired woman, in felt slippers.

"Yes?" she said, expecting nothing. She listened without listening. He could have sworn he had seen her, too, before but knew it was an illusion.

"Salzman—does he live here? Pinye Salzman," he said, "the matchmaker?"

She stared at him a long minute. "Of course."

He felt embarrassed. "Is he in?"

"No." Her mouth, though left open, offered nothing more.

"The matter is urgent. Can you tell me where his office is?"

"In the air." She pointed upward.

"You mean he has no office?" Leo asked.

"In his socks."

He peered into the apartment. It was sunless and dingy, one large room divided by a half-open curtain, beyond which he could see a sagging metal bed. The near side of a room was crowded with rickety chairs, old bureaus, a three-legged table, racks of cooking utensils, and all the apparatus of a kitchen. But there was no sign of Salzman or his magic barrel, probably also a figment of the imagination. An odor of frying fish made Leo weak to the knees.

"Where is he?" he insisted. "I've got to see your husband."

At length she answered, "So who knows where he is? Every time he thinks a new thought he runs to a different place. Go home, he will find you."

"Tell him Leo Finkle."

She gave no sign she had heard.

He walked downstairs, depressed.

But Salzman, breathless, stood waiting at his door.

Leo was astounded and overjoyed. "How did you get here before me?"

"I rushed."

"Come inside."

They entered. Leo fixed tea, and a sardine sandwich for Salzman. As they were drinking he reached behind him for the packet of pictures and handed them to the marriage broker.

Salzman put down his glass and said expectantly, "You found somebody you like?"

"Not among these."

The marriage broker turned away.

"Here is the one I want." Leo held forth the snapshot.

Salzman slipped on his glasses and took the picture into his trembling hand. He turned ghastly and let out a groan.

"What's the matter?" cried Leo.

"Excuse me. Was an accident this picture. She isn't for you."

Salzman frantically shoved the manila packet into his portfolio. He thrust the snapshot into his pocket and fled down the stairs.

Leo, after momentary paralysis, gave chase and cornered the marriage broker in the vestibule. The landlady made hysterical outcries but neither of them listened.

"Give me back the picture, Salzman."

"No." The pain in his eyes was terrible.

"Tell me who she is then."

"This I can't tell you. Excuse me."

He made to depart, but Leo, forgetting himself, seized the matchmaker by his tight coat and shook him frenziedly.

"Please," sighed Salzman. "*Please.*"

Leo ashamedly let him go. "Tell me who she is," he begged. "It's very important for me to know."

"She is not for you. She is a wild one—wild, without shame. This is not a bride for a rabbi."

"What do you mean wild?"

"Like an animal. Like a dog. For her to be poor was a sin. This is why to me she is dead now."

"In God's name, what do you mean?"

"Her I can't introduce to you," Salzman cried.

"Why are you so excited?"

"Why, he asks," Salzman said, bursting into tears. "This is my baby, my Stella, she should burn in hell."

Leo hurried up to bed and hid under the covers. Under the covers he thought his life through. Although he soon fell asleep he could not sleep her out of his mind. He woke, beating his breast. Though he prayed to be rid of her, his prayers went unanswered. Through days of torment he endlessly struggled not to love her; fearing success, he escaped it. He then concluded to convert her to goodness, himself to God. The idea alternately nauseated and exalted him.

He perhaps did not know that he had come to a final decision until he encountered Salzman in a Broadway cafeteria. He was sitting alone at a rear table, sucking the bony remains of a fish. The marriage broker appeared haggard, and transparent to the point of vanishing.

Salzman looked up at first without recognizing him. Leo had grown a pointed beard and his eyes were weighted with wisdom.

"Salzman," he said, "love has at last come to my heart."

"Who can love from a picture?" mocked the marriage broker.

"It is not impossible."

"If you can love her, then you can love anybody. Let me show you some new clients that they just sent me their photographs. One is a little doll."

"Just her I want," Leo murmured.

"Don't be a fool, doctor. Don't bother with her."

"Put me in touch with her, Salzman," Leo said humbly. "Perhaps I can be of service."

Salzman had stopped eating and Leo understood with emotion that it was now arranged.

Leaving the cafeteria, he was, however, afflicted by a tormenting suspicion that Salzman had planned it all to happen this way.

Leo was informed by letter that she would meet him on a certain corner, and she was there one spring night, waiting under a street lamp. He appeared, carrying a small bouquet of violets and rosebuds. Stella stood by the lamp post, smoking. She wore white with red shoes, which fitted his expectations, although in a troubled moment he had imagined the dress red, and only the shoes white. She waited uneasily and shyly. From afar he saw that her eyes—clearly her father's—were filled with desperate innocence. He pictured, in her, his own redemption. Violins and lit candles revolved in the sky. Leo ran forward with flowers outthrust.

Around the corner, Salzman, leaning against a wall, chanted prayers for the dead.

for discussion

1. By which uses of detail and action does the narrator endow Pinye Salzman with magical qualities?

2. Is there any evidence that Salzman has actually contrived the match between his daughter, the fallen Stella, and Leo Finkle?

3. At the story's beginning, the reader is introduced to a rabbinical student whose long and arduous studies have kept him remote from life. What changes occur in Leo as a result of his meetings with the matchmaker?

In what way does the story's time sequence—from winter to spring—provide a kind of mythical background for Leo's gradual transformation?

4. What ceremony or ritual is suggested by the imagery and the events of the story's final scene where "Violins and lit candles revolved in the sky"?

5. What ambiguity exists in the narrator's final reference to Salzman chanting "prayers for the dead"? For whom is he praying?

born 1933

PHILIP ROTH

☐ *Roth's stories unfold in a modern world where
traditional beliefs and ceremonies have survived without
the old faiths that once animated them and gave them
meaning. In his stories, obedience to ancient law is too
often a matter only of duty or guilt or convenience.
Moreover, Roth's characters are the products of a
civilization in which cultural communities—whose unity
was preserved in the past by isolation—have become
increasingly "homogenized." Thus, Roth's characters are
more conscious of what they are not than of what they
are. Whatever sense of older community they manage to
feel is without true solidarity and trust. Roth maintains
that these conditions are "no more true of Jews in our
country than of Christians":*

> *Small matters aside—food preferences, a certain
> syntax, certain jokes—it is difficult for me to
> distinguish a Jewish style of life in our country that is
> significantly separate and distinct from the American
> style of life. (I am thinking of the urban and suburban
> middle classes.) What a Jew wants and how he goes
> after it, does not on the whole appear to differ
> radically from what his Gentile neighbor wants and
> how he goes after it.°*

*Roth affirms the shaping influence of the Jewish past
on his spirit and imagination, but acknowledges as well
"the political and cultural past of America, and the
literary past of England." His heroes sometimes wrestle
with questions of faith and justice that engaged the
ancient Jewish lawgivers but that also invoke a larger,
more inclusive history of "defenders of the faith." The
higher laws to which Roth ultimately appeals are Jewish
in one sense but broadly humanistic in another.*

° Excerpt by Philip Roth from *Commentary*, Volume 31, No. 4, copyright © 1961 by the American Jewish Committee. Reprinted by permission of the publisher.

The meanings of Roth's stories are deeply embedded in realistic details. Roth is a fiercely honest observer who reports things as they are, usually through highly particularized first-person narration. He attempts to uncover essential human values in the new accumulations of fact and experience that make up the life around him. Still a young writer, Roth has already been elected to membership in the National Institute of Arts and Letters.

defender of the faith °

☐ In May of 1945, only a few weeks after the fighting had ended in Europe, I was rotated back to the States, where I spent the remainder of the war with a training company at Camp Crowder, Missouri. Along with the rest of the Ninth Army, I had been racing across Germany so swiftly during the late winter and spring that when I boarded the plane, I couldn't believe its destination lay to the west. My mind might inform me otherwise, but there was an inertia of the spirit that told me we were flying to a new front, where we would disembark and continue our push eastward—eastward until we'd circled the globe, marching through villages along whose twisting, cobbled streets crowds of the enemy would watch us take possession of what, up till then, they'd considered their own. I had changed enough in two years not to mind the trembling of the old people, the crying of the very young, the uncertainty and fear in the eyes of the once arrogant. I had been fortunate enough to develop an infantryman's

"Defender of the Faith" from *Goodbye Columbus and Five Short Stories* by Philip Roth, copyright © 1959 by Philip Roth. Reprinted by permission of the publisher, Houghton Mifflin Company.

° *Defender of the Faith:* the title conferred on Henry VIII by Pope Leo X in 1521 in recognition of the king's support of the traditional Church. Despite the Church of England's subsequent repudiation of papal authority, the title has since been retained by all British monarchs.

heart, which, like his feet, at first aches and swells but finally grows horny enough for him to travel the weirdest paths without feeling a thing.

Captain Paul Barrett was my C.O. in Camp Crowder. The day I reported for duty, he came out of his office to shake my hand. He was short, gruff, and fiery, and—indoors or out—he wore his polished helmet liner pulled down to his little eyes. In Europe, he had received a battlefield commission and a serious chest wound, and he'd been returned to the States only a few months before. He spoke easily to me, and at the evening formation he introduced me to the troops. "Gentlemen," he said, "Sergeant Thurston, as you know, is no longer with this company. Your new first sergeant is Sergeant Nathan Marx, here. He is a veteran of the European theater, and consequently will expect to find a company of soldiers here, and not a company of *boys*."

I sat up late in the orderly room that evening, trying halfheartedly to solve the riddle of duty rosters, personnel forms, and morning reports. The Charge of Quarters slept with his mouth open on a mattress on the floor. A trainee stood reading the next day's duty roster, which was posted on the bulletin board just inside the screen door. It was a warm evening, and I could hear radios playing dance music over in the barracks. The trainee, who had been staring at me whenever he thought I wouldn't notice, finally took a step in my direction.

"Hey, Sarge—we having a G.I. party tomorrow night?" he asked. A G.I. party is a barracks cleaning.

"You usually have them on Friday nights?" I asked him.

"Yes," he said, and then he added, mysteriously, "that's the whole thing."

"Then you'll have a G.I. party."

He turned away, and I heard him mumbling. His shoulders were moving, and I wondered if he was crying.

"What's your name, soldier?" I asked.

He turned, not crying at all. Instead, his green-speckled eyes, long and narrow, flashed like fish in the sun. He walked over to me and sat on the edge of my desk. He reached out a hand. "Sheldon," he said.

"Stand on your feet, Sheldon."

Getting off the desk, he said, "Sheldon Grossbart." He smiled at the familiarity into which he'd led me.

"You against cleaning the barracks Friday night, Grossbart?" I said. "Maybe we shouldn't have G.I. parties. Maybe we should get a maid." My tone startled me. I felt I sounded like every top sergeant I had ever known.

"No, Sergeant." He grew serious, but with a seriousness that seemed to be only the stifling of a smile. "It's just —G.I. parties on Friday night, of all nights."

He slipped up onto the corner of the desk again—not quite sitting, but not quite standing, either. He looked at me with those speckled eyes flashing, and then made a gesture with his hand. It was very slight—no more than a movement back and forth of the wrist—and yet it managed to exclude from our affairs everything else in the orderly room, to make the two of us the center of the world. It seemed, in fact, to exclude everything even about the two of us except our hearts.

"Sergeant Thurston was one thing," he whispered, glancing at the sleeping C.Q., "but we thought that with you here things might be a little different."

"We?"

"The Jewish personnel."

"Why?" I asked, harshly. "What's on your mind?" Whether I was still angry at the "Sheldon" business, or now at something else, I hadn't time to tell, but clearly I was angry.

"We thought you—Marx, you know, like Karl Marx. The Marx Brothers. Those guys are all—M-a-r-x. Isn't that how *you* spell it, Sergeant?"

"M-a-r-x."

"Fishbein said—" He stopped. "What I mean to say, Sergeant—" His face and neck were red, and his mouth moved but no words came out. In a moment, he raised himself to attention, gazing down at me. It was as though he had suddenly decided he could expect no more sympathy from me than from Thurston, the reason being that I was of Thurston's faith, and not his. The young man had managed to confuse himself as to what my faith really was, but I felt no desire to straighten him out. Very simply, I didn't like him.

When I did nothing but return his gaze, he spoke, in an altered tone. "You see, Sergeant," he explained to me, "Friday nights, Jews are supposed to go to services."

"Did Sergeant Thurston tell you you couldn't go to them when there was a G.I. party?"

"No."

"Did he say you had to stay and scrub the floors?"

"No, Sergeant."

"Did the Captain say you had to stay and scrub the floors?"

"That isn't it, Sergeant. It's the other guys in the barracks." He leaned toward me. "They think we're goofing off. But we're not. That's when Jews go to services, Friday night. We have to."

"Then go."

"But the other guys make accusations. They have no right."

"That's not the Army's problem, Grossbart. It's a personal problem you'll have to work out yourself."

"But it's un*fair*."

I got up to leave. "There's nothing I can do about it," I said.

Grossbart stiffened and stood in front of me. "But this is a matter of *religion*, sir."

"Sergeant," I said.

"I mean 'Sergeant,' " he said, almost snarling.

"Look, go see the chaplain. You want to see Captain Barrett, I'll arrange an appointment."

"No, no. I don't want to make trouble, Sergeant. That's the first thing they throw up to you. I just want my rights!"

"Damn it, Grossbart, stop whining. You have your rights. You can stay and scrub floors or you can go to shul—"[1]

The smile swam in again. Spittle gleamed at the corners of his mouth. "You mean church, Sergeant."

"I mean shul, Grossbart!"

---

[1] *shul* (shool): Yiddish for "synagogue."

I walked past him and went outside. Near me, I heard the scrunching of a guard's boots on gravel. Beyond the lighted windows of the barracks, young men in T shirts and fatigue pants were sitting on their bunks, polishing their rifles. Suddenly there was a light rustling behind me. I turned and saw Grossbart's dark frame fleeing back to the barracks, racing to tell his Jewish friends that they were right—that, like Karl and Harpo, I was one of them.

The next morning, while chatting with Captain Barrett, I recounted the incident of the previous evening. Somehow, in the telling, it must have seemed to the Captain that I was not so much explaining Grossbart's position as defending it. "Marx, I'd fight side by side with a nigger if the fella proved to me he was a man. I pride myself," he said, looking out the window, "that I've got an open mind. Consequently, Sergeant, nobody gets special treatment here, for the good *or* the bad. All a man's got to do is prove himself. A man fires well on the range, I give him a weekend pass. He scores high in P.T., he gets a weekend pass. He *earns* it." He turned from the window and pointed a finger at me. "You're a Jewish fella, am I right, Marx?"

"Yes, sir."

"And I admire you. I admire you because of the ribbons on your chest. I judge a man by what he shows me on the field of battle, Sergeant. It's what he's got *here*," he said, and then, though I expected he would point to his chest, he jerked a thumb toward the buttons straining to hold his blouse across his belly. "Guts," he said.

"O.K., sir. I only wanted to pass on to you how the men felt."

"Mr. Marx, you're going to be old before your time if you worry about how the men feel. Leave that stuff to the chaplain—that's his business, not yours. Let's us train these fellas to shoot straight. If the Jewish personnel feels the other men are accusing them of goldbricking—well, I just don't know. Seems awful funny that suddenly the Lord is calling so loud in Private Grossbart's ear he's just got to run to church."

"Synagogue," I said.

"Synagogue is right, Sergeant. I'll write that down for

handy reference. Thank you for stopping by."

That evening, a few minutes before the company gathered outside the orderly room for the chow formation, I called the C.Q., Corporal Robert LaHill, in to see me. LaHill was a dark, burly fellow whose hair curled out of his clothes wherever it could. He had a glaze in his eyes that made one think of caves and dinosaurs. "LaHill," I said, "when you take the formation, remind the men that they're free to attend church services *whenever* they are held, provided they report to the orderly room before they leave the area."

LaHill scratched his wrist, but gave no indication that he'd heard or understood.

"LaHill," I said, "*church*. You remember? Church, priest, Mass, confession."

He curled one lip into a kind of smile; I took it for a signal that for a second he had flickered back up into the human race.

"Jewish personnel who want to attend services this evening are to fall out in front of the orderly room at 1900," I said. Then, as an afterthought, I added, "By order of Captain Barrett."

A little while later, as the day's last light—softer than any I had seen that year—began to drop over Camp Crowder, I heard LaHill's thick, inflectionless voice outside my window: "Give me your ears, troopers. Toppie says for me to tell you that at 1900 hours all Jewish personnel is to fall out in front, here, if they want to attend the Jewish Mass."

At seven o'clock, I looked out the orderly-room window and saw three soldiers in starched khakis standing on the dusty quadrangle. They looked at their watches and fidgeted while they whispered back and forth. It was getting dimmer, and, alone on the otherwise deserted field, they looked tiny. When I opened the door, I heard the noises of the G.I. party coming from the surrounding barracks— bunks being pushed to the walls, faucets pounding water into buckets, brooms whisking at the wooden floors, cleaning the dirt away for Saturday's inspection. Big puffs of cloth moved round and round on the windowpanes. I walked outside, and the moment my foot hit the ground I thought I heard Grossbart call to the others, " 'Ten-*hut!*" Or maybe, when they all three jumped to attention, I imagined I heard the command.

Grossbart stepped forward. "Thank you, sir," he said.

" 'Sergeant,' Grossbart," I reminded him. "You call officers 'sir.' I'm not an officer. You've been in the Army three weeks—you know that."

He turned his palms out at his sides to indicate that, in truth, he and I lived beyond convention. "Thank you, anyway," he said.

"Yes," a tall boy behind him said. "Thanks a lot."

And the third boy whispered, "Thank you," but his mouth barely fluttered, so that he did not alter by more than a lip's movement his posture of attention.

"For what?" I asked.

Grossbart snorted happily. "For the announcement. The Corporal's announcement. It helped. It made it—"

"Fancier." The tall boy finished Grossbart's sentence.

Grossbart smiled. "He means formal, sir. Public," he said to me. "Now it won't seem as though we're just taking off—goldbricking because the work has begun."

"It was by order of Captain Barrett," I said.

"Aaah, but you pull a little weight," Grossbart said. "So we thank you." Then he turned to his companions. "Sergeant Marx, I want you to meet Larry Fishbein."

The tall boy stepped forward and extended his hand. I shook it. "You from New York?" he asked.

"Yes."

"Me, too." He had a cadaverous face that collapsed inward from his cheekbone to his jaw, and when he smiled— as he did at the news of our communal attachment—revealed a mouthful of bad teeth. He was blinking his eyes a good deal, as though he were fighting back tears. "What borough?" he asked.

I turned to Grossbart. "It's five after seven. What time are services?"

"Shul," he said, smiling, "is in ten minutes. I want you to meet Mickey Halpern. This is Nathan Marx, our sergeant."

The third boy hopped forward. "Private Michael Halpern." He saluted.

"Salute officers, Halpern," I said. The boy dropped his hand, and, on its way down, in his nervousness, checked to see if his shirt pockets were buttoned.

"Shall I march them over, sir?" Grossbart asked. "Or are you coming along?"

From behind Grossbart, Fishbein piped up. "Afterward, they're having refreshments. A ladies' auxiliary from St. Louis, the rabbi told us last week."

"The chaplain," Halpern whispered.

"You're welcome to come along," Grossbart said.

To avoid his plea, I looked away, and saw, in the windows of the barracks, a cloud of faces staring out at the four of us. "Hurry along, Grossbart," I said.

"O.K., then," he said. He turned to the others. "Double time, *march!*"

They started off, but ten feet away Grossbart spun around and, running backward, called to me, "Good *shabbus*,[2] sir!" And then the three of them were swallowed into the alien Missouri dusk.

Even after they had disappeared over the parade ground, whose green was now a deep blue, I could hear Grossbart singing the double-time cadence, and as it grew dimmer and dimmer, it suddenly touched a deep memory—as did the slant of the light—and I was remembering the shrill sounds of a Bronx playground where, years ago, beside the Grand Concourse, I had played on long spring evenings such as this. It was a pleasant memory for a young man so far from peace and home, and it brought so many recollections with it that I began to grow exceedingly tender about myself. In fact, I indulged myself in a reverie so strong that I felt as though a hand were reaching down inside me. It had to reach so very far to touch me! It had to reach past those days in the forests of Belgium, and past the dying I'd refused to weep over; past the nights in German farmhouses whose books we'd burned to warm us; past endless stretches when I had shut off all softness I

---

[2] *shabbus* (shä'bis): the Sabbath, which for Jews begins just before sunset on Friday and ends at sundown on Saturday.

might feel for my fellows, and had managed even to deny myself the posture of a conqueror—the swagger that I, as a Jew, might well have worn as my boots whacked against the rubble of Wesel, Münster, and Braunschweig.

But now one night noise, one rumor of home and time past, and memory plunged down through all I had anesthetized, and came to what I suddenly remembered was myself. So it was not altogether curious that, in search of more of me, I found myself following Grossbart's tracks to Chapel No. 3, where the Jewish services were being held.

I took a seat in the last row, which was empty. Two rows in front of me sat Grossbart, Fishbein, and Halpern, holding little white Dixie cups. Each row of seats was raised higher than the one in front of it, and I could see clearly what was going on. Fishbein was pouring the contents of his cup into Grossbart's, and Grossbart looked mirthful as the liquid made a purple arc between Fishbein's hand and his. In the glaring yellow light, I saw the chaplain standing on the platform at the front; he was chanting the first line of the responsive reading. Grossbart's prayer book remained closed on his lap; he was swishing the cup around. Only Halpern responded to the chant by praying. The fingers of his right hand were spread wide across the cover of his open book. His cap was pulled down low onto his brow, which made it round, like a yarmulke.[3] From time to time, Grossbart wet his lips at the cup's edge; Fishbein, his long yellow face a dying light bulb, looked from here to there, craning forward to catch sight of the faces down the row, then of those in front of him, then behind. He saw me, and his eyelids beat a tattoo. His elbow slid into Grossbart's side, his neck inclined toward his friend, he whispered something, and then, when the congregation next responded to the chant, Grossbart's voice was among the others. Fishbein looked into his book now, too; his lips, however, didn't move.

Finally, it was time to drink the wine. The chaplain smiled down at them as Grossbart swigged his in one long gulp, Halpern sipped, meditating, and Fishbein faked devotion with an empty cup. "As I look down amongst the con-

[3] *yarmulke* (yär′məl·kə): the skullcap worn by Jewish males while observing their religion.

gregation"—the chaplain grinned at the word—"this night, I see many new faces, and I want to welcome you to Friday-night services here at Camp Crowder. I am Major Leo Ben Ezra, your chaplain." Though an American, the chaplain spoke deliberately—syllable by syllable, almost—as though to communicate, above all, with the lip readers in his audience. "I have only a few words to say before we adjourn to the refreshment room, where the kind ladies of the Temple Sinai, St. Louis, Missouri, have a nice setting for you."

Applause and whistling broke out. After another momentary grin, the chaplain raised his hands, palms out, his eyes flicking upward a moment, as if to remind the troops where they were and Who Else might be in attendance. In the sudden silence that followed, I thought I heard Grossbart cackle, "Let the goyim [4] clean the floors!" Were those the words? I wasn't sure, but Fishbein, grinning, nudged Halpern. Halpern looked dumbly at him, then went back to his prayer book, which had been occupying him all through the rabbi's talk. One hand tugged at the black kinky hair that stuck out under his cap. His lips moved.

The rabbi continued. "It is about the food that I want to speak to you for a moment. I know, I know, I know," he intoned, wearily, "how in the mouths of most of you the trafe [5] food tastes like ashes. I know how you gag, some of you, and how your parents suffer to think of their children eating foods unclean and offensive to the palate. What can I tell you? I can only say, close your eyes and swallow as best you can. Eat what you must to live, and throw away the rest. I wish I could help more. For those of you who find this impossible, may I ask that you try and try, but then come to see me in private. If your revulsion is so great, we will have to seek aid from those higher up."

A round of chatter rose and subsided. Then everyone sang "Ain Kelohainu"; [6] after all those years, I discovered I still knew the words. Then, suddenly, the service over,

---

[4] goyim (goi'əm): gentiles (plural form of goy).

[5] trafe (trāf): not kosher; not permitted according to Jewish dietary laws.

[6] "Ain Kelohainu": "There is none like our God," a Hebrew song in which the congregation joins during Sabbath services.

Grossbart was upon me. "Higher up? He means the General?"

"Hey, Shelly," Fishbein said, "he means God." He smacked his face and looked at Halpern. "How high can you go!"

"Sh-h-h!" Grossbart said. "What do you think, Sergeant?"

"I don't know," I said. "You better ask the chaplain."

"I'm going to. I'm making an appointment to see him in private. So is Mickey."

Halpern shook his head. "No, no, Sheldon—"

"You have rights, Mickey," Grossbart said. "They can't push us around."

"It's O.K.," said Halpern. "It bothers my mother, not me."

Grossbart looked at me. "Yesterday he threw up. From the hash. It was all ham and God knows what else."

"I have a cold—that was why," Halpern said. He pushed his yarmulke back into a cap.

"What about you, Fishbein?" I asked. "You kosher, too?"

He flushed. "A little. But I'll let it ride. I have a very strong stomach, and I don't eat a lot anyway." I continued to look at him, and he held up his wrist to reinforce what he'd just said; his watch strap was tightened to the last hole, and he pointed that out to me.

"But services are important to you?" I asked him.

He looked at Grossbart. "Sure, sir."

" 'Sergeant.' "

"Not so much at home," said Grossbart, stepping between us, "but away from home it gives one a sense of his Jewishness."

"We have to stick together," Fishbein said.

I started to walk toward the door; Halpern stepped back to make way for me.

"That's what happened in Germany," Grossbart was saying, loud enough for me to hear. "They didn't stick together. They let themselves get pushed around."

I turned. "Look, Grossbart. This is the Army, not summer camp."

He smiled. "So?"

Halpern tried to sneak off, but Grossbart held his arm.

"Grossbart, how old are you?" I asked.

"Nineteen."

"And you?" I said to Fishbein.

"The same. The same month, even."

"And what about him?" I pointed to Halpern, who had by now made it safely to the door.

"Eighteen," Grossbart whispered. "But like he can't tie his shoes or brush his teeth himself. I feel sorry for him."

"I feel sorry for all of us, Grossbart," I said, "but just act like a man. Just don't overdo it."

"Overdo what, sir?"

"The 'sir' business, for one thing. Don't overdo that," I said.

I left him standing there. I passed by Halpern, but he did not look at me. Then I was outside, but, behind, I heard Grossbart call, "Hey, Mickey, my *leben*,[7] come on back. Refreshments!"

"*Leben!*" My grandmother's word for me!

One morning a week later, while I was working at my desk, Captain Barrett shouted for me to come into his office. When I entered, he had his helmet liner squashed down so far on his head that I couldn't even see his eyes. He was on the phone, and when he spoke to me, he cupped one hand over the mouthpiece. "Who the hell is Grossbart?"

"Third platoon, Captain," I said. "A trainee."

"What's all this stink about food? His mother called a damn congressman about the food." He uncovered the mouthpiece and slid his helmet up until I could see his bottom eyelashes. "Yes, sir," he said into the phone. "Yes, sir. I'm still here, sir. I'm asking Marx, here, right now—"

He covered the mouthpiece again and turned his head back toward me. "Lightfoot Harry's on the phone," he said, between his teeth. "This congressman calls General Lyman, who calls Colonel Sousa, who calls the Major, who calls me. They're just dying to stick this thing on me. Whatsa matter?" He shook the phone at me. "I don't feed the troops? What is this?"

---

[7] *leben* (lā′bən): Yiddish for "dear" or "darling."

"Sir, Grossbart is strange—" Barrett greeted that with a mockingly indulgent smile. I altered my approach. "Captain, he's a very orthodox Jew, and so he's only allowed to eat certain foods."

"He throws up, the congressman said. Every time he eats something, his mother says, he throws up!"

"He's accustomed to observing the dietary laws, Captain."

"So why's his old lady have to call the White House?"

"Jewish parents, sir—they're apt to be more protective than you expect. I mean, Jews have a very close family life. A boy goes away from home, sometimes the mother is liable to get very upset. Probably the boy mentioned something in a letter, and his mother misinterpreted."

"I'd like to punch him one right in the mouth," the Captain said. "There's a war on, and he wants a silver platter!"

"I don't think the boy's to blame, sir. I'm sure we can straighten it out by just asking him. Jewish parents worry—"

"*All* parents worry, dammit. But they don't get on their high horse and start pulling strings—"

I interrupted, my voice higher, tighter than before. "The home life, Captain, is very important—but you're right, it may sometimes get out of hand. It's a very wonderful thing, Captain, but because it's so close, this kind of thing . . . ."

He didn't listen any longer to my attempt to present both myself and Lightfoot Harry with an explanation for the letter. He turned back to the phone. "Sir?" he said. "Sir—Marx, here, tells me Jews have a tendency to be pushy. He says he thinks we can settle it right here in the company. . . . Yes, sir. . . . I *will* call back, sir, soon as I can." He hung up. "Where are the men, Sergeant?"

"On the range."

With a whack on the top of his helmet, he crushed it down over his eyes again, and charged out of his chair. "We're going for a ride," he said.

The Captain drove, and I sat beside him. It was a hot spring day, and under my newly starched fatigues I felt as though my armpits were melting down onto my sides and chest. The roads were dry, and by the time we reached the firing range, my teeth felt gritty with dust, though my mouth had been shut the whole trip. The Captain slammed the brakes on and told me to get the hell out and find Grossbart.

I found him on his belly, firing wildly at the five-hundred-feet target. Waiting their turns behind him were Halpern and Fishbein. Fishbein, wearing a pair of steel-rimmed G.I. glasses I hadn't seen on him before, had the appearance of an old peddler who would gladly have sold you his rifle and the cartridges that were slung all over him. I stood back by the ammo boxes, waiting for Grossbart to finish spraying the distant targets. Fishbein straggled back to stand near me.

"Hello, Sergeant Marx," he said.

"How are you?" I mumbled.

"Fine, thank you. Sheldon's really a good shot."

"I didn't notice."

"I'm not so good, but I think I'm getting the hang of it now. Sergeant, I don't mean to, you know, ask what I shouldn't—" The boy stopped. He was trying to speak intimately, but the noise of the shooting forced him to shout at me.

"What is it?" I asked. Down the range, I saw Captain Barrett standing up in the jeep, scanning the line for me and Grossbart.

"My parents keep asking and asking where we're going," Fishbein said. "Everybody says the Pacific. I don't care, but my parents—If I could relieve their minds, I think I could concentrate more on my shooting."

"I don't know where, Fishbein. Try to concentrate anyway."

"Sheldon says you might be able to find out."

"I don't know a thing, Fishbein. You just take it easy, and don't let Sheldon—"

"*I'm* taking it easy, Sergeant. It's at home—"

Grossbart had finished on the line, and was dusting his fatigues with one hand. I called to him. "Grossbart, the Captain wants to see you."

He came toward us. His eyes blazed and twinkled. "Hi!"

"Don't point that rifle!" I said.

"I wouldn't shoot you, Sarge." He gave me a smile as wide as a pumpkin, and turned the barrel aside.

"Damn you, Grossbart, this is no joke! Follow me."

I walked ahead of him, and had the awful suspicion that, behind me, Grossbart was *marching*, his rifle on his shoulder, as though he were a one-man detachment. At the jeep, he gave the Captain a rifle salute. "Private Sheldon Grossbart, sir."

"At ease, Grossman." The Captain sat down, slid over into the empty seat, and, crooking a finger, invited Grossbart closer.

"Bart, sir. Sheldon Gross*bart*. It's a common error." Grossbart nodded at me; *I* understood, he indicated. I looked away just as the mess truck pulled up to the range, disgorging a half-dozen K.P.s with rolled-up sleeves. The mess sergeant screamed at them while they set up the chow-line equipment.

"Grossbart, your mama wrote some congressman that we don't feed you right. Do you know that?" the Captain said.

"It was my father, sir. He wrote to Representative Franconi that my religion forbids me to eat certain foods."

"What religion is that, Grossbart?"

"Jewish."

" 'Jewish, *sir*,' " I said to Grossbart.

"Excuse me, sir. Jewish, sir."

"What have you been living on?" the Captain asked. "You've been in the Army a month already. You don't look to me like you're falling to pieces."

"I eat because I have to, sir. But Sergeant Marx will testify to the fact that I don't eat one mouthful more than I need to in order to survive."

"Is that so, Marx?" Barrett asked.

"I've never seen Grossbart eat, sir," I said.

"But you heard the rabbi," Grossbart said. "He told us what to do, and I listened."

The Captain looked at me. "Well, Marx?"

"I still don't know what he eats and doesn't eat, sir."

Grossbart raised his arms to plead with me, and it looked for a moment as though he were going to hand me his weapon to hold. "But, Sergeant—"

"Look, Grossbart, just answer the Captain's questions," I said sharply.

Barrett smiled at me, and I resented it. "All right, Grossbart," he said. "What is it you want? The little piece of paper? You want out?"

"No, sir. Only to be allowed to live as a Jew. And for the others, too."

"What others?"

"Fishbein, sir, and Halpern."

"They don't like the way we serve, either?"

"Halpern throws up, sir. I've seen it."

"I thought *you* throw up."

"Just once, sir. I didn't know the sausage was sausage."

"We'll give menus, Grossbart. We'll show training films about the food, so you can identify when we're trying to poison you."

Grossbart did not answer. The men had been organized into two long chow lines. At the tail end of one, I spotted Fishbein—or, rather, his glasses spotted me. They winked sunlight back at me. Halpern stood next to him, patting the inside of his collar with a khaki handkerchief. They moved with the line as it began to edge up toward the food. The mess sergeant was still screaming at the K.P.s. For a moment, I was actually terrified by the thought that somehow the mess sergeant was going to become involved in Grossbart's problem.

"Marx," the Captain said, "you're a Jewish fella—am I right?"

I played straight man. "Yes, sir."

"How long you been in the Army? Tell this boy."

"Three years and two months."

"A year in combat, Grossbart. Twelve damn months in combat all through Europe. I admire this man." The Captain snapped a wrist against my chest. "Do you hear him peeping about the food? Do you? I want an answer, Grossbart. Yes or no."

"No, sir."

"And why not? He's a Jewish fella."

"Some things are more important to some Jews than other things to other Jews."

Barrett blew up. "Look, Grossbart. Marx, here, is a good man—a damn hero. When you were in high school, Sergeant Marx was killing Germans. Who does more for the Jews—you, by throwing up over a lousy piece of sausage, a piece of first-cut meat, or Marx, by killing those Nazi bastards? If I was a Jew, Grossbart, I'd kiss this man's feet. He's a damn hero, and *he* eats what we give him. Why do you have to cause trouble is what I want to know! What is it you're buckin' for—a discharge?"

"No, sir."

"I'm talking to a wall! Sergeant, get him out of my way." Barrett swung himself back into the driver's seat. "I'm going to see the chaplain." The engine roared, the jeep spun around in a whirl of dust, and the Captain was headed back to camp.

For a moment, Grossbart and I stood side by side, watching the jeep. Then he looked at me and said, "I don't want to start trouble. That's the first thing they toss up to us."

When he spoke, I saw that his teeth were white and straight, and the sight of them suddenly made me understand that Grossbart actually did have parents—that once upon a time someone had taken little Sheldon to the dentist. He was their son. Despite all the talk about his parents, it was hard to believe in Grossbart as a child, an heir —as related by blood to anyone, mother, father, or, above all, to me. This realization led me to another.

"What does your father do, Grossbart?" I asked as we started to walk back toward the chow line.

"He's a tailor."

"An American?"

"Now, yes. A son in the Army," he said, jokingly.

"And your mother?" I asked.

He winked. "A *ballabusta*.[8] She practically sleeps with a dustcloth in her hand."

"She's also an immigrant?"

"All she talks is Yiddish, still."

"And your father, too?"

"A little English. 'Clean,' 'Press,' 'Take the pants in.'

---

[8] *ballabusta* (bal·ə·boos′tə): Yiddish for "an excellent housewife."

That's the extent of it. But they're good to me."

"Then, Grossbart—" I reached out and stopped him. He turned toward me, and when our eyes met, his seemed to jump back, to shiver in their sockets. "Grossbart—you were the one who wrote that letter, weren't you?"

It took only a second or two for his eyes to flash happy again. "Yes." He walked on, and I kept pace. "It's what my father *would* have written if he had known how. It was his name, though. *He* signed it. He even mailed it. I sent it home. For the New York postmark."

I was astonished, and he saw it. With complete seriousness, he thrust his right arm in front of me. "Blood is blood, Sergeant," he said, pinching the blue vein in his wrist.

"What the hell *are* you trying to do, Grossbart?" I asked. "I've seen you eat. Do you know that? I told the Captain I don't know what you eat, but I've seen you eat like a hound at chow."

"We work hard, Sergeant. We're in training. For a furnace to work, you've got to feed it coal."

"Why did you say in the letter that you threw up all the time?"

"I was really talking about Mickey there. I was talking *for* him. He would never write, Sergeant, though I pleaded with him. He'll waste away to nothing if I don't help. Sergeant, I used my name—my father's name—but it's Mickey, and Fishbein, too, I'm watching out for."

"You're a regular Messiah, aren't you?"

We were at the chow line now.

"That's a good one, Sergeant," he said, smiling. "But who knows? Who can tell? Maybe you're the Messiah— a little bit. What Mickey says is the Messiah is a collective idea. He went to Yeshiva,[9] Mickey, for a while. He says *together* we're the Messiah. Me a little bit, you a little bit. You should hear that kid talk, Sergeant, when he gets going."

---

[9] *Yeshiva* (yə·she′və): since antiquity, a kind of seminary dedicated to study of the compilations of Jewish law (the Talmud) and the rabbinic interpretations of the law. In modern America, the Yeshiva is more likely to be a Jewish parochial school in which both secular and religious subjects are taught.

"Me a little bit, you a little bit," I said. "You'd like to believe that, wouldn't you, Grossbart? That would make everything so clean for you."

"It doesn't seem too bad a thing to believe, Sergeant. It only means we should all *give* a little, is all."

I walked off to eat my rations with the other noncoms.

Two days later, a letter addressed to Captain Barrett passed over my desk. It had come through the chain of command—from the office of Congressman Franconi, where it had been received, to General Lyman, to Colonel Sousa, to Major Lamont, now to Captain Barrett. I read it over twice. It was dated May 14, the day Barrett had spoken with Grossbart on the rifle range.

> *Dear Congressman:*
>
> *First let me thank you for your interest in behalf of my son, Private Sheldon Grossbart. Fortunately, I was able to speak with Sheldon on the phone the other night, and I think I've been able to solve our problem. He is, as I mentioned in my last letter, a very religious boy, and it was only with the greatest difficulty that I could persuade him that the religious thing to do—what God Himself would want Sheldon to do—would be to suffer the pangs of religious remorse for the good of his country and all mankind. It took some doing, Congressman, but finally he saw the light. In fact, what he said (and I wrote down the words on a scratch pad so as never to forget), what he said was "I guess you're right, Dad. So many millions of my fellow-Jews gave up their lives to the enemy, the least I can do is live for a while minus a bit of my heritage so as to help end this struggle and regain for all the children of God dignity and humanity." That, Congressman, would make any father proud.*
>
> *By the way, Sheldon wanted me to know—and to pass on to you—the name of a soldier who helped him reach this decision: SERGEANT NATHAN MARX. Sergeant Marx is a combat veteran who is Sheldon's first sergeant. This man has helped Shel-*

*don over some of the first hurdles he's had to face
in the Army, and is in part responsible for Sheldon's
changing his mind about the dietary laws. I know
Sheldon would appreciate any recognition Marx
could receive.*

*Thank you and good luck. I look forward to see-
ing your name on the next election ballot.*

Respectfully,
Samuel E. Grossbart

Attached to the Grossbart communiqué was another,
addressed to General Marshall Lyman, the post commander, and signed by Representative Charles E. Franconi,
of the House of Representatives. The communiqué informed General Lyman that Sergeant Nathan Marx was a
credit to the U.S. Army and the Jewish people.

What was Grossbart's motive in recanting? Did he
feel he'd gone too far? Was the letter a strategic retreat—
a crafty attempt to strengthen what he considered our alli-
ance? Or had he actually changed his mind, via an imaginary dialogue between Grossbart *père* and Grossbart *fils*?
I was puzzled, but only for a few days—that is, only until
I realized that, whatever his reasons, he had actually decided to disappear from my life; he was going to allow himself to become just another trainee. I saw him at inspection, but he never winked; at chow formations, but he
never flashed me a sign. On Sundays, with the other trainees, he would sit around watching the noncoms' softball
team, for which I pitched, but not once did he speak an
unnecessary word to me. Fishbein and Halpern retreated,
too—at Grossbart's command, I was sure. Apparently he
had seen that wisdom lay in turning back before he plunged
over into the ugliness of privilege undeserved. Our separation allowed me to forgive him our past encounters, and,
finally, to admire him for his good sense.

Meanwhile, free of Grossbart, I grew used to my job
and my administrative tasks. I stepped on a scale one day,
and discovered I had truly become a noncombatant; I had
gained seven pounds. I found patience to get past the first
three pages of a book. I thought about the future more and

more, and wrote letters to girls I'd known before the war. I even got a few answers. I sent away to Columbia for a Law School catalogue. I continued to follow the war in the Pacific, but it was not my war. I thought I could see the end, and sometimes, at night, I dreamed that I was walking on the streets of Manhattan—Broadway, Third Avenue, 116th Street, where I had lived the three years I attended Columbia. I curled myself around these dreams and I began to be happy.

And then, one Sunday, when everybody was away and I was alone in the orderly room reading a month-old copy of the *Sporting News*, Grossbart reappeared.

"You a baseball fan, Sergeant?"

I looked up. "How are you?"

"Fine," Grossbart said. "They're making a soldier out of me."

"How are Fishbein and Halpern?"

"Coming along," he said. "We've got no training this afternoon. They're at the movies."

"How come you're not with them?"

"I wanted to come over and say hello."

He smiled—a shy, regular-guy smile, as though he and I well knew that our friendship drew its sustenance from unexpected visits, remembered birthdays, and borrowed lawnmowers. At first it offended me, and then the feeling was swallowed by the general uneasiness I felt at the thought that everyone on the post was locked away in a dark movie theater and I was here alone with Grossbart. I folded up my paper.

"Sergeant," he said, "I'd like to ask a favor. It is a favor, and I'm making no bones about it."

He stopped, allowing me to refuse him a hearing—which, of course, forced me into a courtesy I did not intend. "Go ahead."

"Well, actually it's two favors."

I said nothing.

"The first one's about these rumors. Everybody says we're going to the Pacific."

"As I told your friend Fishbein, I don't know," I said. "You'll just have to wait to find out. Like everybody else."

"You think there's a chance of any of us going East?"

"Germany?" I said. "Maybe."

"I meant New York."

"I don't think so, Grossbart. Offhand."

"Thanks for the information, Sergeant," he said.

"It's not information, Grossbart. Just what I surmise."

"It certainly would be good to be near home. My parents—you know." He took a step toward the door and then turned back. "Oh, the other thing. May I ask the other?"

"What is it?"

"The other thing is—I've got relatives in St. Louis, and they say they'll give me a whole Passover dinner if I can get down there. God, Sergeant, that'd mean an awful lot to me."

I stood up. "No passes during basic, Grossbart."

"But we're off from now till Monday morning, Sergeant. I could leave the post and no one would even know."

"I'd know. You'd know."

"But that's all. Just the two of us. Last night, I called my aunt, and you should have heard her. 'Come—come,' she said. 'I got gefilte fish, *chrain* [10]—the works!' Just a day, Sergeant. I'd take the blame if anything happened."

"The Captain isn't here to sign a pass."

"You could sign."

"Look, Grossbart—"

"Sergeant, for two months, practically, I've been eating *trafe* till I want to die."

"I thought you'd made up your mind to live with it. To be minus a little bit of heritage."

He pointed a finger at me. "You!" he said. "That wasn't for you to read."

"I read it. So what?"

"That letter was addressed to a congressman."

"Grossbart, don't feed me any baloney. You *wanted* me to read it."

"Why are you persecuting me, Sergeant?"

"Are you kidding!"

"I've run into this before," he said, "but never from my own!"

[10] *chrain* (khrān): Horseradish is usually served with the *gefilte* fish appetizer; but during the Passover supper, or Seder, it is ritually tasted to symbolize the bitterness of Jewish life under Egyptian bondage.

"Get out of here, Grossbart! Get the hell out of my sight!"

He did not move. "Ashamed, that's what you are," he said. "So you take it out on the rest of us. They say Hitler himself was half a Jew. Hearing you, I wouldn't doubt it."

"What are you trying to do with me, Grossbart?" I asked him. "What are you after? You want me to give you special privileges, to change the food, to find out about your orders, to give you weekend passes."

"You even talk like a goy!" Grossbart shook his fist. "Is this just a weekend pass I'm asking for? Is a Seder sacred, or not?"

Seder! It suddenly occurred to me that Passover had been celebrated weeks before. I said so.

"That's right," he replied. "Who says no? A month ago—and I was in the field eating hash! And now all I ask is a simple favor. A Jewish boy I thought would understand. My aunt's willing to go out of her way—to make a Seder a month later. . . ." He turned to go, mumbling.

"Come back here!" I called. He stopped and looked at me. "Grossbart, why can't you be like the rest? Why do you have to stick out like a sore thumb?"

"Because I'm a Jew, Sergeant. I *am* different. Better, maybe not. But different."

"This is a war, Grossbart. For the time being *be* the same."

"I refuse."

"What?"

"I refuse. I can't stop being me, that's all there is to it." Tears came to his eyes. "It's a hard thing to be a Jew. But now I understand what Mickey says—it's a harder thing to stay one." He raised a hand sadly toward me. "Look at *you.*"

"Stop crying!"

"Stop this, stop that, stop the other thing! *You* stop, Sergeant. Stop closing your heart to your own!" And, wiping his face with his sleeve, he ran out the door. "The least we can do for one another—the least . . . ."

An hour later, looking out of the window, I saw Grossbart headed across the field. He wore a pair of starched khakis and carried a little leather ditty bag. I went out into the heat of the day. It was quiet; not a soul was in sight except, over by the mess hall, four K.P.s sitting around a pan, sloped forward from their waists, gabbing and peeling potatoes in the sun.

"Grossbart!" I called.

He looked toward me and continued walking.

"Grossbart, get over here!"

He turned and came across the field. Finally, he stood before me.

"Where are you going?" I asked.

"St. Louis. I don't care."

"You'll get caught without a pass."

"So I'll get caught without a pass."

"You'll go to the stockade."

"I'm *in* the stockade." He made an about-face and headed off.

I let him go only a step or two. "Come back here," I said, and he followed me into the office, where I typed out a pass and signed the Captain's name, and my own initials after it.

He took the pass and then, a moment later, reached out and grabbed my hand. "Sergeant, you don't know how much this means to me."

"O.K.," I said. "Don't get in any trouble."

"I wish I could show you how much this means to me."

"Don't do me any favors. Don't write any more congressmen for citations."

He smiled. "You're right. I won't. But let me do something."

"Bring me a piece of that gefilte fish. Just get out of here."

"I will!" he said. "With a slice of carrot and a little horseradish. I won't forget."

"All right. Just show your pass at the gate. And don't tell *anybody*."

"I won't. It's a month late, but a good Yom Tov [11] to you."

"Good Yom Tov, Grossbart," I said.

---

[11] *Yom Tov* (yun′ tif): a holy day; "good Yom Tov" is the traditional Jewish holiday greeting. However, the greeting has come to be used at any celebration or festivity.

"You're a good Jew, Sergeant. You like to think you have a hard heart, but underneath you're a fine, decent man. I mean that."

Those last three words touched me more than any words from Grossbart's mouth had the right to. "All right, Grossbart," I said. "Now call me 'sir,' and get the hell out of here."

He ran out the door and was gone. I felt very pleased with myself; it was a great relief to stop fighting Grossbart, and it had cost me nothing. Barrett would never find out, and if he did, I could manage to invent some excuse. For a while, I sat at my desk, comfortable in my decision. Then the screen door flew back and Grossbart burst in again. "Sergeant!" he said. Behind him I saw Fishbein and Halpern, both in starched khakis, both carrying ditty bags like Grossbart's.

"Sergeant, I caught Mickey and Larry coming out of the movies. I almost missed them."

"Grossbart—did I say tell no one?" I said.

"But my aunt said I could bring friends. That I should, in fact."

"*I'm* the Sergeant, Grossbart—not your aunt!"

Grossbart looked at me in disbelief. He pulled Halpern up by his sleeve. "Mickey, tell the Sergeant what this would mean to you."

Halpern looked at me and, shrugging, said, "A lot."

Fishbein stepped forward without prompting. "This would mean a great deal to me and my parents, Sergeant Marx."

"No!" I shouted.

Grossbart was shaking his head. "Sergeant, I could see you denying me, but how you can deny Mickey, a Yeshiva boy—that's beyond me."

"I'm not denying Mickey anything," I said. "You just pushed a little too hard, Grossbart. *You* denied him."

"I'll give him my pass, then," Grossbart said, "I'll give him my aunt's address and a little note. At least let him go."

In a second, he had crammed the pass into Halpern's pants pocket. Halpern looked at me, and so did Fishbein. Grossbart was at the door, pushing it open. "Mickey, bring me a piece of gefilte fish, at least," he said, and then he was outside again.

The three of us looked at one another, and then I said, "Halpern, hand that pass over."

He took it from his pocket and gave it to me. Fishbein had now moved to the doorway, where he lingered. He stood there for a moment with his mouth slightly open, and then he pointed to himself. "And me?" he asked.

His utter ridiculousness exhausted me. I slumped down in my seat and felt pulses knocking at the back of my eyes. "Fishbein," I said, "you understand I'm not trying to deny you anything, don't you? If it was my Army, I'd serve gefilte fish in the mess hall. I'd sell *kugel* [12] in the PX, honest to God."

Halpern smiled.

"You understand, don't you, Halpern?"

"Yes, Sergeant."

"And you, Fishbein? I don't want enemies. I'm just like you—I want to serve my time and go home. I miss the same things you miss."

"Then, Sergeant," Fishbein said, "why don't you come, too?"

"Where?"

"To St. Louis. To Shelly's aunt. We'll have a regular Seder. Play hide-the-matzoh." [13] He gave me a broad, black-toothed smile.

I saw Grossbart again, on the other side of the screen.

"Pst!" He waved a piece of paper. "Mickey, here's the address. Tell her I couldn't get away."

Halpern did not move. He looked at me, and I saw the shrug moving up his arms into his shoulders again. I took the cover off my typewriter and made out passes for him and Fishbein. "Go," I said. "The three of you."

I thought Halpern was going to kiss my hand.

That afternoon, in a bar in Joplin, I drank beer and lis-

---

[12] *kugel* (ko͞o′gəl): a noodle or potato pudding.

[13] *hide-the-matzoh* (mät′sə): The Seder ritual prescribes that a piece of matzoh (unleavened bread) be broken at the beginning of the supper and set aside for dessert. It is now customary to make a game of this by hiding the matzoh, so that the children can later search for it. The one who finds it is given a prize.

tened with half an ear to the Cardinal game. I tried to look squarely at what I'd become involved in, and began to wonder if perhaps the struggle with Grossbart wasn't as much my fault as his. What was I that I had to *muster* generous feelings? Who was I to have been feeling so grudging, so tight-hearted? After all, I wasn't being asked to move the world. Had I a right, then, or a reason, to clamp down on Grossbart, when that meant clamping down on Halpern, too? And Fishbein—that ugly, agreeable soul? Out of the many recollections of my childhood that had tumbled over me these past few days I heard my grandmother's voice: "What are you making a *tsimmes*?" [14] It was what she would ask my mother when, say, I had cut myself while doing something I shouldn't have done, and her daughter was busy bawling me out. I needed a hug and a kiss, and my mother would moralize. But my grandmother knew—mercy overrides justice. I should have known it, too. Who was Nathan Marx to be such a penny pincher with kindness? Surely, I thought, the Messiah himself—if He should ever come—won't niggle over nickels and dimes. God willing, he'll hug and kiss.

The next day, while I was playing softball over on the parade ground, I decided to ask Bob Wright, who was non-com in charge of Classification and Assignment, where he thought our trainees would be sent when their cycle ended, in two weeks. I asked casually, between innings, and he said, "They're pushing them all into the Pacific. Shulman cut the orders on your boys the other day."

The news shocked me, as though I were the father of Halpern, Fishbein, and Grossbart.

That night, I was just sliding into sleep when someone tapped on my door. "Who is it?" I asked.

"Sheldon."

He opened the door and came in. For a moment, I felt his presence without being able to see him. "How was it?" I asked.

[14] *tsimmes* (tsim′əs): a stew or dessert requiring elaborate preparation over an extended period of time. *Making a tsimmes:* making more of something than is necessary; inflating matters out of all proportion.

He popped into sight in the near-darkness before me. "Great, Sergeant." Then he was sitting on the edge of the bed. I sat up.

"How about you?" he asked. "Have a nice weekend?"

"Yes."

"The others went to sleep." He took a deep, paternal breath. We sat silent for a while, and a homey feeling invaded my ugly little cubicle; the door was locked, the cat was out, the children were safely in bed.

"Sergeant, can I tell you something? Personal?"

I did not answer, and he seemed to know why. "Not about me. About Mickey. Sergeant, I never felt for anybody like I feel for him. Last night I heard Mickey in the bed next to me. He was crying so, it could have broken your heart. Real sobs."

"I'm sorry to hear that."

"I had to talk to him to stop him. He held my hand, Sergeant—he wouldn't let it go. He was almost hysterical. He kept saying if he only knew where we were going. Even if he knew it *was* the Pacific, that would be better than nothing. Just to know."

Long ago, someone had taught Grossbart the sad rule that only lies can get the truth. Not that I couldn't believe in the fact of Halpern's crying; his eyes *always* seemed red-rimmed. But, fact or not, it became a lie when Grossbart uttered it. He was entirely strategic. But then—it came with the force of indictment—so was I! There are strategies of aggression, but there are strategies of retreat as well. And so, recognizing that I myself had not been without craft and guile, I told him what I knew. "It is the Pacific."

He let out a small gasp, which was not a lie. "I'll tell him. I wish it was otherwise."

"So do I."

He jumped on my words. "You mean you think you could do something? A change, maybe?"

"No, I couldn't do a thing."

"Don't you know anybody over at C. and A.?"

"Grossbart, there's nothing I can do," I said. "If your orders are for the Pacific, then it's the Pacific."

"But Mickey—"

"Mickey, you, me—everybody, Grossbart. There's nothing to be done. Maybe the war'll end before you go. Pray for a miracle."

"But—"

"Good night, Grossbart." I settled back, and was relieved to feel the springs unbend as Grossbart rose to leave. I could see him clearly now; his jaw had dropped, and he looked like a dazed prizefighter. I noticed for the first time a little paper bag in his hand.

"Grossbart." I smiled. "My gift?"

"Oh, yes, Sergeant. Here—from all of us." He handed me the bag. "It's egg roll."

"Egg roll?" I accepted the bag and felt a damp grease spot on the bottom. I opened it, sure that Grossbart was joking.

"We thought you'd probably like it. You know—Chinese egg roll. We thought you'd probably have a taste for—"

"Your aunt served egg roll?"

"She wasn't home."

"Grossbart, she invited you. You told me she invited you and your friends."

"I know," he said. "I just reread the letter. *Next* week."

I got out of bed and walked to the window. "Grossbart," I said. But I was not calling to him.

"What?"

"What are you, Grossbart? Honest to God, what are you?"

I think it was the first time I'd asked him a question for which he didn't have an immediate answer.

"How can you do this to people?" I went on.

"Sergeant, the day away did us all a world of good. Fishbein, you should see him, he *loves* Chinese food."

"But the Seder," I said.

"We took second best, Sergeant."

Rage came charging at me. I didn't sidestep. "Grossbart, you're a liar!" I said. "You're a schemer and a crook. You've got no respect for anything. Nothing at all. Not for me, for the truth—not even for poor Halpern! You use us all—"

"Sergeant, Sergeant, I feel for Mickey. Honest to God, I do. I *love* Mickey. I try—"

"You try! You feel!" I lurched toward him and grabbed his shirt front. I shook him furiously. "Grossbart, get out! Get out and stay the hell away from me. Because if I see you, I'll make your life miserable. *You understand that?*"

"Yes."

I let him free, and when he walked from the room, I wanted to spit on the floor where he had stood. I couldn't stop the fury. It engulfed me, owned me, till it seemed I could only rid myself of it with tears or an act of violence. I snatched from the bed the bag Grossbart had given me and, with all my strength, threw it out the window. And the next morning, as the men policed the area around the barracks, I heard a great cry go up from one of the trainees, who had been anticipating only his morning handful of cigarette butts and candy wrappers. "Egg roll!" he shouted. "Holy mackerel, Chinese egg roll!"

A week later, when I read the orders that had come down from C. and A., I couldn't believe my eyes. Every single trainee was to be shipped to Camp Stoneman, California, and from there to the Pacific—every trainee but one. Private Sheldon Grossbart. He was to be sent to Fort Monmouth, New Jersey. I read the mimeographed sheet several times. Dee, Farrell, Fishbein, Fuselli, Fylypowycz, Glinicki, Gromke, Gucwa, Halpern, Hardy, Helebrandt, right down to Anton Zygadlo—all were to be headed West before the month was out. All except Grossbart. He had pulled a string, and I wasn't it.

I lifted the phone and called C. and A.

The voice on the other end said smartly, "Corporal Shulman, sir."

"Let me speak to Sergeant Wright."

"Who is this calling, sir?"

"Sergeant Marx."

And, to my surprise, the voice said, "*Oh!*" Then, "Just a minute, Sergeant."

Shulman's "*Oh!*" stayed with me while I waited for Wright to come to the phone. Why "*Oh!*"? Who was Shulman? And then, so simply, I knew I'd discovered the string that Grossbart had pulled. In fact, I could hear Grossbart the day he'd discovered Shulman in the PX, or in the bowling alley, or maybe even at services. "Glad to meet you. Where you from? Bronx? Me, too. Do you know So-and-So? And So-and-So? Me, too! You work at C. and A.? Really? Hey, how's chances of getting East? Could you do something? Change something? Swindle, cheat, lie? We gotta help each other, you know. If the Jews in Germany . . ."

Bob Wright answered the phone. "How are you, Nate? How's the pitching arm?"

"Good. Bob, I wonder if you could do me a favor." I heard clearly my own words, and they so reminded me of Grossbart that I dropped more easily than I could have imagined into what I had planned. "This may sound crazy, Bob, but I got a kid here on orders to Monmouth who wants them changed. He had a brother killed in Europe, and he's hot to go to the Pacific. Says he'd feel like a coward if he wound up Stateside. I don't know, Bob—can anything be done? Put somebody else in the Monmouth slot?"

"Who?" he asked cagily.

"Anybody. First guy in the alphabet. I don't care. The kid just asked if something could be done."

"What's his name?"

"Grossbart, Sheldon."

Wright didn't answer.

"Yeah," I said. "He's a Jewish kid, so he thought I could help him out. You know."

"I guess I can do something," he finally said. "The Major hasn't been around here for weeks. Temporary duty to the golf course. I'll try, Nate, that's all I can say."

"I'd appreciate it, Bob. See you Sunday." And I hung up, perspiring.

The following day, the corrected orders appeared: Fishbein, Fuselli, Fylypowycz, Glinicki, Gromke, Grossbart, Gucwa, Halpern, Hardy . . . . Lucky Private Harley Alton was to go to Fort Monmouth, New Jersey, where, for some reason or other, they wanted an enlisted man with infantry training.

After chow that night, I stopped back at the orderly room to straighten out the guard-duty roster. Grossbart was waiting for me. He spoke first.

"You son of a bitch!"

I sat down at my desk, and while he glared at me, I began to make the necessary alterations in the duty roster.

"What do you have against me?" he cried. "Against my family? Would it kill you for me to be near my father, God knows how many months he has left to him?"

"Why so?"

"His heart," Grossbart said. "He hasn't had enough troubles in a lifetime, you've got to add to them. I curse the day I ever met you, Marx! Shulman told me what happened over there. There's no limit to your anti-Semitism, is there? The damage you've done here isn't enough. You have to make a special phone call! You really want me dead!"

I made the last few notations in the duty roster and got up to leave. "Good night, Grossbart."

"You owe me an explanation!" He stood in my path.

"Sheldon, you're the one who owes explanations."

He scowled. "To *you?*"

"To me, I think so—yes. Mostly to Fishbein and Halpern."

"That's right, twist things around. I owe nobody nothing, I've done all I could do for them. Now I think I've got the right to watch out for myself."

"For each other we have to learn to watch out, Sheldon. You told me yourself."

"You call this watching out for me—what you did?"

"No. For all of us."

I pushed him aside and started for the door. I heard his furious breathing behind me, and it sounded like steam rushing from an engine of terrible strength.

"*You'll* be all right," I said from the door. And, I thought, so would Fishbein and Halpern be all right, even in the Pacific, if only Grossbart continued to see—in the obsequiousness of the one, the soft spirituality of the other —some profit for himself.

I stood outside the orderly room, and I heard Grossbart weeping behind me. Over in the barracks, in the lighted windows, I could see the boys in their T shirts sitting on their bunks talking about their orders, as they'd been doing for the past two days. With a kind of quiet nervousness, they polished shoes, shined belt buckles, squared away underwear, trying as best they could to accept their fate. Behind me, Grossbart swallowed hard, accepting his. And then, resisting with all my will an impulse to turn and seek pardon for my vindictiveness, I accepted my own.

for discussion

1. List several possible meanings of the title of this story. Does the title refer to Nathan Marx or to Sheldon Grossbart? Or are they both "defenders of the faith"? In which of its meanings is the title an ironic one?

2. What claim on Sergeant Marx does Private Grossbart subtly establish during their first meeting? In what way does Marx's conversation with Captain Barrett the next morning add another dimension to Marx's dilemma?

3. How does Grossbart's comment on the meaning of the Messiah (pp. 441–2) serve to reveal his conception of religion? What other details in the story illustrate this "modern" conception of religious faith?

4. Is Marx's final action consistent with his earlier statement (p. 450) that "a hug and a kiss" are more fundamental than moral instruction, that "mercy overrides justice"? If Sergeant Marx is the "defender of the faith," what is the faith that he is defending?

born 1933
HUGH NISSENSON

☐ *Hugh Nissenson was born in New York City in 1933. He attended a private school and went on to Swarthmore College, from which he graduated with honors in 1955. He spent a year at Stanford University in 1961 as a Stegner Literary Fellow. Nissenson's stories and articles have been published in* Harper's, Commentary, Holiday, *and other national periodicals. His first book, a collection of stories*

titled A Pile of Stones, *appeared in 1965. It won the
Wallant Award as the best book of Jewish-American
significance published that year. Since 1958 Nissenson has
made several extended visits to Israel. His second book,*
Notes from the Frontier (1968), *is a first-hand report of
life in a kibbutz (a collective farm community) on Israel's
Syrian border.*

*As both a writer of fiction and a reporter, Nissenson is
in search of the meaning of Jewish identity in the
aftermath of an unprecedented destruction and
displacement of the world's Jewish population. The
holocaust in which six million Jews were allowed to perish
is the chief historical fact underlying virtually everything
he has written. The mass murder of European Jews now
stands like a wall that forever divides some Jews from
their religious traditions while it inspires others to see
over it or to turn around and find their traditions
elsewhere than in the past. Thus, Nissenson's stories do
not presuppose the old belief in the fundamental unity of
Jews that informed—sometimes sentimentally—the work
of Jewish writers in the past and that continues to mark
the work of nearly all of Nissenson's contemporaries.*

*Nissenson presents a strikingly varied portrait of
Jewishness: Jews from America, Europe, Israel, and Africa;
worldly, rationalistic Jews who know what they don't
believe and ethereal, intuitive Jews who have discovered
what they can believe. As the critic Robert Alter puts it,
Nissenson's stories "reach out for Jewish experience . . .
in an effort to discover what Jews do with their faith in a
God who so often seems conspicuous by his absence."
Nissenson is governed only by his desire to understand
what is actually happening as he explores the survivals of
Jewish faith, on the one hand, and the signs of its
disappearance, on the other.*

A pile of stones

"Dear Milton," Nina writes.

"We had a tragedy a day or so after the card I sent you. Bill was drowned. He hadn't swum in the ocean for such a long time, he couldn't resist that treacherous water. The undertow knocked him off his feet, and up against some rocks. I know that you will be greatly saddened by the news.

"I am with his family in Greenwich for a few days. Then I will go back to my parents in New Canaan for the rest of the summer. After that, I'm not sure what I will do. Perhaps come to New York, and get my M.S. at the Columbia University School of Social Work. But I'm still terribly shocked. I just wanted to let you know, for I know that you loved him. . . ."

I can't find the card. It was mailed about a week ago, from Bar Harbor, where they had gone to spend the first two weeks of July. According to Bill's last letter, written to me at the beginning of May, they were going on vacation to celebrate his promotion. He had just been made a full partner in his father's law firm in Stamford, in charge of all the corporate litigation. It was his special interest when I knew him at Yale Law School. And he was good at it. Not brilliant, but hard-working, with something of a reputation on campus for being a grind.

It's one of the ways I remember him best: at two o'clock in the morning, with his stockinged feet up on his desk, and a copy of *Wigmore on Evidence* open in his lap, alternately taking a deep drag from his cigarette and scribbling a note on the pad of lined yellow paper fixed to the steel clipboard he always carried with him to class.

As far as I know, the only outside interest he had was a religious study group he had organized with five or six divinity students and two undergraduates who met twice a month, on Sundays, after morning services at a local Presbyterian church. Church-going for its own sake didn't particularly compel him. Sometimes he went, and sometimes he didn't. He never missed a meeting of the study group, though, and in the week before it met spent most of his spare time reading religious books. He pored through Tillich and Niebuhr, somebody or other by the name of Bonhoeffer,[1] and, just after Thanksgiving, a writer, he said, who ought to interest me very much.

"Who's that?" I wanted to know.

"Martin Buber.[2] We're having a discussion next Sunday on his interpretation of Hassidism.[3] What's the matter? He's a great Jewish thinker. You ought to be very proud."

He showed me the photo of the bearded old man on the cover of the paperback edition of his *Tales of the Hassidim.*

"He looks like my grandfather."

---

[1] *Tillich . . . Bonhoeffer:* Paul Tillich (1886–1965), Reinhold Niebuhr (1892–1971), and Dietrich Bonhoeffer (1906–1945) were among the most liberal and fervent voices of the new Protestant theology in the years between the two World Wars. Bonhoeffer, who was executed in a Nazi concentration camp, is regarded by many as a modern saint. Deeply pious scholars who closely scrutinized the world around them, they were leaders of the effort to modify the teachings and the organization of the Protestant churches so as to better meet the spiritual problems of a rationalistic industrial society. They demonstrated to a skeptical world that faith is dependent upon neither miracles nor church authority, that faith may be gained undramatically through one's ordinary experiences.

[2] *Martin Buber:* Jewish philosopher and theologian (1878–1965), who believed that faith grows out of a man's sense of community with other men and is based ultimately upon one's unqualified trust in his personal relation to God.

[3] *Hassidism:* a movement inspired by mystical faith that swept through many Eastern European Jewish communities during the eighteenth and nineteenth centuries. It opposed the traditional Jewish emphasis on exhaustive religious study, and sought instead to find God outside of the synagogue, in nature, and in one's own heart. It exalted simple faith, joyous worship through dancing and singing, and spontaneous prayer over the formal ritual and habitual responses practiced in the synagogue. It proposed a relation to God that was intimate, happy, and within the reach of any man, however poor and ignorant.

"Then why don't you come on Sunday?" Bill said. "All we do is have brunch and sit around and talk. It's very informal. You might enjoy it."

"I'd like to, really, but I can't. I won't be here. I've got a date in New York on Saturday night."

He never asked me to a meeting again. But Buber and Hassidism! It was all I heard from him. He typed over his favorite Hassidic story and thumbtacked it to the wall over his desk.

"Well, what do you think?" he demanded, when I had read it through twice.

"It's very interesting. Very nicely written. Nice and concise."

"But a lot of crap as far as you're concerned."

"No, I wouldn't go so far as to say that."

"Then what?" he insisted.

"Well, for one thing, you have to believe that prayer works."

"And you don't."

"To tell you the truth, I never think about it. I haven't prayed since I was a kid."

"What happened?"

"I grew up."

He grinned—"touché"—and lit a cigarette, blowing the smoke from his nose, while I read the story once again. I can't remember the exact words. It was the one explaining the biblical injunction against using a metal tool to shape a sacrificial altar. The point being that God more often responds to a rough heaping up of stones; that is to say, a spontaneous, unpremeditated cry from the heart.

"Did you ever study any Hebrew?" he asked me, sitting down on the bed.

"Some. For my Bar Mitzvah,[4] when I was a kid."

"Can you read that?" He pointed to the Yale motto emblazoned on the back of the rocking chair he had bought when he was an undergraduate, and still kept in his room.

---

[4] *Bar Mitzvah* (bär mits′və): The ceremony that signifies a thirteen-year-old Jewish boy's arrival at the status of manhood.

"No. Let me see. How do you like that? I don't think I ever noticed it was in Hebrew before."

"It was once a required language here, you know."

"I had no idea."

"Oh yes. And not just for divinity students, either, but for all the undergraduates, along with Latin and Greek. My great-great-grandfather learned his Hebrew at Yale."

"What did he do with it after he graduated?"

"Prayed in it."

"A Presbyterian?"

"You'd be surprised. He came from Vermont, and at that time, in New England, it wasn't that unusual."

"Well, if I could, I'd put in a good word for you myself."

"Yes," he laughed. "It wouldn't do any harm."

And so it went, our whole final year, when we were rooming opposite each other, in Sterling, on the third floor. When Spring vacation came, and I was packing to leave for New York, he wanted to know if my parents were going to celebrate the Passover the following week.

"No. Well, yes, in a way," I said. "We generally have a family get-together, but no religious service, or anything like that. A big dinner."

"And your mother makes gefüllte fish."

"No, Pearl."

"Who's that?"

"The colored maid."

He burst out laughing, and then looked at his watch. "What time does your train leave?"

"Six-fifteen."

"You've got a couple of hours. Why don't you come over to Payne Whitney with me and take a swim. The exercise will do you good."

He was beginning to put on a little weight around his middle, and generally worked out once or twice a week to keep in shape. While I took a quick dip and dried off, he swam his usual twenty laps, and came up the ladder at the deep end of the pool, gasping for breath.

"I want to apologize," he said, jumping up and down

on one foot to get the water out of his ears.

"For what?"

"For asking so many questions."

"Forget it."

We got dressed and strolled back to the dorm. "It's hard for me to explain," he went on, as I opened the door to my room. "It's just that ever since I was a kid, He's been very real to me as a Jew. I mean as an actual Jew who once lived. . . . Have you ever read the *Spiritual Exercises of Ignatius Loyola?*" [5]

"No."

"It's not important." He sat down while I finished packing. "When I was ten or twelve, there was only one Jewish family living in town, or one religious Jewish family. An old man who owned a clothing store, who wore a long black beard, and what-do-you-call-them? You know what I mean. The long curls. . . ."

"*Payis.*"

"Yes, that's the word. The curls tucked behind the ears. I can't even remember his name. He and his wife lived in one of the red-brick houses near the railroad station, on Old Steamboat Road. They never had any kids." He paused for a moment, thinking. "Goldfarb! That was his name! 'A Jew, a real live Jew' was all I could think whenever I saw him. Not so much like Him, perhaps, but maybe Joseph. Yes, why not? It was entirely possible that Joseph looked something like that when he was an old man, with that black skull-cap and scraggly beard. And from there, of course, almost without thinking, it was easier to picture the Son when I prayed. Younger, of course, much younger, and maybe taller and thinner, but with the same bushy eyebrows, and the three furrows on His forehead that made a 'V' when he frowned. You know the way kids are. The kind of pictorial imagination they have. And it was much easier for me to pray with some sort of real picture before

---

[5] *Spiritual Exercises of Ignatius Loyola:* a series of meditations composed by St. Ignatius of Loyola between 1521 and 1548. It was written as a methodical guide for spiritual teachers who wished to assist individuals seeking knowledge of the soul through the making of a "retreat" and the discipline of prayer.

me. Then too, in a certain way, I was right. What I mean to say is, He was human too. That's the mystery of the thing. . . ."

What puzzled me, of course, was why he hadn't gone to Divinity School to begin with, and become a pro.

"That's exactly why," he explained one afternoon, about a month before graduation, when I had gone into his room to borrow some of his class notes.

"I don't understand."

"A professional!" He grimaced. "How can anyone presume to be able to inspire a bunch of people at, say, ten o'clock sharp every Sunday morning for the rest of your life? And particularly if you're getting paid to do it? Hell, no. That's why Buber's anomism is so significant. I'd rather be an ordinary lawyer who only goes to church when he really feels the need."

"What's anomism?" I asked.

"Well, roughly, that it doesn't make so much difference what you do, but how it's done. In what spirit. When you pray, for instance. . . ." But he caught the expression on my face, and let it go at that. "Never mind. It's getting late. What was it you wanted?"

"Yesterday's class notes on *Bennedict versus Ratner.*"

The rays of the late afternoon sun, vibrating with dust, and turning an orange-red, streamed through the slats in the venetian blinds and struck him in the eyes. He raised his hands in front of his face. "On the clipboard. No, to your left, under the manila folder, on the desk. I haven't finished typing them up. . . ."

But I'm almost finished with his story. The trouble is that in reading over what I've written so far—and I've tried to get it all down as accurately as I can—nothing he said makes much more sense to me now than it did then. Nor would it to Nina, either, which just doesn't seem fair. They met after graduation, at a party that following October, to be exact, given by Bill's parents to celebrate his passing the Connecticut Bar Exams. If I remember correctly, her father is a judge. In any case, she was a Sarah Lawrence graduate, a Psych major, who had been brought up as a Congregationalist. The first time that we were introduced, she told me that the only interest she had in religion was in getting Bill to walk down the aisle of a church. He laughed, and gave her a kiss on the mouth. This was after they had been going steady for a couple of months. They came down to New York on a Saturday night, just before Christmas, to go to the theater, and I met them for drinks at the old Sherry-Netherland bar.

"You two ought to get along very well," he said, waving at the waiter for another round.

"I can see it," I told him.

"He's crazy, of course," Nina said to me. "Stark raving mad."

"Of course," I nodded.

"He isn't, though," she added after a pause, with an exaggerated scowl. "That's the problem. He's completely sane. It's very disconcerting. According to the best authorities, a religious maniac ought to have an absolutely rampant Oedipus complex, a desperate need to placate the father. But he doesn't. Not a sign of it. I was absolutely brilliant in abnormal psychology, and I ought to know."

Bill laughed again. The waiter put down three more bourbon and waters. "Of course," she continued, "I'll grant you that I'm not exactly an objective judge of his condition. As far as I can see..." Bill put his hand on her arm.

"Merry Christmas," he said, leaning across the table, and kissing her again. "Merry Christmas, Milt."

"Merry Christmas," I said, raising my glass.

"No. Now there's another thing," said Nina, but the pianist to our right, a fairy with wavy blond hair, began to play "Silent Night" and drowned her out.

The coming June, they were married at the New Canaan Congregational Church. For the next two years, Bill and I kept in touch by mail. I've saved all of his letters. The sprawling handwriting and huge margins on the left side of the page remind me of his class notes.

"... It's lovely," he wrote, just after his father had bought them a home in Greenwich, on Old Bedford Road.

"A converted ice-house, on four and a half acres of land, with a pond and an apple orchard. Nina makes sour applesauce. Milt, I never would have believed it was possible to be so happy. It's a little scary, to tell you the truth. I wonder why? I must ask Nina what Freud would say about that. Right now, she's washing her hair. Tomorrow is Sunday, but I shall sleep late and miss church. No matter. Sometimes I pray here. At night, particularly, when she's asleep. She sleeps on her back, with her hands above her head, the fists clenched. Last night, I woke up, and looked at her, and thought, 'God above, what more can a man want? Just let it go on and on, and when it comes time for it to end, let me be the first one to go. Take me....'"

Etc., etc., dated August 10, 1961. Eleven months later, he was dead.

for discussion

1. A story contains a kind of dramatic irony when a speaker's statements convey a different picture of him than the one he has of himself. At which points in the story do Milton's statements suggest deficiencies in him that he does not himself recognize? Is there, for example, any irony in the fact that Bill is more familiar with Hebrew than Milton is (p. 460), that Milton can only conceive of religion as the concern of a "pro" (p. 463)?

2. What are the principles of Bill's "religion"? Is there evidence in the story that his faith is a highly ecumenical one?

3. Although Milton is a Jew and Nina a Congregationalist, they are represented as similar types. Through what correspondences of outlook and behavior is their similarity established?

born 1917

J. F. POWERS

☐ James F. Powers was born in 1917 in Jacksonville,
Illinois. During his boyhood he lived in two other small
Illinois towns, where he attended public schools first and
then a Catholic academy. But in 1935, the year of his high
school graduation, he moved to Chicago, and found a
variety of unsteady Depression-times jobs. From 1938 to
1941 Powers took night classes at the Chicago branch of
Northwestern University. And in 1943 his first story was
printed in Accent, a "little magazine" published at the
University of Illinois. Powers gained his first real
recognition when his second story, also printed in Accent,
was included in both the Martha Foley and the O. Henry
1944 selections of the year's best short stories. Later his
stories were printed in The New Yorker, Partisan Review,
and Kenyon Review.

The first volume of Powers's short stories, Prince of
Darkness, was published in 1947. A second collection,
The Presence of Grace, appeared in 1956. In 1962 he
completed Morte d'Urban, the novel upon which he had
labored for more than three years and which grew out of
his Church stories written during the preceding decade.
Morte d'Urban won the National Book Award in 1963.
Since 1944 Powers has lived in Minnesota, except for
several years of intermittent residence in Ireland and brief
teaching stints at Marquette University, the University of
Michigan, and Smith College.

Powers's life affords him abundant knowledge of those
Catholics who belong to the American middle classes and
dwell in the Midwest's medium-sized cities. He possesses
an exceptionally sure grasp of rectory life and Church
administration, down to the most intimate qualities of
priestly thought and conduct in the flat, desolate setting
of America's upper plains. Other Irish-American writers
have turned similar experience into literature, but none
has done so as richly and profoundly. And no other Irish

466 PART 3 ETHNIC WRITING COMES OF AGE

Catholic writer in America has achieved Powers's degree of artistry. His Midwestern Catholics are so precisely etched that they dispel the stereotyped notions— unwavering loyalty to the "old sod" and reflex obedience to the Church—which have been commonly employed by other Irish-American writers. With unsparing truthfulness, Powers's ironic vision assesses the disparities between the behavior of his characters and their vows. Showing them as they are, in their full humanity, he is better able to penetrate the blandly ever-present materialism that has corroded and trivialized the national style of life which these characters reflect. And both the smaller and the larger society become Powers's metaphors for the daily commands of the flesh that wear down the Church's ministry to the world. They also serve as his metaphors for the doubt and suffering that illuminate men by revealing to them glimpses of spiritual grace.

Some of Powers's clergy and parishioners are so mastered by their needs to consume, to own, and to dominate that their spiritual sight is entirely obscured. Others fail to see beyond the literal meaning of Christian love and charity, so that their "good works" are self-interestedly performed in the wrong spirit and for the wrong reasons. These characters are the objects of Powers's quietly understated satire, which is sometimes bleakly savage but more often warmed by compassion and humor. The faith demonstrated by Powers's characters seems to burn rather feebly. But they are shown to inhabit a world in which duty and love persist— with divinity still there, hovering just out of sight.

the forks

☐ That summer when Father Eudex got back from saying Mass at the orphanage in the morning, he would park Monsignor's car, which was long and black and new like a politician's, and sit down in the cool of the porch to read his office.[1] If Monsignor was not already standing in the door, he would immediately appear there, seeing that his car had safely returned, and inquire:

"Did you have any trouble with her?"

Father Eudex knew too well the question meant, Did you mistreat my car?

"No trouble, Monsignor."

"Good," Monsignor said, with imperfect faith in his curate, who was not a car owner. For a moment Monsignor stood framed in the screen door, fumbling his watch fob as for a full-length portrait, and then he was suddenly not there.

"Monsignor," Father Eudex said, rising nervously, "I've got a chance to pick up a car."

At the door Monsignor slid into his frame again. His face expressed what was for him intense interest.

"Yes? Go on."

"I don't want to have to use yours every morning."

"It's all right."

"And there are other times." Father Eudex decided not to be maudlin and mention sick calls, nor be entirely honest and admit he was tired of busses and bumming rides from parishioners. "And now I've got a chance to get one—cheap."

Monsignor, smiling, came alert at *cheap*.

[1] *to read his office:* The Divine Office is the Church service for public devotions. It contains psalms; hymns; readings from the Bible, the Church fathers, and saints' lives; and prayers. The Office assembles these into the prescribed forms of public worship for each day of the year. For individual convenience, parts of the Office or shortened forms have been gathered into small books called breviaries.

"New?"

"No, I wouldn't say it's new."

Monsignor was openly suspicious now. "What kind?"

"It's a Ford."

"And not new?"

"Not new, Monsignor—but in good condition. It was owned by a retired farmer and had good care."

Monsignor sniffed. He *knew* cars. "V-Eight, Father?"

"No," Father Eudex confessed. "It's a Model A."

Monsignor chuckled as though this were indeed the damnedest thing he had ever heard.

"But in very good condition, Monsignor."

"You said that."

"Yes. And I could take it apart if anything went wrong. My uncle had one."

"No doubt." Monsignor uttered a laugh at Father Eudex's rural origins. Then he delivered the final word, long delayed out of amusement. "It wouldn't be prudent, Father. After all, this isn't a country parish. You know the class of people we get here."

Monsignor put on his Panama hat. Then, apparently mistaking the obstinacy in his curate's face for plain ignorance, he shed a little more light. "People watch a priest, Father. *Damnant quod non intelligunt.*[2] It would never do. You'll have to watch your tendencies."

Monsignor's eyes tripped and fell hard on the morning paper lying on the swing where he had finished it.

"Another flattering piece about that crazy fellow.... There's a man who might have gone places if it weren't for his mouth! A bishop doesn't have to get mixed up in all that stuff!"[3]

Monsignor, as Father Eudex knew, meant unions, strikes, race riots—all that stuff.

"A parishioner was saying to me only yesterday it's

---

[2] *Damnant ... intelligunt:* Latin for "They condemn what they do not understand."

[3] *A bishop ... stuff:* a reference to the Most Reverend Bernard J. Sheil (1888–1969), senior auxiliary bishop of the Roman Catholic Archdiocese of Chicago, who devoted his life to championing the urban poor, civil rights, and labor unions. Sheil was expected to succeed the late Cardinal Mundelein as archbishop in 1939, but was not chosen.

getting so you can't tell the Catholics from the Communists, with the priests as bad as any. Yes, and this fellow is the worst. He reminds me of that bishop a few years back—at least he called himself a bishop, a Protestant—that was advocating companionate marriages.[4] It's not that bad, maybe, but if you listened to some of them you'd think that Catholicity and capitalism were incompatible!"

"The Holy Father—"[5]

"The Holy Father's in Europe, Father. Mr. Memmers lives in this parish. I'm his priest. What can I tell him?"

"Is it Mr. Memmers of the First National, Monsignor?"

"It is, Father. And there's damned little cheer I can give a man like Memmers. Catholics, priests, and laity alike—yes, and princes of the Church, all talking atheistic communism!"

This was the substance of their conversation, always, the deadly routine in which Father Eudex played straight man. Each time it happened he seemed to participate, and though he should have known better he justified his participation by hoping that it would not happen again, or in quite the same way. But it did, it always did, the same way, and Monsignor, for all his alarums, had nothing to say really and meant one thing only, the thing he never said—that he dearly wanted to be, and was not, a bishop.

Father Eudex could imagine just what kind of bishop Monsignor would be. His reign would be a wise one, excessively so. His mind was made up on everything, excessively so. He would know how to avoid the snares set in the path of the just man, avoid them, too, in good taste and good conscience. He would not be trapped as so many good shepherds before him had been trapped, poor souls—caught in fair-seeming dilemmas of justice that were best left alone, like the first apple. It grieved him, he

[4] *companionate marriages:* a proposed form of trial marriage in which birth control would be practiced.

[5] *The Holy Father:* In 1931 Pope Pius XI issued his encyclical—a papal letter to the entire Church—on social reform. He was critical of unrestrained capitalism, supported labor unions, and urged that workers be more fairly compensated. This encyclical, together with that of Pope Leo XIII in 1891, inspired many Catholics to undertake social action with a sense of papal approval.

said, to think of those great hearts broken in silence and solitude. It was the worst kind of exile, alas! But just give him the chance and he would know what to do, what to say, and, more important, what not to do, not to say—neither yea nor nay for him. He had not gone to Rome for nothing. For him the dark forest of decisions would not exist; for him, thanks to hours spent in prayer and meditation, the forest would vanish as dry grass before fire, his fire. He knew the mask of evil already—birth control, indecent movies, salacious books—and would call these things by their right names and dare to deal with them for what they were, these new occasions for the old sins of the cities of the plains.[6]

But in the meantime—oh, to have a particle of the faith that God had in humanity! Dear, trusting God forever trying them beyond their feeble powers, ordering terrible tests, fatal trials by nonsense (the crazy bishop). And keeping Monsignor steadily warming up on the side lines, ready to rush in, primed for the day that would perhaps never dawn.

At one time, so the talk went, there had been reason to think that Monsignor was headed for a bishopric. Now it was too late; Monsignor's intercessors were all dead; the cupboard was bare; he knew it at heart, and it galled him to see another man, this *crazy* man, given the opportunity, and making such a mess of it.

Father Eudex searched for and found a little salt for Monsignor's wound. "The word's going around he'll be the next archbishop," he said.

"I won't believe it," Monsignor countered hoarsely. He glanced at the newspaper on the swing and renewed his horror. "If that fellow's right, Father, I'm"—his voice cracked at the idea—"*wrong!*"

Father Eudex waited until Monsignor had started down the steps to the car before he said, "It could be."

"I'll be back for lunch, Father. I'm taking her for a little spin."

Monsignor stopped in admiration a few feet from the car—her. He was as helpless before her beauty as a boy

[6] *cities of the plains:* Sodom and Gomorrah. See *Genesis* 18:16–19:29. Note also the pun on "cities of the plains."

with a birthday bicycle. He could not leave her alone. He had her out every morning and afternoon and evening. He was indiscriminate about picking people up for a ride in her. He kept her on a special diet—only the best of gas and oil and grease, with daily rubdowns. He would run her only on the smoothest roads and at so many miles an hour. That was to have stopped at the first five hundred, but only now, nearing the thousand mark, was he able to bring himself to increase her speed, and it seemed to hurt him more than it did her.

Now he was walking around behind her to inspect the tires. Apparently O.K. He gave the left rear fender an amorous chuck and eased into the front seat. Then they drove off, the car and he, to see the world, to explore each other further on the honeymoon.

Father Eudex watched the car slide into the traffic, and waited, on edge. The corner cop, fulfilling Father Eudex's fears, blew his whistle and waved his arms up in all four directions, bringing traffic to a standstill. Monsignor pulled expertly out of line and drove down Clover Boulevard in a one-car parade; all others stalled respectfully. The cop, as Monsignor passed, tipped his cap, showing a bald head. Monsignor, in the circumstances, could not acknowledge him, though he knew the man well—a parishioner. He was occupied with keeping his countenance kindly, grim, and exalted, that the cop's faith remain whole, for it was evidently inconceivable to him that Monsignor should ever venture abroad unless to bear the Holy Viaticum,[7] always racing with death.

Father Eudex, eyes baleful but following the progress of the big black car, saw a hand dart out of the driver's window in a wave. Monsignor would combine a lot of business with pleasure that morning, creating what he called "good will for the Church"—all morning in the driver's seat toasting passers-by with a wave that was better than a blessing. How he loved waving to people!

Father Eudex overcame his inclination to sit and stew about things by going down the steps to meet the mailman. He got the usual handful for the Monsignor—

[7] *Holy Viaticum:* the consecrated bread and wine of the Holy Communion administered to one in danger of death.

advertisements and amazing offers, the unfailing crop of chaff from dealers in church goods, organs, collection schemes, insurance, and sacramental wines. There were two envelopes addressed to Father Eudex, one a mimeographed plea for a missionary society which he might or might not acknowledge with a contribution, depending upon what he thought of the cause—if it was really lost enough to justify a levy on his poverty—and the other a check for a hundred dollars.

The check came in an eggshell envelope with no explanation except a tiny card, "Compliments of the Rival Tractor Company," but even that was needless. All over town clergymen had known for days that the checks were on the way again. Some, rejoicing, could hardly wait. Father Eudex, however, was one of those who could.

With the passing of hard times and the coming of the fruitful war years, the Rival Company, which was a great one for public relations, had found the best solution to the excess-profits problem to be giving. Ministers and even rabbis shared in the annual jackpot, but Rival employees were largely Catholic and it was the checks to the priests that paid off. Again, some thought it was a wonderful idea, and others thought that Rival, plagued by strikes and justly so, had put their alms to work.

There was another eggshell envelope, Father Eudex saw, among the letters for Monsignor, and knew his check would be for two hundred, the premium for pastors.

Father Eudex left Monsignor's mail on the porch table by his cigars. His own he stuck in his back pocket, wanting to forget it, and went down the steps into the yard. Walking back and forth on the shady side of the rectory where the lilies of the valley grew and reading his office, he gradually drifted into the back yard, lured by a noise. He came upon Whalen, the janitor, pounding pegs into the ground.

Father Eudex closed the breviary on a finger. "What's it all about, Joe?"

Joe Whalen snatched a piece of paper from his shirt and handed it to Father Eudex. "He gave it to me this morning."

He—it was the word for Monsignor among them. A

docile pronoun only, and yet when it meant the Monsignor it said, and concealed, nameless things.

The paper was a plan for a garden drawn up by the Monsignor in his fine hand. It called for a huge fleur-de-lis bounded by smaller crosses—and these Maltese—a fountain, a sundial, and a cloister walk running from the rectory to the garage. Later there would be birdhouses and a ten-foot wall of thick gray stones, acting as a moat against the eyes of the world. The whole scheme struck Father Eudex as expensive and, in this country, Presbyterian.

When Monsignor drew the plan, however, he must have been in his medieval mood. A spouting whale jostled with Neptune in the choppy waters of the fountain. North was indicated in the legend by a winged cherub huffing and puffing.

Father Eudex held the plan up against the sun to see the watermark. The stationery was new to him, heavy, simulated parchment, with the Church of the Holy Redeemer and Monsignor's name embossed, three initials, W. F. X., William Francis Xavier. With all those initials the man could pass for a radio station, a chancery wit had observed, or if his last name had not been Sweeney, Father Eudex added now, for high Anglican.

Father Eudex returned the plan to Whalen, feeling sorry for him and to an extent guilty before him—if only because he was a priest like Monsignor (now turned architect) whose dream of a monastery garden included the overworked janitor under the head of "labor."

Father Eudex asked Whalen to bring another shovel. Together, almost without words, they worked all morning spading up crosses, leaving the big fleur-de-lis to the last. Father Eudex removed his coat first, then his collar, and finally was down to his undershirt.

Toward noon Monsignor rolled into the driveway.

He stayed in the car, getting red in the face, recovering from the pleasure of seeing so much accomplished as he slowly recognized his curate in Whalen's helper. In a still, appalled voice he called across the lawn, "Father," and waited as for a beast that might or might not have sense enough to come.

Father Eudex dropped his shovel and went over to the car, shirtless.

Monsignor waited a moment before he spoke, as though annoyed by the everlasting necessity, where this person was concerned, to explain. "Father," he said quietly at last, "I wouldn't do any more of that—if I were you. Rather, in any event, I wouldn't."

"All right, Monsignor."

"To say the least, it's not prudent. If necessary"—he paused as Whalen came over to dig a cross within earshot —"I'll explain later. It's time for lunch now."

The car, black, beautiful, fierce with chromium, was quiet as Monsignor dismounted, knowing her master. Monsignor went around to the rear, felt a tire, and probed a nasty cinder in the tread.

"Look at that," he said, removing the cinder.

Father Eudex thought he saw the car lift a hoof, gaze around, and thank Monsignor with her headlights.

Monsignor proceeded at a precise pace to the back door of the rectory. There he held the screen door open momentarily, as if remembering something or reluctant to enter before himself—such was his humility—and then called to Whalen with an intimacy that could never exist between them.

"Better knock off now, Joe."

Whalen turned in on himself. "*Joe*—is it!"

Father Eudex removed his clothes from the grass. His hands were all blisters, but in them he found a little absolution. He apologized to Joe for having to take the afternoon off. "I can't make it, Joe. Something turned up."

"Sure, Father."

Father Eudex could hear Joe telling his wife about it that night—yeah, the young one got in wrong with the old one again. Yeah, the old one, he don't believe in it, work, for them.

Father Eudex paused in the kitchen to remember he knew not what. It was in his head, asking to be let in, but he did not place it until he heard Monsignor in the next room complaining about the salad to the housekeeper. It was the voice of dear, dead Aunt Hazel, coming from the summer he was ten. He translated the past into the present: I can't come out and play this afternoon, Joe, on account of my monsignor won't let me.

In the dining room Father Eudex sat down at the table and said grace. He helped himself to a chop, creamed new potatoes, pickled beets, jelly, and bread. He liked jelly. Monsignor passed the butter.

"That's supposed to be a tutti-frutti salad," Monsignor said, grimacing at his. "But she used green olives."

Father Eudex said nothing.

"I said she used green olives."

"I like green olives all right."

"*I* like green olives, but *not* in tutti-frutti salad."

Father Eudex replied by eating a green olive, but he knew it could not end there.

"Father," Monsignor said in a new tone. "How would you like to go away and study for a year?"

"Don't think I'd care for it, Monsignor. I'm not the type."

"You're no canonist,[8] you mean?"

"That's one thing."

"Yes. Well, there are other things it might not hurt you to know. To be quite frank with you, Father, I think you need broadening."

"I guess so," Father Eudex said thickly.

"And still, with your tendencies . . . and with the universities honeycombed with Communists. No, that would never do. I think I meant seasoning, not broadening."

"Oh."

"No offense?"

"No offense."

Who would have thought a little thing like an olive could lead to all this, Father Eudex mused—who but himself, that is, for his association with Monsignor had shown him that anything could lead to everything. Monsignor was a master at making points. Nothing had changed since the day Father Eudex walked into the rectory saying he was the new assistant. Monsignor had evaded Father Eudex's

---

[8] *canonist:* a scholarly interpreter of Church law.

hand in greeting, and a few days later, after he began to get the range, he delivered a lecture on the whole subject of handshaking. It was Middle West to shake hands, or South West, or West in any case, and it was not done where he came from, and—why had he ever come from where he came from? Not to be reduced to shaking hands, you could bet! Handshaking was worse than foot washing and unlike that pious practice there was nothing to support it. And from handshaking Monsignor might go into a general discussion of Father Eudex's failings. He used the open forum method, but he was the only speaker and there was never time enough for questions from the audience. Monsignor seized his examples at random from life. He saw Father Eudex coming out of his bedroom in pajama bottoms only and so told him about the dressing gown, its purpose, something of its history. He advised Father Eudex to barber his armpits, for it was being done all over now. He let Father Eudex see his bottle of cologne, "Steeple," special for clergymen, and said he should not be afraid of it. He suggested that Father Eudex shave his face oftener, too. He loaned him his Rogers Peet catalogue, which had sketches of clerical blades [9] togged out in the latest, and prayed that he would stop going around looking like a rabbinical student.

He found Father Eudex reading *The Catholic Worker* [10] one day and had not trusted him since. Father Eudex's conception of the priesthood was evangelical [11] in the worst sense, barbaric, gross, foreign to the mind of the Church, which was one of two terms he used as sticks to beat him with. The other was taste. The air of the rectory was often heavy with The Mind of the Church and Taste.

Another thing. Father Eudex could not conduct a civil conversation. Monsignor doubted that Father Eudex could

[9] *clerical blades:* dashing, stylish young priests.
[10] *The Catholic Worker:* a monthly newspaper founded in New York at the bottom of the Depression in 1933. Its first editorial stated, "It's time there was a Catholic paper printed for the unemployed." The paper has attempted to make American Catholicism live up to the spirit of the papal encyclicals on social reform.
[11] *evangelical:* like the conception of the ministry held by fundamentalist Protestant sects.

even think to himself with anything like agreement. Certainly any discussion with Father Eudex ended inevitably in argument or sighing. Sighing! Why didn't people talk up if they had anything to say? No, they'd rather sigh! Father, don't ever, ever sigh at me again!

Finally, Monsignor did not like Father Eudex's table manners. This came to a head one night when Monsignor, seeing his curate's plate empty and all the silverware at his place unused except for a single knife, fork, and spoon, exploded altogether, saying it had been on his mind for weeks, and then descending into the vernacular he declared that Father Eudex did not know the forks—now perhaps he could understand that! Meals, unless Monsignor had guests or other things to struggle with, were always occasions of instruction for Father Eudex, and sometimes of chastisement.

And now he knew the worst—if Monsignor was thinking of recommending him for a year of study, in a Sulpician seminary [12] probably, to learn the forks. So this was what it meant to be a priest. *Come, follow me. Going forth, teach ye all nations. Heal the sick, raise the dead, cleanse the lepers, cast out devils.*[13] Teach the class of people we get here? Teach Mr. Memmers? Teach Communists? Teach Monsignors? And where were the poor? The lepers of old? The lepers were in their colonies with nuns to nurse them. The poor were in their holes and would not come out. Mr. Memmers was in his bank, without cheer. The Communists were in their universities, awaiting a sign. And he was at table with Monsignor, and it was enough for the disciple to be as his master, but the housekeeper had used green olives.

Monsignor inquired, "Did you get your check today?"

Father Eudex, looking up, considered. "I got *a* check," he said.

"From the Rival people, I mean?"

[12] *Sulpician seminary:* The Sulpicians are a society of priests whose seminary training emphasizes strict orthodoxy of behavior, doctrine, and faith.

[13] *Come, follow . . . cast out devils:* Christ's instructions to the Twelve Apostles. See *Matthew* 10:8. He further directed them not to accept money for their services.

"Yes."

"Good. Well, I think you might apply it on the car you're wanting. A decent car. That's a worthy cause." Monsignor noticed that he was not taking it well. "Not that I mean to dictate what you shall do with your little windfall, Father. It's just that I don't like to see you mortifying yourself with a Model A—and disgracing the Church."

"Yes," Father Eudex said, suffering.

"Yes. I dare say you don't see the danger, just as you didn't a while ago when I found you making a spectacle of yourself with Whalen. You just don't see the danger because you just don't think. Not to dwell on it, but I seem to remember some overshoes."

The overshoes! Monsignor referred to them as to the Fall.[14] Last winter Father Eudex had given his overshoes to a freezing picket. It had got back to Monsignor and— good Lord, a man could have his sympathies, but he had no right clad in the cloth to endanger the prestige of the Church by siding in these wretched squabbles. Monsignor said he hated to think of all the evil done by people doing good! Had Father Eudex ever heard of the Albigensian heresy,[15] or didn't the seminary teach that any more?

Father Eudex declined dessert. It was strawberry mousse.

"Delicious," Monsignor said. "I think I'll let her stay."

At that moment Father Eudex decided that he had nothing to lose. He placed his knife next to his fork on the plate, adjusted them this way and that until they seemed to work a combination in his mind, to spring a lock which in turn enabled him to speak out.

"Monsignor," he said. "I think I ought to tell you I don't intend to make use of that money. In fact—to show you how my mind works—I have even considered en-

[14] *the Fall:* the Fall of Man, resulting from the Original Sin.

[15] *Albigensian heresy:* the unorthodox belief of a medieval Christian sect that the creator and master of the physical world is the Devil, so that the world is not the realm of God, who governs only the realm of spirit. The Albigenses condemned everything material, including the Mass and other religious practices.

dorsing the check to the strikers' relief fund."

"So," Monsignor said calmly—years in the confessional had prepared him for anything.

"I'll admit I don't know whether I can in justice. And even if I could I don't know that I would. I don't know why . . . I guess hush money, no matter what you do with it, is lousy."

Monsignor regarded him with piercing baby blue eyes. "You'd find it pretty hard to prove, Father, that *any* money *in se* [16] is . . . what you say it is. I would quarrel further with the definition 'hush money.' It seems to me nothing if not rash that you would presume to impugn the motive of the Rival Company in sending out these checks. You would seem to challenge the whole concept of good works—not that I am ignorant of the misuses to which money can be put." Monsignor, changing tack, tucked it all into a sigh. "Perhaps I'm just a simple soul, and it's enough for me to know personally some of the people in the Rival Company and to know them good people. Many of them Catholic . . . ." A throb had crept into Monsignor's voice. He shut it off.

"I don't mean anything that subtle, Monsignor," Father Eudex said. "I'm just telling you, as my pastor, what I'm going to do with the check. Or what I'm not going to do with it. I don't know what I'm going to do with it. Maybe send it back."

Monsignor rose from the table, slightly smiling. "Very well, Father. But there's always the poor."

Monsignor took leave of Father Eudex with a laugh. Father Eudex felt it was supposed to fool him into thinking that nothing he had said would be used against him. It showed, rather, that Monsignor was not winded, that he had broken wild curates before, plenty of them, and that he would ride again.

Father Eudex sought the shade of the porch. He tried to read his office, but was drowsy. He got up for a glass of water. The saints in Ireland used to stand up to their necks in cold water, but not for drowsiness. When he came back to the porch a woman was ringing the doorbell. She

[16] *in se:* under Church jurisdiction.

looked like a customer for rosary beads.

"Hello," he said.

"I'm Mrs. Klein, Father, and I was wondering if you could help me out."

Father Eudex straightened a porch chair for her. "Please sit down."

"It's a German name, Father. Klein was German descent," she said, and added with a silly grin, "It ain't what you think, Father."

"I beg your pardon."

"Klein. Some think it's a Jew name. But they stole it from Klein."

Father Eudex decided to come back to that later. "You were wondering if I could help you?"

"Yes, Father. It's personal."

"Is it matter for confession?"

"Oh no, Father." He had made her blush.

"Then go ahead."

Mrs. Klein peered into the honeysuckle vines on either side of the porch for alien ears.

"No one can hear you, Mrs. Klein."

"Father—I'm just a poor widow," she said, and continued as though Father Eudex had just slandered the man. "Klein was awful good to me, Father."

"I'm sure he was."

"So good . . . and he went and left me all he had." She had begun to cry a little.

Father Eudex nodded gently. She was after something, probably not money, always the best bet—either that or a drunk in the family—but this one was not Irish. Perhaps just sympathy.

"I come to get your advice, Father. Klein always said, 'If you got a problem, Freda, see the priest.' "

"Do you need money?"

"I got more than I can use from the bakery."

"You have a bakery?"

Mrs. Klein nodded down the street. "That's my bakery. It was Klein's. The Purity."

"I go by there all the time," Father Eudex said, abandoning himself to her. He must stop trying to shape the conversation and let her work it out.

"Will you give me your advice, Father?" He felt that she sensed his indifference and interpreted it as his way of rejecting her. She either had no idea how little sense she made or else supreme faith in him, as a priest, to see into her heart.

"Just what is it you're after, Mrs. Klein?"

"He left me all he had, Father, but it's just laying in the bank."

"And you want me to tell you what to do with it?"

"Yes, Father."

Father Eudex thought this might be interesting, certainly a change. He went back in his mind to the seminary and the class in which they had considered the problem of inheritances. Do we have any unfulfilled obligations? Are we sure? ... Are there any impedimenta? ... [17]

"Do you have any dependents, Mrs. Klein—any children?"

"One boy, Father. I got him running the bakery. I pay him good—too much, Father."

"Is 'too much' a living wage?"

"Yes, Father. He ain't got a family."

"A living wage is not too much," Father Eudex handed down, sailing into the encyclical style without knowing it.

Mrs. Klein was smiling over having done something good without knowing precisely what it was.

"How old is your son?"

"He's thirty-six, Father."

"Not married?"

"No, Father, but he's got him a girl." She giggled, and Father Eudex, embarrassed, retied his shoe.

"But you don't care to make a will and leave this money to your son in the usual way?"

"I guess I'll have to ... if I die." Mrs. Klein was suddenly crushed and haunted, but whether by death or charity, Father Eudex did not know.

"You don't have to, Mrs. Klein. There are many worthy causes. And the worthiest is the cause of the poor. My advice to you, if I understand your problem, is to give what you have to someone who needs it."

[17] *impedimenta:* Latin for "impediments," bars to the formation of a contract.

Mrs. Klein just stared at him.

"You could even leave it to the archdiocese," he said, completing the sentence to himself: but I don't recommend it in your case . . . with your tendencies. You look like an Indian giver to me.

But Mrs. Klein had got enough. "Huh!" she said, rising. "Well! You *are* a funny one!"

And then Father Eudex realized that she had come to him for a broker's tip. It was in the eyes. The hat. The dress. The shoes. "If you'd like to speak to the pastor," he said, "come back in the evening."

"You're a nice young man," Mrs. Klein said, rather bitter now and bent on getting away from him. "But I got to say this—you ain't much of a priest. And Klein said if I got a problem, see the priest—huh! You ain't much of a priest! What time's your boss come in?"

"In the evening," Father Eudex said. "Come any time in the evening."

Mrs. Klein was already down the steps and making for the street.

"You might try Mr. Memmers at the First National," Father Eudex called, actually trying to help her, but she must have thought it was just some more of his nonsense and did not reply.

After Mrs. Klein had disappeared Father Eudex went to his room. In the hallway upstairs Monsignor's voice, coming from the depths of the clerical nap, halted him.

"Who was it?"

"A woman," Father Eudex said. "A woman seeking good counsel."

He waited a moment to be questioned, but Monsignor was not awake enough to see anything wrong with that, and there came only a sigh and a shifting of weight that told Father Eudex he was simply turning over in bed.

Father Eudex walked into the bathroom. He took the Rival check from his pocket. He tore it into little squares. He let them flutter into the toilet. He pulled the chain—hard.

He went to his room and stood looking out the window at nothing. He could hear the others already giving an account of their stewardship, but could not judge them.

I bought baseball uniforms for the school. I bought the nuns a new washing machine. I purchased a Mass kit for a Chinese missionary. I bought a set of matched irons. Mine helped pay for keeping my mother in a rest home upstate. I gave mine to the poor.

And you, Father?

dawn

☐ Father Udovic placed the envelope before the Bishop and stepped back. He gave the Bishop more than enough time to read what was written on the envelope, time to digest *The Pope* and, down in the corner, the *Personal,* and then he stepped forward. "It was in the collection yesterday," he said. "At Cathedral."

"Peter's Pence,[1] Father?"

Father Udovic nodded. He'd checked that. It had been in with the special Peter's Pence envelopes, and not with the regular Sunday ones.

"Well, then . . . ." The Bishop's right hand opened over the envelope, then stopped, and came to roost again, uneasily, on the edge of the desk.

Father Udovic shifted a foot, popped a knuckle in his big toe. The envelope was a bad thing all right. They'd never received anything like it. The Bishop was doing what Father Udovic had done when confronted by the envelope, thinking twice, which was what Monsignor Renton at Cathedral had done, and his curates before him, and his housekeeper who counted the collection. In the end, each

"Dawn," copyright © 1956 by Partisan Review, from *The Presence of Grace* by J. F. Powers. "Dawn" was originally published in *Partisan Review.* Reprinted by permission of the publisher, Doubleday & Company, Inc.

[1] *Peter's Pence:* at first a tax in medieval England, levied by the Church in Rome but collected by the king; now a voluntary offering of Catholic dioceses to the Pope.

had seen the envelope as a hot potato and passed it on. But the Bishop couldn't do that. He didn't know *what* might be inside. Even Father Udovic, who had held it up to a strong light, didn't know. That was the hell of it.

The Bishop continued to stare at the envelope. He still hadn't touched it.

"It beats me," said Father Udovic, moving backwards. He sank down on the leather sofa.

"Was there something else, Father?"

Father Udovic got up quickly and went out of the office—wondering how the Bishop would handle the problem, disappointed that he evidently meant to handle it by himself. In a way, Father Udovic felt responsible. It had been his idea to popularize the age-old collection—"to personalize Peter's Pence"—by moving the day for it ahead a month so that the Bishop, who was going to Rome, would be able to present the proceeds to the Holy Father personally. There had been opposition from the very first. Monsignor Renton, the rector at Cathedral, and one of those at table when Father Udovic proposed his plan, was ill-disposed to it (as he was to Father Udovic himself) and had almost killed it with his comment, "Smart promotion, Bruno." (Monsignor Renton's superior attitude was understandable. He'd had Father Udovic's job, that of chancellor of the diocese, years ago, under an earlier bishop.) But Father Udovic had won out. The Bishop had written a letter incorporating Father Udovic's idea. The plan had been poorly received in some rectories, which was to be expected since it disturbed the routine schedule of special collections. Father Udovic, however, had been confident that the people, properly appealed to, could do better than in the past with Peter's Pence. And the first returns, which had reached him that afternoon, were reassuring—whatever the envelope might be.

It was still on the Bishop's desk the next day, off to one side, and it was there on the day after. On the following day, Thursday, it was in the "In" section of his file basket. On Friday it was still there, buried. Obviously the Bishop was stumped.

On Saturday morning, however, it was back on the desk. Father Udovic, called in for consultation, had a feeling, a really satisfying feeling, that the Bishop might have need of him. If so, he would be ready. He had a plan. He sat down on the sofa.

"It's about this," the Bishop said, glancing down at the envelope before him. "I wonder if you can locate the sender."

"I'll do my best," said Father Udovic. He paused to consider whether it would be better just to go and do his best, or to present his plan of operation to the Bishop for approval. But the Bishop, not turning to him at all, was outlining what he wanted done. And it was Father Udovic's own plan! The Cathedral priests at their Sunday Masses should request the sender of the envelope to report to the sacristy[2] afterwards. The sender should be assured that the contents would be turned over to the Holy Father, if possible.

"Providing, of course," said Father Udovic, standing and trying to get into the act, "it's not something . . . ."

"Providing it's possible to do so."

Father Udovic tried not to look sad. The Bishop might express himself better, but he was saying nothing that hadn't occurred to Father Udovic first, days before. It was pretty discouraging.

He retreated to the outer office and went to work on a memo of their conversation. Drafting letters and announcements was the hardest part of his job for him. He tended to go astray without a memo, to take up with the tempting clichés that came to him in the act of composition and sometimes perverted the Bishop's true meaning. Later that morning he called Monsignor Renton and read him the product of many revisions, the two sentences.

"Okay," said Monsignor Renton. "I'll stick it in the bulletin. Thanks a lot."

As soon as Father Udovic hung up, he doubted that that was what the Bishop wished. He consulted the memo. The Bishop was very anxious that "not too much be made of this matter." Naturally, Monsignor Renton wanted the item for his parish bulletin. He was hard up. At one time he had produced the best bulletin in the diocese, but now

---

[2] *sacristy:* a small room, beside or behind the altar, where vestments and sacred vessels are kept.

he was written out, quoting more and more from the magazines and even from the papal encyclicals. Father Udovic called Monsignor Renton back and asked that the announcement be kept out of print. It would be enough to read it once over lightly from the pulpit, using Father Udovic's version because it said enough without saying too much and was, he implied, authorized by the Bishop. Whoever the announcement concerned would comprehend it. If published, the announcement would be subject to study and private interpretation. "Announcements from the pulpit are soon forgotten," Father Udovic said. "I mean—by the people they don't concern."

"You were right the first time, Bruno," said Monsignor Renton. He sounded sore.

The next day—Sunday—Father Udovic stayed home, expecting a call from Monsignor Renton, or possibly even a visit. There was nothing. That evening he called the Cathedral rectory and got one of the curates. Monsignor Renton wasn't expected in until very late. The curate had made the announcement at his two Masses, but no one had come to him about it. "Yes, Father, as you say, it's quite possible someone came to Monsignor about it. Probably he didn't consider it important enough to call you about."

"Not important!"

"Not important enough to call *you* about, Father. On *Sunday*."

"I see," said Father Udovic mildly. It was good to know that the curate, after almost a year of listening to Monsignor Renton, was still respectful. Some of the men out in parishes said Father Udovic's job was a snap and maintained that he'd landed it only because he employed the touch system of typing. Before hanging up, Father Udovic stressed the importance of resolving the question of the envelope, but somehow (words played tricks on him) he sounded as though he were accusing the curate of indifference. What a change! The curate didn't take criticism very well, as became all too clear from his sullen silence, and he wasn't very loyal. When Father Udovic suggested that Monsignor Renton might have neglected to make the announcement at his Masses, the curate readily agreed. "Could've slipped his mind all right. I guess you know what that's like."

Early the next morning Father Udovic was in touch with Monsignor Renton, beginning significantly with a glowing report on the Peter's Pence collection, but the conversation languished, and finally he had to ask about the announcement.

"Nobody showed," Monsignor Renton said in an annoyed voice. "What d'ya want to do about it?"

"Nothing right now," said Father Udovic, and hung up. If there had been a failure in the line of communication, he thought he knew where it was.

The envelope had reposed on the Bishop's desk over the weekend and through most of Monday. But that afternoon Father Udovic, on one of his appearances in the Bishop's office, noticed that it was gone. As soon as the Bishop left for the day, Father Udovic rushed in, looking first in the wastebasket, then among the sealed outgoing letters, for a moment actually expecting to see a fat one addressed in the Bishop's hand to the Apostolic Delegate. When he uncovered the envelope in the "Out" section of the file basket, he wondered at himself for looking in the other places first. The envelope had to be filed somewhere —a separate folder would be best—but Father Udovic didn't file it. He carried it to his desk. There, sitting down to it in the gloom of the outer office, weighing, feeling, smelling the envelope, he succumbed entirely to his first fears. He remembered the parable of the cockle. "An enemy hath done this." [3] An enemy was plotting to disturb the peace of the diocese, to employ the Bishop as an agent against himself, or against some other innocent person, some unsuspecting priest or nun—yes, against Father Udovic. Why him? Why not? Only a diseased mind would contemplate such a scheme, Father Udovic thought, but that didn't make it less likely. And the sender, whoever he was, doubtless anonymous and judging others by himself, would assume that the envelope had already been opened and that the announcement was calculated to catch him. Such a person would never come forward.

[3] "An enemy hath done this": see Matthew 13:24–30.

Father Udovic's fingers tightened on the envelope. He could rip it open, but he wouldn't. That evening, enjoying instant coffee in his room, he could steam it open. But he wouldn't. In the beginning, the envelope might have been opened. It would have been so easy, pardonable then. Monsignor Renton's housekeeper might have done it. With the Bishop honoring the name on the envelope and the intentions of whoever wrote it, up to a point anyway, there was now a principle operating that just couldn't be bucked. Monsignor Renton could have it his way.

That evening Father Udovic called him and asked that the announcement appear in the bulletin.

"Okay. I'll stick it in. It wouldn't surprise me if we got some action now."

"I hope so," said Father Udovic, utterly convinced that Monsignor Renton had failed him before. "Do you mind taking it down verbatim this time?"

"Not at all."

In the next bulletin, an advance copy of which came to Father Udovic through the courtesy of Monsignor Renton, the announcement appeared in an expanded, unauthorized version.

The result on Sunday was no different.

During the following week, Father Udovic considered the possibility that the sender was a floater and thought of having the announcement broadcast from every pulpit in the diocese. He would need the Bishop's permission for that, though, and he didn't dare to ask for something he probably wouldn't get. The Bishop had instructed him not to make too much of the matter. The sender would have to be found at Cathedral, or not at all. If not at all, Father Udovic, having done his best, would understand that he wasn't supposed to know any more about the envelope than he did. He would file it away, and some other chancellor, some other bishop, perhaps, would inherit it. The envelope was most likely harmless anyway, but Father Udovic wasn't so much relieved as bored by the probability that some poor soul was trusting the Bishop to put the envelope into the hands of the Holy Father, hoping for rosary beads blessed by him, or for his autographed picture, and enclosing a small offering, perhaps a spiritual bouquet.[4] Toward the end of the week, Father Udovic told the Bishop that he liked to think that the envelope contained a spiritual bouquet from a little child, and that its contents had already been delivered, so to speak, its prayers and communions already credited to the Holy Father's account in heaven.

"I must say I hadn't thought of that," said the Bishop.

Unfortunately for his peace of mind Father Udovic wasn't always able to believe that the sender was a little child.

The most persistent of those coming to him in reverie was a middle-aged woman saying she hadn't received a special Peter's Pence envelope, had been out of town a few weeks, and so hadn't heard or read the announcement. When Father Udovic tried her on the meaning of the *Personal* on the envelope, however, the woman just went away, and so did all the other suspects under questioning —except one. This was a rich old man suffering from scrupulosity. He wanted his alms to be in secret, as it said in Scripture, lest he be deprived of his eternal reward, but not *entirely* in secret. That was as far as Father Udovic could figure the old man. Who was he? An audacious old Protestant who hated communism, or could some future Knight of St. Gregory[5] be taking his first awkward step? The old man was pretty hard to believe in, and the handwriting on the envelope sometimes struck Father Udovic as that of a woman. This wasn't necessarily bad. Women controlled the nation's wealth. He'd seen the figures on it. The explanation was simple: widows. Perhaps they hadn't taken the right tone in the announcement. Father Udovic's version had been safe and cold, Monsignor Renton's like a summons. It might have been emphasized

---

[4] *spiritual bouquet:* the offering by a Roman Catholic of a number of promised or performed devotional acts in behalf of another person on a special occasion.

[5] *Knight of St. Gregory:* One of several papal orders of knighthood, the Order of St. Gregory the Great was founded in 1831 to honor a carefully limited number of exceptionally virtuous men who have made outstanding contributions to society, the Church, and the papal office. Knights of St. Gregory are appointed by the Pope himself upon the recommendations of the bishops in whose dioceses they reside.

that the Bishop, under certain circumstances, would *gladly* undertake to deliver the envelope. That might have made a difference. The sender would not only have to appreciate the difficulty of the Bishop's position, but abandon his own. That wouldn't be easy for the sort of person Father Udovic had in mind. He had a feeling that it wasn't going to happen. The Bishop would leave for Rome on the following Tuesday. So time was running out. The envelope could contain a check—quite the cruelest thought—on which payment would be stopped after a limited time by the donor, whom Father Udovic persistently saw as an old person not to be dictated to, or it could be nullified even sooner by untimely death. God, what a shame! In Rome, where the needs of the world, temporal as well as spiritual, were so well known, the Bishop would've been welcome as the flowers in May.

And then, having come full circle, Father Udovic would be hard on himself for dreaming and see the envelope as a whited sepulcher [6] concealing all manner of filth, spelled out in letters snipped from newsprint and calculated to shake Rome's faith in him. It was then that he particularly liked to think of the sender as a little child. But soon the middle-aged woman would be back, and all the others, among whom the hottest suspect was a feeble-minded nun —devils all to pester him, and the last was always worse than the first. For he always ended up with the old man— and what if there was such an old man?

On Saturday, Father Udovic called Monsignor Renton and asked him to run the announcement again. It was all they could do, he said, and admitted that he had little hope of success.

"Don't let it throw you, Bruno. It's always darkest before dawn."

Father Udovic said he no longer cared. He said he liked to think that the envelope contained a spiritual bouquet from a little child, that its contents had already been delivered, its prayers and communions already . . . .

"You should've been a nun, Bruno."

"Not sure I know what you mean," Father Udovic said,

[6] *whited sepulcher:* like a hypocrite, outwardly virtuous but inwardly corrupt. See Matthew 23:27.

and hung up. He wished it were in his power to do something about Monsignor Renton. Some of the old ones got funny when they stayed too long in one place.

On Sunday, after the eight o'clock Mass, Father Udovic received a call from Monsignor Renton. "I told 'em if somebody didn't own up to the envelope, we'd open it. I guess I got carried away." But it had worked. Monsignor Renton had just talked with the party responsible for the envelope —a Mrs. Anton—and she was on the way over to see Father Udovic.

"A woman, huh?"

"A widow. That's about all I know about her."

"A widow, huh? Did she say what was in it?"

"I'm afraid it's not what you thought, Bruno. It's money."

Father Udovic returned to the front parlor, where he had left Mrs. Anton. "The Bishop'll see you," he said, and sat down. She wasn't making a good impression on him. She could've used a shave. When she'd asked for the Bishop, Father Udovic had replied instinctively, "He's busy," but it hadn't convinced her. She had appeared quite capable of walking out on him. He invoked the Bishop's name again. "Now one of the things the Bishop'll want to know is why you didn't show up before this."

Mrs. Anton gazed at him, then past him, as she had when he'd tried to question her. He saw her starting to get up, and thought he was about to lose her. He hadn't heard the Bishop enter the room.

The Bishop waved Mrs. Anton down, seated himself near the doorway at some distance from them, and motioned to Father Udovic to continue.

To the Bishop it might sound like browbeating, but Father Udovic meant to go on being firm with Mrs. Anton. He hadn't forgotten that she'd responded to Monsignor Renton's threats. "Why'd you wait so long? You listen to the Sunday announcements, don't you?" If she persisted in ignoring him, she could make him look bad, of course, but he didn't look for her to do that, with the Bishop present.

Calmly Mrs. Anton spoke, but not to Father Udovic. "Call off your trip?"

The Bishop shook his head.

In Father Udovic's opinion, it was one of his functions to protect the Bishop from directness of that sort. "How do we know what's in here?" he demanded. Here, unfortunately, he reached up the wrong sleeve of his cassock for the envelope. Then he had it. "What's in here? Money?" He knew from Monsignor Renton that the envelope contained money, but he hadn't told the Bishop, and so it probably sounded rash to him. Father Udovic could feel the Bishop disapproving of him, and Mrs. Anton still hadn't answered the question.

"Maybe you should return the envelope to Mrs. Anton, Father," said the Bishop.

That did it for Mrs. Anton. "It's got a dollar in it," she said.

Father Udovic glanced at the Bishop. The Bishop was adjusting his cuffs. This was something he did at funerals and public gatherings. It meant that things had gone on too long. Father Udovic's fingers were sticking to the envelope. He still couldn't believe it. "Feels like there's more than that," he said.

"I wrapped it up good in paper."

"You didn't write a letter or anything?"

"Was I supposed to?"

Father Udovic came down on her. "You were supposed to do what everybody else did. You were supposed to use the envelopes we had printed up for the purpose." He went back a few steps in his mind. "You told Monsignor Renton what was in the envelope?"

"Yes."

"Did you tell him how much?"

"No."

"Why not?"

"*He* didn't ask me."

And *he* didn't have to, thought Father Udovic. One look at Mrs. Anton and Monsignor Renton would know. Parish priests got to know such things. They were like weight-guessers, for whom it was only a question of ounces. Monsignor Renton shouldn't have passed Mrs. Anton on. He had opposed the plan to personalize Peter's Pence, but who would have thought he'd go to such lengths to get even with Father Udovic? It was sabotage. Father Udovic held out the envelope and pointed to the *Personal* on it. "What do you mean by that?" Here was where the creatures of his dreams had always gone away. He leaned forward for the answer.

Mrs. Anton leaned forward to give it. "I mean I don't want somebody else takin' all the credit with the Holy Father!"

Father Udovic sank back. It had been bad before, when she'd ignored him, but now it was worse. She was attacking the Bishop. If there were only a way to *prove* she was out of her mind, if only she'd say something that would make all her remarks acceptable in retrospect . . . ."How's the Holy Father gonna know who this dollar came from if you didn't write anything?"

"I wrote my name and address on it. In ink."

"All right, Father," said the Bishop. He stood up and almost went out of the room before he stopped and looked back at Mrs. Anton. "Why don't you send it by regular mail?"

"He'd never see it! That's why! Some flunky'd get hold of it! Same as here! Oh, don't I know!"

The Bishop walked out, leaving them together—with the envelope.

In the next few moments, although Father Udovic knew he had an obligation to instruct Mrs. Anton, and had the text for it—"When thou dost an alms-deed, sound not a trumpet before thee" [7]—he despaired. He realized that they had needed each other to arrive at their sorry state. It seemed to him, sitting there saying nothing, that they saw each other as two people who'd sinned together on earth might see each other in hell, unchastened even then, only blaming each other for what had happened.

[7] *"When thou dost an alms-deed . . .":* See Matthew 6:2.

for discussion

1. In "The Forks," what personal contrasts does Powers draw between Father Eudex and the Monsignor? Since Powers offers no actual description of either character, how does he convey the differences between them? Are the characters concretely enough represented?

2. Although Father Eudex—from whose point of view the story is told—is plainly critical of the Monsignor, he does not criticize his superior directly. Does Father Eudex's reluctance to speak out reveal a weakness in him or in his religious faith? Or does it reveal his strength?

3. In what sense may both Father Eudex and the Monsignor be regarded as orthodox churchmen? What implied view of the Church arises from Powers's portrayal of two such conflicting attitudes within the same rectory?

4. What "dawns" upon Father Udovic in the last paragraph of "Dawn"? Does the story's outcome confirm Monsignor Renton's statement (p. 491) that "It's always darkest before dawn"?

5. Is Father Udovic's sudden insight into his motives and instant experience of humility believable? Has the author prepared the reader for this dramatic turn of events?

born 1914

RICHARD HAGOPIAN

☐ *Richard Hagopian was born in 1914 in Revere, a city on Massachusetts Bay near Boston. There he received his early education in public schools and studied voice at the New England Conservatory of Music. Hagopian also spent part of his youth in southern California, where he earned his bachelor's degree in English and religion at Pomona College. He went on to graduate study in English at two schools famous for their creative writing programs, Middlebury College in Vermont and the University of Iowa. His stories have been printed in such magazines as the* Atlantic Monthly *and* Harper's Bazaar. *Several of them were included in the O. Henry and the Martha Foley yearly anthologies of the best American short stories. A collection of Hagopian's stories,* The Dove Brings Peace, *was published in 1944. It was followed by two novels,*

Faraway the Spring (1952) and Wine for the Living (1956). Since 1948 Hagopian has been a professor of rhetoric at the University of California.

Hagopian's outlook is so open and all-embracing that his preoccupation with moral questions seems as naturally attributable to his New England rearing as to his Armenian heritage. His stories reveal a constant impulse to bridge human differences and to understand life in all its strange varieties. The stories grow out of Hagopian's unsentimental memories of the uprooted, melancholy Armenians among whom he was raised. These memories, however, also include his empathy with the immigrant communities that mingled with his own in America's big cities—the Italians, the Irish, and the Jews. And the stories grow as well out of modern American life, in which superficial optimism and grossly materialistic notions of happiness have displaced more difficult questions of doubt and belief. But beyond ethnic and national traits, Hagopian presses his examination of human experience itself—that paradoxical compound of good and evil, of pain and joy.

From this larger perspective, Hagopian notes that persecution and exile have predisposed Armenians to gloom and defeat, while prompt and relatively easy victories have predisposed Americans to unfounded hope and unreal success. Thus, the unification of Armenians and Americans strikes him as an inviting prospect: each thread supplying what the other lacked; each one calling the other into fuller being. The American is reminded of life's darker side by the Armenian's presence; the mournful Armenian, heavy with suffering, derives from America "a measure of lightness and optimism of spirit." In 1944 Hagopian expressed the faith that underlies his stories, his faith that in time the threads of humanity would be "more harmoniously integrated"; he wrote, "Perhaps from a loftier perspective, in a time to come, no single thread will be isolated—the whole embodying a well-patterned unity."

the burning acid

☐ He was already dead like so many others of his dead countrymen. He breathed and walked among them, talked with them, ate food with them, and shared in their beliefs that life for them was past, swept away in the great tide of racial persecution and blood lust [1] which had left a mere handful of his long-tormented people destitute in the unrecognizable sediment of their beautiful churches, music, literature, and the remains of their valiant kin.

The few salvaged men and women who had escaped to the New World had brought with them the look and smell of carnage. Again this curious people had tried to live. Unhappy-faced, they worshiped in their churches, sang their tired laments, married and gave painful birth to their children. And he was one of these—born here; "a triumph of the flesh," as his father put it.

His father was a deep, dead man; and his father's friends were deep, dead people. They existed, but they had forgotten life. They moved now vaguely amidst cigarette smoke and memories. Pain, turned into hatred, had long ago annihilated their spirits; like burning acid it had penetrated through their flesh to the marrow of their bones, and they had cried, "God, we are ready to love anything, only let us love you most, in our own way."

The acid had burned deep into his father, old Haig.

[1] *racial . . . lust:* The Armenians, an ancient Christian nation ruled by Turkish Moslems since the eleventh century, had long been acquainted with religious persecution. But their efforts in the nineteenth century to gain political and cultural independence culminated in a bloody holocaust. In the mid-1890's more than a hundred thousand Armenian men, women, and children were massacred by the Turks and thousands more driven into exile. And in 1915 the Turkish government set in motion a plan to destroy the Armenian people by deportation and massacre. Within a few months between 800,000 and a million Armenians had been murdered; and several hundred thousand more perished during the next few years while undergoing deportation and living as refugees.

They had tied his brother to a tree before his eyes, pulled his beard out from the roots, torn his nails from his fingers and pressed pointed sticks into his kidneys. They had spit upon his dead flesh and mocked his God. Like a thief in the night Haig had come and unlashed his brother from the tree. Then he had carried his precious burden deep into the hills, where he washed him tenderly and buried him deep within the stony earth.

This story impressed itself early upon young Berj's mind long before he could speak or understand the language of his people. At first he felt his uncle's suffering in his father's eyes. Later, when words had meaning, the graphic details were revealed, and this man became a three-dimensional figure of suffering, planted deep behind his eyes.

Old Haig called his son a triumph of the flesh, and as the boy grew into manhood and his father smiled on him, he knew this was true. For his father's smiles were different; they were of the dead. He never laughed flesh-and-blood laughs like the new-countrymen, like the happy fathers of his friends at school—their American neighbors. When he came home from a hard day's work and found his son sitting alone or looking out the window at the laughing, playing children, and he smiled, it merely repeated an old truth:

"And so the acid burns again. You are alone, unlike them. We have given you a body, but not life—the kind that flourished for us amidst plenty and a minimum of pain, when we built our temples and chanted our songs, when we churned our milk and roasted our tender lambs, when we read our books and created beautiful patterns in our rugs. You are alone and suffering, and that is when it burns the most. . . . That is all. As such—we are dead. Let us recognize this and not burn. The only redemption for us is in knowledge—the knowledge of death. We are dead. Only the flesh rebels; but that, too, shall one day succumb."

Then the bad times came for the world again and old Haig read his newspaper with deep philosophic concern. He shook his head and sucked on his cigarette, unconscious of the heavy blue smoke that surrounded him. He was far away, suffering the burning acid again and again, now with the Czechs, now the Poles, now the Jews.

Each evening when he laid down his newspaper, removed his glasses and wiped his tired eyes, his words were always the same: "It has come again. They have commenced the slaughter over again. Europe has become another Der Zor.[2] The little and the weak are dying. The acid is burning again. The little ones of earth are being burned to death."

Each day his flesh grew weaker. And one day his prophecy was fulfilled—the rebellious flesh, that, too, had this day succumbed. The burning acid had eaten its last.

Death for Berj was nothing new. He had been born and raised amidst it. It had hovered about their house as far back as he could remember. Now it was here in person—stamped on the old man's features, complete, expressing weariness. It would hover about this Haig man no longer. This was his man; they were friends of old united.

The house was crowded to the doors the evening before the old man's burial. Few people cried. Some children moved about silently, independent and free of their parents, carrying deep in their eyes a common expression of suffering and deep grief. Occasionally they moved toward the table and self-consciously partook of bits of food.

In a corner of the room, near the bier, an old Armenian played on an ancient instrument. It had a long handle and the end bulged into a bowl similar to the contour of its owner's nose. He stroked the strings awkwardly, moving his gnarled fingers along the obstinate neck of his friend. The music—if you could call it that—went well with the atmosphere, the half-melodious, half-edgy inflections of the language that was being spoken. It neither introduced life into the wake nor took from death any of its solemn dignity. It established its own mysterious language, conversing one-sidedly with any soul who would give ear to it.

---

[2] *Der Zor:* a place of exile and death. Der-el-Zor was the Arab city in the desert between Turkish Armenia and Syria to which thousands of Armenians were deported in 1915 by the Turks. Many died during the forced march to Der Zor, and many others perished owing to the wretched conditions imposed upon them there.

The long neck of the instrument reached clear into the flowers of the dead man's coffin. Berj left his dry-eyed mother with friends. Something about this music appealed to him. It sounded like his father's voice again, expressing old truths for the last time, truths about death and the burning acid, giving his deep advice to all triumphs of the flesh, about redemption through knowledge—the knowledge of death.

The tune went on and on. Berj looked at the player—a silent, dead man too. He watched his hand squeeze and release the instrument's neck and decisive holds. But he noticed that occasionally the Armenian's stiff fingers slipped. The resulting slur seemed to jar on the player's nerves. Only then did his expression change; only then did he seem the least perturbed. Gingerly he removed his left hand from the neck, lighted a cigarette, then replaced his fingers on the proper strings. Before he stroked again, he gazed at his long-necked friend with a deep and steady look of reproval. Then he played as though resolved that no more slips would be permitted. The dead music continued. The silent Armenian's long-necked friend seemed to talk on and on for old Haig. Haig was attentive in death. It was old wisdom. Berj understood the language and knew that his father was in silent agreement with all that was being uttered. Berj fancied his father nodded his head in agreement, from time to time. But then came the two little tones, the curious slur, and the music stopped while the old Armenian collected his wits before starting again. It sounded as though Haig had discovered a new language in death and was trying to express something to his friends, trying to say something more than the musician was willing to admit; and he was interrupting him right in the middle of his story each time he spoke. Something curious was happening. It fascinated Berj.

By early morning the Armenian grew tired. He seemed less careful of his fingering now and played almost with Western abandon. His eyes, filled with smoke and sleep, were half-closed; and now the two mysterious tones, the fanciful slurs, occurred more and more frequently. But the old musician didn't stop.

Berj remained fixed behind this man, wondering, intrigued by the voice of the long-necked speaker. But his body was exhausted; it was tired and needed rest. He sat down, realizing how hard he had been concentrating on the music, the player, and his father's face. Had Haig discovered something, and was he trying to pass it on?

Now the music was a prolonged series of two-tone slurs. They were racing along the long neck of the Armenian's friend, faster and faster, now disengaged, dancing, caressing the strings, linking themselves into long series of major and minor modulations.

Berj felt dizzy. He closed his eyes. He was confused, hypnotized, drunk. . . .

The room was spinning. Old Haig was plowing through the flowers. He was standing amidst the wreckage of wreaths and sprays. He moved with the grace and vigor of a young athlete. He clapped his hands and danced a crazy step. . . . Then he smiled and laughed, opened his mouth and laughed—a flesh-and-blood kind of laugh. He cried out, saying things. His eyes flashed, the color of his cheeks mounted. He was growing younger and younger . . . like Berj. Again he opened his mouth to cry out something, but the music persisted too loudly; the mad two-tone slurs drowned out his voice. Haig nodded his head in happy agreement. . . . "Yes, yes," he seemed to be saying, "Yes, yes, it is the truth!"

Berj opened his eyes with a start. The sweet odor of flowers permeated the room, almost giving its very color to the atmosphere. Everyone was gone, all the dead friends, their wives, and the little sad-eyed children who had nibbled bits of food so self-consciously. Only the old Armenian was left, packing his long-necked friend in an old-country case, preparing to leave. He finished the job, put on his coat and hat, drew his instrument close to him and started out.

Berj was seized with an impulse to talk with this man. "Baron . . ." [3]

He couldn't think of a name to call this man.

"Baron . . ."

If the old Armenian heard him, he paid no attention.

[3] *Baron:* Armenian for "Mister."

Berj tried to rise and go after him, but his legs felt lifeless. He felt drugged. Half-frightened, he looked at the bier. The wreaths and sprays were intact. Old Haig was just as old; death still embraced him jealously.

"What a crazy dream," mused Berj.

His thoughts were interrupted by the touch of a hand on his shoulder. It was his mother. She was telling him to go to bed.

"Who was that man," asked Berj, "the one who played, the Armenian?"

"You remember him?"

"No, I never saw him before."

A half-smile faded across his mother's lips.

"He is an old-country friend. He was a young man with your father. He used to visit us when you were a very little baby. He came many, many miles to be with Haig tonight."

"Where does he live?"

His mother shrugged her shoulder.

"Far away."

"What is his name, what do they call him?"

"You spoke it first. Just 'the Armenian.'" She sighed, as she left the room and quietly closed the door behind her.

One day something happened to the world about Berj, the live, new world where all things dead were buried and forgotten, where life and death flourished in printer's ink; the world of the comic strip and the Gettysburg Address, the Congregational church extolling life and preaching the kingdom of heaven here on earth.

This world with no bullet bearing its name, suddenly found itself within firing range. Suddenly it, too, was faced with the pressing problem of death. Despite its courage and the forces of propaganda which had inculcated into it a kind of conviction which ignored the existence of a magic bullet, it was suddenly forced into the narrowness of its own solitude, and for the first time the possibility of meeting death became a reality.

Seldom had this world thought so earnestly about the future. The few scribbled death notes from its past little battles, though hurried and naive, were sought out, read, reread, and quickly digested. Then, as a thing which has sensed the dynamic of living, the reality of death, it was compelled to utter its thoughts in the face of its narrowing horizon. Excited men and calm men delivered broadcasts, flags waved, bugles blew, and a new premium was placed on youth.

Somewhere far away a dark-eyed young man was marching. It was raining hard, the air was cold, and the distant skies were confused with the alternate rumblings of thunder and cannon. The small detail of men with whom he was marching was picking its way across a puddle-studded field. Silently and smoky-breathed it moved. The men seldom looked at each other. Each seemed to be pressed within himself, beneath the heavy protection of his rain-clothes by the heavy barrage of rain. Occasionally a man stumbled and fell. Only then did the men seem alive. Their progress became temporarily retarded and some turned and looked at the fallen man, while others called, "Watch your step" or "Get a move on" or "Haul it out of there."

Berj moved mechanically. He paused with the others, moved with them, and shifted his rifle when the others made the move. He was pressed deeper within himself than any of the rest. His thoughts were of death—the knowledge of death—now highly accentuated by his recent experience with the men about him—the New World men. He had trained with these men for many months; he knew them, their ways, and their thoughts. They were the laughing children of his childhood grown up. Over them the flesh could win no victories, for there was nothing to overcome. Their spirits demanded a minimum. The chaplain's prayers tided them over long stretches of nothingness, animal living, eating, laughing, and falling into the routines of death with the enthusiasm of children going on a picnic. He knew what they read—crime tabloids and comic books. He saw their eyes bulge to the farfetched perverted stories of crime, adventure, and romance. The few profound monuments of literature and art—their American heritage—were lost to them. They were wide-eyed, and always their gaze penetrated into the present. Death confused these happy men; but instead of submitting to the unknown experience reverently, they considered it a menace and, in their characteristic way, foiled it by turning it into a business, advertising it blatantly on billboards . . . making the funeral ground the final movie house, and the price of admission a pittance. . . .

And now they were marching. They? Berj felt superior and apart. Instinctively he dropped back a few steps. The knowledge he possessed of what they were marching toward—the highly publicized thing—filled him with scorn, some bitterness, a little pain. . . . Yes, he knew where they were going. For him it didn't matter. Old Haig's prophecy would one day have to be fulfilled; tonight he was marching directly into his father's promised release. He felt no desire to call out to the men and say: "Stop! We are heading for certain death. Let us wait. Let us wait an hour at the least. I know, I know. . . ." No, this would only bring rebukes from them. They would joke among themselves, and even if some believed him, they would dismiss the thought and continue. Some would quote the statistics they had been taught earlier about the small percentage killed in actual combat; others would half-jokingly make remarks about the snide insurance companies not allowing death to touch their clients—not with ten thousand drawn on each head. They would kill the essence of Berj's thoughts, his knowledge. And they might think him a coward.

He knew the feeling. He knew rebuke. The burning acid of rebuke had touched him before. Tonight his thoughts went farther back than he had ever allowed them to travel before. But tonight was different. He felt his muscles grow tense. The acid was burning again. . . . But he let it burn. It burns for the last time, he thought. Then he let down the barriers of his mind . . . and pain poured in.

On they marched, half-lost in the shrapnel-like rain. The detail had laughed before this assignment. Of course it was a secret. But they had learned to accept secrets early in life. It was easy for them; they were raised on the happy game where the pocket in which daddy concealed the candy was a secret . . . where the reward was always certain.

They marched on. It wouldn't be long. Berj knew this. He breathed easier and half-audibly welcomed the burning acid. I have waited a long time. . . . But he didn't continue. He felt the sentimentality of his voice. He felt the importance of the hour. The sound of his own voice robbed it of its hallowedness. Tramping feet were different, determined, fatalistic rhythm—inevitable and certain. . . .

He wondered how old Haig had faced the final hour. Surely he knew when he was nearing the end. He remembered now. It had come to old Haig when the world was entering the bad time. He had grown silent—long before his death.

But Berj found himself talking again. . . . I have waited so long, Beatrice. . . . This time his words pressed into the night with deep feeling, and he burned with pain. Like something physical being pressed against him, it forced him to stop. Then everything happened at once. . . . The acid was boiling.

Far away a girl was laughing. Her blue eyes were filled with life. Her voice seemed mingled with the sounds of seashore and surf. "I want to be young, I want to be young. Look at you—" Her voice was drowned out by the noise of mocking gulls. "Don't come back, don't come back. You are dead, you are dead. I am tired of being old with you."

He remembered with anguish how deeply he had loved her—loved her in his shadowy, mysterious way. And she had returned his love kindly, with understanding, accepting his sadness as the heritage of his people, hopeful of his regeneration through their love and its fruits of life.

But time had robbed her of faith, and her love for him revealed itself as an affectation. Reality for her was in youth, in maintaining the illusion of the eternal present— the time of gaiety and laughter, the carefree dissipation of all things, not the suffering which comes with taking the long view, and the silent recognition of man's essential loneliness, the reality of suffering and death. For her there was no compromise. Her mother was an example of the conquest she dreaded. Time had left her frustrated and brittle. To think of the future was to think of herself in terms of her mother—scrawny-dugged, cold, and straining after the last fruits of life. He had become symbolic of the future—and she rebuked him. And he had wept. . . . Now his tears seemed shameful. The thought of them robbed these moments of their strength. Deeper burned the acid.

Again her voice returned. Like angry waves the words engulfed him . . . "I want to be young, I want to be free . . . young, free. I want. . . ."

But before she could finish, the heavens erupted with man-made thunder. He fell on his knees, clutching his stomach. For a moment he remained transfixed looking at the earth as though fascinated by it for the first time. The wet earth. Then he fell upon it and tore at it with his hands, pressed his face into it, now thrashing his mud-filled hands about his hair and neck as though trying to cover up his new and tangible pain.

All around, the music of violence and death grew louder. It exploded against heaven and earth in colossal, jagged gradations of stone and color. It vibrated death. It sought out each pore in the earth and introduced itself; and all who heard died. And those who survived were forced to listen until they could hear no more.

Like a prodigal cell, Berj stuck fast to his matrix, his hands buried in it, half of his face hidden beneath it, the other half, polished to a ghostly mirror by the slashing rain, was highlighted by each event of the night. The puddle about his stomach was dirty with human color. Nothing stirred. The rest of the detail had vanished, smiling; as completely as its smoky breath, it had vanished. The consciousness which had led it, kept it together—its spirit—was spread across the field in ruined fragments.

Only wholeness functioned. Marred, but whole, Berj was experiencing the fast-draining resources of his body and mind. So weak were these impulses that they were almost lost within the blackness of his consciousness. His body remained the same, half-buried, inert. Only the earth around him indicated life. It continued to suck blood.

Slowly into the night of Berj's growing unconsciousness beamed a ray of light, and as he bled it grew brighter. It was impossible for him to move; but now thought came freely—as though, if one could envisage thought as a tangible item—it had been lifted entirely and gently placed on a crystal level, in a glassy-clear atmosphere.

Unable to disregard sound, the diminishing noise of man's corruption still registered with wincing confusion. It made long, dull shadows along the clear stretches of his mind.

But the clear, new mind retaliated with a sound of its own. Like long sunlit avenues his mind radiated into impossibly long spaces, encompassing fantastic areas ... countries, sky, earth, people. The forced shadows the night produced diminished as the light grew brighter and brighter. And with the light came music.

All this, until now a strange phenomenon apart, suddenly engaged itself to the ego Berj. Tantalizing two-tone slurs flashed through his brain, stimulating associations and encouraging a physical desire to respond. The two-tone slurs kept coming stronger and more frequently—like the time the old Armenian, overcome with smoke and weariness, had allowed himself to play freely, with abandon. The music tantalized him, teased him, spun curious patterns about his mind. They were seeking to prick him into motion—life.

But Berj couldn't move. He wanted to sleep. He was tired. . . . He knew this was a dream, like the one he had dreamed at his father's wake, the time old Haig had plowed through the wreaths and sprays and danced like a young man, crying out things which seemed to say, "It's the truth." And the two-tone slurs ... they were the same now. . . .

Berj waited. Soon the dream would be over and the end would come—the thing he didn't fear. He felt within grasping distance of complete knowledge and his ultimate redemption. Yes, the dream would pass ... and those who passed would see another Haig, tired and completely succumbed.

But the two-tone slurs weren't easily discouraged. They changed in rhythms; they modulated into stronger patterns. The two-tone slurs cascaded down in waterfall quantities. And while they lasted, he knew that the flesh was fighting. But his struggles were vain; suddenly it came. . . . Excruciating and maddening pain racked his stomach. Now he knew his victory was not won. Pain pierced his sides. He felt his substance flowing from him like burning acid. The pain radiated throughout his body. His maddened mind pictured little demons rotating pointed sticks in his kidneys in ever-growing circles. He tried to cry out, to bring his hands within the region of his pain. . . . But nothing happened.

Pain frayed the edges of his consciousness, then the whole fabric began to unravel. It grew thinner and thinner. The pattern of twenty-four years' weaving was growing threadbare, quickly, silently, disappearing into nothing. . . . Then he stood in the midst of nothing, shorn of the accretions of time, the forced biases of life, the troublesome protective membrane of flesh and blood.

He was a baby unborn, a faint light half-lost in the shadows of a distant time, in a remote place, pulsating to strange sounds and sights. And the strongest of them took on life proportions and voice. . . . A naked man lashed to a tree, his beardless face torn and bloody, his long white fingers nailless, tortured raw . . . his naked sides pierced with pointed sticks still protruding angrily.

Slowly the beardless face looked up, and the swollen eyes searched into the night until they rested on the dim pulsating light in the shadows. Then the shapeless mouth moved. In soft, clear Armenian the man spoke: "They do not know what they are doing. They do not know."

"Is it enough?" cried one of his tormentors in another language, removing a stick from his side. "Look how thin his blood has become. Like water."

The suffering man looked on his tormentors and tears filled his eyes. But they were not tears of pain; they were not shed for his pierced sides or his ebbing life. His was a weeping that went beyond himself and the earth. They sprang from a far-away well, hidden to the eyes of the world.

The music came softly, in a minor mode, holding Berj back with subtle tenacity, giving him time to think and decide.

But Berj only wept, this time shamelessly, refreshed by the waters of a hidden fountain far away.

The pain was gone now. The little demons had vanished. His stomach felt free, as though purged of the burning acid. And with the pain and acid went hatred, and something else entered his heart; a new feeling for the world of men, the laughing ones who mocked, the child-like and the simple, the men who pursued evil ends and slaughtered for evil purposes, the little ones who died, the men and women in cities and towns who craved passionately for youth and life, the men of his detail now gone, the children of his boyhood grown up, Jack Haley from Oklahoma who loved hillbilly music, Paul Jefferson who read comic books, Ray Hallenback who drank Coca-Colas, Dr. Parks at the Congregational church who preached the kingdom of heaven here on earth.

With this new feeling, he saw new things. He saw wide meadows and happy faces, clear water and untroubled skies. He saw strong women, rich-waisted and fearless. He saw all sorts of men and women, in all walks of life, and the young and old alike carried the dancing Haig's expression in their eyes and happy voices.

Instinctively his fingers moved beneath the wet earth. How frantically he had thrashed it earlier! Now they caressed the strange substance, feeling within it the eternal essence of life, that which transforms the burning acid into fresh blood and life, green trees, flowers, men and women, playing children.

Then his strength ebbed again and his fingers became still. He wanted to weep again. But he didn't fear; but there was no shame. Within him there was light and music. And while these continued to grow in strength, he knew there was hope for himself and the deep, dead men to come.

for discussion

1. How does the description of the performance by the Armenian musician help to define the author's view of the relation between Armenian and American culture?

2. At the story's conclusion, what vision of man's future appears to Berj out of the two-tone slurs that "flashed through his brain" (p. 507)?

INDEX

511

B
C
D
E
F
G
H
I
J

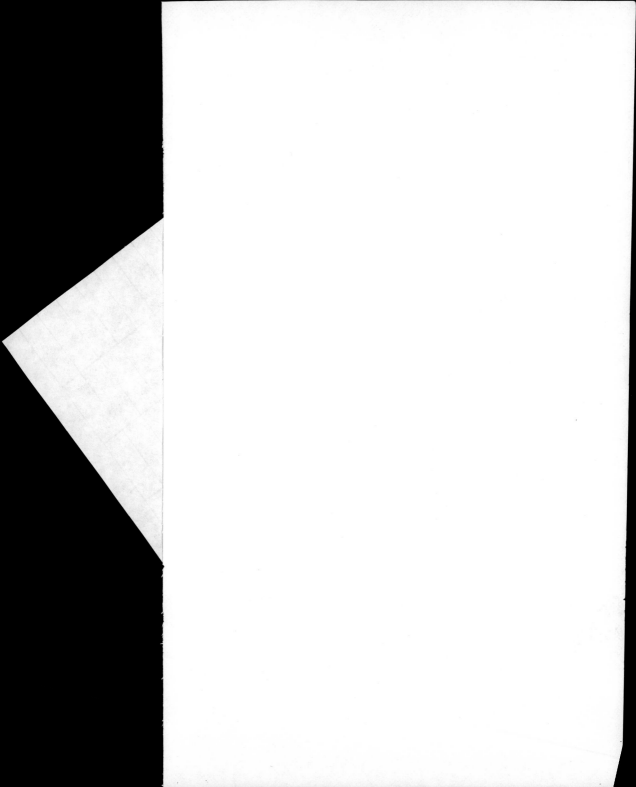

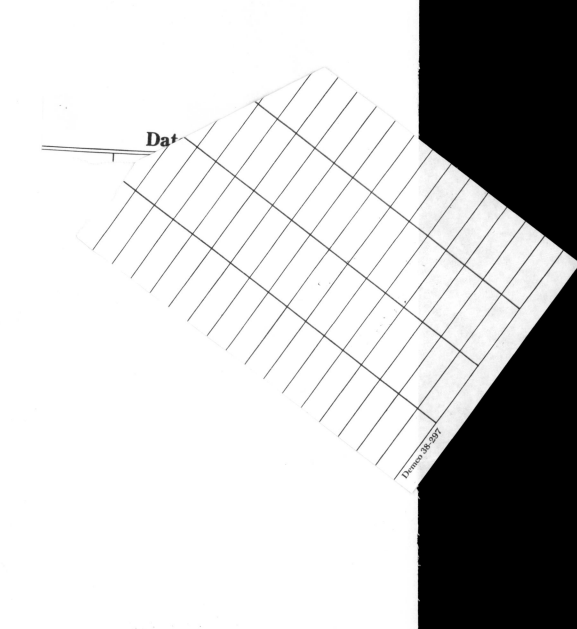

Dat